CAREER OPPORTUNITIES in

TRAVEL AND HOSPITALITY

CAREER
OPPORTUNITIES
in
TRAVEL AND HOSPITALITY

JENNIFER BOBROW BURNS

Foreword by
JOSEPH A. MCINERNEY, CHA
President/CEO
American Hotel and Lodging Association

☑®Checkmark Books®
An imprint of Infobase Publishing

Career Opportunities in Travel and Hospitality

Checkmark Books
An imprint of Infobase Publishing
132 West 31st Street
New York NY 10001

Library of Congress Cataloging-in-Publication Data

Burns, Jennifer Bobrow.
Career opportunities in travel and hospitality / Jennifer Bobrow Burns ; foreword by Joseph A. McInerney.
p. cm.
Includes bibliographical references and index.
ISBN-13: 978-0-8160-7731-1 (hardcover : alk. paper)
ISBN-10: 0-8160-7731-2 (hardcover : alk. paper)
ISBN-13: 978-0-8160-7732-8 (pbk. : alk. paper)
ISBN-10: 0-8160-7732-0 (pbk. : alk. paper) 1. Service industries—Vocational guidance. 2. Travel—Vocational guidance. 3. Hospitality industry—Vocational guidance. I. Title.
HD9980.65.B87 2010
910.23—dc22   2009021814

Text design by Kerry Casey
Cover design by Takeshi Takahashi
Composition by Hermitage Publishing Services
Cover printed by Art Print, Taylor, Pa.
Book printed and bound by The Maple-Vail Book Manufacturing Group, York, Pa.
Date printed: April 2010
Printed in the United States of America

10 9 8 7 6 5 4 3 2 1

This book is printed on acid-free paper.

Dedicated to my daughter Sophie
and all of her limitless career opportunities

CONTENTS

CASINOS AND GAMING

COMMUNICATIONS AND OTHER

APPENDIXES

FOREWORD

First and foremost, I want to congratulate you on taking proactive steps to further your education and professional development by picking up this book. You are on your way to a career in one of the most exciting and diverse international industries. The well-established field of hospitality provides one of the strongest and most interesting functions in the world.

Through upturns and downturns, the American Hotel and Lodging Association (AH&LA) has been the sole national organization representing all sectors and stakeholders in the lodging industry. Our members, who are professionals in the field, receive many benefits that help them to run their businesses effectively, with a separate set of benefits uniquely designed for students of hospitality.

Our Educational Foundation funds approximately $1.3 million in academic scholarships, research grants, school-to-career, and workforce development programs. The Educational Institute provides training DVDs, videos, distance learning programs, and certification in the industry, and also serves as a major source of curricula and textbooks around the world.

In the United States, the tourism industry is currently the third-largest retail industry, and one of America's largest employers. Travel and tourism is the nation's largest services export industry. Residents and international travelers in the United States spend $2 billion a day, $84.5 million an hour, $1.4 million a minute, and $23,500 per second.

There are more than 48,000 lodging properties in the United States, totaling nearly 4.5 million rooms. The industry employs approximately 1.4 million workers at these properties alone and directly supports more than 7.5 million jobs on various other levels. With an overwhelming majority of positions available outside the hotel itself, there will never be a shortage of diverse jobs that need to be filled. Rather than being pigeonholed in one area throughout your career, there is opportunity to switch career categories, often within the same company.

Employment directly generated by travel has grown nearly 30 percent in the last 10 years—a rate almost one and one-half times as fast as that of most other industries. With limited growth, however, a conservative estimate is that the hotel industry will require more than 300,000 new employees by 2014.

The hotel industry has a wide range of opportunities—from advertising to operations, marketing to management, and everything in between. Our industry offers opportunities not only in the United States, but throughout the world. With luck, you will be able to take advantage of an international posting sometime during your career.

Hospitality is not limited to hotels. It encompasses all phases of the travel and tourism industry, from airlines to cruise lines, travel agencies to tour operators, and from hotels to national tourism organizations. In all, when you refer to the "tourism" or "hospitality" industry, you are really talking about more than 15 interrelated businesses.

The diversity in this industry means there is something for every personality, talent, and skill set. And as students of hospitality and future industry leaders, the skills you learn along the way are interchangeable and transferable from job to job.

As a result, now more than ever, there is a greater emphasis placed on education and specialized training. Today, education is an important commodity in our industry. By picking up this book, you have taken a giant step to ensure a successful career.

Optimism about the industry and what you can contribute to it is essential. Employers consider attitude in addition to skills. Once you are in the door, you must work hard, and doing so will allow you the opportunity to qualify for leadership positions with your hotel or company. The nature of our industry is one that offers great opportunities for diverse, robust, and long career growth.

And one more point I would like to add is that hospitality is not merely a profession; it is a way of life. The industry is truly a place where you will make friendships that stand the test of time. With more than 45 years spent working in this industry, I can personally attest to this.

As you embark upon your career, my advice to you is to keep abreast of industry developments and become active in your community and industry associations. As they are great sources for networking, building relationships, and giving back to your community and industry. I wish all of you distinguished careers and the greatest success.

—Joseph A. McInerney, CHA
President/CEO
American Hotel and Lodging Association

INDUSTRY OUTLOOK: INTRODUCTION

People who work in the travel and hospitality industry make their living by helping others to enjoy themselves. Jobs in this field are diverse, encompassing positions in travel and tourism; hotels and lodging; resorts, cruise ships, and recreation; restaurants and culinary arts; casinos and gaming; and communications that can involve roles including management, operations, customer service, human resources, teaching, and more.

There are worldwide opportunities abound for students and career changers interested in travel and hospitality, depending on their interests and strengths. Whether one aspires to be a sommelier at one of the world's premier restaurants, manage a spa on a cruise ship, or lead customized adventure tours through the wilderness, there are many paths to choose.

According to the American Hotel and Lodging Association, tourism is currently the third-largest retail industry in the United States, behind automotive and food stores. Travel and tourism is the nation's largest services export industry, and one of America's largest employers. In fact, it is the first-, second-, or third-largest employer in 30 of the 50 states. The tourism industry includes more than 15 interrelated businesses, from lodging establishments, airlines, and restaurants, to cruise lines, car rental firms, travel agents, and tour operators.

Overall, the employment outlook is excellent for this fast-growing industry. As new hotels and restaurants open and people look for ways to enjoy their leisure time, opportunities grow for workers. Government employment projections predict that over the next 10 years management positions in lodging, food service, tourism, and recreation, and sports will grow by twice the overall rate of employment growth in the economy. Many new jobs in these sectors are projected to be added by the year 2016.

While careers in travel and hospitality are quite varied, there is one thing they have in common: Jobs in this field focus heavily on customer service. The ultimate goal of the CEO of a major hotel chain as well as a bartender at a small restaurant is to make sure that the customer is satisfied. Travel and hospitality professionals enjoy working with people and making sure their expectations are met. Happy guests lead to better profits and then everyone wins.

This book focuses on several different areas of travel and hospitality where individuals can work. Following is some information about each of these career categories as well as current themes and trends.

Travel and Tourism

The U.S. travel industry received more than $645 billion last year, including international passenger fares, from domestic and international travelers. Travel helps people to improve their lives, creating memories and enhancing overall well-being. Opportunities in this sector will keep growing as individuals travel more for business and pleasure. Jobs are available to help plan for this travel, such as those in travel agencies and tour operations, but positions also exist for people who want to explore the world as tour guides, outdoor trip leaders, and directors of visitor centers. They can use their expertise to enlighten others about new places and things. In this sector, employees often enjoy the benefit of free or reduced travel and lodging, one of the biggest perks of the field.

Hotels and Lodging

There are over 48,000 hotels and resorts in the United States. That comes to about 4,500,000 guest rooms that can be sold on a given night, and many opportunities for jobs, especially when you factor in international properties. Lodging includes motels and budget properties, full-service hotels (defined as those with at least one restaurant, generally with room service, meeting spaces, retail shops, and other amenities), bed-and-breakfast inns, guest houses, campgrounds and more.

Positions are broken down to reflect service (including waitstaff, chefs, concierges, counselors, fitness workers), management and finance (general managers, controllers, human resources), and office and administrative support (desk clerks). Career opportunities are also available at the brand/corporate level (such as the Hyatt company) or the unit level (the individual hotels). One can apply specific talents and training to focus on the hospitality industry, such as skill in architecture or marketing, or can explore the different departments such as rooms, food and beverage, or sales to rise to management in the field. Regardless of the job, work days in hotels and lodging establishments are long and nontraditional to reflect the operating hours. Staff must be available for the night shifts to accommodate late arrivals and emergency needs.

To have a successful hotel career, experts advise starting at the bottom, with part-time or summer jobs to gain experience. Entry-level positions do not require substantive education, making these options available for those without a bachelor's degree. However, those who choose to study hotel management can rise within the hotel hierarchy and have an impact on how hotels are run and operated. The American Hotel and Lodging Association provides some excellent resources at www.ahla.com.

Specialty Resorts, Cruise Ships, and Recreation

Each year, more passengers take a cruise holiday, spending billions of dollars to take to the sea. According to the Cruise Lines International Association, over the next three years 51 million North Americans intend to cruise. To date, approximately 19.9 percent of the U.S. population has cruised. Cruise ships provide great employment opportunities for those who want to travel for a fixed period of time. Most contracts for cruise jobs are between six months and one year, so a tremendous commitment is not required. If you love people and want to meet staff and passengers from all over the world, working on a cruise can be the experience of a lifetime. Depending on your special skills and talents, jobs are available performing, serving, babysitting, supervising, and organizing.

The recreation industry includes establishments that provide activities people enjoy during their leisure time. This segment of travel and hospitality includes theme and amusement parks as well as gambling, skiing, and golf facilities. Overall, the recreation industry is characterized by a large number of seasonal and part-time jobs and relatively young workers. According to the Bureau of Labor Statistics, about 40 percent of all workers have no formal education beyond high school. While earnings are relatively low at this level, others who choose this career path can rise to management. Specialty resorts are usually centered around a specific activity such as horseback riding, golf, tennis, or skiing. These environments are ideal for those with unique abilities and a taste for adventure, teaching their craft and leading groups.

Restaurants and Culinary Arts

According to the National Restaurant Association, in 2007 there were more than 935,000 restaurants in the U.S. employing 12.8 million people, making food service the largest private sector employer in the nation. Food services and drinking places include all types of restaurants, from fast-food chains to fine dining establishments. They also include cafeterias, caterers, bars, and food service contractors that operate the food services at places such as schools, sports arenas, and hospitals. As food and drink are often the cornerstones of social interaction and entertainment in our society, this diverse sector creates a multitude of job opportunities. If you are passionate about food and wine, you can be around it all the time as a chef, restaurant manager, sommelier, caterer, maître d', and in many other roles.

Casinos and Gaming

Casinos and Gaming comprise another sector of the hospitality industry that provides a wealth of job opportunities. No longer confined to Nevada and New Jersey, the Bureau of Labor Statistics states that gaming is becoming legalized in more states as an effective way to increase revenues. A substantial portion of this growth in the years ahead will come from the construction of new Indian casinos and of "racinos," which are pari-mutuel racetracks that offer casino games. Furthermore, research conducted on behalf of the National Gambling Impact Study Commission confirmed that casino gaming creates jobs and reduces the level of unemployment in communities that have legalized it. A fast pace and exciting atmosphere surrounds casinos, making them attractive places to work. Opportunities are especially growing in casinos with hotels, providing the full spectrum of hospitality jobs.

Communications and Other

With skills in communications, you can apply your experience to each of the hospitality sectors mentioned above. Hotels, resorts, restaurants, and casinos, as well as tourism-based organizations, need public relations specialists, advertising executives, and writers to bring in visitors and promote their services. Event planners coordinate programs and professors teach the next generation of leaders in the field.

CONCLUSION

As globalization and technology make our world a smaller place, careers in travel and hospitality grow as people want to see the world and have high expectations about the level of service they will receive while doing so. For those with a service attitude, enjoyment of people, flexibility, dedication, and commitment, a career in travel and hospitality can be the ultimate way to keep learning, growing, and experiencing different cultures throughout a lifetime.

ACKNOWLEDGMENTS

I would like to thank all those who participated in some way to the creation of this book. Without their assistance, this book would not have been possible.

First, I extend my appreciation to Joseph A. McInerney, CHA, President and CEO of the American Hotel and Lodging Association (AH&LA) for taking the time to write the foreword of Career Opportunities in Travel and Hospitality. His insight and experience provides readers with an ideal introduction to the industry. I would also like to thank Jessica Soklow, Manager of Media Relations for AH&LA, and Kathryn Potter, Senior Vice President of Marketing and Communications for AH&LA, for all of their help to make this happen.

The numerous travel and hospitality professionals who were kind enough to share information with me are responsible for making this book a valuable resource. The wisdom they shared contributed immensely to my research and helped to make the career profiles both interesting and realistic. In addition to those who prefer to remain anonymous, they include:

Amy Barer, Director, Office of the President, March of Dimes; Joseph Miller, President, International Sommelier Guild; Reneta McCarthy, Lecturer, Cornell University School of Hotel Management; Kathleen Lewis, Executive Director, Court of Master Sommeliers; Sid Wilson, President, A Private Guide tour operation, Denver, Colorado; Traci Hagdis, Executive Casino Host, Planet Hollywood Resort and Casino, Las Vegas, Nevada; Pam Aten, Aten and Associates Event Development and Management; Dr. William Frye, Associate Professor at Niagara University's College of Hospitality and Tourism Management; James Locker, Catering Sales Manager, the Waldorf-Astoria Hotel; David Rosoff, Mozza, Los Angeles, California; Dorothy Dowling, Senior Vice President of Marketing and Sales, Best Western International (Chair, Executive Committee, HSMAI); Marilyn Cafone, Controller, Westminster Hotel, Livingston, New Jersey and President of the Mid-Jersey Chapter of HFTP; Robert A. Gilbert, CHME, CHA, President and CEO, Hospitality Sales and Marketing Association International; Hayley Raphael, cruise performer.

Additionally, I would like to thank editors James Chambers and Sarah Fogarty Dalton, for their patience, assistance, and flexibility, as well as my family, for their love and support.

HOW TO USE THIS BOOK

If you want to explore the world and help people have fun, then the travel and hospitality industry may be the right field for you. The hospitality industry covers a broad range of service providers in the form of accommodation, food and beverage, and entertainment, while travel can encompass tourism services as well as service-oriented work that can take you across the globe. Regardless of the sector, those working in travel and hospitality are service-oriented professionals who are skilled at working with people.

As you can see from the table of contents, travel and hospitality job titles and work environments are quite diverse. This book is broken down into six general categories representing different industry sectors including travel and tourism services; hotels and lodging; specialty resorts, cruise ships, and recreation; restaurants and culinary; casinos and gaming; and communications and other. Many travel and hospitality professionals work in several of these sectors throughout their careers. Additionally, there is much overlap of job titles within this field. For example, "Fitness Instructor" is listed under "Specialty Resorts, Cruise Ships, and Recreation," although it certainly could be listed under "Hotels and Lodging" as well, and a job function such as "Controller," which is listed under "Hotels and Lodging," can fall under many of the other sectors also, including "Restaurants and Culinary Arts" and "Casinos and Gaming." For these reasons, peruse the entire table of contents to read about any job titles that catch your eye.

Because the industry is so varied, no one book could possibly contain the entire potential job titles to be found in travel and hospitality. There are many more positions to be found than the 76 listed by this book. Use this sampling as a starting point for further research into any and all titles and industries of interest.

The Career Profiles

Each of the 76 career profiles in this book describes a different job found in the travel and hospitality industry. It contains useful information that can serve as an introduction to encourage further research into each specific profession and general field. The following sections are included in each career profile.

Career Profile Snapshots and Career Ladders

Each career profile begins with a snapshot of information that will be found in more detail by reading further. At a quick glance, you can get a general sense of basic duties, salary ranges, employment and advancement prospects, and education, training, and skill requirements. The best geographical location to find employment is also included here. Since hotels, restaurants, and tourism services are offered all over the world, the hospitality and travel industry has more geographic flexibility than most. The locations listed are by no means the only options, but are just the areas with the highest concentration of jobs.

Opposite the career profile snapshot is a career ladder, containing three job titles. The profiled job will always be in the middle of the three in order to provide an idea of the typical career path.

Sometimes, advancement occurs by moving from a smaller organization to a larger and more prestigious establishment, having the same job title but enjoying greater responsibility and a higher salary.

Position Description

The position descriptions offer an overview of the basic duties and responsibilities of each career profiled. The goal of the position descriptions is for you to come away with an understanding of what someone in this occupation actually does on a regular basis. Information is included such as daily tasks, type of projects, and how each job fits in with other professions in the field. They may contain insight into typical hours, work environments, and the types of activities involved. Furthermore, the position descriptions share any background information about the industry that is needed to understand the career profile.

Salaries

Salaries within the travel and hospitality industry vary greatly based on several factors. The first factor is geographical location. Hotels and restaurants in major cities pay higher salaries than those located in small towns and rural locations. Additionally, the prestige of each establishment plays a role in staff earnings, as high-end luxury resorts can afford to pay their employees more than budget motels. Furthermore, education and experience also play a role in salaries, as requirements tend to vary greatly among positions. Those with a bachelor's degree might earn more than their counterparts without a college education, but experience may compensate. A first-year bartender will typically earn less than a 20-year veteran who has made a career of the work.

The salary information in this section is compiled from several sources, including the Bureau of Labor Statistics, professional associations, salary surveys, employees in the field, and others. Since salary information becomes outdated very quickly, make sure information is accurate by checking recent sources. As you read over the figures, you can also use salary calculators from sites such as www.salary.com to compare salaries based on region.

Employment Prospects

Employment prospects are variable and often are directly affected by the economy, and travel and hospitality is one of the first expenditures people cut during difficult economic times. As with the salary data, the projections in this section come from the Bureau of Labor Statistics, professional associations, and employees in the field. Be sure to check updated information about the careers that interest you as prospects are constantly changing. They also vary based on the size, budget, and location of the position, as well as by type of organization.

Advancement Prospects

This section covers the advancement prospects for the career being profiled. It may include next steps within the same type of organization, as well as possible moves to other types of organizations that can result in higher salaries or more responsibility. It also discusses any training or other requirements that might be needed for advancement.

Education and Training

While some positions in travel and hospitality require specific educational backgrounds and degrees, others have more flexible requirements. This section includes the required credentials, as well as the credentials that may not be essential, but are widely preferred for employment. It discusses helpful undergraduate majors, course work, and graduate degrees. It also covers any training needed such as certificates or internships.

Skills, Experience, and Personality Traits

Each career that is profiled requires certain skills, experience, and personality traits in order for one to excel in the field. This section discusses necessary skills, such as computer programs, foreign languages, public speaking, or other learned expertise. It also highlights personality traits and innate abilities, such as flexibility, humor, or patience that will enable one to be successful. The positions that are being profiled range from entry level to those that require 10 years or more of experience. This section lets you know about the type of experience that is required for each position as well.

Unions and Associations

Professional associations are an excellent way to gain valuable information about a career field as well as participate in its growth. This section lists associations that may be useful to those in each job.

Special Requirements

Some of the profiled careers have special requirements such as licensure or certification. They might require certain degrees from accredited programs or the passing of specific exams for entry. This section handles these important facts and provides resources such as the Web sites and phone numbers for organizations that offer additional information.

Tips for Entry

Here, you can find helpful tips to learn more about each career. The tips may include insider advice from professionals, useful Web sites, and books. It may also include suggestions relating to course work or internships, and lets you know how to get involved. The information is geared toward offering additional information that can help you learn more about each position and the field. Repeatedly, you will see tips that advise gaining experience through part-time jobs and internships that expose you to the industry.

Additional Resources

Beyond the career profiles, there are several appendixes that have practical information to be used in your exploration. Here you can find contact information and other concrete resources to help you learn more about each field. The appendixes in this book are as follows:

Related Educational Programs

To prepare for a career in travel and hospitality, you might study hotel administration or management, restaurant administration or management, food service, administration, tourism, and more. This section includes degree programs in travel and hospitality management as well as culinary and food

service programs from the American Culinary Federation Foundation Accrediting Commission. All schools are arranged by state and provide addresses, telephone numbers, and Web sites.

Professional Associations

In this section, the associations that are mentioned in the career profiles are listed alphabetically. They can be found nationwide and many have worldwide membership. Each association is listed, along with its mailing address, telephone number, and Web site.

Useful Web Sites, Industry Publications, and Internship Programs

The Internet is one of the best ways to learn about different careers. Web Sites described in this section may provide job listings, industry information, or other helpful tips about travel and hospitality careers. As URLs get updated frequently, check each site to make sure the information is still current. If you find a site is no longer valid, try typing the name into a search engine such as Google or Yahoo! to find an updated link.

Industry publications are also excellent ways to keep up on the travel and hospitality field. They can offer news about current events, networking contacts, job listings, and more. Most have online editions as well.

Bibliography

In order to learn more about the many careers represented in this book, a bibliography for further reading is provided. The bibliography is listed by many of the same categories that are included in the table of contents for easy organization. Most books should be easy to find through local libraries, bookstores, and Web sites such as http://www.amazon.com.

TRAVEL AND TOURISM SERVICES

TRAVEL AGENT

CAREER PROFILE

Duties: Plans travel arrangements for clients, including accommodations, transportation, and more; provides recommendations and advice

Alternate Title(s): Travel Consultant; Travel Counselor; Travel Associate

Salary Range: $20,000 to $60,000 and up

Employment Prospects: Fair to good

Advancement Prospects: Fair

Best Geographical Location(s): All, with the greatest opportunity in large cities such as New York and Los Angeles, as well as popular travel destinations, such as Honolulu

Prerequisites:

Education and Training—High school diploma is minimum credential, but many Travel Agents have bachelor's degrees and some agencies may prefer those with a college degree. Also, completion of a travel agent program from a recognized school may be required

Experience—Prior work in the hospitality/tourism industry or sales helpful

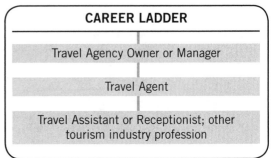

CAREER LADDER

Travel Agency Owner or Manager

Travel Agent

Travel Assistant or Receptionist; other tourism industry profession

Special Skills and Personality Traits—Enterprising and resourceful; excellent communication skills and ability to work well with people; strong organizational skills and attention to detail

Special Requirements—No federal licensing requirement, but designation as a Certified Travel Counselor (CTC) can be helpful and might be required for some positions

Position Description

As a Travel Agent, your job is often helping people to enjoy themselves. Planning a vacation can be overwhelming and people want to make sure they are getting the best deals, as well as choosing the ideal hotels, restaurants, activities, and destinations. Travel Agents help their clients navigate the web of information available, choosing locations and services that meet their clients' needs and budgets.

During initial meetings, which can take place in person or via telephone (or even e-mail), Travel Agents ascertain what their clients want. Some clients want a Travel Agent to help them choose a destination based on certain criteria—honeymoon, family vacation, etc. Others have some idea about their desired location but want recommendations on hotels and activities. Travel Agents also handle logistics including booking flights and rental cars, hotel rooms, restaurant reservations, obtaining tickets for events, and more. Whether clients are traveling for business or pleasure, Travel Agents handle the arrangements so their clients don't have to worry.

The more knowledgeable Travel Agents are about different destinations, the more specific information they can offer their clients. In order to compete with the enormous amount of information on the Internet, savvy Travel Agents can give their clients an insider perspective they can feel confident to trust. Travel Agents advise clients on a wide realm of considerations ranging from the weather and suggested wardrobe to local customs and exchange rates.

Part of the work of a Travel Agent includes securing necessary documentation, including passports, visas, driver's license information, or credit cards. They must pay close attention to detail as they act as liaisons between their clients and airlines, hotels, or tourist bureaus, transferring payment as needed. Prior to the trip, they provide clients with detailed itineraries and all paperwork.

Additional duties may include:

- compiling travel brochures and a library of information
- copying travel documents
- notifying clients of last-minute changes

- trouble shooting travel problems for clients
- promote travel packages to guests of resorts
- recommending tour groups
- changing itineraries mid-trip
- working with U.S. embassies in foreign countries
- updating reservations and travel documents
- using Central Reservation System (CRS) software for bookings
- quoting and collecting payments
- booking reservations for both individual passengers and groups
- ticketing individuals and groups
- preparing in-house sales reports
- being aware of travel advisories and other concerns
- for international travel, knowledge of visas, passports, customs, and vaccination requirements

Travel Agents spend much of their time in an office sitting behind their computer and/or talking on the telephone, but they also travel as well, which many feel is the best part of the job. They take advantage of free or reduced-cost vacations, as well as exploratory trips to research destinations. Their hours may be a regular nine-to-five, Monday-to-Friday workweek, but also can include evenings and weekends to either meet with clients, conduct research, or complete bookings. Flexibility is possible as bookings can take place at non-traditional hours, due to the Internet, time differences, and extended hours of hotels and airlines. Some Travel Agents work from home.

Niche travel is a growing area for Travel Agents and they may specialize in corporate accounts, safaris, adventure travel, destination weddings, ecotourism, or cruises. Others have specific geographic expertise on travel to particular regions. Other Travel Agents work directly for tour operators and promote their programs, presenting them to groups and clients.

In the past, Travel Agents received commissions from the various service providers and frequently did not charge clients. However, this is less common today and most travel agencies charge clients a rate ranging from $50 to $200.

Salaries

According to the Bureau of Labor Statistics (BLS), median annual earnings of Travel Agents were $32,190 as of May 2007. The middle 50 percent earned between $23,480 and $37,890. The lowest 10 percent earned less than $18,250, while the top 10 percent earned more than $47,650. Median earnings in May 2007 for Travel Agents employed in the travel arrangement and reservation services industry were $32,060, while the median for Travel

Agents employed in management of companies and enterprises was $37,790. However, the BLS also states that "experience, sales ability, and the size and location of the agency determine the salary of a Travel Agent."

Salaried Travel Agents typically enjoy standard employer-paid benefits (health insurance, sick days, etc.), while self-employed Travel Agents must provide these for themselves. However, one of the greatest benefits for all Travel Agents is reduced rates for travel. Most Travel Agents get reduced rates on accommodations and transportation when traveling for pleasure. Hotels, restaurants, and sightseeing tours may be eager to provide free or low-cost services for Travel Agents in the hope that they will then recommend them to clients. Some agencies may send their Travel Agents out on free or low-cost trips to learn more about various tourist destinations. Furthermore, resorts, hotels, or cruise lines may invite Travel Agents on such "familiarization" vacations as well. These perks often attract people to the field.

For Travel Agents who own their own agencies, the BLS says that earnings "depend mainly on commissions from travel-related bookings and service fees they charge clients. Often it takes time to acquire a sufficient number of clients to have adequate earnings, so it is not unusual for new self-employed agents to have low earnings. Established agents may have lower earnings during economic downturns."

Employment Prospects

Employment prospects for Travel Agents are fair to good, according to the BLS, but there is little growth expected in the field. The Internet has made travel booking accessible to the general public and with sites such as Travelocity and Expedia, many people receive discounted airfare and hotel rooms by booking plans themselves. Additionally, pleasure travel is an industry affected greatly by the economy, with people cutting back on their vacation plans in difficult financial times.

However, people still seek Travel Agents to save time and money, particularly for luxury or specialty travel. They respect the advice of someone who can guide them and make complicated plans involving multiple forms of transportation, hotel stays, and activities. The best opportunities may be for Travel Agents working in niche areas such as corporate, cruise, or safari travel.

The BLS states that Travel Agents held about 101,000 jobs in May 2006 and are found in every part of the country. Nearly two-thirds worked for travel agencies. Another 13 percent were self-employed. The remainder worked for tour operators, visitors' bureaus, reservation offices, and other travel arrangers.

Advancement Prospects

Travel Agents may advance by moving to management positions at travel agencies and corporations. Furthermore, they may start their own agencies or work as private consultants. They can expand through marketing and advertising their services to clients and hotels, creating their own Web sites, and partnering with hospitality services.

Education and Training

Many vocational schools and community colleges offer Travel Agent programs and training. These programs offer courses in travel sales and trends; agency operations; cruises, tours, hotels, and resorts; reservations and computer systems; destination geography; and niche marketing. Courses can be found at adult education programs, community colleges, and online. The Web site of the American Society of Travel Agents (ASTA) has links to programs at www.asta.org/education/travelschool.cfm?navItemNumber=615.

Additionally, some employers prefer Travel Agents who have college degrees. Useful backgrounds include geography, communication, foreign language, and business/accounting/management. Some schools offer bachelor's or master's degree programs in travel and tourism, such as the University of Denver (www.dcb.du.edu) and Hawaii Pacific University (www.hpu.edu).

Knowledge of Central Reservation Systems (CRS) such as Sabre may be required, and training is often provided since individual agencies may use different computerized booking software.

Special Requirements

According to the BLS, experienced Travel Agents can take courses from the Travel Institute, leading to the Certified Travel Counselor (CTC) designation. They provide the Certified Travel Associate (CTA) and Certified Travel Industry Executive (CTIE) certification programs as well. The Travel Institute also offers marketing and sales-skills development programs and destination specialist programs, which can be increasingly valuable in today's competitive market. Visit the Institute's Web site at www.thetravelinstitute.com for more information.

Furthermore, the National Business Travel Association offers three types of designations for corporate travel professionals—Corporate Travel Expert, Certified Corporate Travel Executive, and Global Leadership Professional. See its Web site at www.nbta.org.

Although there is no federal licensing requirement, some states require a form of registration or certification for Travel Agents, so check with agents and professional associations in your home state for more information.

Experience, Skills, and Personality Traits

Because they are in a service profession, Travel Agents need excellent customer service skills. The ability to develop a rapport with clients and listen to their needs is essential. This ability, coupled with expansive knowledge of travel destinations and services, enables them to earn respect from clients and be seen as experts.

Furthermore, strong computer skills are also a necessary part of the job in order to find out about travel specials, bookings, and more. Travel Agents should be enterprising and resourceful in order to seek out the best deals and resources for their clients. Problem-solving skills are needed to handle unexpected difficulties.

Organization skills and attention to detail help Travel Agents maintain itineraries and ensure that trips go off as smoothly as possible. Good business sense and marketing ability helps them promote different services as well as their own offerings. A love for travel and interest in other cultures is also needed.

Unions and Associations

Travel Agents may belong to professional associations including the American Society of Travel Agents, the National Business Travel Association, the Association of Retail Travel Agents, and more.

Tips for Entry

1. Visit the Web site for the American Society of Travel Agents at www.asta.org. The Society offers a publication called "Becoming a Travel Agent" that discusses how to launch your career.
2. Look into ARC (Airlines Reporting Corporation) Specialist training at www.arccorp.com/products/prod_tra_AST.html; this training may be required for some positions.
3. Immerse yourself in planning a trip. Use the Internet and guidebooks to find information on your own. Then visit a Travel Agent to see how the services he or she provides can offer you better rates or more extensive information.
4. Visit ASTA's links to travel schools at www.asta.org/education/travelschool.cfm?navItemNumber=615.
5. Learn as much about worldwide travel as possible. Surf the Internet to find out about top tourist destinations, adventure travel, honeymoon spots, theme parks, and more. Determine which niche might be right for you.

TOUR OPERATOR

Duties: Arranges tours and travel packages including different elements such as accommodations, transportation, and activities; sells these packages to individuals or travel agents

Alternate Title(s): None

Salary Range: $30,000 to $100,000 and up

Employment Prospects: Fair

Advancement Prospects: Fair

Best Geographical Location(s): All, with special emphasis on major cities and major tourist locations

Prerequisites:

Education and Training—High school diploma is the minimum credential with a bachelor's degree required for many positions, especially management. Courses in travel, tourism, sales/marketing, and business are helpful, as is knowledge of foreign language.

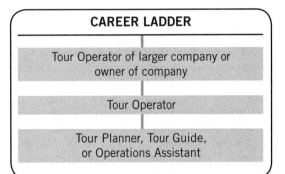

CAREER LADDER

Tour Operator of larger company or owner of company

Tour Operator

Tour Planner, Tour Guide, or Operations Assistant

Experience—Several years of experience in the travel industry, including work as a tour guide, travel agent, or work for a supplier (hotel, airline, etc.)

Special Skills and Personality Traits—Strong written and verbal communication skills, good interpersonal skills, excellent attention to detail and organization, sales and negotiation ability

Position Description

When people plan their trips, they may opt for a vacation package. Vacation packages offer ease by combining multiple travel elements (such as accommodations, transportation, activities, meals) into an all-inclusive price. Due to volume purchasing, this price is often lower than if each element was purchased separately. Tour Operators assemble these vacation packages and offer them to the public, through either individual/group sales or through travel agents.

As organizers and providers for travel packages, Tour Operators make arrangements and negotiate rates with a number of different suppliers, such as hotels, restaurants, attractions, and others. They may conduct market research to determine the best travel destinations and choose the suppliers who have received the most positive feedback. The better informed Tour Operators are about their destinations and package offerings, the better they can market them to the public.

Tour Operators may market and advertise their tours in several ways. Often, they have Web sites that promote their services. They may also develop brochures, direct mail campaigns, and set up booths in hotels and resorts with whom they contract. Tour Operators also work with local travel bureaus and visitors' centers to advertise their packages.

While the tour guide actually conducts the tours, Tour Operators run the business end, ensuring that the tours proceed without a hitch. They handle logistics and operations, including hiring and firing tour guides and other staff, as well as budgeting and planning. They may also develop materials for the tour guides to use, as well as itineraries.

Typically, tours may last between half a day to several weeks and the Tour Operator must determine the budget and scope of operations. There are many options for tour packages. Tours may be grouped by destination, population, or special interest. For example, there are tour packages for teens/students, senior citizens, singles, art enthusiasts, bird-watchers, or foodies, or destination packages such as Caribbean cruises, African safaris, or Australian outback treks. A Tour Operator must determine his or her market and become an expert in that area.

Additional duties may include:

- ensuring proper documentation for clients
- being aware of passport/visa requirements as well as State Department travel advisories
- arranging lodging, meals, and/or transportation
- negotiating rates with suppliers
- working with travel agents

- creating marketing and advertising plans
- supervising staff
- selling tours to travel agents and clients
- selling airline tickets, cruises, or other services

Troubleshooting problems can also be the responsibility of the Tour Operator. If a tour group gets stranded, someone loses his luggage, a tour guide suddenly falls ill, or other issues arise, Tour Operators must solve these dilemmas and make alternate arrangements. They need to be resourceful and help maintain a sense of calm and reassurance for everyone involved.

Most Tour Operators do not go on the trips they arrange, but they may travel to ensure quality of services and research prospective destinations. They also may interact with clients to find out about their experiences: What did they like about the tour and what did they think could be improved? This helps them enhance their services by implementing suggestions and feedback.

Salaries
Salaries for Tour Operators vary depending on their work setting. Some Tour Operators work for large established companies such as Club Med or American Trails West. Others work for smaller, family-owned organizations. Yet other Tour Operators own their own tour operation business themselves. Salaries can range from $30,000 to $100,000 and up.

Employment Prospects
Employment prospects are fair for Tour Operators. Many tour operations are small and family-owned, so not much hiring is done regularly. The best opportunity may be for those who want to begin their own tour operations businesses.

Advancement Prospects
Advancement prospects are also fair. Tour Operators that are employed by smaller companies may move to larger ones, while those at large companies may begin their own businesses.

Education and Training
There is no specific education required to become a Tour Operator, although courses in travel, tourism, business, sales, and hospitality are definitely helpful.

Many Tour Operators do hold bachelor's degrees in a variety of fields. Furthermore, certificate programs are offered by many community colleges and adult-education institutes. The typical curriculum for a tour operations certificate includes courses in hotels and lodging, developing vacation packages, ground transportation, and airfare/reservations. Knowledge of a foreign language is also helpful when dealing with international clients or suppliers.

Experience, Skills, and Personality Traits
Tour Operators should have strong written and verbal communication skills, as well as good interpersonal skills. The success of their business depends on their ability to interact with clients, attract business, and negotiate. Good business sense and knowledge of the tourism industry helps them with their sales and negotiation tactics.

Also, Tour Operators must be highly organized and pay close attention to detail. Travel experiences depend on different elements falling into place and tours must be well planned and thought out. Management experience is also helpful for those who supervise a staff.

Unions and Associations
The main professional association for Tour Operators in the United States is the United States Tour Operators Association. They can be reached at www.ustoa.com. In Canada, the chief association is the Canadian Association of Tour Operators (www.cato.ca). Tour Operators can also join the National Tour Association.

Tips for Entry
1. Take courses through the International Guide Academy at www.igaonline.com.
2. Explore the Tour Operator Company Search on the National Tour Association's Web site at www.ntaonline.com. This will provide a better idea of the multitude of Tour Operators nationwide and the packages they provide.
3. Take a tour targeted to your interests. Speak to the Tour Operator to find out how he or she got started in the field and what advice is available.
4. Learn more about large tour operations such as AAA Member Choice Vacations (www.AAA.com/mcv) and Contiki Holidays (www.contiki.com).

TOUR GUIDE

Duties: Guides groups or individuals on tours of specific sites or activities, overseeing all logistics and details as well as providing narration and information

Alternate Title(s): Tour Escort; Step-on Guide

Salary Range: $50 to $150 per day; $30,000 to $60,000 per year

Employment Prospects: Good to excellent

Advancement Prospects: Fair

Best Geographical Location(s): Major cities and regions with heavily visited tourist attractions, although some Tour Guides are based out of small cities and travel with their groups

Prerequisites:

Education and Training—High school diploma; knowledge of history of specific region; knowledge of foreign languages may be necessary or helpful for some positions

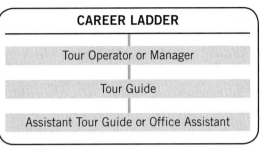

CAREER LADDER

Tour Operator or Manager

Tour Guide

Assistant Tour Guide or Office Assistant

Experience—Prior experience in travel or hospitality or at specific attractions

Special Skills and Personality Traits—Excellent verbal communication and interpersonal skills; good organization and attention to detail; flexibility and patience

Position Description

For many people, travel experiences are enhanced by learning more about the sites they are visiting. Having the history, the details, and the cultural context make sightseeing more pleasurable and interesting. Tour Guides narrate the sightseeing experience for groups and individuals, escorting them on location and providing information about each destination. They also coordinate all logistics, further contributing to the ease for travelers.

Tour Guides may lead groups for their entire travel experience, beginning with a meeting in the airport. They may coordinate transportation from airport to hotel, and then meals, activities, and all transportation for travelers once they arrive at their destination. In this way, Tour Guides are leaders for their group, making decisions and handling the details so travelers just need to be responsible for the time they meet the group.

Other Tour Guides work for specific travel sites, including hotels or cultural/historical attractions. These Tour Guides may pick up groups or individuals at their hotel and escort them to a specific attraction, explaining the significance of what they see all the while. Other Tour Guides may be available for hire (or even provide free tours) once travelers arrive at an attraction, leading them through diverse places ranging from the Roman Coliseum to Niagara Falls.

Some guides commonly called step-on guides, may join an original tour group in order to explain a particular attraction as part of a longer trip. These guides do not handle travel logistics and concentrate only on their specific tour.

It is important for Tour Guides to be knowledgeable about the history, geography, and culture of their region. They interact with people from all over the world and may serve as ambassadors from their home country or town.

Additional duties may include:

- responding to questions
- describing points of interest
- distributing brochures and background information
- explaining tour site operations
- carrying luggage or equipment for travelers
- collecting fees and soliciting new clients
- speaking foreign languages, translating, or interpreting
- planning rest stops and selecting meal options
- arranging entry to museums, government buildings, national parks, or other exhibitions

- checking groups in and out of hotels
- researching various destinations
- assisting passengers with special needs

Whether narrating on a double-decker bus in London or leading a group through the Grand Canyon, knowledge of sights and understanding of local customs is critical. Conducting research helps Tour Guides learn about new locales on multidestination tours.

Tour Guides must ensure the safety of their group at all times. They follow a set itinerary, but sometimes this may change due to weather or other unforeseen conditions and Tour Guides must be able to adapt when needed. Furthermore, they must be able to respond to emergency situations.

Tours may last several hours or several days, depending on the itinerary. Tour Guides may travel to or live in some of the world's most exotic and exciting destinations, enlightening and teaching visitors about their significance. They act as both educators and experts, sharing information and orienting travelers to a particular region or attraction. Tour Guides may focus on specific travel niches, including museums, wine, adventure, or ecotourism.

Tour Guides may spend much time traveling by bus and their hours may be nontraditional, including evenings and weekends. While not usually physically strenuous, they can expect to spend much time on their feet. However, most Tour Guides say they love their work, feeling as though they get paid to travel the world.

Salaries

According to www.payscale.com, the median salary for a Tour Guide with one to four years of experience was $37,500 in 2008, $40,350 for Tour Guides with 10 to 19 years of experience. Other sources say the annual salary range is between $30,000 and $60,000.

Some Tour Guides are paid per day, rather than by annual salaries. These Tour Guides may earn between $50 and $150 per day. Expenses are typically covered while on tour. Tour Guides may also receive travel benefits and perks, including free or reduced cost accommodations or trip packages for personal travel.

Employment Prospects

Employment prospects for Tour Guides are good to excellent. Tour Guides may be employed by tour companies, resorts, or attractions. They may focus on land/sightseeing tours, shore excursions, or adventure/sporting tours. Furthermore, some Tour Guides may work on a freelance basis, typically serving as step-on guides in their hometowns.

Advancement Prospects

Tour Guides can advance in a number of ways. They can move up to become tour directors or tour operators, with responsibility for the operation or management of the tour. Furthermore, they might develop tours or take executive positions eventually as vice presidents or presidents of tour operations. Tour Guides may also seek other opportunities in the hospitality industry promoting hotels or cruise lines.

Education and Training

A high school diploma is the minimum credential for Tour Guides. Some tour companies prefer to hire guides with college degrees. There are a number of schools and programs that offer Tour Guide training, including the International Guide Academy/International Tour Management Academy (www.igaonline.com), Miami-Dade Community College (www.mdc.edu), Professional Tour Management Training (www.tourtraining.com), and West Los Angeles Community College (www.wlac.edu).

With the increase of international travel throughout the world, knowledge of foreign languages may be necessary for some positions. Translating information or serving as an interpreter is an asset in working with travelers from a variety of countries.

Emergency medical training, such as CPR or WFR (Wilderness First Response) certification, might be required for becoming an adventure travel Tour Guide. Furthermore, museums or national parks may require specific degrees such as art, history, or geography.

Experience, Skills, and Personality Traits

Tour Guides should be good listeners, able to pick up social cues from their groups and resolve any issues. Furthermore, they should be flexible and able to deal with difficult personalities without getting flustered.

Additionally, Tour Guides spend virtually all their time with other people. For this reason, they must be outgoing and gregarious, with the ability to entertain as well as inform. Outstanding communication and public speaking skills are needed, as well as the ability to maintain harmony and order among their group.

Prior experience as a camp counselor, ski instructor, or museum docent can be helpful, as is experience with a tour group. Organization and attention to detail helps Tour Guides manage the logistics of their trips.

Unions and Associations

Professional associations for Tour Guides include the National Tour Association and the U.S. Tour Operators Association.

Tips for Entry

1. Explore the course "Get Paid to Travel," offered both online and at 1,300 schools worldwide. For more information, see www.ed2go.com/cgi-bin/ ed2go/newcrsdes.cgi?course=gpt&title=Get^Pai d^to^Travel&departmentnum=PC.

2. Visit the Web site www.jobmonkey.com for more information about interesting jobs in the travel industry.

3. Learn more about becoming a Tour Guide through the International Guide Academy, a training school, at www.igaonline.com.

4. Go on a tour of an attraction in or near your hometown. Pay attention to the Tour Guide's responsibilities and set up an informational interview with him or her afterward.

OUTDOOR TRIP LEADER

CAREER PROFILE

Duties: Leads groups on wilderness trips that may include mountaineering, kayaking, or rafting; ensures safety, plans activities, and delivers curriculum

Alternate Title(s): Outdoor Instructor; Outside Adventure Guide; Wilderness Guide; Outdoor Guide; Field Staff; Outdoor Recreation Guide

Salary Range: $50 to $150 per day for seasonal staff; $25,000 to $40,000 per year for full-time staff

Employment Prospects: Excellent

Advancement Prospects: Good

Best Geographical Location(s): Wilderness locations and areas with multiple national parks, mountains, and rivers

Prerequisites:

Education and Training—No particular educational requirements, but many Outdoor Trip Leaders hold bachelor's degrees or higher; first aid training; CPR training

Experience—Some prior wilderness experience necessary; teaching experience helpful

CAREER LADDER

Course Director, Tour Operator, or Business Owner

Outdoor Trip Leader

Logistics Coordinator or Teacher, Outdoor Enthusiast, College Student, or Recent College Graduate

Special Skills and Personality Traits—Technical skills in climbing, kayaking, or rafting; adventurous spirit; wilderness competence; good judgment; excellent interpersonal and team work skills; sense of humor; ability to stay calm under pressure

Special Requirements—May require Wilderness First Response (WFR) certification

Position Description

Do you love adventure travel and feel confident about your rock climbing, kayaking, or backpacking skills? If you want to share your passion for the great outdoors with other people, explore working as an Outdoor Trip Leader. Outdoor Trip Leaders lead youth, teens, and adults on worldwide wilderness adventures ranging from trekking in Nepal to whitewater rafting down the Colorado River. Trips may last between five days and one semester (72 days). During this time, Outdoor Trip Leaders deliver curriculum and help their groups to work together and brave the elements.

Typically, two Outdoor Trip Leaders and a course director are assigned to each travel group. Groups usually consist of up to 12 people and are frequently called "patrols." The course director does not have full involvement with the trip since he or she is often supervising other adventures simultaneously. It is up to the Outdoor Trip Leaders to work together to create a team environment that will enable their patrol to get the most from their experience.

Before a trip begins, Outdoor Trip Leaders meet to discuss their plans. Since skills in climbing, rafting,

and/or wilderness survival may need to be taught, they discuss teaching styles and methodologies as well as other specifics. In addition, they oversee the packing of equipment and food. Another key aspect is reviewing the forms completed by trip members during registration. This enables Outdoor Trip Leaders to learn more about their group prior to the trip and gain an initial understanding of strengths, weaknesses, and issues that may come up and affect group dynamics.

Many people go on outdoor adventures to learn more about themselves and their capabilities. Because of this self-awareness component, Outdoor Trip Leaders are often charged with promoting personal growth on their trips in addition to the sightseeing and adventure. They run through exercises and initiatives to develop empowering student experiences. Furthermore, they serve to motivate and encourage participants through difficult physical strain.

Once the trip is in full swing, Outdoor Trip Leaders must adhere to high safety standards and ensure course quality. They must be able to challenge their group but not put them at risk in any way. Carrying out their planned curriculum and itinerary, they are also flexible and can tailor activities to meet the needs of their group. Outdoor Trip Leaders must be attuned to each individual group member, especially as they are engaged in dangerous and strenuous activities.

Outdoor Trip Leaders may specialize in one or several of the following areas:

- backpacking
- canoeing
- kayaking
- rafting
- sailing
- skiing/snowboarding/snowshoeing
- dogsledding
- ice climbing
- rock climbing
- hiking/mountaineering
- canyoneering
- biking
- parachuting/skydiving
- swimming/surfing/scuba diving
- horseback riding
- camping
- caving
- fishing

Their duties are diverse, depending on the type of trip they lead. Some responsibilities may include:

- handling natural and emergency medical situations
- carrying equipment, cooking, and pitching tents
- administering first aid and CPR
- learning about the flora and fauna of particular regions
- helping groups work together
- deciding on transportation
- selecting appropriate campsites
- cooking and food preparation
- building fires and pitching tents; setting up and breaking down camp
- respecting natural resources

Many Outdoor Trip Leaders do not lead trips full-time. Their work is contractual and seasonal, depending upon their area of expertise. During the year, Outdoor Trip Leaders may work as public school teachers, ski instructors, or they may be college/graduate students, leading trips during the summer months. However, when they are working, leading a trip is a 24-hour job. When lightning strikes or unexpected weather occurs, Outdoor Trip Leaders need to find a way to make business run as usual no matter what time it is. There is no

such thing as a sick day or vacation time when a trip is in full swing.

The work of an Outdoor Trip Leader can be physically draining and strenuous, even for these outdoor adventure enthusiasts. Another pitfall us that it can be transient work, particularly for those who try to fill a full-time schedule leading trips. Many Outdoor Trip Leaders do not spend more than three to five years doing this kind of work, as they want to establish more permanence in their lives.

Yet for many, it is such a passion that they continue to lead trips on a part-time basis as long as they are able. Outdoor Trip Leaders say that the opportunity to do what they love, combined with the satisfaction they get from seeing the accomplishments of their program participants, is unparalleled by other professions.

Salaries

For Outdoor Trip Leaders that are not year-round staff members, salaries range from $50 to $150 per day. The higher salaries are for Outdoor Trip Leaders with considerable experience and/or those running multiple trips. They may also be paid a flat fee per trip. Annual salaries will depend on how many trips are led per year. Because many outdoor trips are seasonal, most Outdoor Trip Leaders supplement their incomes in other ways.

Outward Bound, the leading adventure-based education program, uses a credit system for overall compensation. Employees can earn salary credits for performance, college degrees, and personal wilderness accomplishments (such as climbing Mount Kilimanjaro on their own time). Outward Bound and other organizations are moving to develop more full-time field staff positions for those who want to make this work their career. Full-time Outdoor Trip Leaders earn about $30,000 and program directors can earn $40,000 or more.

Outdoor Trip Leaders that are not operating through any larger program may devise their own fee schedules, which are usually negotiable rather than set. The fees may vary depending on the type of services, the size of the group, and the guide's reputation.

Employment Prospects

Outdoor Trip Leaders enjoy excellent job prospects. There are numerous adventure travel programs throughout the United States looking to hire strong candidates with the necessary skill sets. Usually one area of outdoor expertise is needed and then programs may provide the necessary training to learn others.

Other Outdoor Trip Leaders work freelance and attract their own clients, developing a following through word of mouth or advertising.

Advancement Prospects

Advancement prospects are good for Outdoor Trip Leaders. While finding full-time fieldwork can be challenging, those who persevere may move into management positions with adventure-based education programs. These management positions include course director, program director, or manager, where they can supervise other leaders and run logistics or operations.

Programs such as Outward Bound run programs for their alumni that enable them to participate in community outreach and speak about their experiences. Having worked for an organization like this can be beneficial for Outdoor Trip Leaders, demonstrating to future employers that they are responsible, confident, and a good leader as well as team player.

Furthermore, other Outdoor Trip Leaders may advance by developing their own adventure travel businesses. They use business and marketing skills combined with their outdoor expertise to advertise their program, build a client base, purchase necessary equipment, plan itineraries, and more.

Education and Training

Outdoor Trip Leaders come from a variety of educational backgrounds. A college degree is not required, although many Outdoor Trip Leaders are college graduates or students, which may lead to higher salaries. Experience teaching, counseling, leading groups, and working with people is helpful, in addition to prior wilderness training. For positions at some organizations, Outdoor Trip Leaders need to be 21 years old to get hired. Younger candidates may gain experience by working in logistics for the organization—packing food, driving, and carrying equipment.

It is necessary for Outdoor Trip Leaders to possess a core set of competencies in wilderness skills. They may have several areas of expertise depending on the trips they plan to lead. If they are hired by an organization, most Outdoor Trip Leaders receive extensive additional training, which may last up to two weeks, prior to their first trip.

Special Requirements

Outdoor Trip Leaders should hold the Wilderness First Response (WFR) certification; it is required for many positions. The WFR is a first-aid certification course lasting 70 to 80 hours that trains outdoor leaders, guides, and rangers to deal with crises in remote settings. It prepares individuals to respond to medical emergencies and issues such as treating hypothermia, administering CPR, and using rescue skills, through education and role playing. Many schools nationwide offer the WFR; two such programs include wildmedcenter.com/courses.html#2 and www.soloschools.com/wfr.html.

Experience, Skills, and Personality Traits

Skills and experience vary depending on the types of wilderness adventures the Outdoor Trip Leader will run. For example, mountaineering courses may require a minimum of 50 days of prior backpacking experience and the ability to carry a load of up to 70 pounds, while rafting and kayaking courses might require leaders to have past documented experience with Class III rapids and with boat operations. The more outdoor competencies one has, the better the chance of finding opportunities. Physical strength, love of nature, and tolerance for working in all types of weather is essential.

Along with wilderness expertise and technical skills, Outdoor Trip Leaders should be natural leaders and teachers. They must be gregarious, confident, and competent in order to work with people and possess self-reliance and environmental understanding. Furthermore, they must have excellent judgment and the ability to stay calm in stressful situations, inspiring leadership and respect. Good communication skills help them work with their groups, minimizing conflict and conveying necessary information. A sense of humor helps Outdoor Trip Leaders make their adventures fun and memorable.

Unions and Associations

Outdoor Trip Leaders may belong to professional associations including the Association for Experiential Education, the Environmental Careers Organization, the National Recreation and Parks Association, and the Outdoor Industry Association. Some states have their own Outdoor Guide Associations; for example, see Vermont's at www.voga.org.

Tips for Entry

1. Take a look at OutdoorEd.com. This site is known as the outdoor education professional's resource and includes articles, trainings, conferences, and jobs.
2. Spend time on the Web site for Outward Bound, the leading nonprofit adventure-based education program in the world, at www.outwardbound.org.
3. Have you ever experienced adventure travel firsthand? If possible, participate in a wilderness

expedition to learn more about yourself as well as the work that goes into leading a group. Many campuses offer programs directly through the school before classes begin in the summer.

4. Hone your wilderness skills in your preferred area, whether it is biking, skiing, or rafting.

5. Learn more about other career opportunities in outdoor/environmental tourism by researching the National Recreation and Parks Association at www.nrpa.org.

DESTINATION MANAGEMENT EXECUTIVE

Duties: Owns and operates a destination management business that coordinates meetings and events for businesses and associations coming to a particular location

Alternate Title(s): Destination Manager; Destination Management Company Owner; Chief Executive Officer; Vice President

Salary Range: $40,000 to $100,000 and up

Employment Prospects: Fair

Advancement Prospects: Fair

Best Geographical Location(s): Major cities; popular tourist or convention locations; resort areas; or areas with many attractions, such as California wine country.

Prerequisites:

Education and Training—No specific requirements, but most Destination Management Executives hold bachelor's degrees in fields such as travel, tourism, hospitality management, sales/marketing, and business

Experience—Several years of experience in the travel industry, including work in tour operations or work for a supplier (hotel, airline, etc.)

CAREER LADDER

Destination Management Executive at a larger company, Owner, or CEO

↑

Destination Management Executive

↑

Sales Manager or other position in the travel or hospitality industry, including Event Planner, Travel Agent, Tour Operator, or work for a supplier

Special Skills and Personality Traits—Excellent management skills; strong written and verbal communication skills; good interpersonal skills; attention to detail and organization; sales and negotiation ability as well as knowledge of budgets, finance, and accounting

Position Description

Each year, companies and associations determine where they are going to host their annual conferences, meetings, conventions, and other programs. As they explore destinations, they need to look at hotels, entertainment, attractions, and other factors to decide if each location meets their needs. Destination management companies provide local resources to these companies and organizations looking to host their programs. Destination Management Executives run these companies, designed to be one-stop shopping for conference planning services.

Destination Management Executives perform many functions of sales, marketing, and public relations. For sales, they are selling their services and bidding on proposals, competing with other destination management companies or individual suppliers. For marketing, they are promoting their business and identifying future clients, pitching to likely candidates. In terms of public relations, they are developing their brand and gaining a reputation with their public, which includes clients as well as area service providers.

Destination Management Executives and their teams coordinate all aspects of convention planning. They handle aspects including airfare and hotels, meeting and greeting at the airport, on-site registration, planning evening events and activities, staffing hospitality tables and more. They work with area vendors and negotiate contracts. A strong relationship with these vendors enables them to get competitive prices and manage schedules and services.

Another big part of the job is prospecting. Destination Management Executives seek business rather than waiting for organizations to approach them. They might conduct research on the Internet, follow leads from local visitor's bureaus, or pitch directly to different businesses. They introduce themselves and their services, trying to show how they can make the meeting process smoother. Furthermore, they develop proposals to showcase their services and show potential clients why hiring them will make their conference planning easier.

As business owners, Destination Management Executives also handle accounting, billing, and paperwork. They may handle staffing, including hiring and firing. They may have full-time employees or bring people in on a contract basis for particular events. Additionally, they may handle meeting planning responsibilities, such as finding keynote speakers and supplying media equipment and technology support.

Either way, Destination Management Executives are involved with every aspect of event planning. They know their city inside and out, and are logistical experts. Working with the best vendors enables them to provide an experience that meets the company's needs. For example, over several months, a Destination Management Executive may work to host a political party's convention, a multinational company's corporate retreat, and a professional association of nurses' annual conference. Each of these groups may want different events and experiences; the Destination Management Executive tailors each program accordingly.

Additional duties include:

- consulting before the event
- discussing and working within different budgets
- negotiating with hotels, airlines, and vendors
- providing supervision and personal service throughout the event
- assisting with air or other transportation
- resolving unforeseen problems
- overseeing all events
- finalizing accounts and handling billing
- developing customized programs and itineraries
- providing site inspections for clients to review venues
- developing brochures, Web sites, and other promotional materials
- planning convention themes and specialty events
- providing transportation and programs for accompanying family members
- visiting area hotels, restaurants, and attractions

Hours may be long and nontraditional, to reflect events that take place on evenings, holidays, and weekends, and could include 15-hour days. However, those in the field love it for the variety in provides. As one Destination Management Executive put it, there is the constant challenge of coming up with new ideas. Rather than a set tour or itinerary, each group needs to be entertained in a different way.

Destination Management Executives typically work in regions with high tourism—big cities, resort areas, or areas with many attractions, such as California wine country. They can work all over the world, as long as they know their destination well.

Salaries
Salaries for Destination Management Executives vary depending on the type of company for which they work. Those who own their own companies in popular tourist locations can earn $100,000 and up. Others who work for other people in smaller operations may earn in the $40,000 to $60,000 range.

Employment Prospects
Destination Management Executives have fair employment prospects. The advantage is that their work is somewhat less economy-driven than pleasure travel; companies and organizations must host their meetings each year in different locations. However, they may scale back their budgets and the types of events they plan during difficult economic times. The best opportunities are for those who have worked their way up in the travel industry and developed relationships to go out on their own.

Advancement Prospects
Advancement prospects are also fair. It can be a challenge for Destination Management Executives to work their way up and make a name for themselves and their business. However, those working for smaller companies may move to larger ones, and those working for other people may advance by starting their own business. Destination Management Executives who own their own businesses can advance by building their client lists through additional sales, marketing, and public relations.

Education and Training
While there are no specific educational requirements to become a Destination Management Executive, courses in travel, tourism, hospitality management, business, and sales are definitely helpful. Many hold bachelor's degrees in a variety of fields. Knowledge of a foreign language is also helpful when dealing with international clients or suppliers. Additionally, training in accounting or finance is beneficial for those who own their own businesses.

Experience, Skills, and Personality Traits

Destination Management Executives should be organized, detail-oriented leaders, with good management skills in order to supervise a staff, oversee consultants/independent contractors, and manage events. Strong written and verbal communication skills enable them to articulate themselves well. Since the success of their business is determined by their ability to attract clients, negotiate with vendors, and meet clients' needs, good interpersonal skills and a customer service orientation are key.

Sales and negotiation ability is important, as well as knowledge of budgets, finance, and accounting. Destination Management Executives should also be flexible, able to troubleshoot when problems arise as well as change plans at a moment's notice. Creativity helps them customize programs, develop themes, and brainstorm ideas to satisfy clients.

Unions and Associations

The main professional association for Destination Management Executives is ADME, the Association of Destination Management Executives. They can be reached at www.adme.org. According to their Web site, they promote professionalism and effectiveness of destination management through education, promotion of ethical practices, and availability of information to the meetings, convention, and incentive travel industries, as well as the general public. They also offer certification programs where one can receive voluntary Destination Management Certified Professional (DMCP) certification.

Tips for Entry

1. Volunteer your time to learn more about destination management. Be flexible and open to different assignments; try to gain exposure to large events.
2. Spend time on the Web site of ADME (www.adme.org) to learn more about the profession and review job listings.
3. How would you advise a business looking to host a convention in your city? Consider all the aspects that might be involved for a four-day program, including accommodations, transportation, and entertainment.
4. Conduct an Internet search for destination management companies to find out more about the services they provide. E-mail an executive and conduct an informational interview to learn about his or her career path.

PARK RANGER

Duties: Protects the flora and fauna of national and state parks; educates and assures the safety of park visitors

Alternate Title(s): None

Salary Range: $25,000 to $60,000 and up

Employment Prospects: Fair

Advancement Prospects: Good

Best Geographical Location(s): Wilderness and rural areas; urban areas with parks and recreation centers and nature preserves

Prerequisites:

Education and Training—Bachelor's degree, or a high school diploma and a minimum of three years of experience in park services

Experience—Internship or part-time seasonal work as a Park Ranger

Special Skills and Personality Traits—Flexibility; love of the outdoors; leadership skills; strong com-

munication ability; physical stamina and outdoor technical skills

Special Requirements—Positions with the federal government are open to United States citizens only; they may also have age limitations, require first-aid certification, and require a valid driver's license

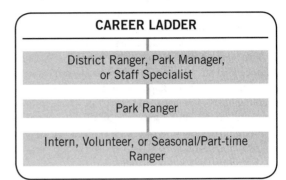

CAREER LADDER

District Ranger, Park Manager, or Staff Specialist

Park Ranger

Intern, Volunteer, or Seasonal/Part-time Ranger

Position Description

Few landscapes in the United States surpass the beauty of national and state parks. Spanning coast to coast, they range from lush mountains to sandy deserts. Overall, there are over 360 national parks in the country, and more than 110,000 state and local parks where visitors come to hike, swim, ski, fish, boat, and find sanctuary from their busy lives. In order for these parks to retain their beauty and their natural resources, they need to be well protected and cared for. Park Rangers orient visitors to these spots of relaxation and recreation as tourism ambassadors, as well as watch over plants and wildlife. Their job is to ensure conservation and safety alike.

The responsibilities of Park Rangers fall into several areas. One area is interpretation, which includes the process of educating visitors about the parks. In addition to knowing the resources of their particular park inside and out, Park Rangers have a wealth of knowledge, encompassing botany, ecology, geology, history, and wildlife. They share this knowledge through tours and other public programs such as lectures and workshops. The mission of education is vast. In one week, a Park Ranger may lead a group on a hike explaining the origin of each tree they pass; lead a nature walk

to see birds of prey; give a lecture about ecosystems and forestry; and complete a nature project with an elementary school group. Also, they may staff a visitor's center, where they answer any questions from the public about park services, as well as park history. Sometimes, they may plan and prepare permanent and alternating educational exhibits in mini-museums at these centers.

Another major component of being a Park Ranger is search and rescue. Park Rangers are trained in first aid, CPR, rescue operations, and other medical techniques in order to respond to emergencies. They must constantly be aware of weather and environmental conditions leading to disasters such as forest fires or avalanches. If hikers don't return by dark or boaters get lost at sea, it is the Park Ranger who puts a plan into action, searching for the missing visitors and mobilizing teams. They investigate all accidents, determining causes and prevention. This is difficult work and requires patience, composure, and physical stamina.

In a related role, Park Rangers also serve as the law enforcers of their parks. They enforce park regulations and in most cases, have the authority to arrest and remove those park guests who break the law. They often must deal with vandals, trespassers, the drunk and disorderly, and the disrespectful visitors who abuse the natural resources. They prevent people from committing acts both intentional and unintentional that will interfere with conservation, such as cutting down trees for firewood, littering, and feeding wildlife.

Furthermore, Park Rangers also handle park maintenance and administration. They answer questions and help establish park policy and procedure. They maintain trails, manage and perform trash collection, and ensure natural resources and habitats remain unspoiled. They may also work in the front office and operate campgrounds.

Additional duties may include:

- developing conservation programs
- writing brochures
- preparing natural, cultural, and historical exhibits
- studying wildlife behavior
- answering correspondence
- hiking on trails
- monitoring air and water quality
- restoring natural habitats
- performing safety inspections
- investigating violations

Park Rangers typically work a 40-hour week, including evenings, weekends, and holidays, but those hours vary tremendously and afford some flexibility. For example, someone may work four 10-hour shifts per week, rather than five eight-hour shifts, or they may alternate between 35-hour weeks and 45-hour weeks. Some Park Rangers choose to work some night shifts, often at the park until 3:00 A.M., in order to free up day schedules. Flexibility is important as Park Rangers at the national level often get moved around several times during their careers, working in different parks around the country. Preferences are taken into consideration, but can't always be accommodated.

Although some parks may close in the winter, most Park Rangers work year round, using the winter months for landscaping, planning exhibits, and preparing for the upcoming season. Furthermore, most Park Rangers have generous vacation time, ranging from four to six weeks depending on experience, and they often take this vacation during the wintertime.

Parks do not only encompass wilderness areas, but also include forests, lakeshores, seashores, historic buildings, battlefields, archaeological properties, and recreation areas. While many Park Rangers work for the National Parks Service (www.nps.gov/personnel), they may also be employed by state and local parks.

Salaries

Since they are government employees, Park Rangers enter the field at various salary grades, depending on their education and experience. A nonsupervisory Park Ranger working full-time would enter as a GS-09 at $45,040 per year, according to a 2008 Federal Salary Table. Supervisory Park Rangers are usually graded GS-11 or higher, with GS-11s starting at S54,494. Most seasonal Park Rangers are hired as GS-05s or GS-07s, earning between $29,726 and $36,822. park guides and visitor use assistants who enter at the GS-04 level earned $26,569 according to the 2008 data. With experience, Park Rangers can earn $60,000 per year or more.

Employment Prospects

Job openings for Park Rangers are quite competitive. The desirable lifestyle and ability to spend much time outdoors attracts many applicants for few positions. Internships and various volunteer programs within the parks are excellent ways to get a foot in the door, as are seasonal or part-time positions. Organizations and programs offering internships include the Student Conservation Association (www.thesca.org) and the Cultural Resources Diversity Program (www.cr.nps.gov/crdi).

Advancement Prospects

Once hired, Park Rangers have good opportunity for advancement. According to the National Parks Service, they may move up through the ranks to become district rangers, park managers, and staff specialists in interpretation, park planning, resource management, and related areas. Also, as they gain more experience and increase their influence over more staff and area, their responsibilities and independence will increase as well. Upper-level Park Rangers are hired for being strong leaders and managers.

Education and Training

While three years of parks service experience will compensate for the lack of a four-year college degree, the vast majority of Park Rangers hold bachelor's degrees. Because of the diversity of their responsibilities and knowledge areas, they may study parks and recreation management, geology, ecology, environmental science, biology, history, archaeology, botany, law enforcement, natural resource management, forestry, public administration, museum studies, or business. Many also hold master's degrees in these areas in order to develop specializations.

Upon hiring, Park Rangers at national parks undergo extensive training through the National Parks Service.

State and local Park Rangers are hired and trained by comparable state and local associations.

Experience, Skills, and Personality Traits

In order to deal with the public every day, Park Rangers must be very customer-service focused and enjoy working with people. They must be strong leaders and excellent communicators, skilled at explaining and engaging visitors. Also, they should have outdoor skills such as hiking, boating, and camping, as well as good physical stamina. Park Rangers are good team players, but they also work well independently.

As a group, Park Rangers generally have extremely high job satisfaction. They spend their days in beautiful surroundings, doing what they love outdoors. However, they need to be comfortable with somewhat stringent regulations of the job, including wearing uniforms and working within a hierarchy. They need to be comfortable with both acting as an authority as well as listening to authority.

To break into the field, internships or volunteer work in park services is very helpful. Seasonal work is a way to pay your dues, gaining experience while helping with basic desk and maintenance work such as answering phones and picking up trash. People also come into the field with prior experience in law enforcement, museums, construction, or grounds management.

Special Requirements

Since Park Rangers hired by the National Parks Service are federal government employees, the jobs have stringent requirements and detailed applications. You must be 18 years old and a United States citizen to apply, and some positions have an age cutoff at 37 years old. Certain positions may require law enforcement credentials, and all require a valid driver's license. Others may require first aid certifications including those for CPR and Emergency Medical Technician (EMT). Background checks and drug testing are also required. Check the National Parks Service Web site for more information at www.nps.gov. State and local parks have their own set of requirements that differ from the federal government and need to be checked individually.

Unions and Associations

Park Rangers may belong to associations including the Association of National Park Rangers, the National Recreation and Park Association, and the National Association of State Park Directors, as well as local and state organizations.

Tips for Entry

1. Visit the Web site www.usajobs.opm.gov, the United States federal government's official job site. This will explain the procedure of completing an application to work for the National Parks Service.
2. Learn more about conservation and natural resource management by visiting Web sites such as www.eco-index.org and www.iisd.org/natres.
3. Explore degree programs in parks, recreation, and tourism management such as the program at North Carolina State University in Raleigh (cnr.ncsu.edu/prtm) and the University of Missouri in Columbia (cafnr.missouri.edu/academics/parks-rec-tour.php).
4. In addition to the National Parks Service, Park Rangers are also employed at the national level by the United States Department of Agriculture Forest Service. Take a look at their Web site at www.fs.fed.us.
5. Visit national, state, and local parks and speak to Park Rangers about their job. Hone your experience in your favorite outdoor skill area.

DIRECTOR OF VISITOR SERVICES

Position Description

Directors of Visitor Services monitor the visitor experience to their institutions. When visitors go to a museum, Directors of Visitor Services want their experience to be inviting and welcoming from the moment they walk in the door. While experts may deem a museum great, it is the people who visit every day that guarantee it a spot in cultural history. Furthermore, it is the contributions from visitors that keep museums flourishing.

Directors of Visitor Services head the department that is responsible for informational materials for visitors. While education departments handle material geared toward educational programs and offerings, not all content produced is educational. There are maps, directories, and other pieces of practical information that are crucial for visitors to receive.

Collaboration is an important part of being a Director of Visitor Services. They collaborate with many other museum departments, such as membership services, where they strive to use the positive visitor experience to turn visitors into members. They also work with the education and public programming departments to ensure that visitors will have a choice of programs to attend to enhance their visit. Tours are often joint efforts between the visitor services and education departments. Furthermore, by working with the communications department, Directors of Visitor Services

are involved in creating brochures, newsletters, press releases, and other content that may affect visitors and their perception of the institution.

Some Directors of Visitor Services may also be involved with public programming. Programs are often targeted to specific audiences such as children, families, or international visitors. This involves even further collaboration with the education department, where they will work together to develop programming that supports the mission and develops audience attendance. The job can also include supervising interns or volunteers, as well as program evaluation.

Since museums bring in such a wide array of visitors, Directors of Visitor Services work to accommodate all populations and meet their needs. Some may specialize in providing services for visitors with disabilities, making sure stairways and exhibits are wheelchair accessible, offering sign language interpreters, and featuring brochures written in braille. Others may work with international guests, coordinating translation services and ensuring the availability of materials in many languages. These services help to enhance the overall visitor experience for everyone.

Additionally, Directors of Visitor Services are strategic. Like others in the tourism industry, they seek not only to provide services for their current visitor base, but also to expand their audience. Indirectly, they can impact the bottom line of the museum by attracting more visitors and donors. They may market their programs through meetings with community groups, advertising, and conducting outreach. It is important for them to be responsive to the needs of various groups and work to create a vision that is inclusive and far-reaching. By evaluating and analyzing current programs, it helps them to determine a direction for the future.

Furthermore, Directors of Visitor Services are managers. Their positions are often part of the management of their institution. They can supervise large staffs, including those who work in admission, coat check, security, and other frontline customer service roles, providing and coordinating work schedules. They also coordinate admission procedures such as ticketing. They can oversee special events as well. Additionally, they manage the budget for their departments.

At many museums and cultural institutions, the gift shop and on-site restaurant are an important part of a visitor's experience, as well as an important area for profitability. The Director of Visitor Services, who makes sure their day-to-day operations are going well, frequently oversees these. Directors of Visitor Services may update menus, order new gift items, and create inviting displays in the windows of these venues to lure visitors in.

Additional duties may include:

- developing research methods to determine visitor expectations
- using technology to create more effective visitor experiences
- writing copy related to visitor information on the institution's Web site
- analyzing inventory of shops and restaurants and preparing quarterly reports
- screening and hiring new employees
- answering visitors' questions, e-mails, and phone calls
- creating phone tree messages for visitors
- overseeing a visitors' center
- planning special events
- assessing public offerings
- writing copy for visitor information materials
- participating in fund-raising goals and initiatives

Like others in the hospitality field, Directors of Visitor Services have a strong commitment to customer service. They need to have a basis in public relations; as a representative of their institution, they should have both the knowledge and the desire to constantly portray it in a positive light. As the frontline professionals for visitors, they should project their museum's mission. They must know all programs and services inside and out.

Also, Directors of Visitor Services need to be excellent troubleshooters. Visitors that have complaints are often referred to them. They must have thick skins to accept criticism and not take it personally. The hours for Directors of Visitor Services may include evenings and weekends, to reflect museum schedules.

Salaries

Salaries vary for Directors of Visitor Services. The main factor influencing earnings is the level of the position combined with the size of the museum. Some Directors of Visitor Services may manage more than 30 employees for a large urban institution that gets millions of visitors each year. Others may serve as coordinators, with little or no supervisory responsibilities and a much smaller visitor base. Therefore, salaries may range from the low $30,000s to the high $70,000s depending on these factors.

Employment Prospects

Employment prospects are fair for Directors of Visitor Services. Opportunities are dependent on the budget of the institution. At smaller museums, jobs may combine visitor services with public programming or education.

However, since museums do depend on visitors to keep running, this position is quite important. Positions are available for those with experience in cultural institutions. The majority of jobs will be found in highly populated and heavily touristed urban areas.

Advancement Prospects

Directors of Visitor Services may pursue different paths for advancement depending on their current position. Those at smaller institutions may look to move to larger ones, while Directors of Visitor Services who manage big departments may seek more leadership as a vice president or senior manager. They may also look to move into the corporate sector of hospitality at tourism agencies or as consultants, as well as government agencies for which they might manage visitors' bureaus for different cities or national parks.

Education and Training

Most Directors of Visitor Services hold a bachelor's degree; many at large institutions have advanced degrees as well. At art museums, common majors include art history, history, fine arts, or museum studies, while at science museums, natural and biological sciences are frequent. Degrees in education and arts administration are also helpful.

For Directors of Visitor Services that work with special populations, specific knowledge and training is required. For example, those who work with people with disabilities should be well versed in the Americans with Disabilities Act regulations, and those who work with international groups may speak several languages. Also, Directors of Visitor Services who work with children may have a background in teaching.

Experience, Skills, and Personality Traits

It is essential for Directors of Visitor Services to have excellent communication skills. They should be able to develop a rapport with many different types of people. Articulate and gregarious, they need to interact with visitors, donors, support staff, and executives with ease.

Directors of Visitor Services also need to be strong managers. It is crucial for them to be well-organized and able to manage many different tasks at once. They must provide distinct leadership that motivates those working in the front line areas to be friendly, yet efficient. Knowledge of managerial principles such as budgeting is also helpful.

Depending on the level of their position, Directors of Visitor Services may have between two and 10 years of experience. Prior work in museums or other cultural institutions, including internships and volunteer jobs, is invaluable.

Unions and Associations

Directors of Visitor Services may belong to a number of associations depending on the institution for which they work. These may include the American Association of Museums or the Association of Science-Technology Centers, or the Nature Conservancy.

Tips for Entry

1. Next time you visit a museum, spend time at the visitors' center. Make an appointment to speak to the Director of Visitor Services to learn about a typical day on the job.

2. To learn more about job descriptions, take a look at sites such as www.museumjobs.com and www.museum-employment.com. Most museums and cultural institutions list their job openings directly on their Web sites, so explore those that interest you.

3. Research educational programs in museum studies. Schools nationwide offer these degrees, including a new online program through Johns Hopkins University (advanced.jhu.edu/academic/museum) and a graduate program at the University of Washington, Seattle (www.museum.washington.edu/museum).

4. Find out about internship and volunteer opportunities at museums using sites such as www.internzoo.com and www.idealist.org. This is a great way to get your foot in the door, as well as to learn about various career paths.

NATURALIST

CAREER PROFILE

Duties: Educates and informs visitors to public parks about the environment; teaches classes and provides tours about wildlife, plants, and the geology of a particular region

Alternate Titles: Teacher Naturalist; Interpretive Naturalist; Environmental Educator; Nature Guide

Salary Range: $20,000 to $30,000

Employment Prospects: Fair

Advancement Prospects: Fair

Best Geographical Location(s): All, particularly regions with parks, water, and conservation needs

Prerequisites:

Education and Training—Bachelor's degree in science or conservation field

Experience—Teaching experience and some knowledge of plants, animals, and geology

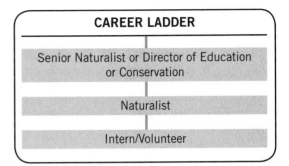

CAREER LADDER

Senior Naturalist or Director of Education or Conservation

Naturalist

Intern/Volunteer

Special Skills and Personality Traits—Love of nature and the outdoors; excellent communication skills, including public speaking and teaching skills; knowledge of the environment, science, and conservation

Position Description

If you are passionate about nature and want to share your enthusiasm with others, consider a career as a Naturalist. Naturalists love the outdoors and are fascinated by the plant and animal life found in different geographical regions. They work for parks, nature centers, wildlife refuges, museums, and other conservation organizations, providing tours and lessons about their surroundings. As experts on the flora and fauna of their particular park, Naturalists study different species and teach others not only about these living things, but also why it is important to protect them.

Many Naturalists spend the bulk of their time teaching. They often work with groups ranging from preschool to older adults, providing programs catered to different age groups. Programs can include lectures, tours, or walks. For young children, for example, Naturalists may offer a program about turtles where children can see them in their natural habitat, followed by an arts and crafts project. For senior citizens, Naturalists may take a group on a bird-watching walk and discuss conservation issues. They develop the plans for these programs and think of ideas that will be interesting to visitors.

For programs with school-age children, Naturalists often collaborate with local school districts. They write curriculum to be used both on their own site as well

as in the schools. They update current offerings and adapt them to meet the needs of teachers and different student groups. As they turn the outdoors into a classroom, Naturalists engage students and help them to see the wonder of nature.

While all Naturalists focus on the conservation and preservation of ecosystems, the topics Naturalists teach will vary depending on their geographical region and organization of employment. For example, a Naturalist working in a beach community will be concerned about wetlands preservation and its related animal and plant species. Those Naturalists employed by organizations such as the Audubon Society have a focus on birds and other wildlife. From the woodlands to the desert, they may run programs about bears, arctic foxes, or cacti, depending on where they live.

In addition to teaching, Naturalists also spend their time interacting with the public in other ways. As resources of information, they may staff visitors' centers and answer questions there. People may bring in interesting plants they have found growing in their backyards that they would like to get identified. Also, Naturalists field telephone calls and E-mails on a variety of conservation issues.

Naturalists may also take on some administrative responsibilities within their organizations. They may supervise volunteers, oversee the care for any on-site animals used for education, and participate in public communication such as writing press releases, program flyers, or newsletter copy. Furthermore, they often travel the trails themselves to notice any changes, as well as new and interesting things to share with visitors.

Some Naturalists also conduct research. They may be involved with projects that study different endangered species or ecology. The projects may be involved with helping to further the known information about these life forms, as well as to set or change public policy. Naturalists may participate in population studies, track bird migration, or sample streams to test water condition. Most research studies are affiliated with universities and based there, so Naturalists collaborate with the university research team.

Other Naturalists may seek positions that enable them to work with special populations, such as young children. At times, they may need to adapt their lessons to serve people with disabilities and other special needs. In parks and preserves with many visitors who speak other languages, foreign language skills are helpful.

Additional duties may include:

- monitoring and preserving plants and animals
- identifying and studying different wildlife species
- leading nature walks and tours
- designing exhibits and display areas for artifacts
- publishing a newsletter
- writing Web copy
- assisting with fund-raising efforts
- gathering information on local ecology
- keeping aware of public policy and issues affecting the environment
- ensuring the safety of guests during nature excursions
- working directly with animals used for visitor programs
- developing programming schedules
- Using multimedia to create and deliver presentations

Naturalists need to enjoy working outside, even in inclement weather. They usually work a 40-hour week, but it may include evenings and weekends for public programs. Even though salaries tend to be low, Naturalists often report high job satisfaction because they are able to earn a living while expressing their passion for nature.

Salaries

Salaries for Naturalists can range from about $20,000 to $30,000. Because of these low numbers, some Naturalists supplement their income with additional teach-

ing or research positions. Naturalists who advance to a senior level within a large organization may earn more.

Employment Prospects

Employment opportunities for Naturalists are fair. There are not a large number of possible employers and positions may be cut due to budget limitations. Those who have interned in the field have a distinct advantage. While most Naturalists work for parks, nature preserves, and conservation organizations, others may find positions in private and public schools.

Advancement Prospects

Naturalists may advance to positions with more responsibility within their organization. Possible next steps can include director of education, director of programming, or director of conservation. Others may decide to become more heavily involved with teaching and research and find positions in schools, colleges, and universities.

Education and Training

Naturalists should hold a bachelor's degree in a scientific field. Popular majors include biology, ecology, environmental science, natural resource management, and botany. Others may have degrees in education, which can also be helpful. Prior teaching experience is an asset and may be necessary for employment. The fieldwork that accompanies the academics is good preparation for practical learning. Additionally, Naturalists have usually spent much time at parks and nature preserves throughout their lives, which provides a background that can't be learned in school.

Experience, Skills, and Personality Traits

Naturalists are committed to environmental issues and the protection of Earth's species and land. They are innate observers who are curious about the world around them, aware of their surroundings, and able to pick up on subtle environmental changes. Knowledgeable about plants, animals, and geology, they are also well-informed about the natural history of their regions.

Furthermore, they are excellent communicators and strong public speakers who are able to work with people of all ages. They are good teachers, with flexibility and patience to answer questions and deal with the public. Those who conduct research need to be adept in this area as well.

Unions and Associations

Naturalists may belong to the Association for Environmental and Outdoor Education, the North American Association for Environmental Education, and the National Science Teachers Association. They also may belong to conservation associations such as the Nature Conservancy, the Sierra Club, and the Wildlife Society.

Tips for Entry

1. Internships are the best way to get involved in environmental education. One site to try is the Student Conservation Association, which contains detailed information for high school and college students about conservation careers. Their Web site, www.sca-inc.org, offers internships, volunteer positions, and seasonal opportunities.

2. Schools such as California State University at Chico offer bachelor's degree programs in recreation administration, focusing on parks and education. For more information, see www.csuchico.edu/catalog/programs/recr/RECRNONEBS.html#PARKENIEPT.

3. Visit a local nature center and participate in an educational program that interests you. Observe the Naturalist who presents the program, and then speak to him or her after the event to learn more about the career.

4. Take courses in science such as biology, environmental studies, conservation, or botany.

5. Take a look at eelink.net, the site for environmental education on the Internet. It is geared to support educators who work with K–12 students. It can give you an idea of professional resources, environmental projects, and grants and jobs available.

HOTELS AND LODGING

GENERAL MANAGER, HOTEL

CAREER PROFILE

Duties: Oversees all operations for a hotel or resort
Alternate Title(s): Hotel Manager
Salary Range: $30,000 to $120,000 and up
Employment Prospects: Fair to good
Advancement Prospects: Good
Best Geographical Location(s): All, with the greatest opportunities in large cities and heavy tourist regions with many resorts and hotels
Prerequisites:
  Education and Training—Four-year college degree; hospitality or hotel management helpful
  Experience—Five to 20 years of experience in the hospitality industry, depending on the property
  Special Skills and Personality Traits—Excellent management and leadership skills; good communication and interpersonal skills; strong financial and organizational ability

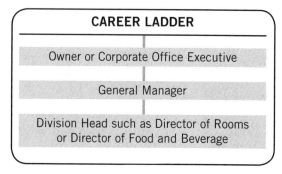

CAREER LADDER

Owner or Corporate Office Executive

General Manager

Division Head such as Director of Rooms or Director of Food and Beverage

Position Description

Every aspect of a hotel can impact its image and reputation, from the beauty of the outer areas and the comfort of the rooms to the quality of the restaurant and courtesy of the service. The General Manager is the "captain of the ship," as one put it. General Managers are responsible for overseeing all operations of a hotel and resort and ensuring that there is smooth sailing all around.

A typical day for a General Manager may begin at 7 or 7:30 A.M., when he or she arrives at work and prepares for an 8 A.M. meeting with the executive committee, made up of the different division heads reporting to the General Manager, such as the rooms director, food and beverage director, sales and marketing director, human resources director, head of accounting, and head of engineering. This committee is essential because it comprises all the key areas of hotel management. It is up to the General Manager to run these daily meetings and determine which tasks will be delegated and which responsibilities he or she will handle. The committee also recaps the positive and negative aspects of the previous day and receives directives for the future, planning for the days and week ahead.

Since most hotel owners are off-property, the General Manager is responsible for the day-to-day running of the hotel. He or she serves as the go-between for the owners and the property, interacting with both to ensure efficient and effective operation. It is up to the General Manager to make sure that the owner receives a return on investment and that strategic objectives are being carried out.

Although the job of a General Manager involves much delegation to the division heads, it also requires much hands-on involvement. At least once a day, General Managers walk through their properties (usually unannounced) in order to check conditions, appearance, and cleanliness, as well as to interact with staff and guests. They may spot-check guest rooms and restaurants along with the executive housekeeper multiple times as well. In addition to monitoring the front-end operations, they also spend time checking the back-end operations, including spaces where guests don't go, such as employee dining rooms, break rooms, or other offices. It is even typical for the General Manager to eat in the employee dining room several times per week as a way of staying connected.

General Managers serve as the face of their hotel, projecting from the top down the overall image and tone of the property. They often represent their hotel off property and are involved with media appearances, along with the public relations director. Furthermore, General Managers interact and develop relationships with groups such as the Better Business Bureau and local chamber of commerce. They also maintain relationships with other surrounding businesses and handle political relations with local governments.

Budgeting is another main area of responsibility for a General Manager. They need to be able to both forecast the budget and meet goals, developing and presenting the operational budget and accomplishments to hotel owners and corporate offices. General Managers must ensure that the budget is being met and revenue is being generated to assure the hotel's success as a business venture.

Additional duties may include:

- responding to calls and/or complaints
- hiring and supervising the management team
- determining and setting business objectives and goals
- handling emergencies and major issues involving guests, employees, or the facility
- negotiating contracts with vendors
- making decisions about the hotel's future, such as upgrades and new plans
- developing a strategic marketing plan
- overseeing guest service functions to ensure customer satisfaction
- identifying areas for improvement and implementing these plans
- providing training and development opportunities for employees

The size of the hotel impacts the extent of the General Manager's responsibilities. At smaller properties, a General Manager might handle functions including accounting, human resources, payroll, and purchasing, while at a larger hotel, these duties are handled by other managers or departments.

Typically, General Managers work a long week (50 to 60 hours) with hours ranging from 7:00 A.M. to 6:00 P.M., but not usually on weekends and evenings. The hierarchy at hotels is usually such that the higher up your position, the more regular your hours are likely to be. However, General Managers are always available for problem-solving should issues arise at any hour, since hotels operate on a 24/7 basis.

Salaries

Salaries for General Managers vary greatly depending on the size, location, and prestige of the property as well as the education and years of experience of the General Manager. According to an Economic Research Institute affiliated salary survey on SalariesReview.com, the mean total compensation for a hotel General Manager in 2008 was $121,050, including base salary, bonuses, and profit sharing. However, according to the Bureau of Labor Statistics (BLS), the mean annual wage for lodging managers in 2007 was $51,140. This discrepancy reflects the range based on the varieties of locations, properties, and education and experience of General Managers.

Furthermore, salaries for General Managers are often impacted by their ability to meet budget objectives. Up to 20 percent of overall compensation is frequently from performance-based bonuses.

Employment Prospects

Employment prospects are fair to good for General Managers with the right combination of education and experience, as the BLS predicts average growth up to 2016. There are approximately 48,000 hotels in the United States, so General Managers need to consider where they want to live and work. A non–full service hotel is a good way to get started, as one will have great responsibility early on. Skills transfer from one hotel to another.

Advancement Prospects

Advancement prospects are good for General Managers who have a proven rate of success. Some move from smaller properties to hotels or resorts that are larger and more prestigious, or from non–full service hotels to full service ones. Yet others develop niche areas such as managing spas or ski resorts. Some General Managers advance to become hotel owners.

Education and Training

A four-year college degree is required for virtually all General Manager positions. While only 50 percent of current General Managers have a degree in hospitality, majors and courses such as hotel or hospitality management are extremely helpful. It is also crucial to gain hotel experience while in college. Many spend their summers interning in hotel management as well as working as waitstaff or desk clerks to learn the field. Insiders say this is the most valuable training one can receive.

Voluntary certification as a Certified Hotel Administrator or Lodging Manager is available through the American Hotel and Lodging Association. For more information, see www.ei-ahla.org/content.aspx?id=112.

Experience, Skills, and Personality Traits

Depending on the size, location, and prestige of the property, there is great variation in the years of experience it takes one to become a General Manager. At a full service hotel, 20 years of experience is average, with one having worked up through the ranks of the hospitality field. Most General Managers begin in hotel operations such as the rooms, food and beverage, or sales and marketing division. They typically work as a division head in two of these three areas before advancing to General Manager, and most General Managers have food and beverage experience. However, at a budget, non–full service hotel, a General Manager may achieve his or her position within five years of finishing school.

Additionally, General Managers must be excellent leaders and supervisors. They must be able to motivate staff and carry out a vision. Their strong budgeting, attention to detail, and administrative skills help operations run efficiently and effectively. Good judgment helps them solve problems and handle emergencies calmly and competently. General Managers must truly enjoy interacting with people and developing ongoing relationships with customers, since that is what the field is all about.

Unions and Associations

The main professional association for General Managers and other hotel executives is the American Hotel and Lodging Association. They provide voluntary certification for executives as well as information for students.

Tips for Entry

1. Insiders say that the best advice for aspiring General Managers is to be prepared to start at the bottom. Without having worked on the front lines as a desk clerk, bellhop, housekeeper, or waitstaff, one will never have true appreciation for the hard work that goes into running a hotel. This experience gives you credibility, empathy, and the ability to better do your job.

2. Get a job at a hotel as soon as possible during a summer/winter break or busy season. This will help you to understand the realities of working behind the scenes in this industry.

3. Educate yourself about the hotel industry. Reading the success stories of pioneers such as Statler, Hilton, and Marriott will inform you and provide a historical context for the field.

4. Conduct an information interview with a General Manager of a hotel to find out about his or her career path, typical day, and advice to someone starting out.

5. Take courses in hotel management that include staffing and finance. These will benefit you throughout your hospitality career path.

DIRECTOR OF ROOMS

Duties: Oversees the front office operations for a hotel, including the front desk, bell stand, valet service, housekeeping, and reservations

Alternate Title(s): Rooms Manager; Rooms Director; Rooms Division Director or Manager

Salary Range: $40,000 to $100,000 and up

Employment Prospects: Fair to Good

Advancement Prospects: Good

Best Geographical Location(s): All, with the greatest opportunities in large cities and heavy tourist regions with many resorts and hotels

Prerequisites:

Education and Training—Bachelor's degree in hotel or hospitality management, business, or related field

Experience—At least five years of experience in the rooms division, including supervisory experience

Special Skills and Personality Traits—Good leadership and management ability; strong financial and communication skills; supervisory experience; customer service orientation; ability to juggle multiple tasks and solve problems

Position Description

When you check into a hotel, you are assigned a room that meets the specifications you requested. Perhaps you wanted a king-size bed, nonsmoking, ocean view or even the honeymoon suite. Overseeing the whole process of room assignment, as well as the entire front office operations of a hotel, is the Director of Rooms.

The Director of Rooms is an important management position within a hotel, as he or she has oversight for all front office responsibilities, which usually includes the front desk, the bell stand and bell/valet services, reservations, housekeeping, laundry, engineering, and security. These divisions are crucial to hotel operations because they involve direct contact with guests. The goal of the Director of Rooms is to ensure that guests enjoy their stay at a hotel, from making their reservation, to having a pleasant check-in experience and assistance with their luggage, to ensuring that their room (as well as all public areas) is kept clean and neat, and that their questions are answered.

A hotel is a business and the Director of Rooms is responsible for selling hotel rooms at the highest cost possible in order to maximize property revenues. Rates must be set and made available that are competitive for the market. Managing the rooms division budget falls to the Directors of Rooms as they hone the business plan, forecast revenues, and look for ways to increase productivity and profits. They also develop plans and goals for their division.

Furthermore, Directors of Rooms are supervisors. They make sure that guests are happy by overseeing all their departments, checking and ensuring that they have all the tools and support necessary to best perform their jobs. Directors of Rooms handle hiring, training, and other staffing issues for the rooms division. They often serve as mentors to their staff, particularly to the entry-level people who are on the front line (such as front desk employees), making sure they are skilled in customer service and know where to direct their questions. In order to ensure that guests are happy, good Directors of Rooms know this begins with making sure their employees are happy.

There is no typical day for a Director of Rooms, since anything can happen on any given day. Much hustle and bustle occurs at hotels, with every moment, someone checking in or out, rooms being prepared, and more. According to one Director of Rooms, those in this position must "have their fingers on the pulse of the hotel." They must be attuned to anything going on the world or community that day that might affect guests and their experience.

Problem solving is part of the job of a Director of Rooms, as he or she must ensure that everything is running properly. Things can go wrong—elevators stop, jewelry is stolen from a room—and the Director of Rooms must resolve the problem and provide guests with the utmost customer service.

Additional duties might include:

- participating in meetings with hotel leadership
- providing performance reviews and other human resources functions
- keeping up on industry trends
- assisting with division marketing plans
- responding to and resolving customer complaints
- managing relationships with outside vendors
- promoting good public relations with guests as well as outside constituents
- implementing emergency procedures
- meeting weekly with all department managers
- coordinating employee schedules to ensure constant coverage

Computer literacy is necessary as computerized systems are the way hotel booking and pricing are done. Directors of Rooms may work extended hours during busy times for hotel stays or staffing. Hours are not usually the typical nine-to-five, since that does not reflect hotel hours. Workweeks can often be 50 hours or more, including evenings, weekends, and holidays. But the work environment can be quite beautiful at resorts, depending on the location of the property.

Salaries

Salaries for Directors of Rooms vary depending on the size and location of the property. A typical salary might be $60,000 to $70,000, but the range can span from $40,000 to $100,000 and up. Experience and skills also play a role in salary. In addition to base salary, Directors of Rooms often receive bonuses, standard benefits, and discounted hotel stays or other travel perks if working for large chains.

Employment Prospects

Employment prospects are fair to good for Directors of Rooms. Since there are many positions reporting to a Director of Rooms, there are many different paths leading up to the position. One may become a Director of Rooms with management experience in front office, housekeeping, guest services, reservations, and other departments. However, the availability of positions can be dependent on the economy and the frequency in which people travel during certain time periods. Networking within the industry and job Web sites such as www.hcareers.com are good ways to discover opportunities.

Advancement Prospects

Advancement prospects are also good for Directors of Rooms. Because of the high level of responsibility in their position, Directors of Rooms often serve as the right-hand people to the general manager of the hotel. Thus, they are likely to be promoted into a general manager position if they have proved themselves. Directors of Rooms may also move to larger properties to have greater responsibilities and higher earning potential.

Education and Training

Directors of Rooms should hold bachelor's degrees in fields such as hotel or hospitality management or business. At larger properties, they may have master's degrees in these or related fields. Formal education in the hospitality field teaches prospective Directors of Rooms about the hotel business, including organization structure, operations, and finance.

Voluntary certification as a Certified Rooms Division Executive is available through the American Hotel and Lodging Association. For more information, see www.ei-ahla.org/content.aspx?id=112.

Experience, Skills, and Personality Traits

Directors of Rooms have worked their way up in the rooms division, usually with five to 10 years of experience, including positions as managers in housekeeping, front office, reservations, guest services, or other areas. Supervisory experience is also necessary to prepare them for this leadership role.

Additionally, Directors of Rooms should have excellent communication and interpersonal skills in order to be able to listen to staff and guest alike and resolve issues. A strong financial background helps them handle the budgetary and accounting responsibilities of the position. Knowledge of foreign languages may be helpful for positions in large international hotels and resorts with employees and guests from all over the world.

Leadership and management ability enables Directors of Rooms to run their teams effectively. Balancing multiple tasks at once, staying calm under pressure, and being an analytical problem solver is also needed. At the heart of the position is a customer service orientation and Directors of Rooms not only display this in their own work, but also train their staff to enhance guest satisfaction.

Unions and Associations

The main professional association for Directors of Rooms and other hotel executives is the American

Hotel and Lodging Association. The association provides voluntary certification for executives as well as information for students.

Tips for Entry

1. Explore the Web site of the American Hotel and Lodging Association at www.ahla.com.
2. A degree in hotel management is excellent preparation for a future career as a Director of Rooms. Explore programs including the Cornell University School of Hotel Administration (www.hotelschool.cornell.edu) and the Northern Arizona School of Hotel and Restaurant Management (home.nau.edu/hrm).
3. Consider an internship at a local hotel. This will provide invaluable insight into the workings of hotel operations.
4. Next time you visit a hotel, observe the different roles and responsibilities that fall under the rooms division. Ask staff about their jobs and overall feelings about the industry.
5. Keep up on industry trends by reading articles on sites such as www.hotel-online.com.
6. Review job descriptions of Directors of Rooms for ideas about roles and responsibilities. You can find jobs listed on sites of major hotel chains such as www.starwoodhotels.com/sheraton/careers/search/index.html.

FOOD AND BEVERAGE DIRECTOR

CAREER PROFILE

Duties: Oversees all functions related to food and beverages for a hotel, including all property bars, restaurants, coffee shops, banquets, and catering

Alternate Title(s): Director, Food and Beverage; Food and Beverage Manager

Salary Range: $50,000 to $100,000 and up

Employment Prospects: Good

Advancement Prospects: Good

Best Geographical Location(s): All, with the greatest opportunities in large cities and heavy tourist regions with many resorts and hotels

Prerequisites:

Education and Training—Bachelor's degree in food service, hotel/restaurant management, business, or related field

Experience—At least five years of experience in the food and beverage division, including supervisory experience

CAREER LADDER

```
General Manager or Assistant General
Manager
          |
Food and Beverage Director
          |
Assistant Food and Beverage Director or
Restaurant Manager
```

Special Skills and Personality Traits—Ability to multitask and solve problems; strong leadership and management ability; good financial and communication skills; supervisory experience; customer service orientation; knowledge of culinary and wine industries

Position Description

When you visit a large hotel or resort, there are typically many different dining options. You might have breakfast at a coffee shop or casual buffet, lunch at the poolside lounge, drinks in the late afternoon at the lobby piano bar, and dinner at the full-service gourmet restaurant. Even at small or business hotels, there are usually several dining options. The Food and Beverage Director oversees everything related to food and drink.

Under the realm of the Food and Beverage Director are not only all the dining establishments, ranging from bars and nightclubs to restaurants and cafés, but also room service and catering/banquets. Their goal is to ensure that all guests have satisfying options for eating and drinking. Depending on the size of the hotel/resort, this can be an exhaustive list. They have oversight of all of these individual establishments and must be aware of what is going on in each at all times.

The Food and Beverage department is made up of a number of subunits. These typically include:

- food production, including the kitchen and all cooking, headed by the executive chef
- food service, often managed by an assistant food and beverage director. This involves managing the

individual managers of each restaurant/bar as well as waitstaff.
- alcoholic beverages, including all stand-alone bars and nightclubs, as well as restaurant bars
- room service
- conventions and catering
- stewarding, which involves cleanup and waste removal

As a manager, the Food and Beverage Director supervises those individuals who run each of the individual restaurants and bars, checking with them to make sure they have what they need to manage their own staffs. He or she oversees the ordering of food, working closely with the executive chef to ensure that the quantity and quality is up to par. They also work with the directors of catering to make sure special events have all specialty items and food and drink needed. Additionally, they may direct sales, delivery schedules, and storage, making sure that pantries and bars are always stocked with the necessary items.

With the bar in particular, both alcoholic and nonalcoholic beverages must be stocked and available for the range of drinks a guest might order. It is important to offer a variety of food and beverages, but not so much that there will be excess, and Food and Beverage Directors must toe that line.

Furthermore, the Food and Beverage Director handles human resources functions for their department, addressing staff concerns as well as training and development. They supervise hiring, firing, scheduling, and other staffing issues for the food and beverage division. Additionally, they often mentor staff members, making sure they have the tools and support to do their jobs. Investing time in staff development makes for happy employees, which in turn affects guest satisfaction and, eventually, the bottom line.

Food and Beverage Directors are part of the executive leadership of their hotels, usually reporting directly to the general manager. They are responsible for quality and service, as well as overall profits. On a regular basis, they review the monthly profit and loss statements and analyze profitability, recommending and implementing changes when necessary. They consider who to control quality and portion size while minimizing waste.

Additional duties may include:

- negotiating prices with suppliers
- estimating food costs
- establishing consistent standards among different dining establishments
- creating divisional budgets
- checking kitchens for cleanliness
- maintaining inventories
- building beverage volume
- ensuring specialty items are in place for functions and events
- ordering items for guests with allergies or special needs
- promoting food and beverage services on the property Web site
- creating marketing programs, working with the sales and marketing department
- achieving or exceeding budgeted revenue and net income operating goals
- generating sales and cost-control procedures
- holding regular meetings with staff and attending executive meetings

Good Food and Beverage Directors have extensive knowledge of food and wine. They may work on planning menus and special promotions, including themes throughout the hotel such as a Hawaiian night, for example. This can include coordinating not only food and drink, but also costumes, decorations, and specialty ordering. They also may circulate through dining rooms, seeking out guest comments and handling complaints.

As typical in the hotel industry, hours are long and nontraditional. Food and Beverage Directors may work extended hours including evenings, weekends, and holidays, when most restaurants are in full swing. They also may be on call during their off hours in order to troubleshoot in case of problems. Work weeks can often be 50 hours or more, but work environments can be quite beautiful at resorts, depending on the location of the property.

Salaries
Salaries for Food and Beverage Directors vary depending on the size and location of the property, as well as the number of bars and restaurants on the site. A typical salary might be $70,000 to $80,000, but the range can span from $50,000 to $100,000 and up, particularly at big city or high-end resorts. Experience and skills also play a role in salary. In addition to base salary, Food and Beverage Directors may receive bonuses, standard benefits, and discounted hotel stays or other travel perks if working for large chains.

Employment Prospects
Employment prospects for Food and Beverage Directors are good. Many positions report to the Food and Beverage Director, so there are a number of different paths leading up to the position. An individual may become a Food and Beverage Director after working as a restaurant manager, chef, or other position within the department. Typically, they are promoted after working as an assistant food and beverage director.

As many hotels and resorts add even more dining choices to their facilities, opportunities for Food and Beverage Directors will grow. Networking within the industry and on job Web sites such as www.hcareers.com are good ways to discover openings.

Advancement Prospects
Advancement prospects are also good for Food and Beverage Directors. As members of the executive team, they may be poised to move up to general managers after a tenure of success on their division. Additionally, they may advance by moving to larger properties that have a greater variety of dining choices and more upscale options, which provides greater responsibility and salary.

Education and Training
Food and Beverage Directors typically have training in the food service industry. Bachelor's degrees are required for most positions, in fields such as restaurant, food service, hotel/hospitality management, or business. At larger properties, they may have master's degrees in

these or related fields. Formal education in the hospitality field teaches prospective Food and Beverage Directors about the hotel business, including organization structure, operations, and finance. Culinary and wine education is also very valuable.

Voluntary certification as a Certified Food and Beverage Executive is available through the American Hotel and Lodging Association. For more information, see www.ei-ahla.org/content.aspx?id=1624.

Experience, Skills, and Personality Traits

The ability to multitask is essential. Simultaneously, a mouse may run through the five-star restaurant, a bartender could run out of sour mix, and a wedding going on in the banquet hall might have melting ice sculptures. The Food and Beverage Director must be able to handle all the issues at once, and more importantly, know to whom and how to delegate.

Additionally, a Food and Beverage Director should be a strong leader and manager who is able to motivate, train, and develop staff. They need good financial and communication skills to work with other departments and manage budgets. Furthermore, they should have a strong customer service orientation and excellent interpersonal skills.

Unions and Associations

Food and Beverage Directors may belong to the American Hotel and Lodging Association, the main professional association for hotel executives. The association provides voluntary certification for executives as well as information for students. They may also belong to the National Restaurant Association.

Tips for Entry

1. Explore degree programs in restaurant and food service management. Some to consider include the bachelor of science degree in restaurant management at Platt College in Tulsa, Oklahoma (www.plattcollege.org/programs/restaurant manag.htm) and the bachelor of applied science in food service management at Arizona State University in Mesa, Arizona (www.poly.asu.edu/saas/nutrition/undergraduate/bas.html).

2. Read job descriptions for Food and Beverage Directors on sites such as www.hospitalityonline.com/jobs.

3. Gain experience working in a restaurant as a member of the waitstaff or as a bartender. Take any opportunity available at a hotel restaurant or bar, as this is a great way to interact with managers and Food and Beverage Directors.

4. Review the Web sites of major hotels as well as smaller local properties. See how many restaurants each of them have and contrast the differences.

PUBLIC RELATIONS DIRECTOR

CAREER PROFILE

Duties: Represents a hotel or resort to the media and manages the relationship between a hotel and the public

Alternate Title(s): Director of Public Relations; Public Relations Manager; Media Relations Director, Director of Communications

Salary Range: $35,000 to $125,000 and up

Employment Prospects: Good

Advancement Prospects: Good

Best Geographical Location(s): All, especially major cities and tourist locations with an abundance of hotels and resorts

Prerequisites:

Education and Training—Bachelor's degree; major in communications, public relations, journalism, hospitality management, or related fields very helpful

Experience—Five to 10 years of prior public relations experience; experience in journalism also very helpful

CAREER LADDER

```
Vice President or President of Public
Relations; General Manager or
Assistant General Manager
                 |
Public Relations Director
                 |
Public Relations or Communications
Specialist; Public Relations
Representative
```

Special Skills and Personality Traits—Excellent verbal communication skills; strong writing and ability; media savvy; good planning and organizational skills; skilled at networking and building relationships

Position Description

The field of public relations (also known as PR) involves helping an organization and its public mutually adapt to each other. Every individual hotel and hotel chain interfaces with the public and wants to represent its image a certain way. Public relations is vital to the hospitality industry because it is the medium through which reputations get built. A good PR campaign impacts overall revenue by encouraging travelers to visit and experience the brand.

Public Relations Directors might work for an individual hotel or in the corporate offices of a hotel chain. Their job is to promote their destination and overall tourism experience. They want their hotels to be in the limelight and get recognition for any new programs or events. In order to do this, Public Relations Directors must be masters of image. They strive to make people aware of their hotels' strengths and offerings. Because they bridge the gap between their hotel and the public, they must fully understand their hotel and its operational goals. Furthermore, they must be equally attuned to the travelers and travel trends, as they seek to improve communication and foster relationships.

Public relations can include components including corporate communications, community relations, employee relations, marketing or product publicity, consumer service/customer relations, managing publications, special events, and public speaking. However, regardless of the specifics, communication is always the key factor. Public relations specialists must be able to effectively communicate and develop a PR strategy through writing, speaking, and visual imagery.

Public Relations Directors may spend much time writing, editing, or overseeing materials including press releases (which inform the media about breaking news and other information), as well as brochures, newsletters, and advertisements. Many use prior experience in journalism to impart information in the most effective way, with attention to tone, style, and key points. They are able to translate hotel industry jargon into language that people can understand. They compile press kits of the most pertinent information to send to their media contacts, including photographs of the hotel and/or any new facilities, upcoming special events, and more.

Once they have written their material, Public Relations Directors find the appropriate outlets for distribution. These outlets can be internal, such as newsletters, or external, such as brochures and Web sites. Additionally, Public Relations Directors try to secure radio or television spots for their hotels, as well as newspaper and magazine articles, in order to promote their services. By developing relationships with journalists and media representatives, they have a built-in network toward which they can pitch stories. Public Relations Directors should have an address book filled with contacts of prominent travel editors, writers, and newspeople.

Verbal communication is equally important. Public Relations Directors may represent their hotel at meetings, at press conferences, and on radio or television. They may serve as the face of their organization, controlling what information is shared. On the flip side, Public Relations Directors serve to conduct damage control when any negative publicity for their hotel emerges.

Additional duties may include:

- serving as liaisons with the media
- attending meetings and making presentations
- managing newsletters and other publications
- coordinating community relations
- negotiating with vendors
- planning and running special events
- handling broadcast communications
- conducting outreach to various public groups
- representing their hotel at events
- writing and editing Web copy, press releases, speeches, and other materials
- managing a PR budget
- creating marketing pieces to help sell projects, services, or ideas
- working with travel agents and inviting them to visit

Public Relations Directors may also be involved with creating surveys and conducting research that lets them know how effective their efforts have been. For example, they may evaluate whether occupancy has gone up after a particularly positive article in a major market. Additionally, they can use research to measure the expectations of the public and adapt accordingly. Public Relations Directors are strategists who manage the short term as they plan for the long term.

Public Relations Directors work closely with communication professionals, such as print and broadcast journalists. They also work closely with other hotel personnel, such as specialists in sales and marketing, special events, and management. Hours will vary depending on the type of hotel or resort, but might often include evenings, weekends, and holidays. Some positions can be quite demanding, requiring workweeks of 45 to 50 hours

and more. Insiders say they need to be "on call 24/7" to deal with any negative publicity that might arise. Some travel might be necessary to attend meetings with clients and evening work might be needed for special events.

Salaries
According to the Bureau of Labor Statistics (BLS), median annual earnings for salaried public relations specialists were $49,800 as of May 2007. The middle 50 percent earned between $37,420 and $69,410; the lowest 10 percent earned less than $29,580; and the top 10 percent earned more than $94,620.

Furthermore, the Public Relations Society of America states the national average salary at the Public Relations Director level, working for a corporation, is $124,000.

Employment Prospects
According to the BLS, employment in public relations is expected to increase faster than the average for all occupations through 2016. With keen competition between hotels in the tourism industry, a good public relations strategy can affect the bottom line. Hotels cannot afford *not* to hire PR firms or in-house staff. For this reason, jobs in public relations are expected to grow.

However, even though employment prospects are good, entry-level jobs remain very competitive. A degree in journalism or communications can be a big help in getting started. Some professionals that eventually become Public Relations Directors at hotels start out in public relations agencies that specialize in travel and hospitality.

Within tourism PR, there are many opportunities outside of hotels. Public relations specialists can work for the tourism branch of government, visitors' bureaus, spas, airlines, cruise lines, theme parks, attractions, museums, restaurant chains, rental car companies, and more.

Advancement Prospects
Advancement prospects are also good for Public Relations Directors. They may advance to hotel management or to corporate offices as vice presidents or presidents of public relations for hotel chains. They may also move to larger and more prestigious hotels and resorts or to agencies focusing on hospitality clients. Additionally, they may work as consultants for a variety of hospitality clients on their own.

Education and Training
Bachelor's degrees are required for Public Relations Directors, with the most valuable majors including

journalism, communications, or English. Some colleges and universities offer public relations courses, minors, or majors, which can also be helpful, and some may include classes in travel and tourism. A business or hotel management background may also be useful for training in marketing and strategy.

While most Public Relations Directors report that much of their training comes on the job and through internships, additional training is available to help professionals advance to the next level. The Public Relations Society of America accredits public relations specialists with at least five years of experience in the field. For this voluntary accreditation, they must pass a comprehensive six-hour examination. Furthermore, the International Association of Business Communicators also has an accreditation program for professionals in the communication field, including public relations specialists. Through this program, which also requires a minimum of five years of experience, qualified professions receive the Accredited Business Communicator (ABC) designation.

Experience, Skills, and Personality Traits

Many public relations professionals say that experience in journalism is very helpful for their job. They believe journalists respect them more knowing that they "used to be on their side" and it also helps them think like a journalist as they pitch ideas and write press releases, determining what type of information a reporter would want to know about each event or item.

Furthermore, a Public Relations Director must be a people person. He or she should be articulate and professional, with the ability to speak to large groups of people with ease. Top-notch communication and writing skills are a necessity. Public Relations Directors should be able to work well under pressure, maintaining calm and projecting confidence for their hotels even in difficult situations. Creativity enables them to create new and innovative PR campaigns. Flexibility, energy, and ambition drive Public Relations Directors to be successful.

Public Relations Directors can handle adversity. They seek out press opportunities and are savvy enough to know how to put a positive spin on a bad situation.

Public Relations Directors are aware of the connection between image and perception. They are able to build relationships with corporate leaders, travelers, and media professionals alike.

Unions and Associations

Public Relations Directors may belong to a variety of professional associations including the Public Relations Society of America, which has a specific Travel and Tourism section, as well as a food and beverage affinity group. They may also belong to the International Association of Business Communicators and the American Hotel and Lodging Association.

Tips for Entry

1. Spend time on the Web site of the Public Relations Society of America, particularly its Travel and Tourism section, at www.prsa.org/networking/sections/travel/. Read their career information, job listings, and definitions of different PR functions.
2. Explore PR firms that focus on travel and hospitality. Quinn & Co., based in New York City, specializes in the real estate, residential hotels and resorts, travel and food, and wine and spirits industries. Visit their Web site at www.quinnandco.com.
3. Many other PR firms nationwide specialize in travel and hospitality clients. See a list at www.odwyerpr.com/pr_firm_rankings/travel.htm.
4. Public relations internships are crucial for a career as a public relations specialist. Visit sites such as www.internships.com, speak with your campus career center, and search your yellow pages for local hotels, resorts, and PR firms to get some ideas.
5. Take courses in journalism, communications, and public relations. Speak to professors who have specializations and/or experience working in travel/hospitality PR-related fields.
6. Look into travel writers' associations, such as the North American Travel Journalists Association (www.natja.org), as a good way to meet journalists in the field.

CATERING MANAGER

Duties: Plans and oversees banquets, functions, and events taking place at a hotel or resort; solicits new business

Alternate Title(s): Catering Sales Manager; Director of Catering Sales; Director of Catering; Banquet Manager

Salary Range: $35,000 to $100,000 and up

Employment Prospects: Fair to good

Advancement Prospects: Fair to good

Best Geographical Location(s): All, with the greatest opportunities in large cities and heavy tourist regions with many resorts and hotels

Prerequisites:

Education and Training—Bachelor's degree; classes in hotel management and sales helpful

Experience—Prior experience in the hotel/event planning industry, especially food and beverage areas

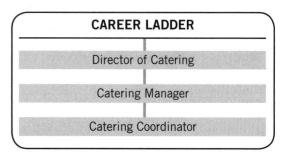

Special Skills and Personality Traits—Excellent sales ability; outgoing personality and strong interpersonal and communication skills; attention to detail; ability to multitask; financial management skills

Position Description

Have you ever been to a wedding, celebratory dinner, meeting, prom, or other event held at a hotel? The Catering Manager plans and organizes these functions, ranging from the initial meeting to sell the space and arrange the deal, to the details leading up to the event and the logistics during the actual function.

Successful Catering Managers do not wait for people to walk into their hotel and approach them. They are strong salespeople, skilled at pursuing business and building relationships. They network with people in various market segments and develop relationships with local businesses. Catering Managers may develop collateral material to help promote and sell their space such as brochures, photographs, and advertisements. Also, they might focus on attracting business from outside groups (professional associations looking to host conventions) or local groups (weddings and other celebrations). For example, Catering Managers might visit local businesses to attract them to hold meetings or parties at their facility.

After an event is booked, the Catering Manager "details" the event with the customer. This involves working through all components of the event including menu planning, setup, audiovisual equipment, decor, security, VIP services, and entertainment. Catering Managers must manage the details of these different

components and coordinate them with the corresponding hotel's operating departments including food and beverages services, housekeeping, reservations, engineering, security and more. All the while, Catering Managers are aware of food and beverages, as well as staffing costs, looking to maximize revenues.

Depending on the size of the hotel, the Catering Manager may oversee the event or pass it over to the banquet service department once the details are in place. At some hotels, there are also convention service departments to detail with conventions and professional meetings. It is important for the Catering Manager to provide exact details to others so he or she can step away from the actual event and work to secure new business.

Furthermore, Catering Managers have significant financial management responsibility. There are financial goals that must be met based on current business as well as projected new business. Hotel space must be booked effectively and make sense in order to achieve financial goals. Catering Managers must juggle new and existing business and make strong decisions in order to use all available space efficiently.

Additional duties may include:

- preparing and presenting contracts
- working with the reservations department to secure blocks of accommodations for event guests

- recommending vendors such as florists, musicians, photographers, and others
- coordinating customer site inspections
- following up with clients
- using computer software to track costs, vendors, and clients
- discussing room availability and prices with clients
- creating menus and organizing tastings
- forecasting future sales

Catering Managers may work evenings and weekends to attend events and/or meet with clients. They may need to be on call to solve emergencies during an event as well. Generally, they should love working with people and be excellent negotiators. Depending on their work setting, they may book events more than a year in advance, and they may juggle more than 10 different events simultaneously.

Salaries

Salaries for Catering Managers vary depending on the size, cost, and prestige of their property. For example, Catering Managers at high-end, expensive resorts sell lavish wedding packages and receive commissions and bonuses accordingly. There may be opportunity to earn more for bringing in new business. The range of salaries can be from $35,000 to $100,000 or even higher. Because only full service hotels need Catering Managers, entry-level salaries might be greater than in other hotel positions.

Employment Prospects

Employment prospects are fair to good for Catering Managers. Opportunities are economy driven in that people will not plan as many or as lavish events during lean times. Also, positions are only available in full-service hotels. However, hotels with banquet and meeting spaces need Catering Managers to sell the space and plan their events. This creates demand, especially for those Catering Managers with experience and who are geographically flexible.

Advancement Prospects

Advancement prospects are also fair to good. Catering Managers may advance to direct catering, conferences, or banquets for their property, or may move to another, more prestigious property. Some may decide to move into the restaurant industry or to country clubs, catering halls, and other facilities outside of hotels. Yet other Catering Managers may decide to start their own businesses, capitalizing on their event planning services.

Education and Training

A bachelor's degree is required for most positions as a Catering Manager. While one does not need to study hotel management, courses in that field, as well as sales and marketing, are very helpful. Computer training is also helpful for scheduling events and tracking sales. Most Catering Managers have a food and beverage background in either the hotel or restaurant industry, which is how they receive their training.

Optional certification as a Certified Professional Catering Executive is offered through the National Association of Catering Executives at www.nace.net/cs/education/cpce.

Experience, Skills, and Personality Traits

Catering Managers should have excellent sales ability and the ability to work well with people. An outgoing personality helps them close deals and network to bring in new business. Strong attention to detail helps them to oversee events and keep track of the different components. Furthermore, multitasking ability and financial management skills are needed.

It is also important to be service-oriented, have food and beverage experience, and be a team player to work with the other hotel departments. Catering Managers need to work well with their clients and make them feel good about the services they are receiving.

Unions and Associations

The National Association of Catering Executives (NACE) is the main professional association for Catering Managers. According to their Web site, www.nace.net, they are the oldest and largest catering association in the world. NACE is focused on promoting career success for its members and the professionalism of the industry with educational programs, professional certification, a job bank, conferences, networking opportunities, and more.

Tips for Entry

1. Cover letters accompany your résumé and provide more detail about your qualifications and interest in a job. View a sample cover letter for a Catering Manager at www.jobbankusa.com/resumes/cover_letters_free_samples/examples_templates_formats/hotel_catering_manager.html.
2. Insiders say that to be effective as a Catering Manager one must have a working knowledge of food and beverage service. Try a job working in a hotel or freestanding restaurant to get started.
3. Next time you attend an event at a hotel, pay attention to the detail and planning involved. If

a friend or family member is planning an event at a hotel, visit the Catering Manager with them to learn and observe the process. If they visit more than one property, take note of the different styles of Catering Managers and which you think is the most effective.

4. Intern in the catering department of a hotel to gain experience and learn if the field is right for you.
5. Gain experience in sales through part-time jobs that involve high people contact and selling, such as retail or telemarketing.

HUMAN RESOURCES DIRECTOR

CAREER PROFILE

Duties: Oversees employee relations functions for a hotel including staffing, recruiting, benefits and compensation, and policies and procedures

Alternate Title(s): Human Resources Manager; Director of Human Resources; Director of Staffing; Recruitment Manager; Employment Manager; Personnel Director; Training and Development Director

Salary Range: $50,000 to $145,000

Employment Prospects: Excellent

Advancement Prospects: Good

Best Geographical Location(s): All, especially major cities and tourist locations with an abundance of hotels and resorts

Prerequisites:

Education and Training—Minimum of a bachelor's degree; master's degree in human resources administration or business may be preferred at larger properties

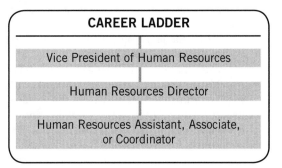

Experience—Prior human resources and supervisory experience, usually between five and 10 years

Special Skills and Personality Traits—Superior interpersonal skills; good verbal and written communication; enthusiasm and professionalism; strong organization and attention to detail; knowledge of federal and state employment regulations

Special Requirements—Voluntary certification is available through several organizations

Position Description

Human Resources Directors manage the "people" concerns for their organizations as the first line of contact for all personnel issues. Their responsibilities range from hiring, firing, and interviewing to mediating problems, administering benefits, and coordinating training. As advocates for their employees, Human Resources Directors work to ensure that their hotels are staffed well and that workers are happy and successful.

There are a number of different aspects of human resources, and Human Resources Directors may be generalists or specialists. The basic human resources functions are as follows:

- hiring, including writing and posting job descriptions, interviewing candidates, and generating job offers; terminations are often handled by human resources as well
- compensation and benefits, including salaries, major medical and dental insurance, vacation time, sick leave, and pensionor 401(k) plans
- training and development, including employee education and programs

- employee relations, including employee assistance programs, counseling, and mediation
- policies and procedures

Human Resources Directors may oversee one or all of these functions. They may also supervise staff members with specific responsibility over each of these functions.

In terms of hiring and recruiting, Human Resources Directors handle or oversee most of the process and identify staffing needs. Working together with the various hiring departments of the hotel, they develop job descriptions and create a recruiting strategy. This strategy may consist of visiting college campuses to conduct interviews or attend career fairs; advertising through professional associations and Web sites; posting jobs on internal and external hiring Web sites; and posting on online search engines both for the hospitality industry as well as general interest.

Human Resources Directors also screen candidates through résumé and cover letter review; either the director or a staff member frequently conducts the initial interview. They see if candidates meet the basic requirements for the job, as well as if they would be a good overall fit for the organization. It is at their discretion that a candidate is then seen by the department. In this way, Human Resources Directors play a major role in shaping and structuring the hotel personnel. After the department makes an employment decision, human resources often generates the offer letter, manages communication with the new employee, negotiates salary, and provides information about benefits.

The compensation and benefits responsibility requires Human Resources Directors to work with insurance companies to process claims and invoices for provider payment. They handle monthly transfers and remittances for 401(k) and pension plans, disability insurance, and medical/dental insurance plans. Furthermore, they maintain benefits records and track usage such as vacation time and sick leave. There may be other unique benefits such as hotel or travel discounts they oversee. Human Resources Directors meet with new employees to orient them about these programs and help them make informed selections. If the hotel has many foreign employees, time must be spent ensuring they understand the procedures. For compensation, Human Resources Directors maintain salary records for all employees and determine appropriate salary ranges and fair compensation guidelines.

Training and development encompasses functions such as developing and implementing training goals and programs for employees. For example, a Human Resources Director may initiate computer system training for the reservations department, or diversity training for the entire hotel staff. Educational seminars and professional growth opportunities help employees to both perform their jobs better and feel more satisfied with their organization.

As employee relations managers, Human Resources Directors are often called on to solve problems and mediate disputes between employees, including supervisors and subordinates. They must be fair and objective in listening to complaints and recommending courses of action. Employees may seek out the Human Resources Director to voice job-related or even personal concerns and issues. Some organizations offer confidential counseling through employee assistance programs or community referrals. Human Resources Directors may also develop and conduct employee performance evaluations. They often work closely with the general manager and hotel management staff, offering advice and assistance.

Policies and procedures are necessary to keep any organization running smoothly and hotels are no exception. From developing procedures to post vacant positions and creating fair hiring policies to developing training manuals, Human Resources Directors document policy and ensure that employees are aware of rules and procedures. This can help in preventing misunderstandings and even lawsuits in the event that an employee is terminated.

Additional duties may include:

- training human resources staff on interviewing techniques
- ensuring compliance with all state and federal laws and regulations that pertain to human resources
- overseeing compliance with an affirmative action program
- managing labor relations activities by administering union contracts and ensuring compliance
- responding to grievances in writing, negotiating settlements, and acting as the hotel representative at all arbitrations
- conducting reference checks and/or mandatory testing such as drug testing
- preparing and monitoring budgets
- using software and databases to track information
- following procedures related to any hotel emergency or security situation
- keeping up to date with employment law and recruitment trends
- maintaining employee records

The typical workweek for Human Resources Directors is 40 to 45 hours, usually on a nine-to-five schedule. Extended hours may be necessary during busy hiring or benefits cycles. Some travel may be necessary to attend career fairs, college campuses, or professional conferences.

Human Resources Directors serve as representatives for their hotel, and must have the energy and enthusiasm to motivate employees. They should feel positive about their jobs in order to recruit and retain a high-quality staff.

Salaries

According to the Bureau of Labor Statistics (BLS), median annual earnings of human resources managers (comparable to Human Resources Directors) were $88,510 as of May 2006. The middle 50 percent earned between $67,710 and $114,860. The lowest 10 percent earned less than $51,810, and the highest 10 percent earned more than $145,600. In May 2006, median annual earnings were $98,400 in the management of companies and enterprises industry.

The highest salaries are found at the most luxurious, high-end properties. Human Resources Directors may also receive discounted hotel and other travel benefits at sister properties or other resorts.

Employment Prospects

The BLS states that employment of human resources, training, and labor relations managers and specialists is expected to grow faster than the average for all occupations, showing excellent job prospects. College graduates who have earned certification should have the best job opportunities. Overall employment is projected to grow by 17 percent between 2006 and 2016, faster than the average for all occupations.

The growth is expected to be due to legislation and court rulings that will set standards in different areas such as occupational safety and health, equal employment opportunity, wages, health care, pensions, and family leave, among others. This will increase demand for human resources, training, and labor relations experts. The BLS also says that "rising health care costs should continue to spur demand for specialists to develop creative compensation and benefits packages that firms can offer prospective employees."

Advancement Prospects

Human Resources Directors can advance in two ways. They may work their way up to become vice presidents of their current organization, taking on a senior management role in their hotel. Or they can move from smaller properties to larger ones, attracting wealthier clients and a higher salary.

Education and Training

Human Resources Directors should hold bachelor's degrees, typically in business or hotel administration. Courses in psychology or organizational development also might be helpful. At some larger organizations, Human Resources Directors have master's degrees, usually in business or hotel administration. This may provide advanced training beneficial for a management role. Knowledge of federal and state employment regulations such as EEO (equal employment opportunity) is also required.

Special Requirements

While there is no required certification for Human Resources Directors, some professionals seek voluntary certification, which can be helpful for hiring or advancement. These voluntary certifications include programs through the American Society for Training and Development (ASTD) (www.astd.org); certification as a Certified Employee Benefits Specialist (CEBP) through the International Foundation of Employee Benefit Plans (www.ifebp.org); certification as a Professional in Human Resources (PHR) or a Senior Professional in Human Resources (SPHR) through the Society for Human Resource Management (www.shrm.org); and the designations of Certified Compensation Professional (CCP), Certified Benefits Professional (CBP), Global Remuneration Professional (GRP), and Work-Life Certified Professional (WLCP) through the World at Work Society of Certified Professionals (www.worldatworksociety.org).

Experience, Skills, and Personality Traits

As they are responsible for recruiting new staff, Human Resources Directors often serve as the face of their hotel. Enthusiasm and energy are necessary to project a positive attitude and motivate others. Furthermore, Human Resources Directors must have excellent interpersonal skills. They deal with people daily and must be objective, fair, and diplomatic in their contacts. Good judgment is needed to make hiring decisions and settle disputes.

Additionally, Human Resources Directors must be highly organized and pay close attention to detail. Computer literacy is needed to work with databases and computer programs that track employee and other information. To reach the level of Human Resources Director, one typically must have between five and 10 years of progressively responsible human resources experience.

Unions and Associations

Human Resources Directors belong to professional associations including the American Society for Training and Development, the Society for Human Resource Management, and the World at Work Society of Certified Professionals.

Tips for Entry

1. Review jobs in human resources at hotels on the Web site www.hcareers.com.
2. Volunteer in your career services office on campus. You may find opportunities to review résumés or help peers prepare for interviews, which would provide useful training for a career in human resources.
3. Ask to shadow a Director of Human Resources for a hotel to see what the job entails on a daily basis.
4. Research graduate programs in human resources management through the Society for Human Resources Management's directory at www.shrm.org/foundation/directory.
5. Consider a summer job at a hotel or resort to learn more about the field and the property's organizational structure.

CONTROLLER (COMPTROLLER)

CAREER PROFILE

Duties: Manages accounting and financial operations for a hotel or resort including budgeting, forecasting, and analysis

Alternate Title(s): Accountant; Director of Accounting

Salary Range: $50,000 to $100,000 and up

Employment Prospects: Good

Advancement Prospects: Good to excellent

Best Geographical Location(s): All, with the greatest opportunities in large cities and heavy tourist regions with many resorts and hotels

Prerequisites:

Education and Training—Bachelor's degree in business, accounting, finance, or hospitality; some Comptrollers have graduate degrees

Experience—At least five years of accounting experience, ideally in the hospitality industry

Special Skills and Personality Traits—Excellent financial and accounting skills; information technol-

ogy and general business knowledge; strong communication and interpersonal skills; good judgment and management skills

Special Requirements—Some Controllers may be certified public accountants (CPAs). Others may hold the Certified Hospitality Accountant Executive (CHAE) credential

CAREER LADDER

General Manager, Chief Financial Officer, or Director/Vice President of Finance

Controller

Assistant Controller

Position Description

The Controller oversees accounting operations for a hotel or resort. While this position might not be the first one hospitality students would consider, it offers an ideal way for those with financial skills to work in the hospitality industry. Controllers are typically members of the executive team and have a very important function in that they keep other departments aware and up to date about all financial information.

Controllers prepare and interpret financial statements in order to analyze the financial operation of their organization. They are sometimes called *controllers* because of the cost control aspect of their position. Central to hotel operations, Controllers keep track of rooms and food/beverage costs and revenues to ensure profits. They work closely with personnel in these departments to make sure information is being reported accurately. Furthermore, Controllers work closely with management and other departments to keep abreast of any developments that will impact financial figures.

A Controller's day may begin by reviewing financial reports from the previous evening including bank reports, cash balances, and more. As part of the

executive team, Controllers meet with other department heads in the morning to review activities and any notable events for the upcoming day as well as recapping events from the previous day. Other daily responsibilities may include reviewing group sales contracts and bids from vendors, reviewing purchase orders, and approving payment requests. They handle accounting functions such as accounts payable, accounts receivable, payroll, and mail orders.

Controllers frequently supervise staff accountants and may also oversee additional areas such as information technology (IT). They also manage purchasing, assistant controllers, food and beverage–specific controllers, storerooms, and credit. As managers, they have responsibility for hiring, firing, evaluating, and training staff.

Furthermore, Controllers prepare financial reports that include summary and detail income statements, balance sheets, forecasts, and cash flow statements. Forecasts may be completed monthly as well as compiled annually. Staff members help them work on these reports each month, which will be submitted to management. These reports are used to make decisions and forecast budgeting and spending for the future. Decision making regarding the hotel is tied into the Controller's role, as the Controller provides the data, statistics, and figures that will be used for these choices.

As financial experts, Controllers offer their insight on hotel operations from a financial perspective. They also review credit applications and monitor accounts receivable reports to make sure that payments are being made and there are no situations that would put their hotel in debt. Controllers are skilled at financial analysis in order to examine the past and look for recommendations for the future.

Additional duties may include:

- reconciling the general ledger account daily
- preparing and reviewing budgets
- recording financial transactions
- valuing inventory
- purchasing new equipment
- responding to inquiries from the corporate office
- handling everything involving audits, including completing the year-end audit process, scheduling auditor visits, reconciling numbers, and responding to auditor requests
- reviewing internal and external audit reports
- reviewing past and future cash flows
- solving problems related to cost controls and revenue enhancement
- investigating, reviewing, and analyzing variance explanations

Controllers typically report to the hotel general manager, but may also have a reporting relationship to the hotel owner/corporate office, in order to offer the hotel corporation additional verification of financial records aside from those provided by the general manager. They tend to work more regular hours than other hotel executives and employees, except during busy hours and tax seasons.

Insiders stress that Controllers at hotels are not just the numbers gurus, but integral parts of the hotel management team. They say their jobs are varied and exciting, and although they don't have the same direct interaction with hotel guests as other personnel, they still feel as if their work is service-oriented.

Salaries

Controllers' salaries vary depending on the geographic location, size, and prestige of their property. Typical salaries can range from $50,000 to $100,000 per year, with most average salaries over $80,000. Overall earnings may include both base salary and bonuses.

Employment Prospects

Employment prospects are good for Controllers, particularly in a good economy. Competent managers are always needed to manage hotel finances. As more hotels are built, opportunities for Controllers will grow, especially those with strong education, experience, and geographic flexibility. The Certified Hospitality Accountant Executive (CHAE) credential can enhance employment opportunities.

Advancement Prospects

Advancement prospects are good to excellent for Controllers. At many hotels (particularly smaller ones), they are next in line to the general manager and can advance to that position with experience. Controllers are particularly well-poised to become general managers because they have such a strong grasp on the hotel's finances. They may also advance by moving to larger, more prestigious properties and by working in the corporate office of a hotel chain.

Education and Training

A bachelor's degree is required to become a Controller, ideally in finance, business, or accounting. However, there are some who come to the field with a hospitality degree, since most hospitality programs require 12 to 15 credits in accounting or finance.

To get started, many begin with hotel accounting positions in order to gain experience and training with hotel operations. The more hotel experience a Controller has, the better he or she is able to perform the job, having had exposure to different areas of hotel operations and their financial implications.

Experience, Skills, and Personality Traits

Typically, Controllers have at least five years of previous accounting/hotel experience. They must have excellent computer, financial, accounting, and statistical skills, as well as the knowledge of specific technical software.

In addition to their numbers skills, Controllers also work with people and must have good communication skills. They work with owners, department heads, clients, and others and must have strong interpersonal ability. Furthermore, Controllers must be good managers who can lead their department and make strong decisions. Also important is good judgment and tact, as Controllers deal with sensitive and confidential information.

Unions and Associations

Hospitality Financial and Technology Professionals (HFTP), headquartered in Austin, Texas, is the global professional association for financial and technology personnel working in hotels, clubs, and other hospitality-related businesses.

Special Requirements

Some Controllers seek the Certified Hospitality Accountant Executive (CHAE) credential, an industry designation showing competency in the area of accounting. While this credential is voluntary, it can make a significant difference when it comes to hiring since it shows dedication to the hospitality industry. Other Controllers are certified public accountants (CPAs).

Tips for Entry

1. Explore the Web site of HFTP at www.hftp.org. Here you can learn about CHAE certification, special events including conferences, and membership.
2. Being a Controller at a hotel or resort is not just about the accounting. Gain hotel experience by working as a desk clerk for the summer to learn more about hotel operations. Current hotel Controllers say this is invaluable preparation for getting into the industry.
3. Learn more about becoming a CPA through the American Institute of Certified Public Accountants (AICPA) at www.aicpa.org.
4. If you are interested in studying accounting, AICPA also has a list of degree programs in accounting on its Web site at www.aicpa.org/collegelist/index.htm.

DIRECTOR OF CONVENTION SERVICES

CAREER PROFILE

Duties: Oversees conventions and meetings occurring at a hotel or resort; once the sale is complete, takes charge of all activities

Alternate Title(s): Convention Services Manager; Director of Meeting Planning; Conference Services Manager; Director of Conference Services; Convention Services Specialist; Director of Catering and Convention Services

Salary Range: $50,000 to $80,000 and up

Employment Prospects: Fair to good

Advancement Prospects: Fair to good

Best Geographical Location(s): The greatest opportunities are in large cities and heavy tourist regions with many resorts and hotels that host conventions

Prerequisites:

Education and Training—Bachelor's degree preferred or required for many positions, but not essential

CAREER LADDER

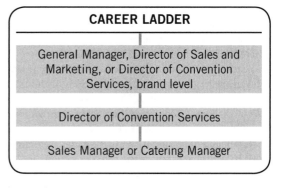

General Manager, Director of Sales and Marketing, or Director of Convention Services, brand level

Director of Convention Services

Sales Manager or Catering Manager

Experience—Prior sales/meeting planning experience; at least three years required

Special Skills and Personality Traits—Excellent organizational skills; strong communication and interpersonal skills; ability to multitask

Position Description

Professional associations and other groups hold conferences year-round and worldwide. Conventions are an important part of belonging to an association as they give members the opportunity to network with others, learn about new developments in the field, receive continuing education credits, and more. Finding a suitable hotel and meeting facility is important in determining the convention's success. The Director of Convention Services for a hotel is instrumental in making sure the conference is a winner.

After the appropriate sales manager seals the deal and the venue is booked, the Director of Convention Services takes over. First, he or she may review the contract to become familiar with it and then send a letter of introduction to the meeting planner at the association. Even if the convention is several months away, this helps the Director of Convention Services develop a working relationship with clients early on and let them know about progress.

Additionally, the Director of Convention Services works closely with other hotel departments that have a hand in serving the convention. They work with department heads from the rooms division to secure guest rooms and the food and beverage division to arrange any on-site meals including buffets and cocktail parties. Coordination is also needed with housekeeping, catering, maintenance/engineering, security, and accounting. The Director of Convention Services prepares information about the convention for department heads in advance so that everyone knows his or her roles and responsibilities. The relationship with sales and marketing is also crucial, in terms of booking the account and implementing programs.

One of the most important jobs of the Director of Convention Services is working with the client. They coordinate with the association's meeting planner and other executives and develop a schedule for the convention, which may last between two to seven days. Daily service requirements are determined and all the necessary service providers are notified. Directors of Convention Services and often present at preconference briefing sessions and greet and tour meeting officials around the property when they arrive. During the convention, they check the facility daily, including function rooms, exhibit areas, and registration areas, and troubleshoot any problems. At the end of the convention, they solicit feedback from the meeting officials and cultivate relationships for future business.

At any given time, a hotel may host several conventions of extremely diverse groups, anything from the American Mathematical Society to the American Association of Zookeepers. Directors of Convention Services must multitask and keep up with all these events simultaneously. In addition to ensuring that the group has all its needs met with regards to rooms, technology, and food and beverage for meetings, they also provide assistance with off-site activities. They work with the local visitor's bureau to coordinate activities, which could be bus tours of cities, passes to the nearby art museum, or tickets to a Major League Baseball game. Therefore, working with groups within the local community is also an important part of the job. Directors of Convention Services must be knowledgeable about the area and its attractions, vendors, and services.

Additional duties may include:

- maintaining records, supplies, inventory, and filing systems
- developing objectives, goals, and policies relating to group business
- working with outside contractors such as audiovisual companies
- facilitating the booking of future business
- ensuring that schedules are maintained and that services go according to plan
- working with the convention bureau and with counterparts in other properties
- informing meeting officials about policy and procedure
- updating operating departments of any schedule changes
- ensuring that event schedules are posted around the property
- securing outside transportation and venues for other convention-related events
- pricing banquet menus

Directors of Convention Services typically work long, nontraditional hours, often 60 to 70 hours per week. They may be a part of the executive committee, reporting to the general manager, or they may report to the sales and marketing director. The Director of Convention Services holds high authority during an event, making decisions about how it should be run. They are responsible for delivering on what the hotel promises and the success of each convention will help drive future business.

Depending on the size of the property, Directors of Convention Services may supervise a staff of convention managers and sales managers. In some locations, they also oversee catering services. Conventions differ from other events such as weddings, with their own unique set of details and specifications to be handled. Those Directors of Convention Services that handle other events are well-versed in both areas.

Salaries
Directors of Convention Services typically earn salaries ranging from $50,000 to $80,000 and up. Earnings vary considerably by size, location, and prestige of the property. Since only full-service hotels host conventions, salaries are at the higher end of the spectrum. Bonuses may also be factored into overall earnings.

Employment Prospects
Convention services came into its own as a profession in the 1980s. However, because not all hotels are equipped to hold conventions, employment prospects are just fair to good. Only large, full-service hotels hire Directors of Convention Services, but those who do are always on the lookout for qualified professionals. Typically, people come into the field through positions in catering or sales as managers; food and beverage experience can also be very useful. Familiarity with different market segments and experience increases employment opportunities.

Advancement Prospects
Directors of Convention Services can advance by moving to larger and more prestigious hotels and resorts in more desirable geographical locations. They also might move into director of sales and marketing positions. Furthermore, at the brand level, there is often one Director of Convention Services that oversees all directors in the various chain hotels; this can be a good advancement opportunity. They may also go to work for meeting facilities outside of the hotel industry.

Education and Training
Educational requirements vary for Directors of Convention Services. Many positions require a bachelor's degree and fields such as sales, marketing, hotel/hospitality management, and public relations are helpful. In other cases, experience can compensate for lack of degrees.

Some Directors of Convention Services have received the Certified Meeting Professional (CMP) credential through the Convention Industry Council. The requirements are based on prior experience and a written exam. For more information, see www.convention industry.org.

the Hospitality Sales and Marketing Association International, and the Convention Industry Council (CIC).

Experience, Skills, and Personality Traits

Directors of Convention Services should be highly organized and detail-oriented. They must be able to multitask and juggle multiple events at once. Additionally, excellent communications and interpersonal skills help them work with people and build relationships. Those Directors of Convention Services who develop good reputations among meeting officials can become known as good to work with, which helps bring in business.

Unions and Associations

The Association for Convention Operations Management (ACOM) is a professional association dedicated to advancing the practice of convention services management (CSM) in the meetings industry and to helping professionals advance their careers. Directors of Convention Services may also belong to the Professional Convention Management Association (PCMA),

Tips for Entry

1. Learn about ACOM and PCMA through their Web sites at www.acomonline.org and www. pcma.org.
2. Explore the Destination Marketing Association International (DMAI) at www.destination marketing.org. This association promotes the long-term development and marketing of a destination, focusing on convention sales, tourism marketing, and service.
3. Are you a member of any professional associations? Get involved with conference preparation and planning, including meeting with a hotel Director of Convention Services.
4. Next time you attend a conference or speak to someone that attended a conference, learn about the schedule and details of the event.
5. Gain sales experience through part-time jobs and internships.

BELLHOP

Duties: Escorting hotel guests to their rooms and assisting with their luggage

Alternate Title(s): Bellman; Bellperson; Bell Attendant; Bellboy

Salary Range: $6.00 to $15.00 per hour plus tips; between $10,000 and $30,000 annually

Employment Prospects: Good

Advancement Prospects: Good

Best Geographical Location(s): All, with the greatest opportunities in large cities and heavy tourist regions with many resorts and hotels

Prerequisites:

Education and Training—High school diploma or equivalent may be preferred or required

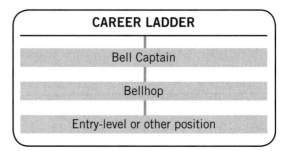

CAREER LADDER

Bell Captain

Bellhop

Entry-level or other position

Experience—Prior hotel or customer service experience

Special Skills and Personality Traits—Strong interpersonal and customer service skills; friendly and courteous; ability to carry heavy luggage

Position Description

When you arrive at a hotel, it is nice to be able to take in your surroundings without having to worry about your cumbersome luggage. Pulling up by taxi or car, a doorman or porter might greet you, open your doors, and remove your bags. After checking in, you can be introduced to an individual who will welcome you with a smile and escort you and your suitcases to your room. This person is a Bellhop.

The name *Bellhop* comes from the tradition of ringing a bell at the front desk when guests require assistance. As guests make their way to their room, which may involve stairs or an elevator, the Bellhop will point out features of interest in the hotel, such as shops, gym/fitness center, swimming pools, business center with fax/computer access, restaurants, and more. Part of his or her job is to make guests feel welcome and to be familiar with the hotel facilities. A brief tour might be on the agenda if the guests are interested. In some cases, guests travel alone to their room and the Bellhop meets them there with the luggage several minutes later.

Once they arrive in the room, the Bellhop will demonstrate the features in the room, such as how to work the television, heat or air conditioner, terrace doors, minibar, lights, and any other amenities. The Bellhop may point out room service menus, explain laundry procedures, and inform the guests about anything else they need to know. With customer satisfaction always in mind, the Bellhop will place the luggage where the

guests prefer and also answer any questions about local attractions or activities. If anything in the room is not functioning properly, Bellhops will report it to the bell captain or maintenance department.

At the end of the stay, Bellhops come to guest rooms to take their luggage down to the entrance and may help guests coordinate transportation, arranging for a taxi to the airport, a rental car, or contacting the valet to retrieve the guests' own car. At this time, Bellhops make conversation with the guests, asking about their visit and making sure it was a positive one.

Additional duties may include:

- bringing up dry cleaning or laundry
- delivering special packages, faxes, or flowers to guest rooms
- hailing taxis for guests
- delivering keys
- running errands for guests
- making reservations for guests
- providing travel directions and assistance

Bellhops are supervised by a bell captain who oversees the bell staff, door people, and everyone else who handles baggage and greets guests. They may assign different Bellhops to guests and coordinate who will escort guests and transport luggage, both at the beginning and end of their stay. Furthermore, they hire and train staff, organize schedules, and keep time records.

The Bellhop should be very friendly and personable in order to make the guests feel at home. Greeting guests by name is a touch that many Bellhops are encouraged to implement. They may be the first in line to deal with complaints if guests are unhappy with their rooms, since Bellhops are the first point of contact once they have seen their room. Bellhops must be able to deal with these complaints respectfully and speak to a manager on behalf of the guests to resolve any problems.

Uniforms are required for Bellhops and they may work a variety of eight-hour shifts that encompass days, evenings, and weekends. Their busiest hours are during hotel check in and checkout times, between 11 A.M. and 5 P.M. Additionally, they must be able to carry heavy bags with ease. For this reason, the majority of Bellhops are male.

Salaries

Salaries for Bellhops vary greatly and may be hard to gauge, since tips can be a strong factor in overall earnings. It is standard for guests to tip the Bellhop after he or she leaves the guest room, and some may tip extravagantly for especially good or more complex service. A median hourly salary for Bellhops is about $9 per hour and yearly earnings can be anywhere between $10,000 and $30,000; bell captains earn more. Bellhops at larger luxury hotels, resorts, and casinos earn more than those at smaller hotels.

Employment Prospects

Bellhops enjoy strong employment prospects. Although only full-service hotels typically employ Bellhops, many are needed to assist guests, especially at larger hotels. There are many opportunities for Bellhops to work in hotels, resorts, and casinos worldwide.

Advancement Prospects

Bellhops can advance in several ways. Those who stand out for their customer service may advance to become bell captains where they supervise other Bellhops and door staff. Also, they may move to larger and more prestigious hotels where earnings and tips can be con-

siderably higher. Furthermore, many college students work as Bellhops during summer and school vacations, as well as part-time during the year. It can be a great way to gain experience in the hospitality industry. Once they finish school, these students can advance to a variety of positions in the hotel field.

Education and Training

Most hotels prefer Bellhops to have a high school diploma; some are college students with degrees in progress. Training often takes place on the job.

Experience, Skills, and Personality Traits

Bellhops should be friendly and personable, with strong interpersonal and customer service skills. Since all of their time is spent interacting with people, the more they enjoy helping others, the more satisfying they will find their jobs. It is also important for Bellhops to be able to handle the physical demands of their job, such as lifting heavy luggage. A valid driver's license may be required for Bellhops who need to drive airport vans or other types of guest transportation.

Unions and Associations

There is no specific professional association for Bellhops, but some may be part of the Unite Here union (www.unitehere.org). The American Hotel and Lodging Association also has more information about jobs in the hotel industry at ww.ahla.com.

Tips for Entry

1. A great site to explore travel-related information is www.petergreenberg.com. Peter Greenberg is a travel expert who serves as the travel editor for NBC's *The Today Show*.
2. Next time you visit a hotel, speak to the Bellhop as he or she assists you. Find out about his or her background and goals.
3. Consider a summer job as a Bellhop; it provides excellent hospitality training due to the extensive customer contact.
4. Read job descriptions on sites such as www.hotel jobs.com.

RESERVATIONS MANAGER

CAREER PROFILE

Duties: Oversees the reservations process for a hotel or resort

Alternate Title(s): Director of Reservations; Reservations Supervisor

Salary Range: $30,000 to $60,000 and up

Employment Prospects: Fair to good

Advancement Prospects: Fair to good

Best Geographical Location(s): All, with the greatest opportunities in large cities and heavy tourist regions with many resorts and hotels

Prerequisites:

Education and Training—High school diploma; some positions may require a college degree, particularly at prestigious properties

Experience—Several years of prior experience in reservations

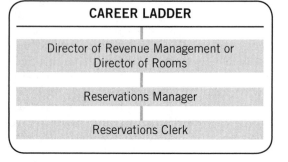

CAREER LADDER

Director of Revenue Management or Director of Rooms

Reservations Manager

Reservations Clerk

Special Skills and Personality Traits—Strong organizational skills; computer literacy and business sense; good communication and interpersonal skills; supervisory skills

---

Position Description

Hotels and resorts run the gamut from small exclusive 10-room inns to huge conference centers with 2,000 rooms or more. At any given time, people make reservations at these properties by calling, using the Internet, and even dropping by. Reservations Managers oversee the reservations process, including supervising the staff who take reservations and analyzing reservation data. Their goal is to maximize occupancy and revenue, all the while ensuring the needs of guests are being met.

As supervisors, Reservations Managers direct the reservations clerks and other staff who take reservations through answering phone calls and gathering online reservations. They hire, train, and evaluate this staff, educating them about the hotel's reservations policies and procedures. Furthermore, they train them on any specific computer systems and online reservation software used by the hotel. Reservations Managers also manage the schedules for the reservations staff, making sure to have all shifts covered with special attention to heavy reservations times related to conferences or other large events.

There are many ways that guests can make hotel reservations, with the Internet increasingly becoming the number-one way. Reservations Managers must ensure that all reservations are centralized, so whether a reservation is made by an individual by phone, by a travel agent, through the hotel's Web site, or through another Web site (such as Travelocity.com or Expedia.com), they all must end up on the same database. It is crucial to stay organized to prevent overbooking and to know what rooms have been assigned for various time frames.

Furthermore, Reservations Managers work with directors of revenue management to control rates and availability. They forecast future occupancy and analyze data of past reservations, cancellations, and occupancy, generating weekly or monthly reports. Reservations Managers note seasonal and other trends, using this information to work with the marketing and advertising departments on special promotions.

Additional duties may include:

- enforcing no-show and cancellation charges and policies
- developing strategies for using Internet distribution channels
- ensuring accuracy of price quotes
- generating e-mails or letters confirming reservations for guests
- using computer software specific to reservations such as PMS (Property Management Systems) and many others
- updating distribution channels for room rates and availability

- creating and maintaining rate codes
- working with annual departmental budgets
- communicating with groups and/or travel agents regarding special requests

Reservations Managers work with other departments such as the sales and catering department in order to reserve room blocks for conferences and special events. Also, they work with the front desk staff to make sure that each day, clerks are provided with a list of all arriving guests, as well as folios providing cost summaries for departing guests. If there are any problems with reservations, Reservations Managers may work directly with guests to upgrade a reservation or solve issues.

Reservations Managers also must be well informed about the hotel rooms, working closely with the rooms director and staff. The entire reservations team must know which rooms have special features including access for people with disabilities, adjoining rooms, special views, kitchenette suites, multiple beds, and more. Furthermore, they must be able to accommodate special requests when taking reservations such as providing a nonsmoking room or a baby's crib.

Salaries

Reservations Manager salaries vary depending on the size, geographic location, and prestige of the property. According to Salary.com, the average salary for a rooms Reservations Manager in the United States as of January 2009 was $38,449. The range can be from $30,000 to $60,000 and up. Experience and education can impact earnings as well.

Employment Prospects

For Reservations Managers, employment prospects are fair to good. Opportunities are best for those with a strong combination of education and experience and for those who are geographically flexible. Reservations Managers at larger properties have more responsibility and higher salaries as they supervise a large scope of rooms and reservations staff. Knowledge of hotel reservations computer software also makes Reservations Managers more employable.

Advancement Prospects

Reservations Managers can advance by moving to larger and more prestigious properties where they supervise a larger staff and have greater management responsibility. Those with degrees in hotel management or related fields may advance to become directors of rooms or directors of revenue management. They may also move over to other departments such as sales and marketing or conference services.

Education and Training

Education and training also varies for Reservations Managers. A high school diploma is required. In some locations, especially large and prestigious properties, a bachelor's degree is preferred or required. Courses in hotel management, business, and sales can be helpful, in addition to training in hotel reservations computer software.

Experience, Skills, and Personality Traits

Good organizational skills are needed to be a Reservations Manager in order to keep track of available rooms in both the present and future. Additionally, supervisory and management ability helps Reservations Managers lead and train their staff. Strong customer service and interpersonal skills are also important. Previous hotel experience is essential for understanding hotel structure, the nature of the job, and computer systems.

Unions and Associations

The main professional association for hotel staff such as Reservations Managers is the American Hotel and Lodging Association. The Association provides voluntary certification for staff and executives as well as information for students.

Tips for Entry

1. Choose a hotel or resort and explore all the different ways to make reservations there, including calling them directly, booking directly through their Web site, or booking through a third party Web site such as www.travelocity.com or www.expedia.com.
2. View jobs for Reservations Managers on sites such as www.simplyhired.com.
3. Begin with a job as a reservations clerk to learn more about the process.
4. Conduct an informational interview with a Reservations Manager to learn about a typical day on the job.

DIRECTOR OF SALES AND MARKETING

CAREER PROFILE

Duties: Oversees the sales and marketing function for a hotel or resort

Alternate Title(s): Sales and Marketing Manager

Salary Range: $50,000 to $120,000 and up

Employment Prospects: Good

Advancement Prospects: Good

Best Geographical Location(s): All, with the greatest opportunities in large cities and heavy tourist regions with many resorts and hotels

Prerequisites:

 Education and Training—Bachelor's degree preferred or required at major hotels

 Experience—Prior sales experience; typically at least five years for director-level positions

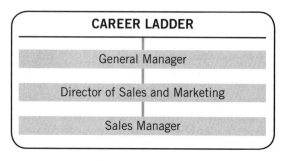

Special Skills and Personality Traits—Excellent communication skills; business knowledge; outgoing personality

Position Description

Sales and marketing is a very important function in the hotel industry. This department is responsible for three main functions: demand creation, demand capture, and demand (revenue) management. Demand creation is the marketing—establishing the hotel as a brand and developing strategic objectives to promote its services through research, public relations, and advertising campaigns. Demand capture is the sales—developing and retaining a client base through sales calls, prospecting, and account management. Third, demand management involves analyzing the process in order to maximize revenues. The Director of Sales and Marketing has responsibility for overseeing all of these functions.

Depending on the size of the hotel, the Director of Sales and Marketing will spend a different breakdown of time on each of these areas. At small, non–full-service properties, virtually all the time and energy is spent on sales. Sales activities can include telemarketing, direct mail, attending trade shows, and prospecting for new accounts. It also involves managing and retaining existing sales relationships in addition to finding new ones. The Director of Sales and Marketing may engage fully in sales activities or direct a team of sales managers based on staff size. Within the sales team, members specialize in different market segments. It is typical at a larger property to have an individual sales

manager responsible for corporate accounts, conventions/associations, and tourism; others may specialize by geographical region.

The marketing function involves directing the brand for their property. The Director of Sales and Marketing, in conjunction with marketing managers, conducts research into different market segments to determine what is effective. They develop collateral materials such as brochures, Web content, and other publicity, in some cases along with an internal or external public relations department. Additionally, the marketing department determines untapped markets and strategies for reaching them. They consider what is unique about their property and how to leverage that into dollars. While larger hotels handle some marketing by unit, the majority of marketing is done at the brand level.

Directors of Sales and Marketing consider how to reach and develop new business. They determine what guests want and how to attract them to their hotel. Research is a key component to developing and maintaining business. The more Directors of Sales and Marketing know about their prospective clients, the better able they are to personalize their sales pitch to them. Sales are different in travel and hospitality than in other fields because instead of selling a product, you are selling a service. Thus, a people-oriented approach is necessary to succeed. In order to be effective, Directors of

Sales and Marketing must be experts about their own brand, as well as their competition.

Additional duties may include:

- traveling to meet clients
- developing and managing a budget
- reviewing proposals and sales contracts
- using specific computer software such as SalesPro
- understanding and matching the needs of the hotel and the customer
- setting and achieving account and revenue goals
- meeting monthly sales objectives
- identifying profit opportunities
- monitoring competition
- running meetings of sales managers
- developing and promoting consumer and trade sales packages
- managing multiple accounts

At smaller properties, the Director of Sales and Marketing might be one person in a department primarily handling sales, while at full-service hotels, the Director of Sales and Marketing might head a department of 12 or more. A large department would consist mostly of sales managers, broken down by several market segments. It would also have a director of sales and a director of marketing. The marketing director would also work with those involved in communications, public relations, and advertising.

Typically, the Director of Sales and Marketing is a member of the executive team along with the director of rooms, the food and beverage director, the human resources director, and the accounting director. Although they are not as involved as other department heads with daily hotel operation and guest interaction, their function is critical as they drive revenue. The Director of Sales and Marketing usually reports to the general manager.

Salaries

Salaries for Directors of Sales and Marketing vary greatly depending on the size and prestige of the hotel. A Director of Sales and Marketing with no or few direct reports at a budget motel might earn $50,000 per year, while a Director of Sales and Marketing with a staff of 12 at a luxury property can earn $120,000 per year and up. Bonuses are common for meeting and exceeding sales expectations.

Employment Prospects

Employment prospects are good for Directors of Sales and Marketing. No matter what the economy, hotels want to fill their rooms. They will always look for skilled professionals who will go out and capture new business and keep the relationship with existing clients so they will keep returning. The best opportunities are for those who have previously worked as sales directors in one or more market segment. Since a Director of Sales and Marketing oversees all market segments—including tourism, corporate accounts, and conventions—familiarity with more than one of these areas is a bonus.

Advancement Prospects

Advancement prospects are also good. Because Directors of Sales and Marketing drive revenue, they might advance to become general managers. Also, they often move from smaller properties to larger and more prestigious ones. They may also move from the unit to the corporate level.

Education and Training

Educational requirements vary for Directors of Sales and Marketing. At smaller properties, a bachelor's degree may not be required, while at larger hotels and resorts, it is necessary. Majors or courses in sales, marketing, business, hotel management, or hospitality administration can be very helpful. Sales training is often offered on the job.

Experience, Skills, and Personality Traits

Prior sales experience is required to be a Director of Sales and Marketing. Professionals have typically worked as sales managers in one or more market segment before achieving this position, between three and 10 years, depending on the property. They may also come to the position from working as a director of convention services. It is important to understand the fundamentals of the sales process as well as marketing competencies.

Sales skills are essential, as is an outgoing personality and the ability to develop relationships. One must be able to pick up the phone and make conversation with complete strangers, and must think on his or her feet. A good memory helps retain clients, and creativity enables Directors of Sales and Marketing to come up with unique branding strategies.

Unions and Associations

Hospitality Sales and Marketing Association International (HSMAI) is a global organization of sales and marketing professionals representing all segments of the hospitality industry. According to its Web site, HSMAI was founded in 1927 and is composed of nearly 7,000 members from 35 countries and chapters worldwide. Learn more at www.hsmai.org.

Tips for Entry

1. HSMAI offers three levels of certification for sales and marketing professionals: Certified Hospitality Marketing Executive (CHME), Certified Revenue Management Executive (CRME), and Certified in Hospitality Sales Competencies (CHSC). Explore these credentials at www.hsmai.org/resources/professional.cfm.

2. Gain experience through a hotel internship or summer job. Working in reservations is a great way to prepare, since that is a form of selling as well.

3. When applying for jobs, be sure to research the company and target your approach, as well as sell yourself on the interview. This will demonstrate to employers the same care you will take to target your sales pitch to individual clients.

4. Gain experience working at a variety of different properties, since each one is different. Do not be discouraged by a bad job and let that affect your impression of the entire field.

5. Hotel-online.com has an interesting article about 12 useful strategies for hotel sales and marketing professionals at www.hotel-online.com/News/PR2006_2nd/Jun06_DoSBakersDozen.html.

EXECUTIVE HOUSEKEEPER

Duties: Supervises the housekeeping function for a hotel or resort, ensuring that guest rooms and public areas are clean and maintained

Alternate Title(s): Director of Housekeeping

Salary Range: $30,000 to $75,000 and up

Employment Prospects: Good

Advancement Prospects: Good

Best Geographical Location(s): All, with the greatest opportunities in large cities and heavy tourist regions with many resorts and hotels

Prerequisites:

Education and Training—A bachelor's degree in hotel/hospitality administration is helpful

Experience—Prior experience in the hotel industry as a floor supervisor or in front office operations

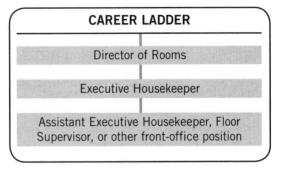

CAREER LADDER

Director of Rooms

Executive Housekeeper

Assistant Executive Housekeeper, Floor Supervisor, or other front-office position

Special Skills and Personality Traits—Excellent supervisory and management skills; good communication skills; strong organization and attention to detail; foreign language skills

Position Description

The cleanliness of a hotel is one of the most important factors in its success. Guests expect to be able to check into an immaculate room with fresh linens, no matter how small or inexpensive the property. Furthermore, they expect the public areas of the hotel to be neat and clean as well. The little touches such as chocolate on a pillow during the turndown service might become the signature by which a property is known. The Executive Housekeeper ensures that these high standards are upheld.

The Executive Housekeeper oversees the housekeeping staff that is charged with cleaning the individual rooms of a hotel. These housekeepers must vacuum, dust, wash windows, scrub the bathroom, make beds, and provide clean linens. Executive Housekeepers train the housekeeping staff to provide consistency in this format. They may inspect rooms for cleanliness, particularly when they are training new staff. Additionally, Executive Housekeepers oversee the cleaning of public areas, including reception, convention/meeting rooms, banquet rooms, and sometimes restaurants.

Housekeeping is an important part of the rooms function and goes hand in hand with other departments. The Executive Housekeeper must keep a close eye on scheduling and track when rooms are cleaned and ready. They communicate with the front office to inform them that these rooms are ready to assign or sell. Furthermore, the front office must keep in touch with the Executive Housekeeper to let him or her know when guests have checked out and their rooms are ready to clean.

Scheduling, organizing, and training is a big part of the job. Executive Housekeepers at large properties may manage staffs of 50 or more; depending on their work environment, they may supervise a few staff members or a few hundred. They must track not only the shifts, both day and night, that each housekeeper must work, but also the block of rooms to which each is assigned. They must stay on top of any problems and issues that arise, troubleshooting and working with guests when necessary. Executive Housekeepers may handle other human resources functions for the housekeeping department, such as hiring, firing, and composing performance evaluations.

Each room must be stocked with amenities that vary by hotel, but can include shampoo, soaps, sewing kits, shoe shine cloths, shower caps, lotions, and more. The more luxurious the property, the more extensive the amenities. Executive Housekeepers make sure that rooms are replenished with what they need daily. Also, they check that the other materials such as menus and daily activity/event printouts are in place.

Additional duties include:

- recruiting new housekeeping staff and conducting background checks

- adhering to OSHA (Occupational Safety and Health Administration) and ADA (Americans with Disabilities Act) regulations
- establishing and maintaining cost control systems for linen and cleaning supplies inventories
- developing systems for inspecting and managing the quality of housekeeping and laundry services to ensure timeliness and efficiency of services;
- supervising inspections of housekeeping/laundry activities to confirm procedures are followed according to standard
- compiling and reporting information on housekeeping activities and expenses
- scheduling staff and work with regard to productivity standards and forecasted occupancy
- meeting special needs of VIP guests
- negotiating prices with vendors
- reporting and replacing malfunctioning items in rooms (i.e. nonworking lightbulbs)
- Maintaining lost and found property

As a manager, the Executive Housekeeper is responsible for budgeting for the department. This can include ordering and estimating supplies, linens, and staff uniforms. An adequate stock of supplies must always be available in case of any ordering glitches. Executive Housekeepers may also oversee the laundry department and must be in frequent communications to make sure towels, sheets, and even napkins and tablecloths are ready when they need to be. They may have oversight for the valet service as well.

While Executive Housekeepers delegate rather than clean individual rooms, they may be required to pitch in when necessary. They work long hours, including evenings, weekends, and holidays, and may be on call during off-hours to respond to problems that can arise at any time. Travel is not typical, except for conferences and to linked properties.

Salaries

Depending on the size, location, and prestige of the property, salaries for Executive Housekeepers can vary greatly. More upscale properties with hundreds of rooms require the Executive Housekeeper to supervise a more substantial staff. A typical salary might be between $40,000 and $50,000, but the range can span from $30,000 to $70,000 and up, particularly at big city or high-end resorts. Experience, education, and skills also play a role in salary. In addition to base salary, Executive Housekeepers may receive bonuses, standard benefits, and discounted hotel stays or other travel perks if working for large chains.

Employment Prospects

Employment prospects are good for Executive Housekeepers. Cleanliness will always be a top priority in the hospitality industry and not an area to skimp on hiring. As the hospitality industry continues to forecast growth, the need for qualified professionals will increase as well. Executive Housekeepers may reach their positions after approximately five years of experience in the rooms division, once they have proven supervisory experience. One of the best ways to find out about job opportunities is through Web sites such as www.hospitalityonline.com.

Advancement Prospects

Advancement prospects are good as well for Executive Housekeepers. Education and experience help them secure positions as Executive Housekeepers at larger or more prestigious properties. Additionally, they may move up to hotel management as directors of rooms.

Education and Training

For success as an Executive Housekeeper and beyond, individuals should hold bachelor's degrees in hotel and hospitality management. While some in the field have reached their position without a degree and by moving up as a housekeeper, most others become Executive Housekeepers through formal hospitality education. This course of study teaches prospective Executive Housekeepers about the hotel business, including organization structure, operations, and finance, which will help them do their jobs and advance.

Two special designations are offered by the International Executive Housekeepers Association (IEHA). The REH (Registered Executive Housekeeper) credential requires a bachelor's degree and the CEH (Certified Executive Housekeeper) credential may be achieved through a certificate program, self-study program, or an associate's degree program. For more information, see www.ieha.org/education/education.htm.

Experience, Skills, and Personality Traits

Executive Housekeepers should have excellent supervisory and leadership skills in order to train, motivate, and mentor staff. Frequently, particularly in areas of the country with many Spanish-speaking immigrants, they work with housekeepers for whom English is not their first language. Foreign language skills can be very helpful in these instances, as can cultural awareness and sensitivity.

Executive Housekeepers should also be good communicators who are well organized and able to juggle multiple tasks at once. This helps them keep track of schedules, resolve problems, and interact with people daily.

Unions and Associations

Executive Housekeepers may belong to a variety of professional associations; the primary organization is the International Executive Housekeepers Association. IEHA has more than 3,500 members who oversee facility housekeeping at the management level. Other Executive Housekeepers may also be members of the American Hotel and Lodging Association.

Tips for Entry

1. Type "job descriptions for Executive Housekeepers" into a search engine to see a broad range of job descriptions. Notice the differences between large and small facilities.
2. Next time you stay at a hotel, take note of the room amenities and everything that must be coordinated in the housekeeping process.
3. Network through professional associations and conduct an informational interview with an Executive Housekeeper.
4. Try an internship at a large hotel chain where you can be exposed to many different departments. For example, see the Westin Hotel and Resorts internship/externship program at www.starwoodhotels.com/westin/careers/recruiting/internships.html.

DIRECTOR OF ENGINEERING

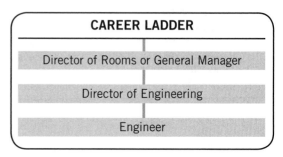

Position Description

Hotel guests often take for granted all the facilities that make their stay possible and pleasant. They expect heat in the winter and air conditioning in the summer, working lights and plumbing, in-room refrigeration, a well-maintained pool and grounds, and more. The Director of Engineering is responsible for overseeing, fixing, and maintaining all these services.

The Director of Engineering may supervise a variety of workers including:

- plumbers
- carpenters
- grounds maintenance workers
- painters
- electricians
- engineers

He or she is responsible for overseeing the entire maintenance staff. This includes hiring, firing, training, and evaluating, as well as scheduling. Training is especially important for maintenance staff because it also encompasses following safety and emergency procedures.

Directors of Engineering handle the appearance of both the interior and exterior areas of a hotel or resort. They oversee landscaping, grounds, pools, and parking lots, as well as the interior common areas used by guests and staff. They ensure that everything looks clean and orderly and is operating properly. Directors of Engineering also make sure that the staff in these areas is completing the necessary tasks to make this happen.

Furthermore, Directors of Engineering make decisions regarding hotel maintenance. They review proposals and contracts, negotiating their terms. They work with vendors, consultants, clients, contractors, and suppliers for these services. Also, Directors of Engineering may explain contract terms to staff and help them understand what needs to be done. As they troubleshoot problems, they use their judgment to decide when issues can be handled internally or when outside contractors must be called in.

It is necessary for Directors of Engineering to make sure the hotel building and all new additions comply with state and federal regulations, including those from OSHA (the Occupational Safety and Health Administration) and ADA (the Americans with Disabilities Act). They take this into account when considering renovations and new projects. Fire protection operations are also an area of concern. Monthly inspections are typically performed to check that everything is working properly and complying with regulations.

Additional duties may include:

- preparing and submitting budget estimates
- developing quality control programs
- managing utility systems
- purchasing equipment
- communicating with corporate staff
- working with building code and planning/zoning officials, as well as community design committees
- consulting with supervisors, owners, contractors, etc. on building openings
- determining ways to cut costs and use energy efficiently
- monitoring vendors to assure quality requirements, delivery times, warranties, exchanges, upgrades, and the like are observed
- overseeing capital construction projects
- maintaining safety manuals

Every lightbulb, faucet, air/heating unit, lock, and sprinkler on property is overseen by the maintenance staff. As supervisors, the Director of Engineering often will handle emergencies and speak to guests to solve problems when necessary. They can expect to work long hours including evenings and weekends to reflect hotel hours.

Salaries
Directors of Engineering can earn between $35,000 and $65,000 per year; salaries are higher at larger and more prestigious properties. Earnings also vary by geographic location. Salaries may be contingent on the amount of staff the Director of Engineering supervises as well. Bonuses may be 10 percent of yearly salary or more.

Employment Prospects
Employment prospects are good for Directors of Engineering. Hotels and resorts need them to oversee maintenance, a critical part of hotel operations. Those Directors of Engineers with the right combination of progressively more responsible supervisory skills and technical ability will find a variety of opportunities nationwide.

Advancement Prospects
Typically, Directors of Engineering report to the director of rooms at most hotels and resorts, although in some cases they may report to the general manager. However, that is not the path one would take for advancement since a different background, skill set, and professional path is required. A Director of Engineering may advance to work at a larger property for a higher salary and more responsibility. Furthermore, he or she may advance by moving to a corporate role, overseeing engineering for several hotels in a chain. Directors of Engineering may also serve as consultants or run their own businesses, advising hospitality maintenance staff and directors.

Education and Training
Education and training requirements vary for Directors of Engineering, but technical training is a definite necessity. At large properties, many Directors of Engineering have bachelor's degrees in engineering or facilities management; others may have two-year or technical degrees.

Experience, Skills, and Personality Traits
First and foremost, Directors of Engineering need strong technical skills. An understanding of HVAC (heating, ventilation, and air conditioning), electrical, mechanical, plumbing, carpentry, and more is essential. They must be familiar with chillers, cooling towers, chemical treatments, control systems, water systems, boilers, refrigeration, compressors, and others.

Additionally, Directors of Engineering should be strong managers. They often supervise large staff and must earn their respect as an authority. The ability to multitask and to stay calm in emergency situations are important, as is problem solving ability and good judgment.

Special Requirements
Some states may require licensure or certification in areas such as HVAC, electrical systems, fire safety, or plumbing for their Directors of Engineering.

Unions and Associations
The Hotel Motel Engineering Association is a professional association for Directors of Engineering and other hotel engineering personnel. Visit its Web site at www.hmea.com/hmea.html. They may also belong to the International Code Council, a membership association dedicated to building safety and fire prevention that develops the codes used to construct residential and commercial buildings. Different states also have their own associations, such as the Building Officials Association of New Jersey (www.boanj.com) and the Washington Association of Building Officials (www.wabo.org).

Tips for Entry
1. Explore jobs on Web sites such as www.bristol assoc.com and www.indeed.com.
2. Consider degree programs in engineering and facilities management. Look at programs

including those at Brigham Young University in Provo, Utah, which offers a degree in facility and property management, at home.fpm.byu.edu.

3. Learn more about hotel engineering at this site, which provides an introduction to hotel engineering: www.maintenanceresources.com/referencelibrary/ezine/hoteleng.html.

4. Is there an area of hotel maintenance that interests you in particular? Become skilled at plumbing, electric work, carpentry, or another technical field through courses and apprenticeships.

FRONT DESK CLERK

CAREER PROFILE

Duties: Greets guests at the front desk of a hotel or resort, checking them in and out, making travel arrangements, and providing necessary information

Alternate Title(s): Desk Clerk; Front Desk Attendant

Salary Range: $14,000 to $25,000 and up

Employment Prospects: Good

Advancement Prospects: Good

Best Geographical Location(s): All, with the greatest opportunities in large cities and heavy tourist regions with many resorts and hotels

Prerequisites:

Education and Training—High school education for most positions; on-the-job training

Experience—Experience in customer service and/or hotel work

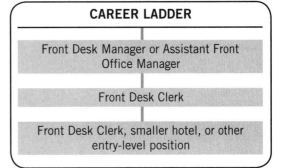

CAREER LADDER

Front Desk Manager or Assistant Front Office Manager

Front Desk Clerk

Front Desk Clerk, smaller hotel, or other entry-level position

Special Skills and Personality Traits—Friendly, personable, professional manner; ability to stay calm under pressure; tact and discretion; strong interpersonal skills

Position Description

When you arrive at a hotel, Front Desk Clerks are often your first point of contact. They greet guests with a smile, check for their reservations, provide keys and necessary materials, and generally orient visitors to the hotel's property. In many ways, Front Desk Clerks are the face of their hotel more than any other employees as they are the staff members that guests interact with immediately. They set the tone for guests and make the first impression.

Because their position is so visible, Front Desk Clerks often serve in a multitude of functions that may overlap with those of reservations, concierges, bellhops, bookkeepers, and housekeepers. Required to be friendly and personable, they field questions on a variety of topics. For this reason, Front Desk Clerks must be knowledgeable about the hotels and all their programs, as well as local attractions. They may be asked to make dinner reservations, recommend activities, and book transportation, especially in smaller properties or when the concierge is off duty.

Front Desk Clerks often receive extensive training to learn all aspects of the property, as well as elements of customer service. Additionally, they must understand the hotel's reservation and billing computer systems thoroughly so they can confirm reservations, check guests in and out, process payments, extend or cancel reservations, and even make new reservations at times.

When Front Desk Clerks arrive for their shifts, they may review what happened during previous shifts to be prepared. They spend virtually all of their time interacting directly with people, both in person and through answering telephone inquiries. Front Desk Clerks direct calls as needed to various areas throughout the hotel. They are on hand to ensure that the process of checking in and out, assigning rooms, and arranging transportation for guests runs as smoothly as possible. Additionally, Front Desk Clerks keep track of room assignments via computer and explain payment processing to guests during checkout.

Like other hotel personnel, Front Desk Clerks must do a great deal of troubleshooting. On a typical day they deal with a multitude of complaints ranging from irate guests who want to switch rooms, reservations that have been misplaced, incorrect charges on a bill, lost luggage, and more. They will eventually delegate many of these issues to the appropriate area—such as the rooms division or reservations—but they are frequently the first to deal with it since they are so visible. They must be able to interact with guests in a calm and professional manner, assuring them that their problems will be addressed.

Additional duties may include:

- taking payment from guests, computing bills, and making change

- coordinating room assignments
- handling incoming packages and passing messages to guests
- making or reconfirming dinner reservations
- using a switchboard to answer phones and track calls
- depositing valuable items into a safe for guests
- issuing room keys, hotel literature, pamphlets, and other material
- working in conjunction with the bell staff to assist guests to their rooms
- arranging transportation for guests
- making coffee in the morning for guests
- arranging for champagne or other special services to be sent to rooms when appropriate
- running reports on the computer for management

Insiders say that Front Desk Clerks keep a log to record the happenings during their shifts. In this way, they are the eyes and ears of the hotel, noting problem guests and those who complain excessively. This can be an important part of their job as they observe and document unusual or troubling events as well, helping their hotels to run more efficiently.

Front Desk Clerks are frequently required to wear uniforms, typically a shirt or jacket with the hotel's logo. They may spend many hours on their feet working behind the front desk. Many hotels staff their front desks 24 hours a day, so Front Desk Clerks may work a variety of shifts, including overnights. Typically, they may choose from three different eight-hour shifts for some flexibility. Front Desk Clerks may work full-time 40-hour workweeks, or part-time.

Salaries
Salaries for Front Desk Clerks vary depending on the size, location, and prestige of the hotel. According to the Bureau of Labor Statistics (BLS), median annual wage-and-salary earnings of Hotel, Motel, and Resort Desk Clerks were $18,950 as of May 2007. The middle 50 percent earned between $16,460 and $22,870. The lowest 10 percent earned less than $14,480, and the highest 10 percent earned more than $27,890. The median hourly wage was $9.11.

Employment Prospects
Overall, employment prospects are good for Front Desk Clerks. The BLS states that employment of hotel, motel, and resort desk clerks is expected to grow 17 percent between 2006 and 2016, which is faster than the average for all occupations. As more properties open, Front Desk Clerks are needed to staff their area

and accommodate guests. The increase of technology streamlines many of the procedures for Front Desk Clerks and enables them to work more quickly and efficiently.

Advancement Prospects
Advancement prospects are also good for Front Desk Clerks, particularly those working for larger hotel chains, those with geographic flexibility, and those interested in achieving additional training or advanced degrees. Some Front Desk Clerks may aspire to management, working at the front desk while attending a degree program in hotel management. Others may seek similar positions at larger or more prestigious hotels and resorts.

Education and Training
A high school education is required for most positions as a Front Desk Clerk. Additionally, Front Desk Clerks received training from managers or those with more experience. They learn about the hotel's policies and procedures, facilities, computer systems, and telephone switchboards, as well as about the local area. Furthermore, courses in bookkeeping or computers can be helpful.

Prior experience through summer or part-time jobs in hotels can be very beneficial. For those Front Desk Clerks looking to advance, more formal coursework or education in hotel management is needed.

Additionally, voluntary certification as a Front Desk Representative is available through the American Hotel and Lodging Association. For more information, see www.ei-ahla.org/content.aspx?id=112.

Experience, Skills, and Personality Traits
Discretion is needed by Front Desk Clerks as they maintain guest privacy and security. Furthermore, the ability to stay calm under pressure is essential. Especially during busy times, such as conventions and holidays, Front Desk Clerks may have lines of people waiting for them, some of them angry. They need to be able to work with these people without losing their cool.

A strong sense of customer service is a necessity. A neat, professional, and personable manner enables Front Desk Clerks to greet visitors with a friendly and approachable image. High energy allows Front Desk Clerks to work long hours on their feet and the ability to multitask is also important.

Unions and Associations
The main professional association for hotel employees is the American Hotel and Lodging Association.

Tips for Entry

1. The Educational Institute of the American Hotel and Lodging Association offers various programs and opportunities for education and training in the lodging industry. Visit its Web site at www.ei-ahla.org.

2. Try a summer job at the front desk of a hotel to get a feel for the work of a Front Desk Clerk.

3. Visit a hotel and speak to a Front Desk Clerk during his or her slow hours. Find out the best and worst parts of the job from an inside perspective.

4. Read job descriptions for Front Desk Clerks on sites such as www.hcareers.com and www.hoteljobs.com.

FRONT OFFICE MANAGER

CAREER PROFILE

Duties: Oversees the front office operations of a hotel or resort, including desk clerks, reservations, bell stand, concierge, and others

Alternate Title(s): Front Desk Manager

Salary Range: $30,000 to $60,000 and up

Employment Prospects: Fair

Advancement Prospects: Good

Best Geographical Location(s): All, with the greatest opportunities in large cities and heavy tourist regions with many resorts and hotels

Prerequisites:

Education and Training—A bachelor's degree is preferred or required for most positions; courses in hotel/hospitality management valuable

Experience—Prior hotel front office experience

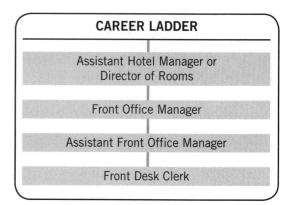

CAREER LADDER

Assistant Hotel Manager or Director of Rooms

Front Office Manager

Assistant Front Office Manager

Front Desk Clerk

Special Skills and Personality Traits—Excellent organizational and supervisory skills; good communication and interpersonal skills; ability to solve problems and multitask

Position Description

The Front Office Manager oversees front-office operations for a hotel or resort. The front office usually includes the front desk, telephones, the bell stand and bell/valet services, and sometimes concierges and reservations. Involving direct contact with guests, these divisions are vital to hotel operations.

When guests check into a hotel, they are greeted by front desk clerks. Bell staff takes their luggage and a valet may park their car. The Front Office Manager ensures these processes are running smoothly. They supervise and evaluate employees, train employees, and set policy and procedure. Furthermore, they are responsible for staffing the front office, including hiring and firing, to create an effective team.

Organization is a key component of working as a Front Office Manager. Front Office Managers need to know which rooms are assigned and which are free, as well as monitoring reservations and looking out for overbooking. They must also make sure all shifts are covered and that staff is in place where needed 24 hours a day. It is up to the Front Office Manager to make sure that staff is on time and presenting the right professional image with regard to uniform and appearance.

Front Office Managers make themselves available to solve customer complaints with regard to reservations,

check-in difficulties, luggage, and other front-office concerns. They try to defuse stress and resolve issues brought to their attention by front desk clerks or guests directly. As managers, they step in when things get difficult and they often have the authority to authorize a room upgrade, refund, or special service. They consider how strong customer service will benefit revenues in the long run.

Additionally, Front Office Managers work closely with other departments within the rooms division such as laundry, reservations, housekeeping, security, and engineering, coordinating activities when appropriate to ensure rooms are clean and ready. They may also work with the sales department on rates to maximize occupancy and revenue.

Additional duties may include:

- handling emergencies
- providing performance evaluations for employees
- analyzing salaries and payroll to maximize revenues
- suggesting and implementing opportunities for improvement
- managing special guest groups, such as conventions or tours
- overseeing audit and controls on a regular basis
- following bank out and cash handling procedures
- processing payments

- sending confirmation letters
- arranging for special services
- greeting important guests personally
- organizing and running staff meetings for front-office staff

Front Office Managers maintain high service standards and work to keep guests, management, and staff satisfied. They must be extremely knowledgeable about hotel policies and procedures and be good managers in order to provide an example and motivate staff. Hours can be long and nontraditional, including evenings and weekends.

Salaries

According to www.cbsalary.com, the United States national average salary for Front Office Managers is $42,660. Salaries vary based on the size, location, and prestige of the property. Also, they vary depending on the education and experience of the Front Office Manager, as well as the scope of their responsibilities. Salaries may range from $30,000 to $60,000 and up. Major hotels (chains or otherwise) typically offer full benefits, including 401(k) programs, sick leave, vacation time, and health plans.

Employment Prospects

Employment prospects are fair for Front Office Managers. The hospitality industry fluctuates with the economy and hotels may open and close depending on the demand for travel. The best opportunities will be for those Front Office Managers who are geographically flexible and have strong education and experience. Jobs are often found through networking and through Web sites such as www.hcareers.com.

Advancement Prospects

Because of the supervisory nature of their jobs, as well as the many areas they cover, advancement prospects are good for Front Office Managers. They have experience working with sales, reservations, the bell station, accounting, housekeeping, etc., which puts them in a strong position to advance to become directors of rooms or assistant general managers. A degree in hotel or hospitality management further enhances advancement prospects. Front Office Managers may also advance to work at larger or more prestigious properties for greater salary and responsibility. Those who work for chains may be promoted to work for different properties within the chain.

Education and Training

Many Front Office Manager positions prefer or require a bachelor's degree, although experience can supplement education in some instances. However, for advancement, a bachelor's degree in hotel or hospitality management is valuable, as are courses in business, communications, public relations, and sales. Larger and more prestigious properties often require extensive education or training.

Voluntary certification as a Certified Front Desk Manager is available through the American Hotel and Lodging Association. For more information, see www.ei-ahla.org/content.aspx?id=112.

Experience, Skills, and Personality Traits

To be an effective Front Office Manager, one should be an excellent leader and supervisor. Front Office Managers must train and motivate their staff, inspiring respect and creating a team atmosphere. Furthermore, they should have strong organizational skills as they need to develop schedules and keep track of multiple projects and staff members at once.

Good customer service and interpersonal skills are essential. Front Office Managers should be effective communicators who like to work with people and help others. Skills with computers and/or foreign languages can also be beneficial.

Unions and Associations

For Front Office Managers, the main professional association is the American Hotel and Lodging Association. They provide voluntary certification for staff and executives as well as information for students.

Tips for Entry

1. Review the organizational structure of hotels to understand the different departments and reporting structures.
2. Take courses in hotel management to learn more about the industry.
3. Explore job listings on the Web sites of major hotel chains such as www.hilton.com and www.hyatt.com.
4. Practice your customer service skills through fast-paced summer jobs that require strong interpersonal contact.
5. Hone your résumé using sites such as jobstar.org/tools/resume/index.php and resume.monster.com/archives/dosanddonts.

CONCIERGE

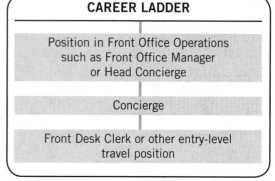
Special Skills and Personality Traits—Superior interpersonal and communication skills; ability to be diplomatic, tactful, resourceful, and detail-oriented; good at solving problems

Position Description

The word *concierge* translated from French means "the keeper of the candles," coined for those who tended to visiting nobles in medieval Europe. Concierge today is essential to all aspects of guest service and satisfaction. By answering questions and assisting guests with personal services, Concierges serve to enhance the visit of guests staying in their hotel.

Out of all the jobs in the hospitality industry, Concierge is probably the one that most defines "hospitality." Concierges are on the front line, working with people and trying to meet their needs every day. Their role is to serve as a resource for hotel guests and the scope of their responsibilities can be quite varied. Depending on the circumstances, Concierges can do anything from making restaurant recommendations and dinner reservations to finding an after-hours pharmacy to obtain medication.

Most Concierges spend most of their time at a stand that is part of or near the front desk of their hotel or resort. However, for some guests, their interaction with the Concierge begins before they even check in. They may e-mail or call the Concierge to have plans arranged, including dinner reservations, tours, and activities, before they arrive. Concierges may also field pre-trip questions about weather, packing advice, and suggestions for itineraries.

Concierges must be good listeners to assess their guests' desires. Based on their experience and familiar-

ity with local commerce, they develop a repository of information that is tried and true. However, by speaking to their guests, they will know which recommendations might be most appropriate for them. For example, in terms of restaurants, Concierges can offer advice about the best restaurant to celebrate an anniversary, dine with children, or bring a large party. Their knowledge is such that they can describe a variety of places to their guests in order to help them make the best decisions. Anything they do not know, a Concierge will find out; having menus e-mailed or faxed over or speaking to a maître d' are just some of the possibilities.

Some of the responsibilities of a Concierge might be similar to those of a travel agent. They often book tours, arrange transportation or rental cars, and overall, help visitors with the burden of planning their trips. Concierges should be local experts as they are often called upon to give directions as well as suggest activities ranging from art museums and shopping to parks and recreation. They need great knowledge of their particular hotel or resort as well as all local services, venues, events, and transportation options.

Additional duties may include:

- taking messages for guests and ensuring guest mail and fax delivery
- monitoring guest requests for other hotel services
- providing directions and maps

- securing transportation such as rental cars, taxis, or limousines
- providing tickets for sporting events
- interacting with other departments to make sure guests' needs are being met
- following up with guests to see how services have worked out
- handling special or unique requests
- tracking down lost luggage
- confirming airline tickets
- maintaining a clean reception area
- maintaining a database with information about city highlights
- acting as a personal assistant, such as picking up food or dry cleaning
- visiting new restaurants, shops, and galleries in their city for information
- planning events

The role of a Concierge can vary greatly depending upon the property where he or she works. At a world-class big city hotel, visitors come from all over the world and may have unique requests, including theater tickets and cultural events. At hip, trendy boutique hotels where guests inquire about the hottest clubs, or sprawling family resorts where patrons want to know about babysitting services, Concierges try to anticipate the needs of their particular guests. However, they cannot generalize and will sometimes be surprised by what guests ask for and need. They use their network to fulfill any requests they cannot meet on their own.

Developing relationships with people is what being a Concierge is all about. Some hotels may have regular guests and Concierges ensure they have their favorite activities and services lined up. Building and maintaining relationships with staff at local venues including restaurants, ticket bureaus, theaters, and tourist attractions is equally important. It is these contacts that enable Concierges to best help their patrons.

Hotels are bustling around the clock, and during peak travel times Concierges may work long or non-traditional hours, often on their feet. Some hotels have Concierges staffed during the nine-to-five hours and on call for after-hours emergencies. Like other hotel employees, they should expect to work some evenings, holidays, and weekends.

Salaries

According to Les Clefs d'Or USA, a national organization for hotel lobby Concierges, annual salaries are generally between $20,000 and $50,000. However, they also state that salaries vary widely from hotel to hotel and from region to region. The highest salaries are in large cities and luxury resorts and properties.

Additional salary information comes from the December 2005 issue of *Condé Nast Traveler* magazine, which states that Concierges earn from $50,000 up well into six figures, including tips.

Concierges often receive tips from many guests they assist, which can significantly affect their earnings.

Employment Prospects

The Bureau of Labor Statistics (BLS) projects faster than average growth in employment for Concierges through 2016. As people travel more and have higher expectations for service when they travel, the need for knowledgeable Concierges will be strong.

Opportunities can be found by applying directly to hotels and resorts, or from within for those already employed in hotels. Typically one year of hotel experience is required. Networking through the industry or through educational programs can also be helpful. Concierges can work in hotels all over the world, with opportunities increasing if they can speak more than one language.

It is interesting to note that while worldwide, the Concierge profession is male-dominated, in the United States, Les Clefs d'Or Concierges are 70 percent female and 30 percent male.

Advancement Prospects

Because of the heavy customer service orientation of their jobs, Concierges prepare themselves to advance to a variety of roles. They may become head Concierges or Concierges at more high-end properties. Others may hold or be studying for degrees in hospitality management and advance to positions in front-office operations.

Education and Training

Concierge positions require a minimum of a high school education. At many big city or luxury properties, Concierges with college degrees are preferred for hiring. Courses or degrees in hotel and hospitality management can be very valuable.

Much of the training for Concierges comes on the job, as they learn the specifics about their particular hotel. However, knowledge of the local area is often required to start out.

Experience, Skills, and Personality Traits

Concierges should be friendly, patient, and approachable, making a positive impression on guests. Virtually all of their time is spent speaking to people, so strong interpersonal and communication skills are essential.

They also need to be detail-oriented and organized as they make arrangements.

Knowledge of one or more foreign languages can be a huge asset, especially at large properties with multinational guests. Many job descriptions require or prefer this skill. Concierges should also be resourceful; as good problem-solvers, they can find difficult information for guests quickly and efficiently. As they work with many different types of people, Concierges need the ability to be diplomatic and tactful, as they may occasionally serve as personal confidants. They can stay calm and polite even when faced with adversity.

Knowledge of computer software such as the Microsoft Office products and property management systems is beneficial as well.

Unions and Associations

Les Clefs d'Or USA is a national organization for hotel lobby Concierges. To become a member, applicants must have at least five years experience within the hotel industry and at least three years experience as a full-time hotel Concierge.

Concierges may also belong to the National Concierge Association and American Hotel and Lodging Association. Different cities, states, and regions have their own professional associations as well, such as the Los Angeles Concierge Association or the Seattle Hotel Concierge Association. Professional associations can be great networking tools as Concierges can share tips and recommendations as well as develop contacts in other cities.

Tips for Entry

1. Explore the Web site for Les Clefs d'Or USA at lcdusa.org. Here, you can learn more about the role of a Concierge, including the history of the job.
2. Try helping friends and relatives when they visit your hometown. Recommend restaurants and make reservations, suggest and plan events, and gather maps and other information.
3. Talk to a Concierge at a local hotel or a resort to find out how he or she got started in the field.
4. Work in the customer service industry to gain experience interacting with people.
5. See other Concierge association Web sites such as www.thelaca.com and www.seattlehotel concierge.com.

SPA MANAGER

CAREER PROFILE

Duties: Supervises the overall operations of the spa facilities for a hotel or resort

Alternate Title(s): Health Club Manager; Director of Health and Fitness Services; Spa Director

Salary Range: $30,000 to $80,000 and up

Employment Prospects: Good to excellent

Advancement Prospects: Good to excellent

Best Geographical Location(s): All, particularly big cities and heavy tourist areas; regions with major hotels, resorts, and spas

Prerequisites:

Education and Training—Degree in related field, including spa/resort management

Experience—Prior experience in management of a spa or health club

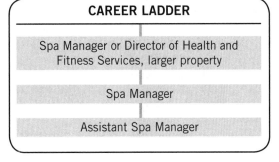

Special Skills and Personality Traits—Excellent communication and interpersonal skills; good business sense and knowledge of spa operations; ability to multitask and stay calm under pressure; strong management and leadership skills

Position Description

Many travelers like to have a haven where they can relax when they are away from home. Some like to swim or exercise; others seek pampering where they can enjoy massages, facials, and additional treatments. For this reason, health clubs and spas at hotels and resorts are growing at an exponential rate. Spa Managers oversee these facilities and ensure that guests are well cared for.

Spa Managers oversee the spa and health club facilities for hotels, resorts, and cruise ships. These facilities can include gyms with exercise equipment and fitness classes; pools, saunas, and hot tubs; beauty salons; and special treatments such as massages and facials. They supervise the staff in these areas including fitness instructors, massage therapists, aestheticians, lifeguards, and front desk staff. Overall, their goal is to promote a sense of relaxation and wellness for guests, thus increasing profitability by bringing in more satisfied clients.

The job of a Spa Manager touches many facets of the hospitality industry. Spa Managers may oversee marketing and sales of spa services, retail operations, food and beverages sold and served in the spa, housekeeping and laundry, staffing, ordering, and more. In terms of marketing and sales, Spa Managers make sure that their spa programs are well promoted. They work to devise new treatments and services and bring in guests who

will pay for them. The spa may have a balance of transient members (hotel guests who use the facilities during their stay) and permanent members (local members of the community who are members of the gym). Spa Managers work to assist both clients and increase profits by attracting new members.

Some spas also have retail stores as part of their facility. These stores may sell exercise clothing, robes, and soaps and lotions, particularly those that were used in treatments. The Spa Manager promotes these products and oversees the store and its staff. The fruit and water found in the waiting area of a spa is also overseen by the Spa Manager. They also supervise the laundry and housekeeping to ensure that the spa and health club are clean and that fresh towels and robes are always provided.

Handling human resources for their department, Spa Managers hire, train, and evaluate staff. They must be knowledgeable about the health and wellness industry in order to train staff on proper policies and procedures. It is necessary for employees to have the proper licensure when needed to perform their jobs. Good Spa Managers are able to inspire leadership and manage those who have credentials different than their own. Although they will likely not be certified fitness instructors or massage therapists themselves, they know enough about the industry to distinguish those professionals who are. Spa Managers also may manage scheduling to ensure coverage for classes, treatments, and other services.

Like other hospitality employees, Spa Managers strike the balance between customer service and the bottom line. They strive to increase profits as they develop budgets for their department. Furthermore, Spa Managers understand the impact of customer service as affecting profits as well. They often interact with customers, providing prospective guests and members with facility tours and explanations. They must be well aware of all the spa services and equipment in order to demonstrate the options.

Additional duties may include:

- ordering products and supplies
- taking and maintaining inventories
- identifying areas for growth
- working with vendors to negotiate prices and choose services
- ensuring that equipment is functioning properly and ordering repairs when needed
- keeping up with industry trends and introducing new services
- resolving guest issues, complaints, and problems
- evaluating current programs and services and analyzing success
- developing literature and promotional materials about spa services
- creating content for the spa Web site
- monitoring daily sales activities
- planning special media events and interacting with the press
- establishing spa policy and procedure manuals

Spa Managers are also responsible for the overall aesthetics of the spa. They look to create a warm and inviting environment that may include soft colors, subtle lighting, candles and aromatherapy, plants, and more. Some spas may have themes, such as Asian, and Spa Managers are constantly looking for new ways to make their facility attractive and desirable to guests.

Health and safety is a primary concern at spas and health clubs, and Spa Managers should be knowledgeable about CPR, first aid, and other emergency procedures. A typical workweek is usually 50 hours or more and may include evenings and weekends.

Salaries

Salaries for Spa Managers vary depending on the size, geographic location, and prestige of the facility they manage. For Spa Managers at small or midsize hotels offering a limited array of services, salaries might be in the $35,000 to $45,000 range. However, for Spa Managers at luxurious high-end properties offering a wide variety of spa services and treatments, salaries can be $70,000 to $80,000 and more. These Spa Managers often supervise a large staff of 10 to 20 employees or more.

Employment Prospects

Spa Managers currently enjoy good to excellent employment prospects. The spa, health, and wellness industry is growing quickly and even the smallest hotels are now including health clubs and fitness centers. Additionally, adding a high-end spa can be a way for large resorts to distinguish themselves. The need for qualified Spa Managers to run these facilities is quickly growing. The best opportunities will be for those Spa Managers with a combination of education and experience in the field.

Advancement Prospects

Advancement prospects are also good for Spa Managers. With their organizational and operations skills, they can move into other management areas if they desire within the hotel or resort structure. They can also move to direct spas at larger and more high-end properties where they manage larger staffs and earn more money. Furthermore, they may oversee more than one facility for a hotel/resort chain.

Education and Training

Most Spa Manager positions require a college degree in addition to work experience. Fields such as hospitality and resort management, as well as business and health or nutrition are useful. Some colleges of hospitality management offer degree programs focusing on spa management. Lynn University in Boca Raton, Florida, offers a bachelor of science in hospitality management with a specialization in spa management. For more information, see www.lynn.edu. Also, the University of Minnesota in Crookston offers a bachelor of science and associate of applied science degree with an emphasis in resort and spa management; see www.umcrookston.edu/academics/bus/HRI/Undergrad programs.htm.

Curriculum is a balance of hospitality management and customer service, business management and marketing, nutrition, health, and wellness. Courses in operations management are also very helpful. Some Spa Managers will work their way up from positions as desk clerks or fitness instructors, but education becomes useful or necessary for advancement.

The International Spa Association (ISPA) offers a voluntary certification for spa supervisors and managers worldwide: the Certified Spa Supervisor Program.

For more information about this program, see www.experienceispa.com/ISPA/Education/Certified+Spa+Supervisor+Program/.

Experience, Skills, and Personality Traits

Spa Managers come to their positions through progressively more responsible positions in spa management. They are usually promoted from assistant spa manager positions where they have familiarity both with spa operations and managing staff.

It is essential for Spa Managers to be well organized and be able to juggle multiple responsibilities at once. They must know everything going on in the different spa departments and be efficient leaders to hire qualified staff to delegate responsibility. Spa Managers should be able to stay calm in difficult situations and relate well to people. Their interpersonal and communication skills promote the excellent customer service environment that makes spas successful.

Furthermore, it is necessary to be a good salesperson with strong financial sense. Spa Managers must understand the business of running a profitable spa and must be innovative at finding ways to increase visibility. Interest in and commitment to the mission of health and wellness also helps them believe in their work and foster that sense in both employees and guests.

Unions and Associations

Spa Managers may belong to professional associations including the International Spa Association (ISPA).

According to its Web site, since 1991, ISPA has been recognized worldwide as the professional organization and voice of the spa industry, representing more than 3,000 health and wellness facilities and providers in 75 countries. An additional professional associations is the Day Spa Association.

Tips for Entry

1. You can receive an associate of occupational studies degree in spa management and leadership through the Southwest Institute of Healing Arts in Tempe, Arizona. For more information, see the Web site at www.swiha.edu/Programs/Degree-Programs-Spa-Management-and-Leadership-AOS-Degree.html.

2. Additionally, Arizona State University's Polytechnic campus in Mesa, Arizona, offers a Spa Management Certificate Program. Learn more at www.poly.asu.edu/saas/wellness/spa.

3. Visit a variety of spas, both in hotels and outside, to determine which you like best. Each will have a different vision and focus. Why do you think some are more successful than others? What would you do differently if you ran your own spa? Which ideas would you build on?

4. Take a look at SpaTrade, a spa business resource, at www.spatrade.com.

ARCHITECT

CAREER PROFILE

Duties: Designs hotels, resorts, casinos, and other properties in the hospitality industry

Alternate Title(s): None

Salary Range: $40,000 to $110,000 and up

Employment Prospects: Fair to good

Advancement Prospects: Fair to good

Best Geographical Location(s): All, with the greatest opportunities in large cities and heavy tourist regions with many hotels and resorts

Prerequisites:

Education and Training—Degree in architecture plus internship (see text)

Experience—At least three years of post-degree internship experience

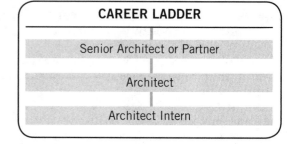

CAREER LADDER

Senior Architect or Partner

Architect

Architect Intern

Special Skills and Personality Traits—Technical and artistic skill; good communication ability; patience and interpersonal skills; detail-oriented

Special Requirements—All states require individuals to be licensed (registered) to use the title Architect and contract to provide architectural services

Position Description

There are a wide range of hotels and resorts throughout the world with unique designs. From chic minimalistic urban boutique properties and sprawling tropical beach resorts to themed structures with detail built into every angle, the design of these buildings is what gives them their character. Architects are the professionals who develop these design visions and turn them into concrete reality.

The design of hotels and resorts can be especially interesting and creative. Many details must be considered, including how many rooms the property will have, and what features the public areas, restaurants, pools, spas, and other areas will have. It is also important for the Architect to understand the demographics of the population. Who will be visiting this property and what are their needs?

Architects work with clients in order to develop plans for buildings. They consult with them to get a sense of the needs and functions of the property and its users, as well as other details such as budget, materials, location, and design. Furthermore, they plan the building structure including plumbing, electrical wiring, AC/heating, and more. Architects may also develop plans that include landscaping, furnishings, and other considerations. To create these plans, Architects develop drawings and models using Computer-Aided Draft and Design (CADD) and Building Information Modeling (BIM) Technology.

Much of Architects' time is spent meeting with clients in person, talking on the phone, and going back and forth until a plan is finalized. Working with clients can be frustrating at times and Architects must be able to sell and explain their ideas in nontechnical language that clients can understand. Many revisions go into the final process and Architects need patience to be able to complete a project that satisfies everyone.

Using skills that combine arts and science, Architects oversee the building process from start to finish. They may help clients select a building site by providing various analyses that compare factors such as costs or environmental impact. On the building sites, Architects work with contractors and subcontractors to ensure that building is going according to plan. They may also help clients select construction staff.

Post-construction, Architects make sure that the building is structurally sound and that their vision was translated correctly. They may provide advice to clients regarding facility management, energy efficiency or any changes that must occur. The best properties are those where the visions of the Architect and clients merge and the resources are used effectively.

Additional duties include:

- presenting proposals and reports to clients
- working with engineers, urban planners, interior designers, electricians, plumbers, and landscape architects

- researching and adhering to zoning laws, building codes, and fire regulations
- filing legal documents
- marketing their services

Architects specializing in hotels and resorts typically work long hours and may work on projects both large and small in scope. At the beginning of their careers, they will be assisting other Architects and carrying out their ideas, rather than developing their own. Furthermore, rather than designing entire buildings, they may be responsible for parts of hotel buildings such as a lobby, bathrooms, or even a doorway. However, after years of hard work, Architects are able to have control over their projects and see their visions take life. As people enjoy their hotels and resorts for years to come, the legacy of Architects produces something tangible for everyone to share.

Salaries

According to the Bureau of Labor Statistics (BLS), median annual earnings of wage-and-salary Architects were $67,620 as of May 2007. The middle 50 percent earned between $52,030 and $88,360. The lowest 10 percent earned less than $40,250, and the highest 10 percent earned more than $112,990. Those just starting their internships can expect to earn considerably less.

Salaries vary by geographical location as well as experience. Partners in established firms may see salary fluctuations due to the economy and business conditions. The period of establishing his or her own practice can be a difficult financial time for an Architect, but if the practice becomes successful, it can have strong payoff later on.

Employment Prospects

Employment prospects are fair to good for Architects. The BLS projects employment for Architects to grow faster than the average for all occupations through 2016. However, building is determined by the economy and difficult times will mean that fewer hotels and resorts will be built. Those Architects with experience as well as expertise on environmentally friendly architecture will have the best opportunities.

Advancement Prospects

Architects have a number of areas in which they can work and advance. They may aspire to become partners in existing architectural firms or to open their own firms and become self-employed. Furthermore, they may become professors who teach architecture students or work as consultants. Others may write books, give

lectures, and work on private design. They may move to or from the hospitality industry.

Education and Training

According to archcareers.org, a site created in conjunction with the American Institute of Architects, there are three educational and training steps needed to become an Architect. First, one must earn an accredited degree in architecture. The National Architectural Accrediting Board (NAAB) accredits more than 100 U.S. programs, and graduating from one of these programs will ensure you will meet the educational qualifications necessary to take the Architectural Registration Exam (ARE). Students can complete a bachelor of architecture (B.Arch.), master of architecture (M.Arch.) or doctor of architecture (D.Arch.) degree. Some students may receive degrees in different disciplines and then complete a master of architecture program. To see this list of programs, visit NAAB's Web site at www.naab.org.

The next step is to participate in the Intern Development Program (IDP). The IDP is a national program for architecture interns to gain practical work experience; a typical internship may last three to five years. In order to become a licensed Architect, it is necessary to complete these educational and training requirements, and in most U.S. states, this training requirement is fulfilled by completing the IDP. The IDP is offered by the National Council of Architectural Registration Boards (NCARB)—for more information, see www.ncarb.org/idp/index.html.

Finally, Architects are ready to sit for the Architect Registration Exam (ARE). One cannot take the exam without fulfilling the required amount of professional experience, usually at least three years.

Majors in architecture include courses in architectural history and theory, building design (emphasis on CADD), construction methods, structures, technology, engineering, professional practice, math, physical sciences, and liberal arts, as well as the design studio.

Experience, Skills, and Personality Traits

To be a successful Architect, one must be able to combine art and science. It is necessary to have the technical skills combined with the artistic sensibility to create ideas, plans, and models that are innovative yet structurally sound. Furthermore, Architects should be strong communicators with good interpersonal skills. They must sell their ideas to clients and work with all types of people throughout the construction process. Patience helps them put the time into their work and meticulous attention to detail ensures that nothing has gone unnoticed.

Additional Information

According to the BLS, all states and the District of Columbia require individuals to be licensed before they may call themselves architects and contract to provide architectural services. Licensing requirements include a professional degree in architecture, a period of practical training or internship, and a passing score on all divisions of the Architect Registration Examination (ARE).

The BLS maintains that most states also require some form of continuing education to maintain a license. Requirements vary by state but usually involve the completion of a certain number of credits annually or biennially through workshops, formal university classes, conferences, self-study courses, or other sources.

Unions and Associations

The American Institute of Architects (AIA) is known as the "voice of the architecture profession." They are based in Washington, D.C., and have over 83,000 members. Students may become members of the American Institute of Architecture Students at www.aias.org.

Tips for Entry

1. AIA has extensive career information on its companion Web site, www.archcareers.org. Learn more about the profession and its educational requirements here.

2. Many firms specialize in the hospitality industry. The Cornell Hotel School in Ithaca, New York, maintains a list of many of them across the country at www.hotelschool.cornell.edu/research/library/tools/links/hslinks.html?scid=138&name=Lodging+Industry&scname=Architects+&+Designers&id=6.

3. Read architecture publications such as *Architectural Digest* (www.architecturaldigest.com), *Architectural Record* (archrecord.construction.com), and *Dwell* (www.dwell.com).

4. Design Intelligence publishes an annual book on America's Best Architecture and Design Schools. For more information, see www.di.net/archschools/schools.html.

5. View different extreme design hotels on this feature on the Forbes Traveler Web site: www.forbestraveler.com/resorts-hotels/extreme-design-hotels-story.html.

BED-AND-BREAKFAST OWNER

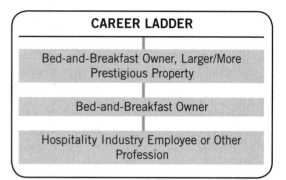

Position Description

Running a bed-and-breakfast (also called a B&B) is one of those jobs that sounds like a dream come true to many. You get to work out of your home as a gracious host to guests from all over the world. For many Bed-and-Breakfast Owners, their work is extremely fulfilling, but there are also many realities that go along with the vision. Owning and running a bed-and-breakfast is a 24/7 job.

According to the Professional Association of Innkeepers International (PAII), there are three types of B&Bs:

- **Bed-and-breakfast inn:** A lodging establishment that also functions as a residence for the owner-hosts. Breakfast is served to overnight guests.
- **Country inn:** This kind of lodging property has all the characteristics of a B&B inn, but serves an evening meal in addition to breakfast. Dinner may be served to overnight guests only and included in the room rate, or served in a full-service restaurant open to the general public. Most country inns have 10 or more rooms.
- **Home-stay (host home):** An owner-occupied private home where the business of renting rooms is secondary to its use as a private residence. Most home-stays rent three or fewer rooms, and many operate for a limited season. Breakfast is the only meal available and may be self-serve.

Visitors seek bed-and-breakfast inns as alternative to larger hotels for many reasons. For one, they may like the cozy atmosphere and personal attention that comes from staying in a home or inn with a limited number of rooms. They may enjoy meeting and dining with other guests and talking to people. Also, in some locations, particularly scenic and rural areas, there are few large hotels. Bed-and-breakfast inns offer a way to stay in beautiful, sometimes romantic surroundings that blend with their environment. Furthermore, some bed-and-breakfasts are in historic homes that attract travelers looking for a unique spot.

Bed-and-breakfast inns vary tremendously in terms of size, amenities, and services. A small inn may have less than five rooms and a larger one can have 20 or more. Some inns are luxurious, with rooms including fireplaces, balconies, and flat screen televisions, while others have no television, no Internet, and not even a private bathroom. People may actually seek out bed-and-breakfasts to get away from it all, ones that have no television or cell phone reception. Some serve a gourmet breakfast, tea or wine and cheese in the afternoon, and an optional dinner in the evening in a full-scale restaurant. Others have a casual breakfast only prepared by the innkeeper.

Bed-and-Breakfast Owners have a vast array of responsibilities. To begin, prospective owners either may start their own inn or buy an existing bed-and-breakfast to take over. If they are converting their home or buying a home to convert to an inn, they must acquire the zoning permits in their state that are needed to operate any commercial lodging establishments. Next, they must make a number of decisions about their inn. Will it be seasonal or year-round? Open daily or weekends only? How will they decorate the rooms—will there be a theme? What will they charge per stay? These are just a few of the questions they tackle as they plan to furnish, staff, and organize their new inn.

To turn their inn into a lucrative business, Bed-and-Breakfast Owners must consider their marketing and public relations campaign. Either doing it themselves or hiring consultants to create it for them, they often develop Web sites as a way to get their inn discovered and take reservations. They may also pay to be included in guidebooks or online guides, send press releases to local media inviting them to visit, register with local chambers of commerce, speak with travel agents, develop brochures, and more.

Furthermore, Bed-and-Breakfast Owners must decide how much of the work they will take on themselves and what staff they will hire. They may hire a chef, housekeeper, landscaper, maintenance crew, an assistant to help with luggage, and more. Other Bed-and-Breakfast Owners, particularly by those with smaller inns, may take on all or some of these responsibilities themselves.

In a large hotel, there are different staff members to meet the various needs of travelers. A Bed-and-Breakfast Owner may be a reservationist (booking reservations), front desk clerk (checking guests into their rooms), bell person (helping guests with their luggage), and concierge (recommending activities, tours, and restaurants) all in one. Bed-and-Breakfast Owners need to be local experts who know about the major tourist attractions and can recommend as well as arrange for activities and outside meals for their guests. Frequently, they have an array of literature about local attractions on the premises for guests.

Each day is a long one for Bed-and-Breakfast Owners as they decide what time breakfast will be served and how it will be structured. At some bed-and-breakfasts, all guests are asked to come down at 9 A.M., while at others, breakfast might be served on an ongoing basis from 8 to 11 A.M. It can be an elaborate meal of French toast, eggs Benedict, and homemade jams or a more casual selection of pastries and cereal. Time for food preparation, shopping, and serving all must be taken into consideration. Bed-and-Breakfast Owners are usually available at this time as well to talk with guests about their plans for the day.

During a typical day, Bed-and-Breakfast Owners field questions from guests as well as oversee operations, such as cleaning the rooms, performing maintenance, gardening, shopping, bookkeeping, etc. They may join guests for afternoon tea and cookies or wine and cheese, chatting about their activities and sightseeing. Some bed-and-breakfasts operate restaurants that serve dinner to guests and outside visitors, so in those cases, Bed-and-Breakfast Owners must prepare accordingly. In the evenings, they are usually on hand to answer questions and resolve problems and are on call for emergencies after hours.

Additional responsibilities may include:

- handling bookkeeping, accounting, and payroll
- meeting health department standards
- setting policies and procedures such as check-in and checkout
- providing specialty services for guests on the premises such as bicycle rentals
- interviewing potential employees and completing paperwork
- providing tours of the inn and surrounding property

In the past, owning a bed-and-breakfast was something of a retirement hobby as older couples opened their homes to travelers. Today, it is a thriving lifetime career business for younger couples or individuals who want to own and run an inn. Additional revenue can come from operating retail shops on the premises that sell homemade or local goods or even renting out the property for weddings and other events. According to PAII, weddings, family reunions, and special events are regular features at over half of all inns.

Bed-and-Breakfast Owners may run their inn on a part-time basis or as their primary career. The hours and location of the inn dictate their work hours, although even when the inn is closed, Bed-and-Breakfast Owners still have a myriad of responsibilities to make the inn run smoothly. Like any other business, when the Bed-and-Breakfast Owners are on vacation, the inn must be closed or operated by another manager.

Salaries

According to PAII, the bed-and-breakfast/country inn business is a $3.4 billion industry with more than 20,000 inns operating in the United States as of 2006. However, another interesting statistic from PAII states than 58 percent of Bed-and-Breakfast Owners are dependent on outside income. Income will depend on mortgage, operating costs, additional salaries to be paid out, and other annual expenses. Salaries for Bed-and-Breakfast

Owners can range from less than $20,000 to $100,000 or more depending on these factors.

Employment Prospects

Employment prospects are fair to good for those who want to own and operate B&Bs. PAII states that 82 percent of inn owners are couples and 88 percent live on the premises. In terms of geographical location, bed-and-breakfasts have the best chances of success in popular tourist areas and on scenic properties.

For success as a Bed-and-Breakfast Owner, one needs a good business sense to find the right opportunity. According to PAII some common mistakes that Bed-and-Breakfast Owners make are not having enough capital, having invested too much in the business to make it profitable, failing to market actively, and not providing quality service and product.

Advancement Prospects

Advancement can come when Bed-and-Breakfast Owners get more recognition for their inns. Perhaps they might bring a well-known chef on board, be photographed for a national magazine, or produce cheese for distribution on the premises that will impact revenue. Also, they may move to take over larger inns or buy additional properties.

Education and Training

Bed-and-Breakfast Owners come to their positions from a variety of backgrounds. Some owners quit their corporate jobs to leave the rat race and move to the country to run an inn, while others have formal education and training in the hotel industry. They might have advanced professional degrees or a high school education, but courses in hotel management and innkeeping are very helpful. PAII offers workshops and information about other organizations running workshops and classes for aspiring innkeepers nationwide at www.paii.org/workshops.asp.

Experience, Skills, and Personality Traits

To dedicate your days to hosting guests, one must truly be a people person. Bed-and-Breakfast Owners should be energized by speaking to others. They must enjoy getting to know and serving people with genuine interest. Furthermore, Bed-and-Breakfast Owners need to be good managers. They may supervise a large staff and must keep organized and abreast of all operations. Strong accounting and financial skills are needed as well.

Unions and Associations

The main professional association for Bed-and-Breakfast Owners is the Professional Association of Innkeepers International. For more information, visit its Web site at www.paii.org. There are also professional associations by state for Bed-and-Breakfast Owners.

Tips for Entry

1. Read books such as *The Complete Idiot's Guide to Running a Bed and Breakfast* by Susannah Craig and Park Davis, *How to Start and Run Your Own Bed and Breakfast Inn* by Ripley Hotch and Carl A. Glassman, and *So—You Want to Be an Innkeeper: The Definitive Guide to Operating a Successful Bed and Breakfast or Country Inn* by Mary E. Davies with Pat Hardy, Jo Ann M. Bell, and Susan Brown.

2. Learn more about how to run a B&B on About.com at bandb.about.com/od/running/How_to_Run_a_Bed_and_Breakfast.htm.

3. There are many Web sites that rate B&Bs. Take a look at some of these sites and then the individual inns at www.bedandbreakfast.com/Awards-Winners.aspx, www.bnbfinder.com, and www.iloveinns.com, among others.

4. Stay at a bed-and-breakfast and speak to the innkeeper(s). How did they get started in the field? When you visit the Web sites of many B&Bs, it provides a bio of the owner as well.

5. Try running a B&B through a program called Vocation Vacations, which allows people to test-drive their dream jobs: vocationvacations.com.

6. Check out innstar.com, a ratings guide to bed-and-breakfast guidebooks on the Internet.

HOTEL ATTORNEY

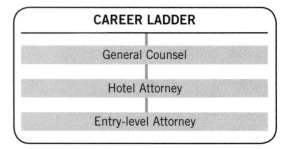

Position Description

Within the hospitality industry, there are many legal issues and agreements to be negotiated. Therefore, Hotel Attorneys can work in a variety of capacities. They may represent hotel owners, developers, or lenders in the process of buying and managing hotel properties. Hotel Attorneys help owners to find the right management team and financing. They help their clients identify their goals and find the right property, overseeing real estate transactions and flow of capital.

Hotel Attorneys work as both defenders and counselors for their clients. As defenders and champions, they represent them by presenting evidence and arguing in court if necessary. As counselors, they talk with clients about their legal rights, recommending courses of action. A large part of their work involves researching law and judicial decisions, and then applying the law to specific aspects of their clients' cases.

Hotel Attorneys may also work as the general or in-house counsel of a hotel unit or brand. The job of general counsel is to protect the hotel's legal interest. General counsels maintain hotel operations within the scope established by law. Working closely with the hotel unit and/or brand's executive leadership such as general

managers, vice presidents, CEOs, etc., the general counsel ensures that legal issues are identified, handled, and managed.

As in-house counsel, Hotel Attorneys are on-site and employed by the hotel corporation or unit as an integral part of the management team. In this capacity, they know their property inside and out. While Hotel Attorneys in private practice may have a number of hospitality industry clients, those working as general counsel serve the needs of one hotel or brand.

Problems can arise with unhappy guests staying at hotels of all calibers. Perhaps jewelry was stolen from their room or they slipped on an icy walkway on the property. When disputes cannot be settled, people may take legal action. The general counsel and other Hotel Attorneys protect the hotel's interest, working with the legal team and preparing necessary materials to represent the hotel in these lawsuits.

To prepare for these lawsuits, Hotel Attorneys conduct extensive research, checking for interpretation of the law, precedents, and the outcomes in previous cases. They may interview a variety of people involved in the charges. Then they discuss options with their client for possible resolution. Sometimes, cases will need to go to trial. Some Hotel Attorneys represent their clients/

hotels in trials, while others bring in outside counsel trained in trial work.

Frequently, Hotel Attorneys are involved with mergers and acquisitions, especially at the brand level. They advise hotels on new deals and help them seek out fiscally wise opportunities. Hotel Attorneys may spend a large portion of their time on transactional work, which includes real estate investments and new management contracts. Also, they work with boards of directors on corporate governance of the hotel unit or brand.

Additionally, Hotel Attorneys may handle labor and employment concerns within the hospitality industry. They may represent union workers and collective bargaining agreements to ensure fair wages, policies, and procedures, working closely with human resources departments. Additional issues include workers' compensation and complying with nondiscriminatory hiring practices.

Additional duties may include:

- drafting key documents
- assuring legal compliance
- presenting clear recommendations
- planning and accomplishing goals
- handling securities filings
- negotiating contracts
- overseeing insurance issues

Hotel Attorneys must be familiar with concepts, practices, and procedures in the hospitality field. They may lead or direct the work of others, depending on whether they are in-house counsel or work for a private firm specializing in hospitality. Typically, Hotel Attorneys work between 40 and 60 hours per week. Above all, their goal is to protect the interest of their client.

Salaries

According to the Bureau of Labor Statistics, the median annual earnings of all wage-and-salaried lawyers were $106,120 as of May 2007. The middle half of the occupation earned between $72,060 and $145,600. Hotel Attorneys, particularly those with considerable experience, often earn more than $150,000 per year. Chief legal officers earn an average compensation of approximately $280,000 per year, including bonuses.

Employment Prospects

Employment prospects are good for Hotel Attorneys. As the number of hotels continues to grow, so will the need for in-house counsel to represent the hotels' interests. Additionally, hotels will need to retain Hotel Attorneys in private practice to represent them as well.

The best opportunities will be for those with the combination of legal expertise and hospitality industry work experience.

Advancement Prospects

Advancement prospects are also good. Since the industry is specialized, Hotel Attorneys with experience create a valuable niche for themselves. Hotel Attorneys may advance to be the senior general counsel, chief legal officer, or head of the legal team for a hotel, as well as a partner in a law firm specializing in the hospitality industry.

Education and Training

To become a Hotel Attorney, one must complete an undergraduate degree as well as a law degree from an accredited law school. As of June 2008, a total of 200 institutions were accredited by the American Bar Association (ABA). For a complete list of ABA-approved programs, see www.abanet.org/legaled/approvedlawschools/approved.html. Law school lasts typically three years, after which the Juris Doctor (JD) degree is awarded. The Law School Admission Test (LSAT) is a standardized exam required for admission to law school. For more information about the LSAT, see www.lsat.org.

Undergraduate majors can include anything, but often courses in English, history, political science, and economics are helpful, along with hospitality management. It can be beneficial to take time off between college and law school, particular to gain hospitality work experience. For an eventual career in the hotel industry, this is very valuable. Some Hotel Attorneys, particularly those handling real estate transactions and tax issues, also hold degrees in finance, real estate development, or accounting.

Experience, Skills, and Personality Traits

Hotel Attorneys need excellent analytical and research skills. They should be strong writers and communicators who are comfortable with public speaking and can articulate well in speech and writing. Interpersonal skills help them instill trust in their clients. Furthermore, Hotel Attorneys should have detailed knowledge of the hotel industry, including work experience. Knowledge of tax and finance is helpful for work in these areas.

Special Requirements

In order to practice law, Hotel Attorneys (as well as other lawyers of any kind) must be admitted to the bar of the state in which they want to work by passing a written bar examination. To qualify to take the bar exam, candidates must graduate from a law school accredited by the ABA.

Unions and Associations

Hotel Attorneys may belong to professional associations including the American Hotel and Lodging Association, the American Bar Association, and the Association of Corporate Counsel (for those who practice in-house).

Tips for Entry

1. Visit the Web site of the Law School Admission Council (LSAC), a nonprofit corporation whose members include more than 200 law schools in the United States, Canada, and Australia. It was founded in 1947 to coordinate, facilitate, and enhance the law school admission process. LSAC administers the LSAT and its Web site (www.lsac. org) provides considerable information about the law school admissions process.

2. If you are interested in learning more about hotel law, check out the blog published by the Global Hospitality Group at hotellaw.jmbm. com, as well as the Hospitality Lawyer blog at blog.hospitalitylawyer.com.

3. How much do you know about the law school process? Princeton Review offers valuable information, including time lines and essay tips, at www.princetonreview.com/opinionAdvice. aspx?type=law&RDN=1.

4. To be a successful Hotel Attorney, a combination of hospitality and legal experience is best. Try a summer job at a hotel to learn more, and speak to the in-house counsel while you are there.

RETAIL MANAGER

CAREER PROFILE

Duties: Oversees operations of a hotel or resort store or gift shop

Alternate Title(s): Retail Supervisor; Store Operations Manager

Salary Range: $21,000 to $60,000 and up

Employment Prospects: Fair

Advancement Prospects: Fair

Best Geographical Location(s): All, with the greatest opportunities in large cities and heavy tourist regions with many hotels and resorts

Prerequisites:

Education and Training—Varies; college degree helpful for advancement

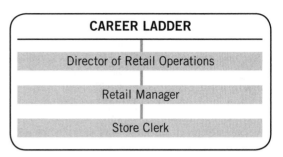

Experience—Prior retail work experience

Special Skills and Personality Traits—Excellent customer service skills; good business and management skills; communication and interpersonal ability; organization

Position Description

Large hotels and resorts often have a number of different retail options. In addition to a traditional gift shop that may sell hotel logo merchandise and pharmaceuticals, snacks, and toiletries, many properties offer considerably more shopping choices. Beach resorts often sell warm weather apparel and bathing suits; family resorts may have elaborate toy stores. Spas showcase the lotions and other skin care products they use; hotels known for their sports facilities will have a pro shop that sells equipment; and large casino hotels often sell jewelry and luxury goods. Each of these diverse types of stores has a Retail Manager who directs operations for their store.

While the duties of Retail Managers depend on the size and type of hotel store for which they work, their responsibilities can divided into four categories: merchandising (including buying and selling store inventory); store operations (including staffing and receiving goods); accounting and bookkeeping (tracking sales figures); and advertising and promotion (bringing in customers through publicizing offerings). In small stores, the Retail Manager is involved with all of these aspects.

Since stores contribute to the hotel's overall bottom line, Retail Managers have a responsibility to increase profitability. One way to do this is through hiring and supervising staff. Depending on the size of the store, they may hire part-time workers or full-time workers, one or several. Retail Managers train the staff and set store policy. For example, they may teach them how to demonstrate products or fold certain items according to standard. Additionally, Retail Managers must terminate staff if the situation is not working, as well as arrange schedules.

Furthermore, Retail Managers use their marketing skills to arrange the store in a pleasing way that will draw in customers. They develop and oversee window and in-store displays, promoting the most visible products. Developing special promotions can also be a way for Retail Managers to entice customers. They make decisions about putting items on sale in order to drive up revenue.

Financial skills are also necessary for Retail Managers. They maintain their store's budget, analyzing sales figures on a regular basis (daily, weekly, monthly, and annually) and forecasting future sales. They keep aware of industry trends in order to plan the store's needs and stock for the future. As needed, Retail Managers may make decisions such as extending hours to improve performance. At all times, Retail Managers are aware of their stock, making sure the right amount of inventory is on hand. They also keep track of merchandise and enforce procedures to prevent theft.

Additional duties may include:

- ordering and maintaining inventory
- conducting interviews with prospective staff members
- ensuring standards of the hotel are met
- responding to customer complaints and comments

- monitoring the local competition
- working the cash register and direct sales when needed
- attending merchandise trade shows

Retail Managers also spend time interacting with customers. They tour the sales floor regularly, talking to shoppers to see if their needs are being met. Additionally, Retail Managers meet with hotel executives to report on performance. If the hotel has numerous shops, the Retail Managers all meet regularly to share ideas and best practices. Some retail shops in hotels are part of a chain (such as Starbucks). These Retail Managers are accountable to that company and may report to a regional manager.

Stores may be open for more than 40 hours per week, definitely including weekends and possibly evenings. Retail Managers work long hours but in some cases can also delegate hours to staff members and not be on the premises at all times.

Salaries

Salaries for Retail Managers vary depending on their experience as well as the type of store they manage. According to the Bureau of Labor Statistics, salaried supervisors of retail sales workers (Retail Managers) had median annual earnings of $34,470, including commissions, as of May 2007. The middle 50 percent earned between $26,950 and $45,300 a year. The lowest 10 percent earned less than $21,760, and the highest 10 percent earned more than $60,550 a year. In addition to base salary, most Retail Managers also earn commissions and/or bonuses depending on performance. They may also receive additional travel perks, especially if they work for a large hotel chain.

Employment Prospects

As more hotels and resorts are built, Retail Managers will be needed to manage their shops. The best opportunities will be at large properties and specialty resorts that have more than one store, creating the need for several Retail Managers. Additionally, those with retail and supervisory experience will have the greatest options.

Advancement Prospects

Retail Managers can advance by moving to manage larger stores with more staff and responsibility. Further-

more, they can also become directors of retail operations for large hotels and resorts where they oversee all the managers of each of the stores. They may work at the unit or brand level. Others may decide to leave the hospitality industry for different retail opportunities.

Education and Training

Education and training varies for Retail Managers. Some enter the field with a high school diploma and experience in progressively more responsible retail positions. Others have bachelor's degrees, which can be necessary for advancement. Useful fields of study include business, marketing, sales, and merchandising.

Experience, Skills, and Personality Traits

Excellent customer service skills are needed to be a successful Retail Manager. Additionally, one needs good business sense as well as management and financial skills to oversee transactions, inventory, and staff. Communication and interpersonal skills enable Retail Managers to work well with customers, staff, and management. A knack for sales and the ability to be positive and persuasive is also beneficial.

Unions and Associations

Retail Managers may belong to the National Retail Federation, the world's largest retail trade association, with membership that comprises all retail formats and channels of distribution including department, specialty, discount, catalog, Internet, and independent stores, chain restaurants, drug stores, and grocery stores, as well as the industry's key trading partners of retail goods and services.

Tips for Entry

1. Explore different hotel Web sites to see the types of shops they feature. How do they vary depending on the property? For example, Caesars Palace Las Vegas Hotel and Casino has more than 120 luxury shops on its premises: www.caesars palace.com/casinos/caesars-palace/casino-misc/ shopping-at-caesars-palace-detail.html.
2. Visit hotel gift shops to see the type of merchandise they sell.
3. Gain experience in retail sales, especially working in a store that is part of a hotel or resort.
4. Take courses in sales and marketing to learn more about the field.

INTERIOR DESIGNER

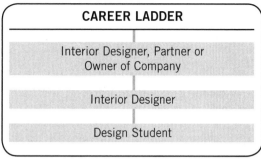
Position Description

When you walk into the lobby of a luxury hotel, you immediately get a feel for the image it is trying to project. The furniture may be modern, with soft lighting, earth-toned walls, subtle artwork, mirrored panels, and elegant floral arrangements. This feeling that the decor conveys is the work of an Interior Designer. Interior Designers create the look and feel of hotels, resorts, casinos, and other properties in the hospitality industry in order to make each unique.

Interior Designers have a hand in every aspect of the public space. They offer recommendations related to furniture selection; colors; materials, fabrics, and textures; artwork; flooring; lighting; and more. Analyzing each design component, they consider quality, cost, maintenance, safety, and overall appearance. They meet and consult with clients to determine their vision, budget, and plan for the interior, much the way architects meet with clients to discuss the exterior. During these client meetings, it is important for Interior Designers to understand the goals the property is trying to achieve and the needs of their targeted clientele.

After meeting with clients, Interior Designers prepare plans for their review. They may use sketches or software programs (such as CAD—computer-aided design) to create these visions and may even include three-dimensional modeling to show furniture and other aspects of room design. Within hospitality properties, Interior Designers may work on lobbies, restaurants, guest rooms, meeting rooms, and other areas of the facilities. Some may work on all areas, while others may have specialties, such as kitchen, bathroom, or restaurant design.

Frequently, Interior Designers collaborate with architects, engineers, contractors, and others involved with the overall look and feel of the property. They work together to ensure the plan is adhering to safety codes and regulations and that the selected materials will work well together and can be properly installed. In addition to decorating, Interior Designers may also be involved with design details that affect the building structure, such as built-in shelves.

Furthermore, Interior Designers develop relationships with vendors who sell paint, furniture, light fixtures, flooring and carpeting, fabric, and other items. These relationships help them to get the best prices on merchandise as well as to negotiate consistent and reliable quality and service. They often visit many retailers and attend design shows to add to their stable of contacts.

Additional duties may include:

- maintaining awareness of federal and state building codes
- selecting contractors and other project staff

- developing a project time line
- coordinating work schedules
- shopping for and purchasing furniture and room accessories
- estimating costs, obtaining bids, and preparing contracts
- inspecting quality of finished products
- keeping billing records

Interior Designers working for a hotel or restaurant chain must ensure that all properties have consistent design themes. Within an individual hotel or resort, they create a scheme where different rooms complement each other. Details such as where to place mirrors, floral arrangements, beds, and tables may seem insignificant, but have an overall impact on the entire image of a property. All areas must be both functional and aesthetically pleasing.

Hours for Interior Designers vary and may be long and nontraditional in order to meet the schedules of clients and contractors. Travel may be required to visit properties and suppliers.

Salaries

The Bureau of Labor Statistics (BLS) states that median annual earnings for wage and salaried Interior Designers were $43,970 as of May 2007. The middle 50 percent earned between $33,480 and $60,200. The lowest 10 percent earned less than $25,920, and the highest 10 percent earned more than $81,800. Salaries vary depending on geographic location and the scope and budgets of their projects. Also, those Interior Designers who are self-employed may earn considerably more.

Employment Prospects

According to the BLS, job prospects for Interior Designers are expected to grow faster than average through 2016. Demand from businesses in the hospitality industry—hotels, resorts, and restaurants—is expected to be high because of an expected increase in tourism. Opportunities can also grow from developing a specialized niche. The BLS also states that about 26 percent of Interior Designers are self-employed. When on the job market, Interior Designers use portfolios that have examples of their past work.

Advancement Prospects

Interior Designers can advance by taking on larger projects in size and scope. They may become partners in design firms or start their own companies. Furthermore, they may be contracted by large hotel, resort, or restaurant chains to work on many properties at once.

Education and Training

For the greatest opportunity as well as professional licensure, Interior Designers should have a bachelor's degree from an accredited program. The National Association of Schools of Art and Design has approximately 287 accredited institutional postsecondary school members with programs in art and design. Most of these schools award a degree in interior design. Furthermore, the National Council for Interior Design Accreditation also accredits interior design programs that lead to a bachelor's degree. For updated information about these programs, see the Web site at www.accredit-id.org/accreditedprograms.php.

Special Requirements

The BLS states that 23 states, the District of Columbia, and Puerto Rico register or license interior designers. The National Council of Interior Design Qualification administers the licensing exam for interior design qualification. To be eligible for the exam, applicants must have at least six years of combined education and experience in interior design, of which at least two years must be postsecondary education in design. After passing the qualifying exam, Interior Designers are granted the title of certified, registered, or licensed interior designer, depending on the state.

Experience, Skills, and Personality Traits

Overall, Interior Designers need artistic ability and vision. They need a trained eye to walk into a space and have a sense of the way it should be arranged to maximize attractiveness and functionality. Additionally, CAD training and the ability to create drawings and models to bring these visions to life is important.

Along with artistic sense, Interior Designers need solid business sense. Good organizational and planning skills keep projects on schedule. Excellent sales skills enable Interior Designers to market their talents to clients. Interpersonal and communication skills help them develop relationships with both clients and suppliers.

Unions and Associations

Interior Designers may belong to a variety of professional associations including the American Society of Interior Designers (ASID), the oldest and largest professional association for Interior Designers (over 40,000 members), and the International Interior Design Association (IIDA), a networking and educational association with more than 13,000 members. Those interested in the field can also get information from the Interior Design Educators Council (IDEC) and the National Council of Interior Design Qualification (NCIDQ).

Tips for Entry

1. Read *Becoming an Interior Designer: A Guide to Careers in Design*, by Christine M. Piotrowski, FASID, IIDA.

2. Learn more about what makes a beautiful space. Visit hotels and restaurants and note which properties and features stand out in terms of design. Read travel magazines that showcase these interiors.

3. There are interior design groups that specialize in the hotel industry. View their Web sites and contact the Interior Designers for informational interviews. Several groups can be found at www.interiordesignerworld.com/commhotel.htm.

4. Another great Web site to explore is Hotel Designs (www.hoteldesigns.net), a hotel design resource for Interior Designers, architects and hoteliers. It includes a directory of manufacturers and suppliers, as well as industry news and events.

5. Review Careers in Interior Design (www.careersininteriordesign.com/index.html), a site compiled by a number of professional associations in order to provide career information.

SPECIALTY RESORTS, CRUISE SHIPS, AND RECREATION

CRUISE DIRECTOR

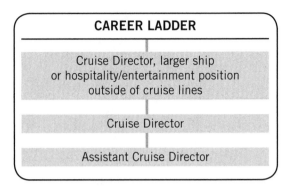

Position Description

Vacationers take cruises in order to relax and get away from it all. On a cruise, they expect a certain quality of accommodation, food, and activities. Furthermore, because of the nature of cruise vacations, they expect to be entertained.

Cruise Directors are responsible for the on-ship entertainment. Made most famous by Julie, the Cruise Director on the 1970s television series *The Love Boat*, Cruise Directors serve to make sure guests have fun and enjoy themselves. They lead and organize daily recreational activities ranging from wine tastings and magic shows to karaoke and trivia games. Along with their staff of assistants, they plan these activities to ensure that guests always have something to do on the ship and offshore.

Working with their team of staff to develop programming that meets the unique needs of passengers, Cruise Directors must understand the demographics of their passenger base and what types of programming this group needs and wants. Itineraries and activities may fluctuate depending on the different groups of guests. The Cruise Director must be sensitive to these changes and plan accordingly. In fact, Cruise Directors say that each voyage is a totally different experience

depending on the passenger group and the dynamics on board.

Furthermore, different cruise lines are known for catering to different clientele. Some have reputations for being "party ships," while others are more sophisticated. Cruise lines often have very different requirements for their Cruise Directors, based on the nature of their ship and what they want the Cruise Director to achieve.

While on board, Cruise Directors plan the daily activities and generally generate excitement and enthusiasm for the ship's offerings. They may schedule lecturers, performers, variety shows, and other programming, developing ideas and hiring staff. Cruise Directors serve as the master of ceremonies for events, announcing programs during meals and shows, as well as overseeing all loudspeaker announcements.

When it comes time to disembark at the cruise's featured destinations, Cruise Directors earn revenue for their cruise line by selling tour packages to passengers. They make passengers aware of the various excursions at each port—snorkeling sessions, shopping trips, ATV riding, etc.—and let them know how they can sign up for these tours. Cruise lines work hand in hand with these tour companies so both can make a profit.

Cruise Directors also need to be experts both on ship and off. They know their ships from top to bottom and can advise passengers on activities for every minute of the day to fit every mood. Cruise Directors must know details about each port destination, including activities, currency, and more to assist passengers with itineraries.

Additional duties may include:

- liaising with other cruise department heads to coordinate social programming
- developing policies and procedures for social activities and programs
- overseeing production shows, variety shows, musicians, lectures, and activities, and establishing guidelines for improvement
- developing social budget proposals and recording expenditures
- managing and maintaining departmental finances within budgetary requirements
- leading passengers through safety demonstrations
- providing a disembarkation lecture
- working with vendors in the various ports
- performing in various shows and events
- attending VIP and other passenger functions and cocktail parties/receptions
- developing a contingency plan for rainy day activities
- producing a daily newsletter of activities

On large ships, Cruise Directors often have a staff that includes assistant cruise director(s) and social hosts/hostesses. They also work closely with entertainers, youth counselors, stage managers and other personnel and departments in order to plan and coordinate activities.

The work of a Cruise Director continues around the clock when the ship is in motion. For this reason, jobs tend to operate on a six-month or other type of contract, such as four months on, six weeks off. However, most Cruise Directors love their work as it enables them to be in the spotlight to perform and entertain others, as well as travel the globe.

Salaries

According to Cruiseshipjobs.com, the salary for Cruise Directors ranges from $3,800 to $7,500 per month, depending on the cruise line. Earnings can vary greatly based on the experience of the Cruise Director as well as the size of the cruise line.

Employment Prospects

Employment prospects are fair to good for Cruise Directors. All cruise ships need them, but competition is tight for those on desirable ships. The positions are contract based, usually for a six-month period or so, and many do not stay in their positions for more than a few years. Usually, Cruise Directors come to their positions from being promoted within, from assistant cruise directors, disc jockeys, onboard entertainers, hosts/hostesses, and other jobs.

Advancement Prospects

While Cruise Directors typically report to the onboard hotel manager as well as entertainment directors, they are usually interested in different types of advancement. Cruise Directors may move to different ships/cruise lines that are larger and more prestigious, or choose options that allow them to see other parts of the world. Others may move to positions outside of cruise ships as actors/actresses, dancers/musicians, or to different hospitality careers.

Education and Training

The path to becoming a Cruise Director begins with cruise staff positions such as a host or hostess who greets and mingles with the guests. A job as an assistant cruise director would be the ideal preparation needed as one would have extensive training working with passengers and learning the ropes firsthand. The Cruise Director is frequently an entertainer who performs several times in various capacities during a voyage. For this reason, a background in entertainment and performing arts can be very helpful.

While in the past, most Cruise Directors were musicians, performers, and other types of entertainers, today Cruise Directors come from all types of backgrounds. Since there is no type of formal education required, there are Cruise Directors with graduate degrees as well as those with just a high school education (some job listings do require a bachelor's degree, however). Courses in hospitality as well as knowledge of foreign languages can be helpful. Cruise Directors receive training on the job related to the policies and procedures of their cruise line and particular ship.

Experience, Skills, and Personality Traits

Different cruise lines look for varying qualities in a Cruise Director, depending on the nature of the ship, but all Cruise Directors must be highly outgoing and enjoy working with people. They get very little downtime during a voyage and must love constantly being "on" and in the spotlight. Also, Cruise Directors must be charismatic leaders who can command the attention of large groups of people naturally and with a sense of humor.

Additionally, Cruise Directors need high energy for their work at motivating and entertaining passengers. They must be good at developing relationships and excellent communicators and speakers, whether dealing with individuals or making announcements to larger groups. Cruise Directors should be good leaders and managers for supervising staff and need the ability to multitask.

Unions and Associations

There is no professional association specifically for Cruise Directors. Cruise Lines International Association (www.cruising.org/about.cfm) is an association that promotes the cruise industry.

Tips for Entry

1. View cruise ship jobs and read job descriptions on sites including www.cruiseshipjob.com and www.cruisejobfinder.com.

2. *Sealetter Cruise* magazine at www.sealetter.com is the Internet's oldest and most established publication, featuring cruise reviews, port reviews, shore excursion reviews, cruise articles, cruise discussion boards, cruise news, and cruise humor.

3. Have you been on a cruise? If you have traveled different cruise lines, note the differences in style between various Cruise Directors. See if you can shadow a Cruise Director for a day to see if you have what it takes to get into the field.

4. CruiseCritic.com (www.cruisecritic.com) is an interactive community comprised of avid and first-time cruisers who enjoy the fun of planning, researching, and sharing their passion for cruising. It also features helpful interviews with cruise staff.

CAPTAIN, CRUISE SHIP

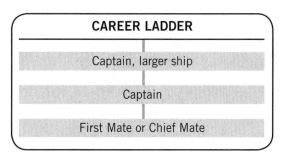

Position Description

If you have a passion for boating, spending your days navigating the ocean at the helm of a cruise ship may be a dream come true. While passengers on board are eating, sleeping, swimming, and dancing the night away, Captains adeptly steer their vessels through the water, making the ships feel as if they are barely moving at all.

Captains are the highest ranking personnel on a cruise ship. They maintain charge of their ships and crew as a captain would in the navy. They are responsible for the entire crew, as well as the safety of the passengers. Captains make the final decisions about which course to take and they have authority over rules and regulations.

In order to steer and navigate a ship, Captains need extensive training. They are responsible for setting the course and the speed of the ship and they use navigational aids including computers, charts, and observation to determine direction. Furthermore, they monitor conditions such as weather at all times. Captains must keep the ship on a course that avoids hazards, using radar and lighthouses, among other tools to guide their way.

While Captains are in command, they also delegate responsibilities to their crew, and often hire, train, and supervise this staff. Living and working together often creates a familylike atmosphere, and trust and respect are essential. The mates and crew assist with maintenance, engine operation, and passenger embarkation and disembarkation.

Additional duties may include:

- hiring and training the crew
- administering payroll and benefits (in smaller operations)
- tracking expenses for repairs and cleaning
- providing ship tours for passengers
- assigning responsibilities
- purchasing navigational equipment and making recommendations
- understanding international maritime laws

Even once the ship docks, the Captain's job continues with paperwork and port regulations. Captains are responsible for maintaining activity logs that include such details as weather, fuel usage, navigational decisions, and more.

On cruise ships, Captains also may socialize with the guests at special dinners and receptions. The Captain is seen as somewhat of a celebrity and passengers may be excited to get a glimpse of this seemingly glamorous role. The Captain may also make announcements. On smaller ships, passengers may have even more interaction with the Captain. Captains may work on cruise ships, yachts, ferries, and other types of boats that transport passengers ranging in all sizes. On smaller vessels such as yachts, Captains may also be owners of their ships.

Being a Captain is the ultimate way to see the world, as Captains may sail in all global waters. Hours are long and shifts may run from four hours to 12 hours at a time. At sea, Captains work seven days and may rotate with other Captains. Typically, cruise ship Captains work for two months at a time and then enjoy one month off. Some Captains' families live aboard with them during these work periods, while others do not.

The job of Captain is a stressful one, as Captains have people's lives at stake. They need sound judgment and maritime expertise. Many Captains take seriously the old saying about Captains going down with their ship, and they put the safety of passengers and crew at top priority.

Salaries

Once one has worked up to becoming a Captain, salaries are high. Captains of cruise ships typically earn in the six-figure range ($100,000 and up), with room and board also part of the package. On a cruise ship, they may be paid a monthly salary of between $6,000 and $10,000 per month. Captains of other passenger vessels may earn less, ranging between $50,000 and $100,000 per year.

Employment Prospects

Employment prospects are very limited for cruise ship Captains, and there is much competition for jobs. Qualified candidates compete from all over the world, and many Captains of international cruise lines are from European countries with long seafaring traditions. Captains may come to cruise lines after working on ferries or other passenger vessels and need extensive experience as a chief mate before becoming a Captain. Additional job opportunities may be available for Captains on commercial ships.

Advancement Prospects

Captains can advance by moving to larger ships, or moving to different types of vessels that fit with their goals and interests. Some Captains aspire to work on cruise ships, while others want to own their own yacht or charter service.

Education and Training

Captains must hold a bachelor's degree from an accredited maritime program. There are a limited number of

U.S. schools that offer maritime degree programs. The list of schools includes the following:

- United States Merchant Marine Academy (www.usmma.edu)
- State University of New York Maritime College (www.sunymaritime.edu)
- California Maritime Academy (www.csum.edu)
- Great Lakes Maritime Academy (www.nmc.edu/maritime)
- Maine Maritime Academy (www.mainemaritime.edu)
- Massachusetts Maritime Academy (www.maritime.edu)
- Texas Maritime Academy (www.tamug.edu/corps)

Special Requirements

Captains must have a STCW-95 license to operate a ship as well as a U.S. Coast Guard license (for a U.S. registered vessel). Standards of Training, Certification and Watchkeeping provides information about the steps needed to obtain this license at www.stcw.org.

Experience, Skills, and Personality Traits

Captains must have excellent technical maritime knowledge to operate their ship. Years of experience in progressively more responsible positions (including at least five years as a chief mate) provides the expertise needed for this stressful job. Captains must be able to stay calm under pressure and have very strong leadership and management skills. Communication and interpersonal skills help them to work well with passengers and mathematical ability enables them to understand their course. Attention to detail and observation is also important and knowledge of shipboard safety is essential.

Unions and Associations

The American Maritime Officers Union (www.amo-union.org) is the largest union of merchant marines in the United States. Information about working on a cruise ship can be obtained from Cruise Lines International Association at www.cruising.org.

Tips for Entry

1. A Career Afloat is a site that provides information about maritime careers, from the U.S. Department of Transportation's Maritime Administration. Learn more at marweb.marad.dot.gov/acareerafloat/index.html.
2. Learn more about cruise ship positions through sites such as www.cruiseshipjobfinder.com.

3. Get as much experience as possible working on boats and learning the rules and regulations.
4. Research maritime degree programs. Admissions representatives can put you in touch with current students to learn about their curriculum and career plans.
5. Speak to cruise ship Captains to learn how they got started in the field.

STAGE MANAGER

CAREER PROFILE

Duties: Oversees all shows on a cruise ship or resort; manages the technical staff and operations

Alternate Title(s): Production Manager

Salary Range: $2,200 to $3,100 per month, plus room and board

Employment Prospects: Fair

Advancement Prospects: Fair

Best Geographical Location(s): Any locations that cruise ships sail, including the Caribbean, the Atlantic/Pacific coast, Alaska, the Mediterranean, and more; resort locations worldwide

Prerequisites:

Education and Training—Background in theater performance and technical operations

Experience—Prior experience in theater, most recently as an assistant stage manager

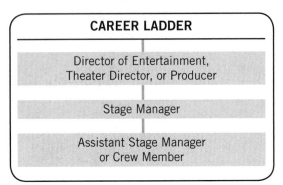

CAREER LADDER

Director of Entertainment, Theater Director, or Producer

Stage Manager

Assistant Stage Manager or Crew Member

Special Skills and Personality Traits—Technical knowledge; ability to stay calm under pressure and multitask

Position Description

Cruises and resort hotels are known for the elaborate shows they produce every evening. Ranging from Broadway-style theater to dancers, jugglers, magicians, and more, these productions may be performed on large stages for hundreds of guests. Stage Managers oversee these shows and ensure that they run smoothly backstage and onstage, as well as before, after, and during the performance.

Many factors go into producing a successful show. One of the main responsibilities of a Stage Manager is to "call" the show, which means calling the cues for the different crew members. This is how all cast and crew—including sound operators, lighting, effects, and performers—know what they are supposed to do at each moment. This is crucial to the production running seamlessly, as sound and light appears when the actors are reciting their specific lines.

Stage Managers lead and supervise rehearsals, ensuring the performers and crew are there on time and that all is running well. Furthermore, they record everything that happens during rehearsals in a prompt book. This often massive notebook becomes the guide for the performance, as well as future performances. Notes are kept here about props, costumes, cues, and more, and they may include diagrams and records. The timing of light and sound cues are also recorded.

Stage Managers use this prompt book to run each show.

After rehearsals, the Stage Manager may run reports to share with the production team. Also, additional reports may be run after each performance. This is another way Stage Managers track the details and communicate between departments. Coordinating between cast and crew and the director is an essential part of being a Stage Manager.

Overall, the Stage Manager takes over where the director leaves off. He or she ensures that the performance looks and sounds the way it is supposed to, according to the artistic vision. To make this happen, Stage Managers track and coordinate information and production details. They are in constant coordination with the stage crew in different areas overseeing props, costumes, scenery, effects, sound, lighting, performers, dialogue, and more.

Additional duties may include:

- scheduling meetings with guest entertainers
- work with engineering staff to report and fix broken equipment
- ordering supplies and maintaining inventory
- supervising the construction of scenery
- recording the blocking (where performers are positioned on stage)

- making sure performers stay on script
- tracking down performers who forgot cues
- assisting the director
- coordinating scene changes
- handling discipline problems

On a cruise ship or at a resort, performances may change frequently. Additionally, on a seven-night cruise, there will be a different performance each night. Stage Managers must coordinate these different performances and keep track of the unique needs of each one. They supervise the crew and schedule their hours, as well as serve as the main point of contact for the entertainers.

Hours for Stage Managers are long, as rehearsals are held during the day and shows go into the night. However, for those with a passion for the stage, the job is very rewarding. To combine a love for performance with the appeal of working on a cruise ship or in a resort makes this position a desirable one.

Salaries
On a cruise ship, salaries for Stage Managers average between $2,200 to $3,100 per month. While aboard, expenses are quite low, with housing and food included, so Stage Managers can save money. Stage Managers who work outside of cruise ships and resorts might earn yearly salaries of $40,000 to $80,000 and up, depending on the size and scope of the performances they oversee.

Employment Prospects
Employment prospects are fair for Stage Managers. Cruise Ships hire a limited number of Stage Managers each year, but due to the high turnover and relatively short contracts (eight to 12 months), opportunities keep arising. Resorts may hire Stage Managers that stay for longer durations. Stage Managers with technical and theater experience will have the best job prospects.

Advancement Prospects
Stage Managers can advance within the cruise/resort industry or the theater industry. Some may want to direct entertainment for a cruise line or resort, while others aspire to become directors of productions. Some Stage Managers gain experience through a cruise line or resort but their ultimate dream is to work as a Stage Manager for the world's largest stages, such as those on

Broadway. Also, after working on a ship, Stage Managers may want more permanence and settle down with a regular job at a theater.

Education and Training
Stage Managers often have professional theater education and training. They may hold a bachelor's degree in theater, or have degrees in other subjects but have taken many acting classes. Training in the technical aspects of theater management, as well as acting, directing, and producing, is very helpful. Some Stage Managers may have a master of fine arts (M.F.A.) degree as well.

Experience, Skills, and Personality Traits
Stage Managers need technical skills to handle sound and light operations. Experience running a mixing board for musical groups is helpful and familiarity with computerized mixing boards is useful on newer ships with state-of-the-art equipment. Experience as an assistant stage manager is crucial before they can run the show as Stage Managers.

Additionally, Stage Managers need to be able to stay calm under pressure. They must pay close attention to detail and use organizational skills to maintain the prompt book. Management skills help them oversee cast and crew and help everyone to remain on point.

Unions and Associations
Stage Managers may belong to a variety of professional associations including the Stage Managers' Association (www.stagemanagers.org), Actors' Equity Association, and the American Guild of Musical Artists.

Tips for Entry
1. Get involved with theater as early as possible. Work on high school and college productions, gaining experience in lighting, sound, and production.
2. Speak to Stage Managers working on cruise ships. Ask them how they found their jobs and what type of prior experience they needed.
3. Pay attention to the different details required when watching a production, noting the work of the Stage Manager.
4. Visit the Web site of the Actors' Equity Association at www.actorsequity.org. Actors' Equity is the labor union that represents more than 48,000 actors and Stage Managers in the United States.

MASSAGE THERAPIST

CAREER PROFILE

Duties: Provides massages (structured techniques for manipulating muscles and tissue) for clients, performed for relaxation or medical purposes

Alternate Title(s): Masseuse; Masseur

Salary Range: $20,000 to $40,000 per year and up; $16 per hour on average

Employment Prospects: Good to excellent

Advancement Prospects: Good

Best Geographical Location(s): All, particularly regions with major resorts, hotels, and spas

Prerequisites:

Education and Training—Formal schooling or training program in massage therapy

Experience—Hands-on experience in massage therapy required through school or training program

Special Skills and Personality Traits—Good communication skills; independence and flexibility; interest in working with people; some physical strength

Special Requirements—Varies by state

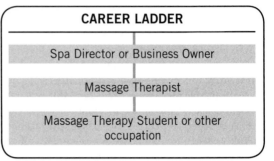

CAREER LADDER

Spa Director or Business Owner

Massage Therapist

Massage Therapy Student or other occupation

Position Description

Have you ever received a professional massage in order to ease tension, relax, or soothe sore muscles? Massage Therapists are skilled technicians schooled in the art of manipulating muscles in a way that can reduce stress, treat ailments, or promote circulation. They provide clients with a relaxing or therapeutic experience that helps promote overall well-being.

Working by appointment, Massage Therapists see a variety of clients on any given day. Appointments are typically between 30 and 90 minutes, depending on the type of massage. There are a number of different types of massage that Massage Therapists offer. Some are specialists in a particular modality only, while others are trained to perform several modalities. According to the Bureau of Labor Statistics (BLS), there are over 80 different types of massage.

Types of massage include therapeutic massage, Swedish (Western) massage, Reiki, and reflexology; all require different techniques. Some Massage Therapists also specialize with certain features such as pregnancy massage, sports massage, hot stone, or aromatherapy. In most forms of massage, Massage Therapists apply pressure to different points on the body using their fingers and hands. They also knead muscles to provide the most effective stress and/or pain relief, depending on the clients' stress zones, including the neck, shoulders, or back.

Additional duties may include:

- promoting overall health and wellness
- assessing the condition of clients' muscles
- discussing clients' medical histories and areas of stress or pain
- maintaining treatment records
- developing client treatment plans
- conferring with health professionals and referring clients for additional treatment when necessary
- traveling to clients' homes and offices
- buying or selecting equipment or supplies, including pillows, tables, linens, and lotions

Massage Therapists can work in a wide variety of hospitality industry settings. They can be employed by hotels and resorts, spas, and cruise lines. Additionally, they may have the opportunity to work worldwide at these different facilities. While Massage Therapists in other settings such as hospitals or clinics might focus on injuries or therapeutic massage, in the hospitality industry most Massage Therapists strive to provide a relaxing and enjoyable experience for their clients.

Facilities in spas and resorts can be quite luxurious. A Massage Therapist may use an array of lotions and oils, scented and unscented, and use aromatherapy as one of the options. Often in massage rooms, soothing new age or classical music is playing and candles may be burning, with dim lighting. Massage Therapists may have freedom in selecting the products for their therapy room, choosing those that create the most soothing image. In some resorts, in-room massage is also an option. Massage Therapists bring materials to set up and provide massages for individuals or couples in their own room.

Many Massage Therapists work part-time or flexible schedules. Most of their time is spent standing and using their strength and technique with their hands. Because of the demanding physical nature of their work, most Massage Therapists do not work a 40-hour workweek and may consider 20 to 30 hours full time. Some work at several different spas or hotels as independent contractors. Weekend work and holiday work is typical, and some evenings may be required.

Salaries

As of May 2007, the BLS lists the mean hourly wage of Massage Therapists as $19.39 and the mean annual wage as $40,330.

According to BLS research, the median hourly earnings of Massage Therapists, including gratuities, were $16.76 as of May 2006. The middle 50 percent earned between $11.18 and $24.74. The lowest 10 percent earned less than $7.69, and the highest 10 percent earned more than $34.06. Massage Therapists typically earn 15 to 20 percent of their income as gratuities. Gratuities are typically 20 percent of the cost of the massage.

The BLS also notes that the U.S. districts where Massage Therapists receive the highest pay are Washington, New Hampshire, the District of Columbia, Oregon, and Connecticut.

Employment Prospects

Employment prospects are very good to excellent for Massage Therapists. The BLS projects growth in the field to be faster than average through 2016, with a 20 percent increase in employment since 2000. Whereas massages used to be considered a luxury, their benefits are now more widely known. Also, as people travel more for business and pleasure, many hotels now include spas and massage services, and not just in the luxury sector.

The best opportunities are for those Massage Therapists who pass licensing and certification exams. Many work part-time until they can build up a substantial client basis. Additionally, job opportunities are slightly better for female Massage Therapists, as many clients express preference by gender. In 2006, 84 percent of all U.S. Massage Therapists were female, according to the BLS.

Advancement Prospects

Massage Therapists can advance by building their client base; this typically occurs through word of mouth. They may also move to more luxurious properties where massages are more expensive, thus making gratuities higher. Networking through professional associations as well as through additional training can increase clients and income.

Furthermore, entrepreneurial Massage Therapists can leave or supplement their jobs at hotels, resorts, cruise ships, and spas by starting their own businesses and taking on private clients. This may provide the highest income range for Massage Therapists. They may work as independent contractors at several different locations, with even greater options if they can bring in their own clientele.

Education and Training

Massage Therapists must complete some type of formal education/training in massage therapy. Programs vary from six- to nine-month courses to two- to four-year degrees.

Typically, the massage therapy degree includes extensive opportunities to perform basic hands-on techniques under the supervision of a massage professional. Courses include anatomy and physiology, aromatherapy, kinesiology, massage theory and techniques, pathology, palpation, musculoskeletal treatments, clinical and case studies, and more. Students also learn and practice the different massage modalities such as Swedish, sports, and deep tissue as well as professional standards and ethics and client counseling.

For directories of accredited massage therapy schools, see the Commission on Massage Therapy Accreditation at www.comta.org or the Accrediting Commission of Career Schools and Colleges of Technology at www.accsct.org.

Experience, Skills, and Personality Traits

In order to be a Massage Therapist, one must enjoy working with people. One needs to be patient and genuinely want to help others. As a service professional, a Massage Therapist must be attuned to his or her clients and responsive to their needs.

Although Massage Therapists are working with people, massage therapy is largely solitary work. Massage Therapists are on their feet for hours, working usually in silence when a client is on the table. Most clients seek massages looking for relaxation and to decompress. Massage Therapists should be independent and flexible, enjoying quiet peaceful surroundings without feeling the need to interject with conversation unless the client specifically asks. They should also be good listeners if clients decide they want to talk or share problems.

Also, Massage Therapists need some physical strength, depending upon the type of massage they practice. They must be comfortable touching people and manipulating their bodies. Furthermore, they must be discreet as they are working with people in an intimate setting.

Special Requirements

For Massage Therapists, training standards, licensure, and certification can vary greatly by state, so be sure to check information on licensing, certification, and accreditation on a state-by-state basis for the most current requirements.

According to the BLS, as of 2007, 38 states and the District of Columbia had laws regulating massage therapy in some way. Most of the boards governing massage therapy in these states require practicing massage therapists to complete a formal education program and pass a national certification examination or a state exam.

The National Certification Examination for Therapeutic Massage and Bodywork (NCETMB) is the exam required by many states in order to practice massage therapy. The exam is administered by the National Certification Board for Therapeutic Massage and Bodywork (NCBTMB); for more information see www.

ncbtmb.org. For additional licensure information, see the Federation of State Massage Therapy Boards at www.fsmtb.org.

Unions and Associations

Massage Therapists may belong to a variety of professional associations including the American Massage Therapy Association and Associated Bodywork and Massage Professionals.

Tips for Entry

1. Have you ever received a professional massage? If time allows, speak to your Massage Therapist or schedule a time to speak to him or her to learn more about the career path.
2. Research massage therapy schools and programs to determine options and requirements in your home or desired state.
3. Visit the Web site of Natural Healers, an education resource for those pursuing careers in the healing arts. Their directory of educational programs can be viewed at www.naturalhealers.com/feat-massage.shtml?src=goo_anh_032007_01299.
4. Explore the spa area next time you stay at a hotel. Speak to the receptionist and find out how many Massage Therapists they employ.

NUTRITIONIST

Position Description

The food we eat has a major impact on our overall health and wellness. Nutritionists are experts on the effects different foods have on the human body. They advise individuals and groups about their food choices and explain how these choices can affect their long-term health. Additionally, they plan and prepare menus for organizations, ensuring that the quality of food meets the highest nutrition standards.

In the hospitality industry, Nutritionists may work for hotels, resorts, restaurants, spas, and cruise lines, among others. They may oversee and plan menus to make sure healthy choices and variety of foods are available. They also can supervise the preparation of meals to limit unsanitary practices to prevent disease or illness.

At specialty resorts, Nutritionists might be on staff to work with guests individually or in groups. They serve as advisers, counselors, and educators. For example, at a yoga retreat, a Nutritionist might offer classes or seminars about healthy eating, as well as individual appointments to promote health, weight loss, sports performance, and more. Classes may include topics such as monitoring metabolism, healthy cooking, and managing stress.

Nutritionists may have many different areas of special interest. These can include:

- weight management
- vitamins, minerals, and nutritional supplements
- children and families
- cardiovascular health
- sports enhancement
- education
- older adult nutrition
- preventive nutrition
- menu planning
- pregnancy
- exercise
- disease management and prevention, including diabetes, hypertension, etc.
- vegetarian eating
- dining out
- eating for energy/stress management
- allergies

It is important for Nutritionists to be good listeners as they work closely with people. They consult with clients and take food histories, asking them about their habits and preferences. They then develop customized eating plans that fit each client and promote overall good health. Nutritionists also help clients to understand how making changes in their food intake will impact their lifestyle for the better.

For Nutritionists that are employed by restaurant or hotel chains, much menu planning and supervision is part of their work. They might recommend methods of food preparation that will reduce calories and maximize nutrients. Additionally, they can analyze the nutritional content of meals to determine its value. If you've ever seen "heart healthy" choices listed on a menu, Nutritionists were likely consulted to confirm that the dish in question met the standards to promote cardiovascular health. They also spend much time observing in the kitchen and ensuring hygienic conditions to reduce bacteria.

Frequently, Nutritionists consult with other health professionals, including doctors and nurses, as well as with chefs and kitchen staff. Together, they make decisions that will help guests enjoy the best choices. Furthermore, they help those with health problems adopt diet changes that will reduce the negative effects of their condition, whether it is reducing salt intake, adding more fiber, or choosing fresh fruits and vegetables.

Additional duties may include:

- working with hotel staff and management to encourage healthy eating (such as bowls of fruit on each floor, etc.)
- modifying menu items
- consulting about food preparation and grocery shopping
- creating special menus for guest on diets
- responding to guests with special needs and altering menus accordingly
- checking refrigerator temperatures to ensure proper levels
- reviewing all food as it arrives to make sure it is clean and fresh
- ordering food for hotels and restaurants
- developing classes based on guest response and needs

Nutritionists may be employed full-time by specific hotels or resorts, or they may work for chains. They may also consult at several different properties, working 40 hours per week or more. Some Nutritionists also maintain private practices where they work with individual clients. Also, they may specialize with different populations, including pregnant women, the elderly, or children.

Salaries

Salaries for Nutritionists vary depending on their work setting as well as their education level. According to the Bureau of Labor Statistics (BLS), median annual earnings of dietitians and nutritionists were $49,010 as of May 2007. The middle 50 percent earned between $40,180 and $59,580. The lowest 10 percent earned less than $31,830, and the highest 10 percent earned more than $71,130.

According to the American Dietetic Association, median annualized wages for registered dietitians in 2005 was $53,800 in consultation and business and $60,000 in food and nutrition management. Some Nutritionists supplement their salaries with consulting work, private practice, teaching, or writing; this can increase salaries substantially in some cases.

Employment Prospects

Employment prospects are fair to good for Nutritionists in the hospitality industry. Not all hotels, restaurant chains, and resorts hire Nutritionists, so competition for positions can be great. However, as awareness of the importance of healthy eating continues to grow, so will opportunities. Those Nutritionists who are licensed, certified, and hold advanced degrees will benefit, as well as those who focus on specialty areas.

Advancement Prospects

Advancement prospects are also fair to good. Nutritionists can go on to become directors of nutrition for their organization, with a staff of Nutritionists working for them. They can also develop private practices, consult, or teach. Some Nutritionists utilize their expertise to write columns for magazines or Web sites, articles, or even books about healthy eating, recipes, and lifestyles. Additional education and training can help Nutritionists to advance. They can also move to larger properties with higher salaries.

Education and Training

Nutritionists must hold either undergraduate or graduate degrees in nutrition or dietetics. These courses cover the physiology of the human body, including digestion, food balance, and vitamin needs. They may focus on food science, biology, physiology, chemistry, biochemistry, and institution management, and take courses that develop an understanding of human behavior such as psychology and counseling. Some nutrition degree programs in academic departments also cover food service management. Both undergraduate and graduate programs include required clinical internships.

As of 2007, there were 281 bachelor's degree programs and 22 master's degree programs approved by the American Dietetic Association's Commission on Accreditation for Dietetics Education (CADE). To meet necessary clinical experience for licensure as registered dietitians (RDs), Nutritionists must either complete a CADE-accredited program or complete 900 supervised hours in a CADE-accredited internship program. See this link for more information: www.eatright.org/cps/rde/xchg/ada/hs.xsl/career_401_ENU_HTML.htm.

Special Requirements

According to the BLS, of the 48 states and jurisdictions with laws governing dietetics, 35 require licensure, 12 require statutory certification, and 1 requires registration. Requirements vary by state. The American Dietetic Association (ADA) awards the registered dietitian credential to those who pass a certification exam after completing their academic course work and supervised experience. Since requirements vary by state, see the ADA's Web site at www.eatright.org.

Also, the Clinical Nutrition Certification Board (www.cncb.org) of the International and American Associations of Clinical Nutritionists offers licensure as a clinical Nutritionist. While this licensure is not required to work in most states, it can be a helpful credential for employment.

Experience, Skills, and Personality Traits

To work with a wide variety of clients and colleagues, Nutritionists need excellent communication skills. They must be persuasive and able to be seen as an authority figure, while being approachable and sympathetic to concerns and issues. Also, many positions involve public speaking and presentations, so comfort with speaking in front of groups is essential.

Furthermore, Nutritionists need to be experts about food and the human body. They need to understand different food combinations and their chemical breakdowns, as well as the effects of diet on overall health. In order to work with different populations, they must be good listeners, sensitive, and skilled at counseling.

Unions and Associations

The nation's largest professional association for food and nutrition practitioners is the American Dietetic Association. Nutritionists may also belong to the International and American Associations of Clinical Nutritionists.

Tips for Entry

1. Review the Food Guide Pyramid, developed by the United States Department of Agriculture (USDA) to learn more about what makes a serving and what types of daily food combinations are recommended: www.mypyramid.gov.
2. Visit a spa that employs a staff of Nutritionists. Ask them about their career path and what their job is like.
3. Take courses in nutrition and food science to get a feel for the subject. Speak with the professors of these courses about career options.
4. Try an internship in food service or nutrition to get a feel for the profession.
5. Read magazines and other publications focusing on nutrition including *Prevention* and *Better Nutrition*.

TENNIS PRO

Duties: Teaches tennis to groups and individuals at a hotel, resort, country club, camp, or other sports facility

Alternate Title(s): Tennis Instructor

Salary Range: Varies from $10 per hour to $100 per hour and up; yearly earnings $30,000 to $65,000 and up for a Head Tennis Pro

Employment Prospects: Good

Advancement Prospects: Good

Best Geographical Location(s): All, particularly large cities with many hotels, resorts, and clubs; greater opportunities may be in warm climates where tennis can be played outdoors year-round

Prerequisites:

Education and Training— Varies, but some formal tennis training required

Experience—Prior experience playing and teaching tennis

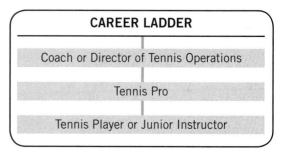

CAREER LADDER

Coach or Director of Tennis Operations

Tennis Pro

Tennis Player or Junior Instructor

Special Skills and Personality Traits—Excellent tennis skill; strong interpersonal skills and interest in helping others; good communication and teaching skills

Special Requirements—Voluntary certification available through professional associations; can be valuable for employment

Position Description

Some people are able to turn their favorite pastime into a career. After years of playing tennis and reaching a high level, some translate this ability into helping others develop this passion and skill. Tennis Pros get paid to play tennis and teach others the sport that they have mastered. In fact, the name Tennis "Pro" is short for "professional," implying the level of skill involved.

Tennis Pros work in a variety of settings, including private country clubs, tennis clubs, public parks and recreation departments, summer camps, hotels, resorts, and cruise ships. They provide instruction to people of all ages ranging from toddlers to senior citizens. Some Tennis Pros specialize in teaching specific age groups, such as children, but most can teach players of all ages. Working with groups and individuals, they teach the mechanics of the game including rules and techniques.

Tennis Pros must be skilled in the game of tennis as well as have the patience to teach others. They provide instruction on strokes, serving, and the structure of the game. Often, they provide their students with drills to keep honing in on specific skills and techniques until the students master them. A good Tennis Pro can play tennis in a variety of styles and can be flexible in the way they teach, adapting different styles to the needs of the players.

During a typical day, a Tennis Pro may give lessons lasting between a half hour to two hours, lead groups, play tennis games, and staff the tennis shop. The more experienced Tennis Pros get to work with the better players and find the games to be challenging themselves. While the hours are not especially long, they are nontraditional, with weekends and holidays often as prime time for play.

Additional duties may include:

- maintaining the tennis courts
- assisting with merchandise and equipment sales
- performing public relations duties for the establishment to market the tennis programs
- running tennis clinics

Depending on their work setting, Tennis Pros will develop long-term or transient relationships with students. At a resort, they work with vacationing guests who typically do not stay longer than one week. In this time, what can be accomplished through teaching is limited. At a club, however, members might take lessons for one year or longer, even several years with the same Tennis Pro. In this environment, the Tennis Pro can truly chart the progress of these students and impact their game.

At a resort or club, Tennis Pros are important parts of the staff and they have much guest and management interaction. They often attend dinners, functions, and parties to mingle with guests and make them feel comfortable. Frequently, they also play tennis with people in management.

Salaries

Salaries of Tennis Pros can vary greatly, depending on their experience. Beginning instructors can earn as little as $10 per hour, while experienced professionals can earn $100 per hour and up for private instruction. Head Tennis Pros at resorts might earn between $40,000 and $65,000 per year. Those who are self-employed can earn more depending on how much business they are able to generate.

Employment Prospects

Tennis is a sport that many people of all ages enjoy—one doesn't have to be overly adventurous or athletic to play. Therefore, employment prospects for Tennis Pros are good since they can find opportunities at resorts, clubs, and camps all over the world. While not all resorts have golf courses, for example, most do have tennis facilities. Many resorts are located in warm climates where people play tennis year-round without an off-season; Tennis Pros working at private clubs often teach and play indoors during the winter months. Additionally, some Tennis Pros are self-employed, contracting their services out to camps, clubs, and resorts.

Advancement Prospects

Tennis Pros may advance to become coaches. While Tennis Pros teach the game, coaches usually step in after a player has reached a certain level of skill and want to become competitive at the high school, college, or professional level. Tennis Pros may also go on to direct tennis operations for a major tennis resort.

Education and Training

Education for Tennis Pros may range from a high school diploma to an advanced degree. To get started in the field, many begin by taking years of lessons from Tennis Pros themselves. They may then move on to assist the Tennis Pro. Also, it is very valuable to gain experience teaching tennis at a summer program, either through a parks and recreation department or at a summer camp focused on tennis or with a dedicated tennis program. While there is no specific educational background required, many Tennis Pros played tennis on their high school or college teams.

There are a limited number of colleges and universities that offer professional tennis management programs. Hampton University in Virginia offers a bachelor of science degree in marketing with a professional tennis management emphasis; visit www.hamptonu.edu/academics/schools/business/undergrad/tennis.htm. Tyler Junior College in Texas offers a tennis tech associate's degree program at www.apacheathletics.com/tennisTech.php.

Experience, Skills, and Personality Traits

Prior experience playing tennis is an absolute must in order to develop the skills and techniques to teach others the game. Tennis Pros typically have worked teaching tennis for several years as assistants, specialists, or instructors. However, skill at the sport is not enough and not all good tennis players make strong teachers. Tennis Pros must have excellent interpersonal skills as well as a friendly, outgoing personality to work with all different types of people. Furthermore, they need patience, especially when working with beginners or those who get easily frustrated. Good business skills help Tennis Pros who want to market their own services. Knowledge of a foreign language can be an asset for Tennis Pros at international resorts.

Additional Information

Certification is voluntary for Tennis Pros but it can be helpful for employment and advancement. Benefits include liability insurance; access to job listings; specialized resources, courses, and workshops for members; help with the business of the profession including hosting for a Web site to promote individual teaching services; and eligibility for tournaments. The U.S. Professional Tennis Association (USPTA) and the Professional Tennis Registry (PTR) provide training and certification for Tennis Pros; learn more at www.uspta.org and www.ptrtennis.org.

Unions and Associations

In addition to the USPTA and the PTR, the United States Tennis Association (USTA) has much useful information for Tennis Pros and those involved with the sport.

Tips for Entry

1. Attend teaching clinics that are offered nationwide to improve your game.

2. Explore tennis jobs at sites such as www.play tennisjobs.com and www.tennisjobs.com.

3. Spend time on the Web sites of the USPTA and the PTR at www.uspta.org and www.ptrtennis. org. They offer information about certification, teaching, workshops, and events.

4. Research tennis camps at sites such as www. ussportscamps.com/camps/tennis_camps.html, www.tenniscamper.com, and www.kidscamps. com/sports/tennis.html.

5. Tennis Resorts Online, at www.tennisresorts online.com, offers a guide to tennis camps as well as resorts.

SKI INSTRUCTOR

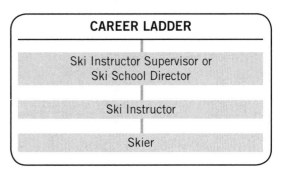

CAREER LADDER

Ski Instructor Supervisor or Ski School Director

Ski Instructor

Skier

Position Description

Do you have a passion for skiing? Is the idea of spending your work hours doing what you love appealing to you? Ski Instructors are typically longtime skiers who want to share their passion by teaching others this skill. Essentially, they get paid to train others in their hobby and vocation.

Ski Instructors work at ski resorts and mountains teaching individuals and groups the fundamentals of skiing. They may begin at the lowest level: teaching children and beginners in groups. Ski Instructors work on techniques, drills, and basics with those who have not skied before, such as getting on and off a chairlift, stopping, and more. Advanced Ski Instructors work with more talented skiers, which give them the opportunity to ski the more varied and challenging terrain. They work with students on speed, moguls, jumps, and other advanced techniques.

In addition to being expert skiers, Ski Instructors also need excellent interpersonal skills. Their objective is not only to teach people to ski, but also to enhance their overall resort experience and to ensure that they are having fun on the slopes and meeting their goals. Ski Instructors try to instill enjoyment and dispel fear. Like others in the hospitality industry, their ultimate goal is customer satisfaction with the services received.

A typical workday for Ski Instructors might begin with setting up the instruction area with cones, ropes, and other teaching tools. Ski Instructors may spend time at the base of the mountain waiting for groups to begin. They can teach from four to eight hours per day, in combinations of group and private lessons. A day could end by attending clinics to help improve their teaching and technique. Frequently, Ski Instructors work six to seven days per week during the ski season, with hours that including early mornings.

Creativity is required to devise lessons and teaching methods to fit the population. A good Ski Instructor can work with senior citizens, children, and young adults alike. Ski Instructors who work with children develop games and activities that are age-appropriate. Their job has more of a teaching/child care approach to it, while Ski Instructors who give private lessons to strong skiers gear their work toward advancing skills and technique. It is important for Ski Instructors to be flexible and able to adapt to the needs of different groups. Some instructors may specialize in snowboarding rather than skiing. Since less technique is required, more lesson time is devoted to learning the sport and having fun.

Additional duties may include:

- representing their resort at preseason shows, promotions, special events, or races

- serving as an ambassador for their mountain
- accompanying students on chairlifts
- dealing with emergency situations and calling for help if necessary
- training students on safety precautions

The work conditions for a Ski Instructor can be harsh, as they are out in very cold weather, often with high windchill factors, snow, sleet, and/or strong sun. Ski Instructors need to be able to brave the elements and be comfortable with these factors. They typically dress in the ski attire required by their mountain—for example, each Ski Instructor might wear the same red jacket.

Ski Instructors may work part-time or full-time, and their work is seasonal. Many ski resorts operate for about five to six months of the year, from November to March or April. Some Ski Instructors are college students who work during their school breaks or days off, as well as recent graduates taking some time off before entering the "real world." Others work in the adventure travel industry, as Ski Instructors during the winter and white-water rafting guides during the summer. Yet others are professional career Ski Instructors who love the work and couldn't imagine doing anything else. Nothing beats the experience of going to work each day and it not feeling like work.

Salaries

Ski Instructors do not usually pursue this career for the money, and salaries can vary greatly depending on the ski area and experience of the instructor. Ski schools have varying pay structures based on experience, hours, and certification. A first-year noncertified Ski Instructor may earn $7.25 per hour, while a certified full-time Ski Instructor with experience can earn $25 per hour or more.

Teachers of private lessons are at the top of the earning scale and some Ski Instructors report earning almost $300 per week in tips alone. Other financial perks come with the job apart from salary, including free ski time, free meals in the cafeteria, and in some cases, employee housing.

Employment Prospects

According to Jobmonkey.com, only about 6 percent of the 304 million people in the United States ski, and of those, only about 10 percent take instruction. However, the recreation industry overall does a lot of hiring and job opportunities are always available for qualified Ski Instructors. Opportunities tend to vary annually based on weather conditions as well as the economy. The more experience one has, the better the odds of being hired. Previous work as a Ski Instructor offers the flexibility to move to different mountain and resort areas.

Opportunities are available at ski areas throughout the United States, as well as around the world. When the season is over in Colorado, it may just be beginning in Australia. Ski Instructors who are looking to work abroad may need to be sponsored by North American Ski Companies. Snowboarding instructor opportunities may be easier to find because they are less regulated and there is generally less competition for available jobs.

Jobs can be found through applying directly to ski areas. Some mountains run hiring clinics where prospective Ski Instructors register and participate at the beginning of the season to have their skills evaluated and learn how to become instructors. Even if they are then not hired by that particular mountain, it can still be a good experience to improve skills.

Advancement Prospects

Advancement prospects are good for Ski Instructors. By receiving certification from the Professional Ski Instructors of America (PSAI), Ski Instructors enhance their employment options. They can move to different ski resorts, experiencing skiing all over the world.

Some Ski Instructors advance to become instructor supervisors or directors of ski schools. They may also consider options such as ski coaching. Yet others use the position to launch their careers in the ski resort industry. Many marketing directors or area managers started as Ski Instructors with their passion for skiing as their entry into the field.

Education and Training

There is no typical educational path to becoming a Ski Instructor, other than prior ski experience and training. Many Ski Instructors are college students or graduates who have studied a vast variety of fields.

Experience, Skills, and Personality Traits

The job of a Ski Instructor requires equal parts technical acumen and people skills. Prior ski experience is crucial; although Ski Instructors who teach children need basic ski skills, those who teach advanced groups need much more expertise on the slopes. All Ski Instructors need patience and the ability to impart information in a fun and effective way.

Teaching and communication skills are essential, as is the ability to work with different types of people. A Ski Instructor must be able to tolerate the physical demand of the job as well. Knowledge of foreign languages can be helpful, especially at certain resort areas and world regions.

Special Requirements

Ski Instructors may need to become certified by PSIA. Certification is designated as level I, level II, and level III certified. Certification involves passing exams and can lead to better pay and job opportunities.

Unions and Associations

The Professional Ski Instructors of America is the main professional association for Ski Instructors. According to its Web site (www.psia.org), its mission is to help members (who are both part-time and full-time Ski Instructors), as a part of the snow sports industry, to develop personally and professionally, create positive learning experiences, and have more fun.

Snowboarding instructors may belong to the American Association of Snowboard Instructors. For more information, see www.aasi.org.

Tips for Entry

1. Explore the Web sites for some of the nation's largest ski areas such as Vail, Colorado (vail.snow.com/home) and Stratton, Vermont (www.stratton.com/index.htm). These sites offer information about employment as well as internships for those who want to explore various aspects of the ski industry.

2. Spend time learning more about PSIA and membership. Read about certification requirements and the impact they have on employment.

3. Go skiing! Ski Instructors have a passion for the sport, so take as many lessons as possible, even if you are already an experienced skier. Speak to your instructors about their backgrounds and how they got involved in the field.

4. Consider another position at a ski resort in order to gain entry. When positions have not been available, some Ski Instructors have gotten started with waitstaff restaurant positions as a way to ski at the resort and get to know supervisors.

5. If you are interested in a professional role in the ski resort industry, consider degree programs such as the associate's degree in ski area management/operations offered by Colorado Mountain College (www.coloradomtn.edu).

GOLF COURSE SUPERINTENDENT

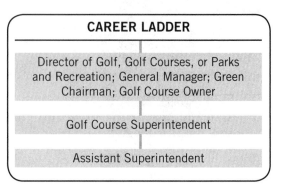

Position Description

Imagine spending every day out on a golf course, making sure that the conditions are just right for playing. This is the job of a Golf Course Superintendent. These professionals maintain, operate, and manage golf courses using a combination of scientific and agricultural knowledge, communication and leadership skills, and commitment to and passion for the sport of golf.

A typical day for a Golf Course Superintendent begins as early as five A.M., when he or she checks the weather report. Arriving at the course by six, Golf Course Superintendents travel the course to see what needs to be done that day and delegates responsibilities. The greens may need to be mowed, irrigated, sprayed; sand traps may need to be raked. The Golf Course Superintendent analyzes the conditions and makes sure the work gets done.

The science of maintaining a golf course is important and involves extensive knowledge of turf grass management, agronomy, and plant science. Golf Course Superintendents need to know what pesticides to use and in what quantities in order to maintain the course. They must understand the threats to the course such as weeds, bugs, and weather and how to minimize these threats. All the while, they take into consideration environmental concerns with regard to chemical applications.

Additionally, Golf Course Superintendents oversee the golf course's surrounding properties, which may include pools and tennis courts, wooded areas, and open spaces, as well as all golf course equipment and grounds. They are responsible for construction and capital improvements of the course. They develop plans to submit to management regarding renovation and other projects, and when these plans are approved, they supervise the construction projects, either using in-house staff or outside contractors. Golf Course Superintendents use their knowledge to determine which projects make the most sense financially and aesthetically.

As managers, Golf Course Superintendents supervise assistant superintendents as well as the maintenance staff responsible for caring for the property. Frequently, these are large staffs of 20 employees or more. They interview, hire, and train their staff and work closely as part of a team. They are responsible for scheduling and delegating responsibility. Golf Course Superintendents also prepare budgets and decide where to best allocate funds.

Additional duties include:

- overseeing inventory control
- approving spending
- keeping records of pesticide and chemical applications
- maintaining records of payroll and inventory
- understanding safety laws, rules, and regulations
- playing golf regularly

- advising management with regard to construction and improvement
- maintains course equipment
- planting shrubs and applying fertilizer
- preparing the course for tournaments

Golf Course Superintendents may work for golf courses that are part of resorts, hotels, and country clubs, private membership-based golf courses, or public golf courses that are city owned. Depending on the setting, the reporting structure varies. At a public course, they may report to a director of parks and recreation, while at a private course, they report to a green chairman. Either way, Golf Course Superintendents can expect to play golf with management regularly. This is a way for Golf Course Superintendents and management to develop a good working relationship and communicate in a more casual setting, since golf is the game that has brought them all there. At private clubs, Golf Course Superintendents also attend green committee meetings and board meetings.

Golf Course Superintendents work long hours beginning early in the morning, especially holidays and weekends when people are apt to play golf. A typical workweek might range from 41 hours per week in the winter to 60 hours per week in the summer. They deal with demanding golfers and must meet their challenging expectations, working outdoors in a variety of weather conditions. However, for those in the field, it is a way to constantly be around the sport they love. The beautiful surroundings and the ability to be involved with golf make the work of a Golf Course Superintendent a dream for many.

Salaries

According to the Golf Course Superintendents Association of America (GCSAA), in 2007, the average base salary for Golf Course Superintendents was $73,766. This was a 7 percent increase over the base salary reported in 2005 and a 49.7 percent gain since 1995. In 2007, half of all Golf Course Superintendents earned $66,000 or more annually, 25 percent earned more than $87,550, and the top 10 percent earned $115,000 or more annually.

In addition to base salary, more than half of all Golf Course Superintendents receive bonuses, which increase their overall compensation. The GCSAA offers certification and states that certified Golf Course Superintendents who responded to their 2007 survey reported earning an average salary of $87,225, as compared to noncertified Golf Course Superintendents who reported earning an average salary of $68,464—a 27 percent difference.

Salary can vary based on the education and experience of the Golf Course Superintendent, as well as the facility and geographical location in which they work. Golf Course Superintendents working at $1 million typically earn in the six figures. The GCSAA states that at least 14 percent of all certified Golf Course Superintendents with a bachelor's degree or higher earn $125,000 or more.

Employment Prospects

There is competition for Golf Course Superintendent jobs, but opportunities are available for those with the right education and experience. Those with a bachelor's degree and internship experience will have an advantage, as the internship enables prospective applicants to network and develop relationships with potential employers. Professional associations are a good way to find out about job openings as well. The best opportunities are for those who are geographically flexible and are willing to work at different types of courses, both public and private.

Advancement Prospects

Advancement prospects are good for Golf Course Superintendents. As they gain more experience, they can become eligible for voluntary certification and higher salaries. A move from a smaller course to a larger one might also be a next step. Furthermore, they may move into management in positions such as director of golf, director of parks and recreation, general manager, or green chairman.

Education and Training

While some Golf Course Superintendents have worked their way up from the maintenance crew, a minimum of a two-year degree in a related field is required. A bachelor's degree or even a graduate degree can help create more opportunities as well as flexibility for advancement. Related fields include golf course management, turf grass management, agronomy, horticulture, and others. According to the GCSAA, in 2007, 91.8 percent of Golf Course Superintendents 34 or under earned a college degree, reflecting the need for a degree in today's market.

The GCSAA maintains an online college guide of colleges and universities that offer two-year associate/applied science degrees, four-year bachelor of science degree, graduate programs and certificates in golf course management, turf grass, or related fields. Search this database at www.gcsaa.org/students/CollegeGuideSearch.aspx.

Internships are an essential part of the training process, according to insiders. Spending a summer or semester working alongside Golf Course Superintendents, trying out different grasses, seeing different courses, and learning the ropes is invaluable. These programs may provide housing and additional perks, such as free golf.

Additionally, the GCSAA offers a professional certification program for Golf Course Superintendents enabling them to be recognized for their superior levels of achievement in golf course management. For more information, see www.gcsaa.org/cm/contentm/modules/display_dynamic.ahtml?params=MSwxMTks MDAwMDQuMDAwMDU=.

Experience, Skills, and Personality Traits

Golf Course Superintendents typically begin as second or first assistants after graduation. This position builds on the basic skills they learned during their internship and they gain more exposure to supervising others, budgeting, chemical applications/managing turf, preparing for tournaments, and other key skills. Golf Course Superintendents may work as assistants for several years or longer depending on their learning curve. It is also common for them to move around to different golf courses in order to gain a broad range of experience and training.

Technical skills are required for the job in order to understand turf grass management, irrigation techniques, plant physiology, and chemical applications. As managers, Golf Course Superintendents should have excellent leadership and communication skills. They need to work with staff, management, and players. Furthermore, they need to have experience playing golf, with knowledge of the rules and strategies of the game.

Unions and Associations

The Golf Course Superintendents Association of America (GCSAA) is the major professional association for Golf Course Superintendents. According to its Web site at www.gcsaa.org, GCSAA is dedicated to serving its members, advancing their profession, and enhancing the enjoyment, growth, and vitality of the game of golf. Other information is available through the United States Golf Association (USGA).

Tips for Entry

1. Explore bachelor's degree programs in golf course management such as the ones offered by Ferris State University in Big Rapids, Michigan (www.ferris.edu/bachelor-degree-professional-golf-management.htm) and the State University of New York in Delhi, New York (www.delhi.edu/academics/catalog_08/bachelor_degrees/golf_course_management_superintendent_bba.php).

2. During the job application process, make sure to target your résumé and cover letter toward each particular course and Golf Course Superintendent. Photographs of your projects can be helpful supplemental material that can demonstrate your knowledge of maintenance.

3. Get a summer job working at a golf course as soon as possible. This will give you an important background and help you to decide which position is right for you.

4. Both the GCSAA and the USGA have extensive career information on their Web sites—be sure to explore both at www.gcsaa.org and www.usga.org.

5. Search for Golf Course Superintendent jobs and career information on search engines such as Google. Much career information is out there, including "day in the life" pieces and other features.

THEME PARK MANAGER

CAREER PROFILE

Duties: Oversees daily operations for an amusement/ theme park

Alternate Title(s): Guest Experience Manager; Rides and Operations Manager; Attractions Manager; Theme Park Supervisor

Salary Range: $35,000 to $60,000 and up

Employment Prospects: Fair

Advancement Prospects: Fair

Best Geographical Location(s): All; theme parks can be found in regions around the United States and all over the world

Prerequisites:

    Education and Training—Bachelor's degree typically required for executive positions; background in business very helpful

    Experience—Prior theme park experience at multiple levels

    Special Skills and Personality Traits—Good business, sales, and marketing ability; customer service orientation; ability to multitask and think strategically; knowledge of theme parks

CAREER LADDER

General Manager

Theme Park Manager

Area Supervisor

Position Description

There are a wide variety of theme and amusement parks throughout the United States and all over the world. Guests travel to these theme parks to see attractions, experience rides, and enjoy family fun during their leisure time. Theme Park Managers run the daily operations for these parks and ensure customer satisfaction and safety.

Many responsibilities go into overseeing the day-to-day activities of a theme park. Above all, Theme Park Managers want to make sure that guests have a positive experience. They work closely with the front line employees, providing training and guidelines, since these concession workers, ride operators, and others are the ones who interact with guests and make an impression of the park. Theme Park Managers are responsible for supervising, hiring, firing, and evaluating seasonal and full time employees.

Furthermore, Theme Park Managers are involved with strategic planning and development. Regardless of the type of park, all want to grow and continue to meet and exceed goals. Theme Park Managers analyze the status quo and explore areas for growth and improvement. Market research such as focus groups and customer surveys help them learn what the public wants. Theme Park Managers identify areas for new attractions that are consistent with trends and market needs. They make decisions about the new directions the park will take and oversee big development projects

that eliminate old or worn-out attractions, replacing them with modern innovations.

Health and safety is a big issue facing theme parks, as it makes headline news several times each year when someone is inadvertently harmed on a ride. Theme Park Managers are constantly monitoring health and safety standards as well as checking the rides and their performance regularly and assessing their operation. They also make sure that frontline staff operates the rides correctly and with supreme attention to detail, such as enforcing height requirements and other precautions. Risk assessment is a big part of reviewing current attractions and adding new ones.

Depending on the size of the park, Theme Park Managers may have specialized or general responsibilities. At small parks, they typically handle many functions such as human resources, marketing, and more, while at larger properties they may have staff for delegation. Their responsibilities will also vary if they manage a park that is part of a chain, as opposed to an independent property. Chain parks are upheld to consistent standards throughout each property and Theme Park Managers must adhere to those rules and regulations.

Additional duties may include:

- preparing budgets and setting financial goals
- working with vendors and contractors, as well as negotiating contracts

- keeping informed about industry trends and new developments
- overseeing projects related to general park developments, including ride design
- working with human resources on personnel issues
- serving as a liaison with the community
- authorizing repairs and maintenance
- evaluating ride performance
- monitoring competition
- marketing the park and its attractions
- tracking and analyzing ride/attraction usage

Theme Park Managers may start by overseeing one location within the park, such as a gift shop or ride. Typically, they will have worked as an employee in this area previously. Responsibilities include supervising workers, creating schedules, and opening and closing the location. Next, Theme Park Managers may become area or region supervisors, responsible for a group of related attractions. Full park supervisors manage an entire park area and general managers oversee all the supervisors and the entire park as a whole.

Hours for Theme Park Managers are quite long during the park season, and do not follow a traditional schedule. Since amusement parks do most business on weekends, hours reflect the operation. The summer months are typically the high season and some parks are closed during the winter, depending on geographic location. Theme Park Managers report that 70 percent of their time is spent in the park and 30 percent in the office, with most office time during the slower season.

One challenge for Theme Park Managers is organizing the changing schedules for the park based on the season, as well as relying on part-time and seasonal workers. However, theme parks are places that people come purely to have fun, and making a career out of providing, facilitating, and supporting this entertainment can be very rewarding.

Salaries

Salaries for Theme Park Managers vary based on the level of their position as well as the size and location of their park. Entry-level management positions might pay $15,000 to $25,000 per year, while upper level management positions can pay six figures. A typical range might be $35,000 to $60,000 and up.

Employment Prospects

According to the International Association of Amusement Parks and Attractions (IAAPA), there are more than 400 amusement parks and traditional attractions in the United States. The IAAPA Web site states that in 2006 amusement parks in the United States entertained 335 million visitors who enjoyed more that 1.5 billion rides. There are also 300 amusement parks in Europe.

With these statistics, employment prospects are fair for Theme Park Managers at the executive level. Since there are a limited number of parks, competition is tight for top positions. Many more jobs exist at the lower management level, since each park needs numerous area supervisors. The best opportunities for Theme Park Managers are for those with experience and for those who are geographically flexible.

Advancement Prospects

Theme Park Managers can advance by moving to larger parks for more responsibility. They may also move up the corporate ladder to become general managers or executives at a corporate theme park chain. With their transferable business skills in human resources, marketing, and strategic development, they can be poised to move into other hospitality industry positions as well. Since there are a limited number of U.S. theme parks, the willingness to relocate may increase advancement opportunities.

Education and Training

Educational requirements vary for Theme Park Managers. At the location supervision level a high school diploma is required, while at the executive and management level a bachelor's degree or higher may be necessary. Degrees or courses in business and marketing can be very helpful.

Experience, Skills, and Personality Traits

To be a Theme Park Manager, one should have experience working in a theme park. Many begin with summer jobs while in high school that lead to careers. It is very helpful to have worked in some of the various positions that you will supervise. Theme Park Managers should have a good business background with a sales and marketing perspective as well as the ability to drive growth and revenue. Excellent communications and interpersonal skills are also needed; the theme park experience is all about ensuring that the guests are enjoying themselves. Supervisory and management skills are also required.

Unions and Associations

Theme Park Managers may belong to a variety of professional associations including the Themed Entertainment Association and the International Association of Amusement Parks and Attractions (IAAPA).

Tips for Entry

1. Explore job listings on sites such as www.themeparkjobs.com.
2. Each year, the IAAPA offers an Institute for Emerging Leaders as a professional development opportunity for managers. For more information, see www.iaapa.org/expos/attractions/Emerging_Leaders_Institute.asp.
3. Research employment opportunities at some of the nation's largest amusement park chains such as Six Flags (www.sixflags.com/national/Jobs/index.aspx), Anheuser-Busch Adventure Parks (www.becjobs.com/Scripts/Index.aspx) and the Walt Disney Company (corporate.disney.go.com/careers/index.html).
4. Spend a summer working at a theme park in areas such as concession, retail, or ride operation. This is the way many people get into management.
5. JobMonkey.com has a section on theme park jobs which encompasses seasonal jobs as well as management careers at www.jobmonkey.com/themeparks.

THEME PARK DESIGNER

CAREER PROFILE

Duties: Designs rides, attractions, and/or overall park layout for an amusement or theme park

Alternate Title(s): Ride Designer; Imagineer (Disney)

Salary Range: Variable; $50,000 to $100,000 per year and up

Employment Prospects: Poor

Advancement Prospects: Fair

Best Geographical Location(s): Theme parks can be found in regions around the United States and all over the world, but the best opportunities are in cities such as Los Angeles, California, Orlando, Florida; and Cincinnati, Ohio

Prerequisites:

Education and Training—Bachelor's degree in fields such as art, engineering, architecture, design, and others

Experience—Prior theme park experience and expertise in one of the fields above

CAREER LADDER

Theme Park Designer, larger park, or Director of Creative Services, or Chief Creative Officer

Theme Park Designer

Entry-level Designer

Special Skills and Personality Traits—Passion for theme parks and knowledge of the industry; skills in a specific discipline; excellent communication and interpersonal skills; creativity and imagination

Position Description

When you walk into a theme park, you are frequently transported into a fantasy world. Whether the idea is small town America, the Far East, outer space, or when dinosaurs walked the earth, parks and attractions take their visitors to different places and times. Overall park design and rides all reflect the theme and transforming experience. Imagine having a job where you were responsible for creating these fantasies. This is the work of Theme Park Designers.

Theme Park Designers are trained in a variety of disciplines and have different creative functions in making attractions come to life. Some are responsible for conceptualizing and illustrating the attractions, sketching rides that they imagine including the details. Other Theme Park Designers have training in architecture and engineering to bring these visions to life. They build the rides and attractions and determine how to make them work, while landscape architects and planners utilize the outdoor space and create an atmosphere that fits.

In addition, Theme Park Designers work on backgrounds and sets for attractions, using training in design to create scenery and props. Film and video production specialists develop the graphics and video components that are now part of so many rides and attractions, and writers develop the words and stories that accompany the visuals. Theme Park Designers with all of these special skills and backgrounds collaborate to create this magical entertainment for guests.

After developing the concept, Theme Park Designers then create models in both 3-D and video to guide construction. The construction process involves extensive testing and tweaking to make sure plans are brought to life as envisioned. Theme Park Designers often maintain files of information for each ride and attraction about production, design, and concepts to be used for future innovations.

Behind the wonder of each attraction is a good story. Theme Park Designers are storytellers who can put guests in the center of the action and make them forget that it is all an illusion. Their creativity enables them to determine ideas for rides and shows based on movies, mythical places, and other fanciful notions. Rides may be indoor or outdoor, involve water, thrills, video, interaction, and more. The best attractions are considered immersive in that they impact all senses, incorporating lights, sounds, set, and mood. Theme Park Designers combine creativity and technology to develop ideas that will appeal to target audiences and remain relevant and modern to today's theme park guests.

Additional duties may include:

- keeping up on the theme park industry and trends
- visiting a variety of theme parks
- conducting focus groups and tests on rides and attractions
- working with theme park managers and executives
- writing guest experience outlines and scripts
- developing concepts and designs for themed restaurants and shops
- implementing a "show," the whole attraction and all of its components
- pitching ideas and developing proposals

Theme Park Designers get their ideas from all different sources in popular culture, media, and literature. They may travel the world for inspiration and research. Many jobs are on a project basis, so some Theme Park Designers move on to other projects after an average time of 18 months, while others are employed by major corporations such as Disney or Thinkwell Group.

Salaries

Salaries for Theme Park Designers vary depending on their background and role as well as the type of company for which they work. At large corporations, Theme Park Designers may earn six figure salaries, while other Theme Park Designers who get paid per project may earn considerably less. Earnings are also variable depending on job function such as engineering, architecture, design, writing, etc. An average starting salary at a large corporation may be between $50,000 and $100,000 per year.

Employment Prospects

Theme park design is a highly competitive field. Many jobs are found through word of mouth and networking, since this is a small industry. Insiders say that prior theme park experience is essential, as is knowledge of and familiarity with many parks. To be marketable, prospective Theme Park Designers should have expertise in one functional area, but also the ability to be flexible with many general skills. While themed parks are found everywhere, the majority of jobs are found in southern California and the Orlando, Florida region where Disney and many other theme parks are based, with additional opportunities in Cincinnati, Ohio. Resources such as the themed attractions career page at www.

themedattraction.com/careers.htm have job listings for Theme Park Designers.

Advancement Prospects

Advancement prospects are fair as Theme Park Designers who have established strong reputations can be sought after in the industry. They may move onto larger projects or full-time employment for large companies. Additionally, they can advance to leadership positions as creative executives.

Education and Training

Education varies greatly for Theme Park Designers but industry experts agree that it is very difficult to succeed without a college degree. Depending on their area of expertise, Theme Park Designers hold bachelor's degrees in design, fine arts, architecture, engineering (structural, mechanical, or electrical), industrial design, film/video production, landscape architecture, creative writing, theater, and more.

The Ringling College of Art and Design in Sarasota, Florida provides unique degree programs such as a major in motion design. Learn more at www.ringling.edu.

Experience, Skills, and Personality Traits

Prior theme park experience is needed for Theme Park Designers. Hourly summer jobs to become familiar with rides and attractions can go a long way in preparing for a theme park design career. Creativity and imagination is a key component needed in all aspects of the field, combined with technical skills in engineering, design, illustration, writing, planning, or film/video.

Theme Park Designers also need excellent communications and interpersonal skills. They must understand what makes attractions successful and keep audiences entertained. Theme Park Designers must pay close attention to detail and have artistic and creative vision.

Unions and Associations

Professional associations such as the International Association of Amusement Parks and Attractions (IAAPA) and the Themed Entertainment Association (TEA) are excellent resources for Theme Park Designers. Attending their meetings and conventions is valuable for networking.

Tips for Entry

1. For many prospective Theme Park Designers, becoming a Disney Imagineer is their ultimate

goal. *Imagineer* is Disney's trademarked term for creative team members. Learn more about becoming an Disney Imagineer at corporate.disney.go.com/careers/who_imagineering.html.

2. Thinkwell Group, headquartered in Burbank, California, provides immersive experiences for clients throughout the world. See its Web site at www.thinkwelldesign.com.

3. Themedattraction.com is a Web site devoted to theme park design. Explore its resources at www.themedattraction.com.

4. Read as much as possible about the theme park industry through publications such as *Amusement Today* (www.amusementtoday.com) and *Theme Park Adventure* (www.themeparkadventure.com).

5. Are you interested in roller coaster design? Check out the Web site for S&S Worldwide, headquartered in Logan, Utah (www.s-spower.com).

6. Read up on Walt Disney and pioneers in the field. Recommended books include *Walt Disney's Imagineering Legends and the Genesis of the Disney Theme Park* by Jeff Kurtti.

7. Visit as many theme parks as possible to experience a variety of attractions. Note the ones that you find work best as well as the least successful ones and explain why.

DUDE WRANGLER

Position Description

Images of cowboys and the Wild West are embedded in American culture. As people consider how to spend their leisure time, visiting a dude ranch is often a popular vacation option. Anyone who has seen the movie *City Slickers* won't forget the life-changing experience Billy Crystal's character and his friends had on their trip. Scattered across the United States, particularly in the West and Southwest, dude ranches vary from family-oriented destinations to upscale resorts with high-end amenities, to adults-only hard-core cattle driving experiences.

Working ranches raise livestock to produce a product, such as meat or wool. A guest ranch, or dude ranch, is one that is oriented toward visitors and tourism. Visitors get a ranch experience that includes riding horses and may also include cattle drives, roundups, and branding. Horses are an integral part of a ranch and Dude Wranglers work with horses in all capacities.

Dude Wranglers are one part outdoor trip leader, one part tour guide, and one part social director, while serving as experts on horses as well. They entertain guests of a dude ranch and provide opportunities for them to interact with horses. Their role is twofold in their care of both visitors and horses.

On the visitor side, Dude Wranglers provide patrons with an enjoyable ranch experience. They lead guests on trail rides, using their knowledge of terrain to plan itineraries geared toward different skill and interest levels. While on rides, Dude Wranglers share history, information about the sights, flora, and fauna, as well as amusing anecdotes, jokes, and funny stories. At all times they must also be aware of the guests' safety while riding. Their experience with horses guides them to match the right person with the right horse depending on his or her ability.

At some ranches, Dude Wranglers may lead guests on more challenging courses, including cattle drives and roundups. They may also take them out of the ranch for one or several days to camp, where they pitch tents, build fires, and prepare food. Dude Wranglers should be skilled in outdoor and wilderness education as well as knowledgeable about conservation and wildlife laws.

Dude Wranglers also work extensively with horses. They perform horse and tack maintenance, such as saddling and unsaddling horses, corralling horses, grooming horses, caring for sick horses, and barn management. It is important for Dude Wranglers to know how to adjust saddles for guests as well as assist with mounting and dismounting.

Additional duties may include:

- rounding up the horses each morning
- packing horses with supplies and provisions for extended or overnight trips
- driving or leading pack horses
- entertaining guests by singing, telling stories, or playing a guitar or other instrument
- escorting female guests to dances and other social functions
- participating in rodeos provided by ranch management
- cleaning stalls and the barn area
- eating meals with guests
- leading hikes, rafting, or fishing trips
- making repairs around the ranch
- answering questions about horses
- pitching in for other areas such as dishwashing, cleaning, etc.

Some Dude Wranglers work particularly with children, especially at family-oriented ranches. These professionals must be skilled at teaching and have a gift for commanding the attention of little ones. They are extra cautious with the horses and adapt all activities to the skill level of the children. If they work with children, Dude Wranglers may plan curriculum and daily activities and supervise fishing, arts and crafts, and other programs as well.

Dude Wranglers participate in all ranch activities such as barbeques, campfires, and other social events for guests. They may also be asked to eat meals with guests. Since ranches are often in isolated areas, they frequently live on the premises and socialize with the other ranch workers. The work is often seasonal, with Dude Wranglers working during the summer months, the high season for most dude ranches. Each dude ranch has a different horse program and philosophy and Dude Wranglers must be able to subscribe to the philosophy of their particular ranch.

Hours are usually 40 to 60 hours per week, usually spread over six-day workweeks with varying hours (and anything over 40 hours may qualify for overtime). Dude Wranglers are required to wear specific types of Western dress (typically jeans and cowboy boots) and they need to be prepared for the sometimes taxing physical demands of their job. Virtually all of their time is spent outdoors and they must be able to carry heavy equipment.

Salaries

Most ranch positions are salaried, with a monthly stipend that is supplemented by overtime pay and tips. Overtime pay may be time-and-a-half after 40 hours of work; tips can vary tremendously, but in some cases exceed the monthly stipend. Depending on the ranch, monthly salaries may be between $500 and $1,500 per month. End-of-season bonuses may also be common and add to overall earnings.

Additionally, Dude Wranglers typically receive room and board, so overall, those who work for a summer can come away with significant earnings, since they will spend very little money during their time on a ranch.

Employment Prospects

Employment prospects are good for Dude Wranglers. Frequently, this is a seasonal job, ideal for college students. During the summer season, which can range from May to October (peaking in June, July, and August), dude ranches look to hire Dude Wranglers. Hiring can start as early as January and February for peak season. However, some ranches do operate on year-round basis and hire throughout.

Hiring is serious business as many ranches are family-owned operations. Ranchers want to hire Dude Wranglers who will fit in and take their job seriously. The best opportunities are for those with prior experience with horses and who are very personable. Since in-person interviews are often not possible with ranches being in isolated areas, some employers may require potential Dude Wranglers to send in videos stating their qualifications and selling themselves, or photographs at the very least. During interviews, prospective Dude Wranglers should expect to answer specific questions about horses to demonstrate their knowledge.

Advancement Prospects

Dude Wranglers may advance in different ways, depending on their career goals. Some Dude Wranglers are college students looking for an adventurous way to spend the summer and plan to pursue totally different career paths. Other Dude Wranglers plan to stay in the field, advancing to become head wranglers with management responsibility. Additionally, others might aspire to run or own their own ranch one day.

Education and Training

There is no specific educational background required of Dude Wranglers, since some may be right out of high school and others are college students or graduates. While prior experience with horses is necessary, much of the training occurs on the job at an orientation before the season. Ranches that are members of the Dude Ranchers' Association expect Dude Wranglers to successfully complete a standard wrangler safety course during the orientation.

Experience, Skills, and Personality Traits

Dude Wranglers should be very customer-service oriented, with excellent communication skills. They spend extensive time working with people and must be friendly and genuinely enjoy the contact they have, including playing with children, talking to the elderly, and everything in between. A sense of humor and a positive attitude enables them to entertain guests as well as enjoy their work.

Furthermore, Dude Wranglers need to be comfortable with working under difficult physical demands. Often, ranches are in areas with high altitudes and weather conditions can vary from extreme heat to bitter cold. Dude Wranglers need to be able to withstand the elements and be outdoors, carrying heavy equipment. A love for horses and experience in riding and animal care is also needed.

A valid driver's license may be required to escort guests off property. The minimum age requirement for Dude Wranglers ranges between 18 and 21 years old. Dude Wranglers may also need to be CPR and first aid certified.

Unions and Associations

Dude Wranglers may belong to the Dude Ranchers' Association, which according to its Web site (www. duderanch.org/index.cfm?) represents over 100 ranches fostering the Western way of life. The Web site offers information about dude ranching and how to select a ranch based on individual needs.

Tips for Entry

1. There are several Web sites dedicated to dude ranch employment. Explore listings on www. duderanchjobs411.com and www.duderanch jobs.com.

2. There are dude ranches all over the country that cater to different specialties. Try looking at Web sites such as www.bucksandspurs.com, www. doubleeranch.com, and www.rockinghorseranch. com.

3. Get experience working with horses through horseback riding lessons and volunteering at local stables.

4. The Web site www.jobmonkey.com has an extensive section on dude ranch jobs. Learn more about dude ranches and available positions by visiting www.jobmonkey.com/duderanch.

5. Working in the kitchen can also be an option to get the dude ranch experience if you do not have expertise with horses. View the job search Web sites and look for positions other than Dude Wrangler.

YOUTH COUNSELOR

CAREER PROFILE

Duties: Duties: Supervises children ranging in age from infants to teenagers attending children's programs on a cruise ship or resort; plans activities for children

Alternate Title(s): Child Care Worker; Program Coordinator

Salary Range: $1,800 to $2,100 per month

Employment Prospects: Good

Advancement Prospects: Good

Best Geographical Location(s): Any locations that cruise ships sail, including the Caribbean, the Atlantic/Pacific coast, Alaska, the Mediterranean, and more

Prerequisites:

Education and Training—Classes in education; bachelor's degree required for some positions, especially supervisory positions

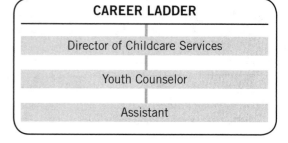

CAREER LADDER

Director of Childcare Services

Youth Counselor

Assistant

Experience—Prior experience working with children as a camp counselor, teacher, or nanny

Special Skills and Personality Traits—High energy and enthusiasm; patience; ability to work well with children; good communication skills

Position Description

When traveling on a cruise ship, children's programs are a major part of the experience for many families. Travelers want to make sure each member of the family enjoys the trip with plenty of fun and appropriate activities. Cruise ships run children's programs that may begin as early as 8 or 9 A.M. in the morning and run throughout the day until midnight. Youth Counselors staff these programs.

Youth Counselors work with children and teenagers ranging in age from two to 17. Like camp counselors, they organize games and plan and supervise activities. They may be responsible for developing curriculum with new activities themselves, in addition to carrying out the schedule planned by the youth program director. Since children's programs are broken down by age group (such as two to four year olds, five to seven year olds, and so on), Youth Counselors are assigned to work with specific groups. Some Youth Counselors always work with certain groups—for example, teenagers—while others work with different ages depending on the voyage.

The youth programs are chock-full of activities beginning in the morning. Parents drop off their children and Youth Counselors ensure that parents complete any kind of paperwork necessary, especially notifications of food allergies and signed emergency waivers. Youth Coun-

selors may even be involved in writing and developing some of that paperwork, especially flyers about the daily activities available so parents and children can choose what they want to attend. Frequently on cruise ships, parents receive pagers so they can be notified immediately if their children need them.

The day of a Youth Counselor is an extremely busy one. They may be involved with organizing scavenger hunts, painting and drawing, holding sports competitions, swimming, arranging theme parties, trivia games, movie nights, and much more. Serving as the host of karaoke sing-along or the judge of a talent show would not be uncommon. All the while, they engage children in the activities, making sure they are having fun and that no one is unhappy. Youth Counselors may supervise children during meals held in the main dining room, or meals that are specifically in the youth room such as pizza or ice cream sundae parties.

While supervisors are involved with scheduling, budgeting, and planning, Youth Counselors spend their time more directly engaged with the children. It is a hands-on job, as Youth Counselors engage in the same activities as their charges, whether it be playing soccer or tie-dying a sweatshirt. Parents depend on Youth Counselors to keep their children safe, so they keep a careful watch on their group as they move to activities.

Additional duties may include:

- ordering supplies for the youth room
- comforting children who are crying
- dealing with confrontations and resolving fights
- administering minor first aid, such as adhesive bandages
- taking inventory
- distributing prizes
- changing diapers (although many cruise lines won't allow children in diapers to participate in the youth programs)
- stepping in for hosting duties if necessary
- cleaning and sanitizing spaces and objects

Youth Counselors typically work more than 50 hours per week and may receive overtime pay for additional hours. Youth program directors may work 70 hours per week or more. Many cruise ships require Youth Counselors to work seven days per week during their contracts, which usually last three months. Youth Counselors usually wear uniforms provided by the cruise line, and as shipboard employees they may also be required to dress up for theme nights. While the majority of Youth Counselors are female, there are males as well, particularly to work with older boys playing sports.

Although they work long hours, Youth Counselors usually have some downtime when the ship is in port. In fact, many cruise lines encourage staff to go out and enjoy themselves so they can learn more about their destinations in order to answer guests' questions. Some Youth Counselors may lead children on land excursions, but this is not always an option. Some may close their youth program when the ship is in port, while others will keep it running on a limited basis. If Youth Counselors feel burned out after a particularly difficult voyage with challenging children, the good news is that, the next week brings a whole new group of guests to meet and get to know.

Working as a Youth Counselor can be a great option for college students majoring in education who want to travel for a summer job, as well as anyone else interested in both working with children and traveling on a cruise. Insiders say that the atmosphere is fun and they meet people from all over the world. Downtime is spent snorkeling, diving, and seeing new and exotic places. Some Youth Counselors complain about the ship housing, as most staff must share a room; however, many feel it is very worthwhile and a wonderful experience.

Salaries

Salaries for Youth Counselors typically range from $1,800 to $2,100 per month. Youth Counselors may earn more through overtime and tips. Some cruise lines allow Youth Counselors to provide private in-room babysitting services as well, which could generate extra income. Overall, Youth Counselors can do well on a cruise ship; since their room and board is covered, expenses are kept to a minimum. Therefore, Youth Counselors can come away at the end of their contract with considerable savings.

Employment Prospects

Employment prospects are good for Youth Counselors. Most ships hire the majority of their Youth Counselors on three-month contracts for the summer months, when children are off from school and more likely to travel extensively with their families. The size of the staff of the youth department varies depending on the size of the ship, and this area does need to be staffed all year round. Childcare experience is essential for getting hired, and applicants should stress this background during the interview process. Since many interviews are held by telephone, prospective Youth Counselors should be very personable and able to sell themselves. Opportunities can be found on the Web sites of the individual cruise lines as well as general cruise job sites such as www.cruisejobfinder.com.

Advancement Prospects

Advancement prospects will vary depending on the professional goals of the Youth Counselor. Some Youth Counselors are college students who work on a cruise ship as their summer job and plan to pursue careers in teaching or other areas of education and other fields. Other Youth Counselors may be experienced teachers or day-care providers taking a break from their work or working during vacations, or they may leave cruise ships to work in schools or day-care centers. Still others plan more of a long-term career on cruise ships, and they may advance to become youth program directors and supervisors. Youth Counselors may work at hotels and resorts that have children's programs in additional to cruise ships.

Education and Training

Formal educational requirements vary depending on the position and the cruise line. Many jobs require a bachelor's degree, usually in education, early childhood, psychology, or related fields. Others will supplement childcare experience for degrees. Supervisory positions usually require a college degree.

Experience, Skills, and Personality Traits

Youth Counselors need prior childcare experience, either through teaching/student teaching, babysitting, working as a nanny, working as a camp counselor, working with youth groups, or working in a daycare center. They must love children and work well with them, treating them with kindness but also being able to command their attention. Additionally, they need strong communication skills to work with parents as well.

Furthermore, Youth Counselors need high energy and enthusiasm due to the long hours and taxing physical demands of their job. They need to be flexible and adaptable, as well as extremely patient. A sense of humor and organization is essential. Youth Counselors should also be CPR and first aid certified. Knowledge of more than one language can also be beneficial in working with international guests.

Unions and Associations

The Cruise Lines International Association (www.cruising.org) promotes the cruise industry. Youth Counselors may join this association, and may opt to belong to the National Association of Childcare Professionals at www.naccp.org.

Tips for Entry

1. To learn more about cruise ship employment, see following article on the Web site Transitions Abroad: www.transitionsabroad.com/publications/magazine/0507/cruise_ship_jobs.shtml.

2. Spend a summer working as a camp counselor to hone your skills at interacting with youth.

3. Take an early childhood education class to learn about the theories behind working with children.

4. Volunteer at a local youth group or Big Brother/Big Sister program to develop long-term relationships with older children. This experience can be very valuable when highlighted on a résumé for employment.

5. Research the various children's programs offered by different cruise lines. See how they differ and are similar in philosophy and activities.

DIVING INSTRUCTOR

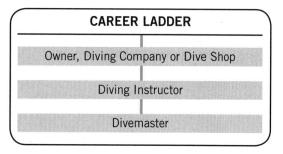

Position Description

If you have a passion for scuba diving, exploring the world, working with people, and being outdoors in the water, then work as a Diving Instructor can be a dream come true. You can get paid for pursuing something you love, sharing your interest with other people and teaching them about how to experience the wonders of the ocean.

Diving Instructors both instruct people in order for them to become certified divers as well as lead certified divers out on dives. In order to learn to dive, one must complete a certification course that teaches the fundamentals of diving. The courses may be condensed into several days at a resort or cruise, or be completed part-time over several weeks. Diving Instructors teach this "open water" course to groups ranging in age from 15 and above (children 10 to 15 years old may complete a junior open water course). They instruct the fundamentals of diving in several components.

First, Diving Instructors teach their students the basics of diving to be learned through gathering knowledge. This session may take place in a classroom and require reading a manual and watching videos. Here, students learn about techniques, safety, equipment, and more, and they must pass a written test to move onto the next level. Next, Diving Instructors teach their students in confined waters such as a swimming pool. In this setting, they impart the basic skills and students master techniques before graduating to the final step, open water training. Diving Instructors finally take their students to open water to apply what they have learned. Once the students pass the final test, they will be able to be independent divers throughout their lives.

In addition to teaching these courses, Diving Instructors lead divers on excursions. They may work for cruise ships or resorts such as Club Med, or they may work for independent dive shops that contract with hotels and resorts or develop their own client base. Diving Instructors plan and organize these dives, deciding where to go, how long to stay out, and how deep to dive. These groups can range in size from five or six to 20 or more. They may dive off a beach or go out by boat.

Before leading a dive, Diving Instructors ensure that every diver is paired with a buddy. They also provide an orientation about using the equipment and a safety review. Additionally, they let patrons know about what they can expect to see on the dive—exotic fish, interesting shipwrecks, colorful coral, and more. Once they are down below, they communicate with their group via hand signals and watch out at all times to make sure everyone is safe.

Additional duties may include:

- driving boats
- cleaning supplies
- working part-time in a dive shop
- talking with clients
- refilling oxygen tanks
- completing paperwork
- selling dive trips and lesson packages

Diving Instructors have great responsibility. Unlike most other positions in the hospitality industry, this is one where people's lives are in your hands. Diving Instructors need a combination of maturity and technical acuity to handle the work. There is huge liability in the field, and while the employer typically carries the liability and insurance, there is still a lot of pressure.

Diving Instructors spend about 75 percent of their time in the water. While most images of Diving Instructors are in beautiful tropical climates and warm waters, Diving Instructors also work in Alaska, Canada, and all over the world in some freezing conditions. Wet suits help protect them, but they must be able to withstand the physical demands of the job. However, this is job that people do purely because they love it, and most Diving Instructors find that it doesn't feel like work. They feel the exhilaration not only of diving themselves, but also of teaching others how to experience the underwater world.

Salaries

Salaries for Diving Instructors vary. While some say that it is difficult to earn a living in the field and one must do this part-time combined with another job, others manage to work as Diving Instructors full-time. For example, cruise ships may pay between $1,700 and $2,400 per month, with resorts paying a similar but slightly higher $2,000 to $3,000. Diving Instructors who work full-time may earn between $18,000 and $30,000 per year and up.

Employment Prospects

Employment prospects are excellent for Diving Instructors. With the necessary certification, there are jobs to be found all over the world. In fact, many contracts are for six months at a time and Diving Instructors may move from one resort to another in the same chain once their contract is up—say, six months in Mexico and then six months in the Philippines. The opportunities are truly boundless for skilled Diving Instructors.

Advancement Prospects

Diving Instructors may advance by running their own dive shop as an entrepreneurial venture. They might own equipment, boats, and hire other instructors. Also, Diving Instructors may advance by moving from smaller resorts to larger ones, or by moving to more geographically desirable areas.

Other Diving Instructors advance to positions within diving outside of hospitality, such as technical diving, commercial diving, media diving, or scientific diving.

Education and Training

There are several levels of certification and training needed to become a Diving Instructor. Becoming dive master is the first level of professional certification. Dive masters have achieved a level of diving where they understand safe diving practices, physics and decompression theory, and equipment use and medical aspects of diving; they can lead trips and assist instructors. However, in order to teach certification courses, one must reach the level of Diving Instructor, which is the highest level of certification offered by the two main associations, the Professional Association of Dive Instructors (PADI) and the National Association of Underwater Instructors (NAUI). Proof of 60 to 1,000 logged dives may be required to take the instructor development course which is quite intense. It teaches advanced diving theory, as well as how to teach in both the confined water session as well as the open water skill evaluations. Written and skill exams will follow, and may exceed more than 20 hours total over several days. However, this certification is required in order to teach other divers.

Diving internships can be a key way to achieving certification and many in the field recommend this path to becoming a Diving Instructor. The fee of the internship includes accommodations, equipment, and diving costs, as well as exams and placement services.

In terms of other education, Diving Instructors come to the field with all levels of formal study ranging from no high school diploma to graduate degrees. It is a field people come to typically because of their passion, regardless of what they studied in school.

Experience, Skills, and Personality Traits

In addition to the technical skills required to be a Diving Instructor, one must also be a good teacher and truly enjoy working with people. Diving Instructors teach individuals a skill that can be dangerous and must be able to do so with clarity. They should also be able to stay calm under pressure and have patience. An outgoing personality helps them motivate their students and other divers on trips.

Furthermore, Diving Instructors must be able to meet the physical demands of their job, spending most of their time submerged in waters of all temperatures. In many cases, Diving Instructors are selling their services; for example, if they work for a dive shop or resort, they try to get vacationers to sign up for their classes or dives. Therefore, they should have good sales and communication skills as well as a professional manner. Knowledge of a foreign language is also an advantage.

Additional Information

Diving Instructors must be certified; the two main associations that certify divers are the Professional Association of Dive Instructors (PADI) and the National Association of Underwater Instructors (NAUI). However other organizations such as Scuba Schools International also provide certification. Many believe PADI is the leading association for divers; see their Web site at www.padi.com. Diving Instructors may also need CPR and first aid certification.

Unions and Associations

The above professional associations, PADI and NAUI, are the main professional associations for diving instructors.

Tips for Entry

1. There are many job sites for Diving Instructors to explore. The following sites are just a sample: www.jobs4divers.com, divehappy.com/category/scuba-diving-jobs, and www.best-scuba-diving-tips.com/scuba-diving-jobs.html.

2. Spend time exploring the Web sites of PADI at www.padi.com and NAUI at www.naui.org. They will both give you a comprehensive idea about the requirements to become a Diving Instructor.

3. Consider different world regions where you would like to work and research those areas—this can give you an advantage when applying for jobs there.

4. When you go out on a dive, speak to your Diving Instructor extensively and learn about his or her career path.

5. By simply typing "Diving Instructor" or "Scuba Guide" into a search engine such as Google you will find articles, blogs, and many other sites with valuable insight and tips.

PERFORMER

CAREER PROFILE

Duties: Performs in shows on a cruise ship including acting, singing, dancing, and other special talents

Alternate Title(s): Entertainer; Cast Member

Salary Range: $1,600 to $5,000 per month and up

Employment Prospects: Good

Advancement Prospects: Good

Best Geographical Location(s): Any locations that cruise ships sail, including the Caribbean, the Atlantic/Pacific coast, Alaska, the Mediterranean, and more

Prerequisites:

Education and Training—Varies, but often includes performing arts training

Experience—Prior experience acting, singing, dancing, or performing

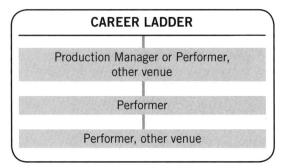

CAREER LADDER

Production Manager or Performer, other venue
Performer
Performer, other venue

Special Skills and Personality Traits—Performing arts talent; flexibility; good communication and interpersonal skills

Position Description

Entertainment is a major part of the cruising experience. Each evening, as passengers filter into the onboard theater to await their nightly show, Performers are behind the scenes preparing. These actors, singers, musicians, dancers, and other artists constitute the entertainment portion of a cruise, performing each night for guests to enjoy.

Whether their talent is singing, dancing, juggling, or magic, Performers work hard at their craft. On some ships, it is standard for Performers to attend rehearsals prior to sailing—for example, Disney cruises train their staff one month in advance, providing room and board for eight-hour rehearsal days while learning their programs. Rehearsals are also necessary while on board to practice and perfect the shows. Production managers, directors, and choreographers lead rehearsals and teach Performers their roles.

Most cruise ships typically have two shows per night, lasting approximately one hour in length. Performers work between five and six hours each night, including the time before and after each performance. The shows may be Broadway-style revues, variety shows, and more, depending on the cruise demographic. Family-oriented cruises will often have more child-friendly performances, while adult or singles cruises will feature comedians and other performers to cater to that crowd.

Additionally, as crew members, Performers have other responsibilities on a cruise ship. They receive extensive safety training and are called upon to participate in drills and assemblies to teach passengers about ship safety. Furthermore, they may appear in other ship programs, including dinner activities and theme nights.

While many Performers also serve as crew members, cruise ships also employ guest Performers. These entertainers join the ship for a short period of time, ranging from one night to several weeks, flying in and out of various locations. Sometimes these Performers have a specific talent, such as juggling, magic, comedy, or singing, so that they are a featured act on their own. Performers who are crew members are typically part of an ensemble, with bigger and smaller parts depending on the performance.

Performers must be flexible in order to adapt to different roles as assigned. No matter what their specialty—music, singing, or dance—they must be able to perform in a variety of styles. On a seven-night cruise, there will be a different show each night, with the ensemble likely performing in three to four of them. They must also be able to perform under rough sea conditions.

Additional duties may include:

- learning choreography from veteran performers
- calling bingo, hosting social events, and other non-performance tasks
- posing for photos with passengers, especially in costume

- participating in children's programs
- assisting with luggage pickup and delivery
- working with the cruise director to engage passengers in activities
- attending safety training

Contracts for Performers may range between four and 10 months, on average. While on board, Performers can expect to work six days per week. However, they do report enjoying free time to visit different ports and relax. There are specially designated areas for crew only on board, and Performers can enjoy their own pools, gyms, and other areas not open to passengers. Performers wear costumes while on stage and may be required to wear uniforms or adhere to a dress code during other times.

Salaries

Performers are well compensated for their work, and many feel that earnings are one of the perks of the job. Insiders say that singers earn more than dancers, but an expected range can be anywhere between $400 and $800 per week, or $1,600 to $4,000 per month. Since room and board is provided, most Performers are able to save a considerable amount during their time aboard.

Guest performers may earn up to 50 percent more than regular crew members. However, they are typically more experienced professionals who are known for headlining shows.

Employment Prospects

Because cruises are growing in popularity for leisure travel, employment prospects are good for Performers. While other arts and theater programs are cut, cruises need Performers to entertain passengers. Hiring managers receive hundreds of recordings each week featuring singers, dancers, and musicians. The hiring process is done through these audition tapes or live auditions, which are the opportunity for Performers to showcase their talent.

The best opportunities are for those with talent and general public appeal, as they will have a more interactive and customer-service role than most stage Performers not working on a cruise. Jobs also have to do with demand for specific talent, as cruise ships want to diversify their entertainment repertoire. Experience is required to get these competitive positions, but due to the high standards for cruise ship Performers, this job can be a great way for a Performer to build his or her résumé.

Advancement Prospects

With a prestigious cruise ship job on a résumé, Performers can advance in a number of directions, depending on their goals. Since cruise ships provide the opportunity to meet people from all over the world, and have a strong reputation for their entertainment standards, having such a position can help a Performer. Some are drawn to life on a cruise ship and want to work as entertainment directors, production managers, or cruise directors. For many Performers, however, a cruise job is one stop in their career to gain experience. After leaving their ship, Performers often continue to audition for theater, television, and film, as well as professional dance and music companies. Others, such as comedians and magicians, continue to market themselves to find work in entertainment venues throughout the world.

Education and Training

Performers have a variety of educational backgrounds, depending on their specialty. Many hold degrees in related subjects such as theater or music, while others have unrelated bachelor's degrees. Yet others have non-degree professional training in their art.

Experience, Skills, and Personality Traits

Prior experience is needed to work as a Performer on a cruise ship. Auditions and tapes reflect the work that the Performer has done in dance, song, music, or another area. Performers not only need talent, but they must also be able to showcase their talent to hiring managers. They must appeal to a wide variety of people and have excellent interpersonal skills.

Performers should also be flexible in order to adapt to cruise travel. They should be willing to pitch in as part of the crew and become part of the ship family. Also, Performers need high energy and stamina to keep up their schedule of rehearsals and performances.

Unions and Associations

Performers may belong to a variety of professional associations, including Actors' Equity Association, the American Guild of Musical Artists, the Screen Actors Guild (SAG), and Dance/USA.

Tips for Entry

1. Theater Web sites and publications such as www. playbill.com and www.backstage.com/bso/index. jsp have sections for cruise ship auditions. These auditions are frequently held in larger cities such as New York and Los Angeles.
2. Jobs can also be found through individual cruise lines Web sites as well as general sites. Try www.

cruiseshipjob.com, as well as Princess Cruise Lines (www.princess.com/employment/index.jsp) and Norwegian Cruise Lines: (www.ncl.com/nclweb/cruiser/cmsPages.html?pageId=JoinOurTeam).

3. Be sure to get everything in order before even applying for cruise ship employment, including passports and other travel documents. Also, take care of personal appointments such as doctor or dentist visits before the ship sails.

4. Hone your art through local performances to build up your audition tape.

CRUISE SHIP PHYSICIAN

CAREER PROFILE

Duties: Treat passengers and crew on a cruise ship for illness and injury

Alternate Title(s): Maritime Physician; Cruise Ship Doctor

Salary Range: $4,600 to $6,400 per month or $48,000 to $62,000 per year

Employment Prospects: Fair to good

Advancement Prospects: Fair

Best Geographical Location(s): Any locations that cruise ships sail, including the Caribbean, the Atlantic/Pacific coast, Alaska, the Mediterranean, and more

Prerequisites:

Education and Training—In addition to a bachelor's degree, medical degree and residency training

Experience—At least three years of post-residency work experience

Special Skills and Personality Traits—Excellent analytical and diagnostic skills; strong communication, interpersonal, and listening skills; scientific knowledge

Special Requirements—Medical degree and board certification in a specialty such as emergency medicine, family medicine, or internal medicine, and advanced life support and advanced cardiac life support certification are required

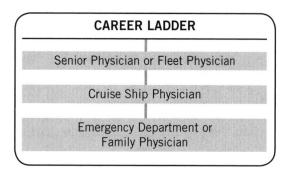

CAREER LADDER

Senior Physician or Fleet Physician

Cruise Ship Physician

Emergency Department or Family Physician

Position Description

Including passengers and crew, large cruise ships may have up to 5,000 people on board at any given time. During each voyage, some of these people will need medical care. Cruise Ship Physicians provide this care, treating the illnesses and injuries of cruise ship passengers and crew.

A typical large cruise ship may employ two Cruise Ship Physicians and four nurses. Cruise Ship Physicians work a combination of office hours (about four to six hours per day) and on-call hours, when they are required to carry a pager for emergencies. During office hours, they treat a spectrum of concerns ranging from on-ship conditions, such as seasickness and cuts and bruises, as well as preexisting problems such as sore throats, common colds, influenza, and more. Cruise Ship Physicians report seeing the spectrum from minor concerns to serious and severe illnesses requiring immediate treatment, and they see patients of all ages. Nurses help Cruise Ship Physicians by treating passengers and crew when they can and only passing along the necessary cases.

Most large ships that sail for one week or longer are equipped with state-of-the-art medical equipment including defibrillators, external pacemakers, ECG machines, ventilators, cardiac monitoring systems, and infusion pumps. They also have wheelchairs, stretchers, spinal boards and immobilization devices on board. The ship's infirmary may include in-patient beds, emergency rooms, X-ray rooms, critical care wards, treatment rooms, and dispensaries for medication. Dispensaries are stocked with a wide variety of medications, including thrombolytics to help heart attack victims.

While infirmaries are stocked to handle a comprehensive range of situations, Cruise Ship Physicians prefer to stabilize patients and get them on land as soon as possible. Sometimes, patients may need to travel by medical helicopter to the nearest land-based medical facility. In emergency situations where helicopters are not an option, the ship may have to divert its course to arrive at a different port sooner than expected. Cruise Ship Physicians develop partnerships with hospitals in the United States as well as the countries they visit in order to facilitate care in these circumstances.

Additional duties for Cruise Ship Physicians may include:

- prescribing and dispensing medicine such as antibiotics
- examining patients
- performing minor surgeries

- diagnosing illnesses
- supervising nurses
- mingling with passengers more informally
- documenting follow-up services and notes for patients' records

One of the major concerns for Cruise Ship Physicians is an outbreak of bacteria or a virus on board, which can be potentially deadly. They have the right to refuse boarding of passengers who exhibit symptoms and work to ensure that all cleanliness standards with regard to food preparation are upheld. Cruise Ship Physicians are also concerned about litigation from passengers who get sick on board and so must be careful with all treatment procedures.

Cruise Ship Physicians are able to enjoy free time on board and in port, traveling the world and meeting and treating people of all nationalities. Caring for the crew takes up more time than caring for the passengers, as crew members are on board for up to one year at a time. Cruise ship crews hail from all over the world and Cruise Ship Physicians find that they learn about people of all nationalities.

Contracts range from four to eight months for Cruise Ship Physicians. After completing the first contract, some ships allow Cruise Ship Physicians to bring their spouse and family on board. Those working full-time may enjoy several weeks off between each contract shift. Most Cruise Ship Physicians are required to wear uniforms during their working hours.

Salaries

Salaries for Cruise Ship Physicians are considerably lower than physicians working in other environments. Ranges are between $4,600 to $6,400 per month or $48,000 to $62,000 per year, while average salaries for family physicians or emergency physicians, the typical specialties of Cruise Ship Physicians, are between $150,000 and $200,000 per year. However, many Cruise Ship Physicians feel that the benefit of being able to travel the world compensates for the lower earnings.

Additionally, expenses are quite low while on ship, as room and board are included. Some Cruise Ship Physicians work part-time to supplement their income during vacations and other slow times.

Employment Prospects

Employment prospects are fair to good for Cruise Ship Physicians. To find job opportunities, they can search both medical journals and cruise ship employment sites. They can also contact cruise lines directly. Some insiders say that the best Cruise Ship Physician jobs are found through word of mouth, with currently employed Physicians who are ready to move on passing along the opportunity to a friend or colleague. Many Cruise Ship Physicians work part-time, while others choose it as a full-time career for several years. Turnover is high in that many Cruise Ship Physicians don't want to choose the erratic lifestyle for many years, especially if they want to have a family.

Advancement Prospects

Cruise Ship Physicians might advance to become senior physicians or fleet physicians, where they work directly for the cruise line, supervising a number of different shipboard physicians. Others will return to land positions including private practice, academic medicine, and staff hospital positions. In addition to cruise ships, opportunities are available at ski and vacation resorts.

Education and Training

Extensive education and training is required for all physicians, including Cruise Ship Physicians. The first educational step is a bachelor's degree. Students can major in any field, but must take the premed requirements in order to apply to medical school. In addition, the Medical College Admission Test (MCAT) is required. For information about the MCAT and applying to medical school, see www.aamc.org/students/mcat.

After four years of medical school, physicians are required to complete a residency in a specialized area. As residents, they work as physicians in a hospital under the supervision of senior doctors. After completing an internship and residency lasting between two and five years, they are eligible to become board certified in that specialty area. Most Cruise Ship Physicians are board certified in family practice, emergency medicine, internal medicine, or critical care.

Special Requirements

Cruise Ship Physicians need a degree and license to practice medicine as well as board certification or the international equivalent in a specialty. Additionally, advanced life support (ALS) and advanced cardiac life support (ACLS) certification is also required.

Experience, Skills, and Personality Traits

Excellent diagnostic skills are needed for Cruise Ship Physicians as they determine ailments and treatment plans in patients. Scientific and medical knowledge is required. Good communication and interpersonal skills help Cruise Ship Physicians work with passengers and crews of all different nationalities. While fluency in English is required, knowledge of other languages can also be helpful.

Before becoming a Cruise Ship Physician, at least three years of postgraduate experience are required as well.

Unions and Associations

Physicians in the United States belong to the American Medical Association, as well as associations related to their specialties such as the American Academy of Family Physicians. The American College of Emergency Physicians has a section of membership for cruise ship and maritime medicine at www.acep.org/ACEPmembership.aspx?id=24928.

Tips for Entry

1. Take a look at Adventure Medics, the Web site where doctors can find interesting and international adventure travel jobsm at www.adventure medics.com.

2. Learn about applying to medical school from the Association of American Medical Colleges at www.aamc.org/students/applying/start.htm.

3. Ask to shadow an emergency room physician to see the range of cases that come in on a typical shift. This is similar to cruise ship medicine in that you do not typically develop long-term relationships with your patients.

4. Speak to Cruise Ship Physicians and find out how long they have been in their position, and how long they plan to stay with this type of medicine. What do they see as the pros and cons of the job?

FITNESS INSTRUCTOR

CAREER PROFILE

Duties: Teaches exercise and fitness classes at a hotel, resort, or cruise ship fitness center

Alternate Title(s): Exercise Instructor; Aerobics Instructor

Salary Range: $18,000 to $40,000 and up

Employment Prospects: Good

Advancement Prospects: Good

Best Geographical Location(s): All, particularly big cities and heavy tourist areas; regions with major hotels, resorts, and spas

Prerequisites:

    Education and Training—Varies, but a degree or certificate in exercise or fitness is required for many positions

    Experience—Experience taking and teaching fitness classes

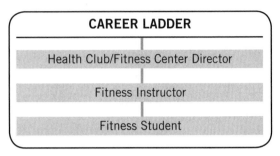

CAREER LADDER

Health Club/Fitness Center Director

Fitness Instructor

Fitness Student

Special Skills and Personality Traits—Energetic and enthusiastic; good stamina and technical ability in type of exercise taught (e.g., yoga knowledge); strong communication and teaching skills; patience

Special Requirements—Accreditation and/or certification may be required for many positions

Position Description

Exercise is an integral part of many people's lives and their daily routines. When they are on vacation or away on business, this is no exception. Hotel guests expect to continue their normal workout even when they are not at home. The fitness centers in hotels, resorts, and cruise ships often have state-of-the-art equipment where guests can run on treadmills or lift weights and train. Additionally, many offer exercise classes to motivate and tone visitors. These classes are taught by Fitness Instructors.

Fitness Instructors lead classes that might range from 20 minutes to one hour or more. Classes may be in aerobics (step or regular), spinning, cardio, yoga, martial arts, Pilates, and more. Classes may use equipment such as bicycles or balance balls, or take place on the floor using mats. Fitness Instructors are trained to teach these classes and maximize health benefits and minimize injury. They may be experts in one of these specific areas or several.

Before each class, Fitness Instructors set up the room if necessary and bring out the equipment. They develop fitness routines targeted to different skill levels or populations. For example, there are fitness classes designed for senior citizens and those developed for pregnant women. Part of creating each class might include selecting music and choreographing sequences of moves. Fitness Instructors use their knowledge to develop a

workout that meets the target goal of the class, whether it is to raise heart rate or tone stomach muscles. This becomes the fitness class curriculum.

Classes need to reach that happy medium where they are challenging but not too difficult. Fitness Instructors need to be expert at all the required moves and must be able to help students achieve them, particularly in classes like yoga and Pilates that require specific stretching positions. They need to be able to motivate and instruct others to engage them in participation.

Also, Fitness Instructors often take histories from the guests who sign up for their classes. People complete forms about their medical background and Fitness Instructors try to ensure safety and take special needs into account. They may recommend a different class for someone with a health condition or make other accommodations when necessary.

It is important for Fitness Instructors to enjoy working with people. In the hospitality industry, they contribute to a guest's overall experience and must be a positive representative of their property. To be helpful when they speak with guests, Fitness Instructors must know about all the property amenities and special events. Furthermore, they need to be able to address all feedback and problems calmly and confidently, with a customer-service orientation, to ensure that the guest is satisfied.

Additional duties may include:

- providing coverage for assigned classes and/or filling in for other instructors
- ensuring that guests complete necessary paperwork
- handling special requests and paperwork
- promoting special services and programs within the hotel
- being knowledgeable about property policies and procedures
- explaining benefits of different types of exercise
- reporting any problems to management
- teaching aquatic fitness
- keeping up on new fitness trends and equipment
- keeping equipment clean and working properly

Fitness Instructors should be knowledgeable in CPR and other first aid and emergency procedures. They must adhere to safety standards at all times. At times, they may be asked to stand in for other staff, from desk attendants to managers. They may also be knowledgeable about other health-related areas such as weight management or nutrition.

Hours usually include weekends and might also include some evenings. Fitness Instructors may have some flexibility over their schedules. Insiders say that there is high job satisfaction, and many Fitness Instructors feel they are getting paid to stay in shape.

Salaries

According to the Bureau of Labor Statistics (BLS), median annual earnings of fitness trainers and aerobics instructors as of May 2007 were $27,680. The middle 50 percent earned between $18,850 and $42,610. The bottom 10 percent earned less than $15,550, while the top 10 percent earned $58,990 or more. Many Fitness Instructors are paid hourly; the mean hourly salary was $13.31.

Employment Prospects

Employment prospects for Fitness Instructors in the hospitality industry are good. Most hotels have gyms now and are expanding their repertoire of services. The need for qualified people to staff these fitness centers and teach classes will grow. For those Fitness Instructors with certification and specialty areas, opportunities will be best.

Advancement Prospects

Advancement prospects are also good for Fitness Instructors. They can move to more prestigious properties or to spa facilities where they may teach more classes, earn more money, and have more responsibility. Some may move up to manage the fitness center at a hotel, or manage all its fitness services. Others might seek certification as a personal trainer, where they can take on private clients and earn considerably higher incomes.

Education and Training

Education and training varies depending on the type of classes a Fitness Instructor teaches. Most Fitness Instructors that teach group classes begin by taking many classes themselves and developing their own style. Those Fitness Instructors who teach yoga or Pilates must receive specialized training in these disciplines. According to the BLS, both Pilates and yoga require training programs that may last one weekend, but more typically require at least 200 hours of participation. The Web sites for the Pilates Method Alliance (www.pilatesmethodalliance.org) and the Yoga Alliance (www.yogaalliance.org) provide more information.

Additionally, many Fitness Instructors have college degrees in fields such as exercise science, physical education, recreation, health, and other subjects. Some employers prefer to hire instructors with bachelor's degrees in addition to or in place of certification.

Experience, Skills, and Personality Traits

Fitness Instructors usually come to the field from years of taking and enjoying fitness classes themselves. Exercise is a passion that they have chosen to turn into a vocation.

To be a good teacher, a Fitness Instructor must be friendly and patient, with excellent communication skills. He or she must be able to lead by example and motivate others. Also, he or she must be able to improve the performance of students and correct mistakes while being encouraging rather than critical.

Extremely high energy and enthusiasm are needed, as well as the ability to keep these up for the duration of not only one class, but several classes in the same day. This requires being in good physical shape and health with extended stamina. Technical skill in their fitness discipline is essential, as well as commitment to health, wellness, and exercise.

Special Requirements

Most employers require Fitness Instructors to be certified or work toward becoming certified. Several national organizations certify Fitness Instructors, including the Aerobics and Fitness Association of America (www.afaa.com), the American Fitness Professionals and Associates (www.afpafitness.com), the American Council on Exercise (http://www.acefitness.org/), the Health and

Fitness Association (www.ideafit.com), and the International Sports Sciences Association (www.issaonline.com). They should have CPR certification as well.

Unions and Associations

Fitness Instructors may belong to a variety of professional associations including the National Strength and Conditioning Association, the Aerobics and Fitness Association of America, American Fitness Professionals and Associates, and the International Sports Sciences Association.

Tips for Entry

1. Take many different types of fitness classes. Pay attention to what you like and dislike about the structure and style of the class.
2. There are CPR certification courses offered frequently nationwide. Use some of the following sites to locate a class near you: www.cprtoday.com, www.redcross.org, and www.americanheart.org.
3. Explore bachelor's degree programs in fitness such as the health and fitness major at Purdue University in West Lafayette, Indiana (www.cla.purdue.edu/academic/hk/hkadvising/HealthFitness.htm) and the health and fitness major at the University of Southern Maine in Portland (www.usm.maine.edu/sportsmed/hefcurriculum.html).
4. Find your passion for a specific type of fitness discipline and pursue training in that area. Look into yoga, Pilates, tai chi, aquatics, aerobics, weight training, and others.
5. Develop a musical playlist for your workout that can be used for future classes you might teach. Consider the types of songs that energize and motivate you to work harder.

DISC JOCKEY

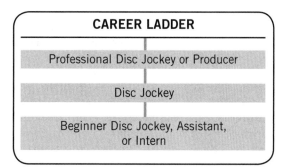
Position Description

Entertainment is a big part of the travel and hospitality industry. Whether checking out a club on a cruise ship, hotel, or casino, or attending a party in a restaurant or banquet hall, many guests like to dance and have a good time. Disc Jockeys announce and play music in these venues. They determine the best music to play for each audience, trying to engage the crowd and create a festive atmosphere.

Cruise lines and resorts like their Disc Jockeys to have a broad music base to span the generations of their clientele. Cruises attract a wide variety of passengers ranging from children and teens to senior citizens, so knowledge of music across the decades is essential. Prior hospitality experience is also useful since cruise ship Disc Jockeys need to socialize and interact with passengers. On a cruise ship, experience with lighting and sound can be very helpful as well, since some Disc Jockeys work closely with the stage manager in assisting with show production.

Disc Jockeys select songs to play during certain hours that appeal to their audience. For example, they may select oldies for a themed cruise night and pop for a Sweet Sixteen party. Different playlists are created that they can use over again. Disc Jockeys use their knowledge of and experience with music to choose the right songs to get the crowd excited and dancing.

Disc Jockeys also serve as entertainment personalities. They might announce each song they play, as well as organize games to energize the audience. At a party, they may announce the guest of honor and serve as master of ceremonies for any speeches being given. They may give out prizes such as glow sticks, beads, and other accessories. A strong desire to entertain people and get them dancing and motivated is required.

In addition to merely selecting and playing songs, Disc Jockeys also use their technical skills to mix music, which means blending together different songs. This remixing of music creates new and unique songs. Disc Jockeys typically work in a booth with their equipment, including mixers, turntables, amplifiers, CD decks, and headphones.

Additional duties may include:

- taking requests from the crowd
- creating Web sites, business cards, and other self-marketing material
- developing playlists of various musical genres
- researching and listening to new music
- creating a music library
- networking and developing relationships to find opportunities
- studying musical styles and music videos

On a cruise ship and in most other venues, Disc Jockeys typically work only at night, leaving their days open and free. However, they must enjoy working weekends and late nights until the wee hours of the morning. They are passionate about their work, reveling in the idea of being responsible for people having a good time and dancing, and even having an impact on the music that becomes popular with a certain crowd.

Many Disc Jockeys are self-employed and they promote their services to get hired to play for individual jobs at clubs, restaurants, and special events. Often they have their own equipment, which they bring to each booking. Sometimes Disc Jockeys may get hired to play every weekend in a certain club for a set period of time.

Salaries

On a cruise ship, the typical Disc Jockey salary is between $1,700 to $2,000 per month. While on board, expenses are very low, with room and board included. DJs can come out at the end of a cruise ship contract with a substantial amount of money saved.

On the professional Disc Jockey circuit, salaries can vary greatly depending on experience. They are usually paid per job, rather than a yearly salary. A top DJ can get between $1,000 and $3,000 for a huge event, but beginners may earn $100 to $300 instead.

Employment Prospects

Employment prospects are good for Disc Jockeys, since they have several different areas of opportunity. On a cruise ship, contracts generally last six months and pay is salary-based. For self-promotion to work clubs and special events, Disc Jockeys market themselves through business cards, Web sites, word of mouth, etc. A demo CD that showcases mixing skills is required to get hired. Some Disc Jockeys may work for agencies or hire managers who work to book them with job opportunities each weekend.

Advancement Prospects

Disc Jockeys can advance by building their business. After a stint on a cruise ship, they may promote themselves to work at clubs or parties, developing a strong reputation. Experience will help them book bigger venues for more money and recognition. They may even advance to run a company that hires and books other Disc Jockeys as well. Additionally, some Disc Jockeys may want to work as radio personalities where they not only announce and select music on the radio, but also provide news, entertainment, and commentary on current events and popular culture. Others may advance within the music industry to become music or record producers.

Education and Training

While there is no specific educational requirements for Disc Jockeys, training in the technical aspects of job is certainly needed. Disc Jockeys must know how to mix music and use other necessary equipment. Some Disc Jockeys have a high school education, while others have bachelor's degrees. Useful fields of study include broadcasting, media production, business, and music. Disc Jockey training courses are also available and can be very beneficial.

Experience, Skills, and Personality Traits

First and foremost, Disc Jockeys need a passion for music. Their knowledge of different types of music should be vast and varied. Disc Jockeys should like being the center of attention and the life of the party. They need the outgoing personality, communication, and interpersonal skills to motivate a crowd and get them dancing.

Breaking into the field does require an initial investment, so good financial and business skills are useful, as well as the ability to promote yourself. Sales and marketing techniques help Disc Jockeys develop business cards, Web sites, flyers, and other publicity materials to let people know about their services.

Unions and Associations

Disc Jockeys may belong to professional associations including the American Disc Jockey Association. The association has many local and state chapters that can be helpful resources for networking.

Tips for Entry

1. Find a mentor. Insiders say this is the best way to learn about being a Disc Jockey. Watch an experienced professional in action and gain his or her advice about how to succeed in the field.
2. A mentor can also offer advice about how to get started without overspending. Insiders say that one should be careful not to spend too much money on equipment early on.
3. Take a DJ training course. By searching the Internet, you can find a multitude of online and local courses.
4. Develop your own unique style as a Disc Jockey.
5. Check out DJ Advantage, a Web site that offers professional DJ resources (www.djadvantage.com) as well as the videos offered by Expert Village.com at www.expertvillage.com/video-series/7476_how-be-professional-dj.htm.
6. Search for cruise ship Disc Jockey positions on sites such as www.cruisejobfinder.com and www.shipjobs.com.

ACTIVITIES DIRECTOR

Duties: Plans, organizes, and oversees all activities for a hotel or resort, including sports, games, and other special programs

Alternate Title(s): Hotel Activities Director; Hotel Recreation Director; Resort Activities Director

Salary Range: $30,000 to $70,000 and up

Employment Prospects: Fair

Advancement Prospects: Fair

Best Geographical Location(s): All, with the greatest opportunities in large cities and heavy tourist regions with many resorts and hotels

Prerequisites:

Education and Training—Bachelor's degree in recreation, physical education, or tourism valuable

Experience—Several years of resort activities experience

CAREER LADDER

General Manager or Director of Recreation

Activities Director

Assistant Director or manager of one specific activity

Special Skills and Personality Traits—Strong communications and interpersonal skills; good leadership and organization; knowledge of recreation and leisure activities; creativity

Position Description

Large hotels and resorts known for their robust programs employ full-time Activities Directors to coordinate and supervise these offerings. During a typical day, a resort may offer tennis clinics for people of all ages, water aerobics geared toward senior citizens, and nature walks for children.

Activities Directors are responsible for designing and shaping the activities program for their resort. These programs play a large role in attracting guests, so the Activities Director has an integral part in influencing the resort's reputation and revenue. They use their expertise in the recreation field to develop programs geared for the resort's various demographics, based on age, skills, and interest.

Depending on the type of resort, activities can be quite diverse, including games, crafts, hayrides, bonfires, nature walks, fishing tournaments, and horseback riding. A full schedule of indoor and outdoor sports may also be provided, such as tennis, golf, basketball, surfing, and many others. Additionally, Activities Directors may plan evening events, booking comedians, magicians, and performers, or scheduling karaoke parties. They may provide a full spectrum of both children and adult programs each day and evening. A typical day for an Activities Director might be arranging events as diverse as a scavenger hunt, "Name That Tune," a home run derby, a relay race, "Family Feud," design your own birdhouse, a diving competition, a beach volleyball game, a wine tasting, and an evening Broadway-style show.

Another responsibility for Activities Directors may be planning programs for specific visiting groups, such as convention attendees or corporate executives. They may coordinate team-building events, bring in outside speakers, arrange day trips to local attractions, and more.

Activities Directors plan activities that take place at the resort as well as outside. They develop relationships with local services that provide such activities as horseback riding, go-carting, biking, snorkeling, zip lining, and many others. By working with local vendors, they create a spirit of cooperation instead of competition that can be financially beneficial to everyone.

Activities Directors work to publicize and promote their events. At many resorts, a daily calendar is available during breakfast; sometimes it may be delivered to guest rooms at night. Activities Directors might write the copy for these flyers in a way that will engage guests and make them want to participate. They may also publicize programs through boards in the lobby, announcements, closed-circuit television on a resort channel, and the resort Web site. On the Web site, listing the activities is a way of advertising and promoting the resort experience.

Additional duties may include:

- arranging athletic or family game competitions
- managing activity registration or sign-up
- purchasing supplies and equipment
- designing a program of activities
- working with outside vendors
- socializing with guests

Supervising staff is also part of being an Activities Director. Some staff members may be seasonal or part-time, hired to work with children or other populations related to a specific skill such as tennis. The Activities Director is responsible for hiring, terminating, training, and scheduling these workers, making sure they have the necessary tools to perform their jobs. An enthusiastic activities department can go a long way toward contributing to guest satisfaction, so Activities Directors look to hire staff who are both knowledgeable and personable, with a customer-service orientation.

As managers of an activities department, Activities Directors also have financial responsibilities. They may plan, budget, and forecast for each year, analyzing which activities work best for their desired goals. Additionally, they may make recommendations for new sports complexes, equipment, or other plans that will enhance the activities department.

Resort Activity Directors may work for luxury hotels, convention centers, casinos or resorts. Hours are long and nontraditional to reflect weekend and evening activities at resorts. They may wear uniforms or costumes provided by the resort for different programs. Activity Directors strive to provide visitors with memories that will encourage them to return.

Salaries

According to data on PayScale.com, the median salary for a resort Activities Director in the United States with five to nine years of experience is $38,527. For one to four years of experience, the median salary is $33,000 and for 10 to 19 years, it is $40,064. Additional data showing a higher salary range can be found on Salary.com, which shows that the average annual salary for a hotel recreation director falls between $46,236 and $68,526. Like other hospitality positions, salary varies depending on the experience and education of the Activities Director, as well as the size, location, and prestige of the resort.

Employment Prospects

Employment prospects are fair for Resort Activities Directors. Not all resorts employ Activities Directors, making opportunities limited to large properties with full activities programs. The best way to get involved with the field is through summer jobs at resorts that have activities departments. Others gain experience planning activities in different sectors, such as retirement homes, and then move into the hospitality and resort industry. They may also work for departments of parks and recreation.

Advancement Prospects

Advancement prospects are also somewhat limited for resort Activity Directors. Many stay in the position for a long time, particularly at family-owned resorts. Resort Activity Directors may move to larger and more prestigious resorts in geographically desirable areas. They also may go on to direct activities for a chain of hotels or resorts.

Education and Training

Many Activity Directors hold a bachelor's degree in recreation, physical education, or tourism. These fields focus on helping people to enjoy their leisure time and provide training in customer service, leadership, and planning. Courses in physical education are helpful for Activity Directors who lead athletic programs. Schools such as the University of Illinois at Urbana-Champaign feature a department of recreation, sport, and tourism (www.rst.uiuc.edu) as does the University of North Carolina, with its degree program in parks, recreation, leisure, and fitness studies (www.northcarolina.edu/content.php/apps/disted2/searchresults.php?inv_type=T&browse=rec).

Experience, Skills, and Personality Traits

Activity Directors should have excellent interpersonal skills. They must enjoy working with people of all different types, interacting with them and helping them have fun. Creativity enables them to plan an array of activities that will stimulate guests, both mind and body, as well as target activities appropriately to different age groups. As good communicators, they can articulate their ideas to staff and guests, as well as use their writing skills to advertise their programs.

Furthermore, Activities Directors need to be strong leaders who are well-organized. They should be able to motivate others and manage schedules so that many things can take place at once but without conflicts. Knowledge of recreation, sports, and leisure activities helps them to design appropriate curriculum.

Unions and Associations

The Resort and Commercial Recreation Association is a professional association specifically for Activities

Directors working at resorts. Additionally, they may be part of the National Recreation and Park Association, the American Alliance for Health, Physical Education, Recreation & Dance, and the American Hotel and Lodging Association.

Tips for Entry

1. Visit a full-scale resort with an activities program and take note of the variety of activities that take place in one day.
2. Conduct an informational interview with an Activities Director. What constitutes a typical week on the job?
3. Try a summer job at a resort to learn more about the programs and activities. This can be a good way to get your foot in the door for future employment.
4. Take courses in recreation, leisure, and tourism.
5. Gain experience by coaching a local youth sports league and working as a camp counselor.

RESTAURANTS AND CULINARY ARTS

CATERER

CAREER PROFILE

Duties: Provides food and beverages for special events; may also provide staffing, decor, linens, dishes, flatware, and other accompaniments

Alternate Title(s): None

Salary Range: $20,000 to $200,000 and up

Employment Prospects: Fair to good

Advancement Prospects: Good

Best Geographical Location(s): All, with the best opportunities for growth in larger cities or more affluent areas

Prerequisites:

Education and Training—Varies, from degree programs to culinary school

Experience—Prior experience in the food service industry

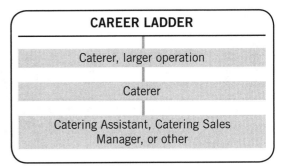

Special Skills and Personality Traits—Strong culinary skills; creativity; excellent interpersonal skills; good business sense; managerial ability and attention to detail

Position Description

When planning a special event, choosing the right menu is a huge part of what makes the party successful. Caterers provide food and related services for special events from planning the menu and providing the waitstaff to cooking and breakdown. They may work on events ranging from elaborate large-scale weddings for 300 people to small, intimate dinner parties for eight.

First, Caterers meet with clients to determine their needs. They establish the budget within which they need to work and then offer menu ideas and suggestions based on the event and venue. Caterers typically have written material for clients to review that lists their food options and prices—appetizers, main dishes, desserts, and specialty items. These pamphlets or brochures may also have different types of menu suggestions (brunch, cocktail party, themes, etc.). Together with the clients, Caterers come up with an individualized plan that works for each event. During this process, they may also allow clients to taste the food.

After the initial consultation, Caterers gather all the inventory and staff necessary for each of their events. They often work on many events simultaneously and must keep their calendars well-organized. In one weekend, they may be catering a first birthday party held in a backyard and a Sweet Sixteen taking place on a yacht. It is important to be prepared with not only the food and

beverages but also the linens, flatware, and staff to work each event.

Most Caterers are self-employed, and many get started in the business because they love to cook and catering is an opportunity to showcase their skills. Some Caterers do all the cooking themselves, while others have a team to help. Caterers may have waiters and waitresses, bartenders, and other staff working for them on a contract basis or full-time (depending on the size of their business) to help with events.

Caterers must be skilled in culinary arts, business, and interpersonal relations. They must be able to not only prepare food, but to present it in a pleasing way. Skilled in the art of entertainment, Caterers make their clients happy and make their events successful; by the nature of their work, they are taking part in important moments in their clients' lives. In addition to working with customers, Caterers must develop good working relationships with food suppliers in order to get the best ingredients at reasonable prices.

Additional duties may include:

- supervising food preparation and event setup
- developing themes for events
- evaluating cooking ingredients and kitchen products
- ensuring safety, cleanliness, and hygiene standards
- accommodating special dietary needs
- developing recipe lists and custom menus

- stocking a professional kitchen and determining whether to buy or rent equipment
- preparing estimates and contracts
- transporting prepared food
- obtaining board of health certification
- working with event planners, wedding coordinators, and other professionals

As they begin a business, Caterers must decide on their projected size and scope. They may need to put together a business plan and obtain financing for startup costs. Some Caterers rent or own space where they prepare food and meet with clients, while others have meetings at client homes and prepare food in their own kitchens (for small operations). Also, Caterers must do their research to set prices that are fair in the market but will lead to profit.

To expand their businesses, Caterers must be skilled at marketing themselves. Success may depend on word of mouth, as well as advertising and publicity in local media outlets. Caterers may develop brochures, Web sites, direct mail campaigns, and other material to let the community know about their services.

Hours are long for Caterers, as they work events that usually take place on evenings and weekends. After becoming very established, some Caterers might not attend all events; rather, they may delegate the responsibility, especially with smaller events and trusted waitstaff. However, Caterers still go to many events to supervise and assist the client.

Caterers may also work in hotels and resorts, overseeing catering operations. Additionally, large catering businesses may contract with big companies or nonprofits to provide the sole catering services for their events. A Caterer may have two or three employees, or a staff of 50 or more. Food may be prepared in the catering kitchen or the kitchen of the party venues.

Salaries

As for any business owner, salaries for Caterers are dependent on the size and profits of their operation. During their first few years of owning a business, average salaries may be in the $20,000 to $40,000 range, but after several years of success, Caterers can earn between $40,000 and $80,000 per year. Additionally, Caterers in affluent areas who establish strong reputations can earn six-figure salaries, the top echelon earning $200,000 and up.

Employment Prospects

Private and social catering is considered to be one of the fastest-growing segments of the restaurant industry. Growth is expected as business and individuals hire Caterers for various parties and events. However, growth is also dependent on economic conditions, as people plan fewer events during downturns. Furthermore, this business is risky, with many catering operations failing during their first few years.

Advancement Prospects

Caterers may come from the food service industry and decide to open their own private business, or they may decide to go to the industry if they are tired of business operations. Caterers may become executive chefs at restaurants, catering managers at hotels, or they may expand their business or work for event-planning companies. Successful catering businesses may also expand to own restaurants, write cookbooks, and teach classes or lecture.

Education and Training

Individuals typically get into the catering field because they love to cook and entertain. Caterers come from a variety of educational backgrounds, including those with bachelor's degrees in unrelated fields, and graduates of restaurant management or culinary arts programs. Courses in culinary arts are extremely helpful to learn about a variety of food preparation, and business classes are useful for the financial and management end of the job.

Experience, Skills, and Personality Traits

Caterers need excellent culinary skills and the ability to produce large quantities of food without sacrificing quality. Creativity is also important to develop themes, personalized menus, and special touches for events that people will remember. Caterers may have signature dishes or a dessert for which they become known. Prior experience working in the food service industry, such as positions as a chef or catering sales manager, is very valuable.

Additionally, customer service and good interpersonal skills are paramount. A good Caterer listens to clients and understands their needs. He or she enjoys pleasing people and works with them using tact and diplomacy. Business savvy is needed to run an effective operation, as are organizational skills and attention to detail. Caterers must be able to multitask and handle numerous events at once. Furthermore, they must be flexible enough to handle last-minute changes.

Unions and Associations

The National Association of Catering Executives (www.nace.net) is the oldest and largest catering professional association in the world. Caterers involved with industrial catering may also belong to the Convenience Caterers and Food Manufacturers Association (CCFMA). Additional information may be obtained from the National Restaurant Association.

Tips for Entry

1. Take a look at *Catering Magazine,* the only national business-to-business trade magazine dedicated to the professional catering industry, at www.cateringmagazine.com.
2. Catersource.com is a Web site that provides education, products, and news for caterers at www.catersource.com.
3. Gain as much cooking experience as possible. Take culinary and wine courses to learn about food and beverage pairing, learn to bake and make desserts, and explore different specialty areas.
4. Shadow an experienced Caterer to see what the job involves. Observe the difference between working small and large events.
5. Read books such as Joyce Weinberg's *Everything Guide to Starting and Running a Catering Business: Insider's Advice on Turning Your Talent into a Career* and *Catering Like a Pro: From Planning to Profit* by Francine Halvorsen.

SOMMELIER

CAREER PROFILE

Duties: Advises customers on wine selections in restaurants and hotels; oversees all alcohol purchasing for establishment; wine and spirit management

Alternate Title(s): Wine Steward; Cellar Master; Wine Captain

Salary Range: $20,000 to $160,000 and up

Employment Prospects: Fair

Advancement Prospects: Fair

Best Geographical Location(s): Major cities, upscale resort areas, and major wine regions such as Napa and Sonoma valleys, California

Prerequisites:

Education and Training—Sommelier training courses requiring over 300 contact hours; some Sommeliers hold bachelor's degrees in hospitality/restaurant management or other fields as well

Experience—Prior experience in the restaurant/hospitality industry

CAREER LADDER

Master Sommelier, Wine Director, Food and Beverage Director, Restaurant Owner

Sommelier

Wine Assistant, Assistant Sommelier, Apprentice, Other Food/Beverage Service Position, Student

Special Skills and Personality Traits—Excellent knowledge of wine and food; strong interpersonal skills; good management ability; foreign language ability

Position Description

Sommelier (the French translation is *cellar master* or *wine steward*) is an ancient profession, and has been around as long as people have been drinking wine. Sommeliers advise people on wine selection in restaurants and hotels. Their role is critical in the restaurant industry equivalent to that of the chef. Sommeliers have a tremendous impact on the profit margin of their establishment based on the wines that they choose and sell.

The job of a Sommelier includes acquisition, service, and recommendations. A typical day may begin by coming in wearing casual attire around three in the afternoon. The Sommelier might create the wine specials for the evening or work on the master wine list. He or she may also assess the inventory, meet with suppliers and wholesalers, and purchase new wines. Meeting with the chef each day is essential. Sommeliers taste all specials and menu items personally and analyze the best food and wine pairings. Before the dinner hour, around 6 P.M., Sommeliers change into a suit or professional dress and get ready to spend several hours working the floor.

A good Sommelier is available when needed, but spends much time training his or her waitstaff about the different wines and pairings. Each day Sommeliers review the specials with the staff so they will be able to advise customers. Some customers will ask to see the Sommelier specifically if they have questions that the waitstaff cannot answer. However, since it is impossible for most Sommeliers to visit every table, an important part of their job is training staff to be experts and knowledgeable salespeople.

Many people are uncomfortable ordering wine because they do not feel knowledgeable about it. Sommeliers help guide them through the process. Most Sommeliers will say that their goal is to ensure that customers are happy and get the most out of their gastronomic experience. If they can make good sales and increase profits as well, it is an added bonus.

Sommeliers must be able to recommend wines for different budgets as well as different tastes. They get people to talk about likes and dislikes without being condescending. By learning how to read people and ask the right questions—to gauge their tastes, budget, and whether they may be celebrating a particular occasion—they can make the most appropriate recommendations. As they visit tables, Sommeliers pour the wine and encourage customers to experience it through smell and taste, describing the aromas and subtleties to enhance their enjoyment and understanding.

A Sommelier is a trained expert in everything about wine. In order to develop and grow wine lists, Sommeliers must sometimes taste up to 30 wines per day. They keep up with new vintages and trends, as well as travel to different regions when new wines are produced. They must understand the different wine regions, grapes, and everything about making wine. However, Sommeliers must know about food as well. To recommend the optimum food and wine pairings, they must see the complementary intersections between the two. Years can be spent acquiring and training their palates.

Additional duties may include:

- working with wine distributors
- presenting wines to customers
- educating customers as well as waitstaff about wines
- decanting wines when necessary
- keeping up on trends in the industry—both food and wine
- tracking the aging process of certain wines
- giving lectures to private groups or wine societies; hosting wine tastings or dinners
- teaching and mentoring new and aspiring Sommeliers
- stocking bars and ensuring all types of drinks are served properly in addition to wine
- attending professional wine tastings
- overseeing the dining room
- participating in wine competitions
- recommending popular or new wines
- developing curriculum and/or training programs for wineries, restaurants, or colleges/universities
- hosting wine tours abroad
- maintaining relationships with wineries
- negotiating prices

Sommeliers work in some of the most luxurious properties in the world. Only the finest restaurants, hotels, resorts, and bars employ Sommeliers, and their clientele are upscale and demanding. For this reason, Sommeliers must be passionate about both people and wine, and committed to matching the two. Good Sommeliers treat every customer as the biggest spender, providing each with the utmost customer service and enhancing their dining experience.

A plus for many Sommeliers is the opportunity to travel the world to increase their ever-expanding knowledge of wine. It is a dynamic industry that is always training. Work includes evenings, weekends, and holidays and can be very consuming. However, for most Sommeliers, their passion makes it worthwhile. It is not just a career, but a lifestyle.

Salaries

According to an article at www.culinaryed.com, a typical Sommelier can earn between $45,000 and $60,000 a year. The article states that for master Sommeliers, salaries can rise to between $80,000 and $160,000 a year, and even higher. Industry insiders believe that typical starting salaries are around $60,000 and can more than double with experience. Some Sommeliers earn extra income through consulting, lecturing, and writing about wine.

Culinaryed.com also offers the following base pay information by city for Sommeliers:

- Los Angeles, California: $25,700
- Chicago, Illinois: $24,500
- New York, New York: $39,400
- Miami, Florida: $24,600
- Washington, D.C.: $26,300
- Houston, Texas: $26,000
- Seattle, Washington: $30,600

Employment Prospects

Sommeliers that already work in the food and beverage industry often find employment through their experience and personal contacts. For example, a Sommelier who had previously been a bar manager may end up working as a Sommelier at the same restaurant or a similar one. Word of mouth through suppliers and others in the industry is a huge resource. Additionally, Sommeliers may find jobs through their vocational training program. They may also be hired by hotel and restaurant chains as consultants.

Advancement Prospects

Sommeliers can advance to become master Sommeliers, the highest distinction in the field. Advancement can also occur through moves to more prestigious restaurants with more focus on wine education and diversifying the list. Sommeliers may also teach, lecture, or consult about wines, earning extra income and recognition. Achieving expert status is important and top Sommeliers strive to be known and quoted as wine authorities. Furthermore, having responsibility for developing the wine list of their restaurant, accommodating the variety of tastes and budgets, is an honor beginning Sommeliers often aspire to. Others may want to open their own restaurants or have a financial stake in those restaurants where they work.

According to the Court of Master Sommeliers, there are 96 professionals who hold the title Master Sommelier in North America. Of those 81 are men and 15 are women. There are 167 professionals worldwide who have earned the title master Sommelier since the first Master Sommelier Diploma Exam.

Education and Training

There are two main paths that people follow to enter the Sommelier profession. Many new Sommeliers are people who have had careers or experience in the restaurant or hotel industry. It is common for managers, assistant managers, and bar and waitstaff to find through their experience that they want to learn more about wine. The others tend to come into the profession as an initial career path. Experts say that approximately one quarter of Sommeliers come to it as a first career path—those who thought, "I want to be a Sommelier when I grow up." Typically, these professionals have had extensive exposure through the wine and hospitality industry throughout their lives, such as family-owned restaurants or vineyards.

Insiders believe that the best training is to have prior experience in the restaurant and hotel industry. Many experts think the combination of work in the industry and vocational courses is the ideal mix to acquire a firm knowledge base.

About 50 percent of Sommeliers hold bachelor's degrees. Programs in hospitality, hotel, or restaurant management usually provide initial exposure and courses in wines, although vocational education will still be needed. Within professional wine training, programs vary in scope and credibility. While there are many classes throughout the country at culinary schools and college extension programs, only a few organizations offer certification.

The Court of Master Sommeliers (www.master sommeliers.org) conducts education and testing for restaurant wine professionals throughout the world. There are four levels of certification within the organization: introductory, certificate, advanced, and MS diploma (master). The master Sommelier diploma is the highest distinction a professional can attain in fine wine and beverage service. To achieve master Sommelier status, one must pass an extensive test that includes restaurant service, theoretical information, and tasting.

Additional organizations offering certification include the International Sommelier Guild (www.inter nationalsommelier.com) and the Culinary Institute of America's professional wine studies (www.ciaprochef. com/winestudies/index.html).

Experience, Skills, and Personality Traits

In addition to their extensive knowledge of wine and food, Sommeliers should have excellent interpersonal skills. At the core of their profession is service and hospitality, so they need to enjoy working with people and helping to teach, inform, and entertain them. Good communication skills enable Sommeliers to interact well with all their constituents ranging from chefs and vineyard owners to distributors and customers.

Knowledge of one or more foreign languages can be helpful for Sommeliers as well, particularly the languages of major wine growing regions, such as French or Italian. Sommeliers also use their management ability to oversee staff and make decisions that have financial impact.

Unions and Associations

Sommeliers may belong to professional associations including the Sommelier Society of America (www. sommeliersocietyofamerica.org), the International Sommeliers Association, or the Court of Master Sommeliers.

Tips for Entry

1. Experts agree that the best preparation to become a Sommelier is to spend considerable time working in a restaurant. Experience as a waiter/waitress or bartender provides an excellent introduction to the industry and you can have access to a Sommelier to learn from his or her background.

2. Learn as much as possible about wine by attending wine tastings. These can be found through local wine shops and wine associations.

3. Consider beginning by taking some culinary and wine courses through a community college or extension program. This can provide a good introductory base to determine if you'd like to go further.

4. Visit wineries to learn about the process of making and aging wines.

5. Read magazines such as *Decanter* (www.decanter. com) and *Food and Wine* (www.foodandwine. com).

6. Learn about what it takes to become a master Sommelier by visiting the Web site for the American chapter of the Court of Master Sommeliers at www.mastersommeliers.org.

7. The Sommelier industry has been male-dominated in the past, but women have recently made strides. See the book *Women of Wine* by Ann B. Matasar and the Web site of Andrea Immer Robinson, a renowned female Sommelier, at www. andreaimmer.com.

EXECUTIVE CHEF

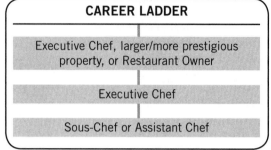

Position Description

Have you ever dined at a restaurant and been surprised by a dish on the menu, wondering how its unusual ingredients would blend together and being amazed when you discovered that they did, quite deliciously? Executive Chefs are masters at not only cooking and preparing food, but also at recipe creation, with knowledge and training that enable them to create memorable and tasty meals for their customers. In a hotel, casino, resort, or on a cruise ship, Executive Chefs have responsibility for all the restaurants on the property and all the individual chefs. It is their vision that comes to life in their restaurant or restaurants.

Executive Chefs oversee cooking for the multitude of kitchens that might be on site at a hotel or resort. Creativity helps them come up with new and innovative menu items. They may create their own recipes and adapt existing recipes to fit their style. Also, they experiment with different tastes and try to meet the needs of their customers as well. Furthermore, they train cooks and sous-chefs (who are the second in command) on how to prepare these dishes. They use their aesthetic sense for pleasing presentation as well.

Many Executive Chefs have specialties in certain types of cuisine based on their background and training. They may be experts in Cajun cuisine, northern Italian cooking, southern barbeque, or pan-Asian fusion. Some Executive Chefs become known for their specialties and receive recognition for their restaurants or dishes. Yet Executive Chefs should be able to prepare a variety of cuisines as well.

Management and supervision is another big part of the job at the Executive Chef level. Many Executive Chefs delegate the cooking to cooks and individual restaurant chefs as they oversee the process for all restaurants. At a large property, this may include dining establishments ranging from coffee shops to five-star gourmet restaurants. They are responsible for hiring and staffing, and also training, which is an ongoing process as new menu items and specials are added constantly. Executive Chefs ensure that items are prepared uniformly, consistently, and always meet the same high standards.

Executive Chefs are also responsible for ordering food and kitchen supplies. They are instrumental in affecting profits, so they must work within a budget to order the appropriate amounts of food as to not have a surplus. In order to estimate quantities, Executive Chefs must have a good idea about their customers and what dishes will be the most popular. They understand culinary trends and the market-driven aspect of the business. Using this knowledge, they also may set prices for menu items.

When chefs first begin professional work, they often start off with cold items such as salads or appetizers and work their way up. Eventually, they will be ready for entrée preparation, the main part of the meal. The role of Executive Chef is equal parts administrative and culinary, as they typically delegate much of the actual cooking.

Additional responsibilities include:

- meeting health regulations and quality control standards
- taking inventory
- developing work schedules for kitchen staff
- preparing budgets
- tasting food
- speaking with customers
- working with food and beverage managers and other staff
- instilling safety and sanitation habits in kitchen employees
- negotiating prices for purchasing
- standardizing recipes and portion sizes
- participating in culinary competitions

In the hospitality industry, Executive Chefs work at restaurants, hotels, resorts, and cruise ships. Depending on their work setting, they may travel for additional training. Hours are long and nontraditional, with weekends and evenings as heaviest work times to reflect dinner as the signature meal at most establishments.

The work can also be physically grueling, as Executive Chefs are on their feet most of the time. They lift heavy pots, deal with extreme temperatures, and use technical skills such as slicing and dicing where there is room for injury. However, for most Executive Chefs, their work is their passion. They are spending their days doing what they love.

Salaries

Salaries for Executive Chefs can vary greatly depending on their work setting, geographical location, and experience. According to annual average base salary information on Culinaryed.com, an Executive Chef earns $85,900 in Los Angeles; in New York, $90,000; and in Houston, $78,900.

According to the Bureau of Labor Statistics (BLS), median annual wage-and-salary earnings of chefs and head cooks were $37,160 as of May 2007. The middle 50 percent earned between $28,020 and $49,790. The lowest 10 percent earned less than $21,560, and the highest 10 percent earned more than $64,550.

For the lucky few Executive Chefs that establish strong reputations and become "celebrity chefs" or work in the nation's top restaurants and resort properties, salaries can be considerably higher.

Employment Prospects

Employment prospects are fair to good for Executive Chefs, with tough competition for the top jobs. With more restaurants and hotels opening and competing for customers, the need to hire quality chefs will grow. The BLS states that the largest market for growth will be in family-oriented establishments rather than in fine dining. Many Executive Chefs find opportunities through professional associations, their culinary institutes or training programs, networking/word of mouth, and job listing Web sites.

Advancement Prospects

Executive Chefs enjoy good advancement prospects. Some may advance to work at larger and more prestigious properties where they might oversee a greater number of different restaurants, chefs, and kitchen staff. Many Executive Chefs eventually aspire to own their own restaurants. That is a way to make their mark based on their specialty cooking and also have a larger stake in the profits.

Other Executive Chefs branch out into other areas including catering or food writing. The most successful Executive Chefs can become household names and write cookbooks or host programs on channels such as the Food Network.

Education and Training

Most Executive Chefs have degrees or certificates from culinary schools, institutes, or academies. While experience provides great training, many employers require degrees, increasingly from accredited programs. For a list of programs accredited by the American Culinary Federation, see Appendix I of this book on page X. Executive Chefs may also complete apprenticeship programs. The American Culinary Federation also offers certification in specialty areas such as executive chef or master chef.

One of the best-known schools is the Culinary Institute of America, located in Hyde Park, New York. It offers bachelor's degrees, associate's degrees, and certificates, with courses held in New York and California. See its Web site at www.ciachef.edu for more information.

Experience, Skills, and Personality Traits

Executive Chefs come to their positions with several years of experience in the industry assisting other chefs before they are given the leadership of a kitchen on their own. For this reason, Executive Chefs should have excellent managerial and supervisory skills to lead other chefs and kitchen staff. They must be able to motivate and inspire them, as well as train and teach.

Additionally, Executive Chefs need good attention to detail and strong organizational skills. They must be able to multitask and stay calm under pressure as they oversee many different things at once. Good communication skills help them work with staff as well as customers, talking with them about likes and dislikes.

Most importantly, Executive Chefs should be expert in the technical skills of their job. They should love food and being around food, with good creative and aesthetic sense. Most also have knowledge of wines. Foreign language skills may be useful for international work or recipes as well as work with international clientele.

Unions and Associations

The American Culinary Federation is one of the main professional associations for Executive Chefs, credited with changing the designation of chef from a service occupation to a professional one. Additionally, Executive Chefs may belong to the International Association of Culinary Professionals and the National Restaurant Association.

Tips for Entry

1. Insiders say that the best tip for those considering the field is to experience working in a kitchen before attending culinary school. Enjoying cooking at home as a hobby is different from the profession of being a chef. They advise that it is important to have that hands-on experience before making a commitment.

2. Explore the Web site of the American Culinary Federation at www.acfchefs.org. It provides information about accredited schools, apprenticeship programs, certification, jobs, and more.

3. Many books have been written about the career path to becoming a professional chef. Try *Becoming a Chef* by Andrew Dornenburg and Karen Page or *The Complete Idiot's Guide to Success as a Chef* by Leslie Bilderback.

4. Take a culinary course at a local community college to experience cooking in a more professional capacity.

5. Pay attention to menus as you go to restaurants, taking note of specials and any notes or interactions with the Executive Chefs.

SOUS-CHEF

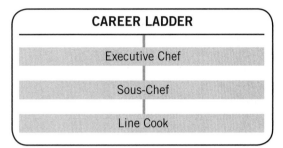

Position Description

While the executive chef has the vision, it is usually the Sous-Chef that turns that vision into a reality. Sous-Chefs are the right-hand people to the executive chef, in the kitchen every day, slicing, dicing, and sautéing. Under the direction of the executive chef, they prepare menu items, create specials, watch over the kitchen staff, and in general perform much of the hands-on work that occurs within a kitchen.

Sous-Chefs may be able to use their creativity on a limited basis. They must prepare dishes exactly the way the executive chef specifies. Sometimes, they may be able to experiment with recipes and their own style, but usually must get permission from the executive chef. In this way, they are still paying their dues, learning from the executive chef before having the responsibility for a kitchen all to themselves. Many have the flexibility to plan menus and create specials.

Once they have mastered a dish, they may be responsible for training line cooks on preparation, ensuring consistency throughout the restaurant. Sous-Chefs may also manage kitchen staff, serving as a direct contact while the executive chef may be overseeing several restaurants. For this reason, although the position is a second-in-command, it typically involves a high level of management and leadership skill. In the absence of the executive chef, the Sous-Chef steps in as the leader. The Sous-Chef also often has direct responsibility for staff supervision, including training, managing, and scheduling.

Furthermore, the Sous-Chef often serves as an expediter, the liaison between the customers in the dining room and the line cooks. This job requires an excellent grasp of time management as scheduling must be coordinated so that all diners at a table receive their food at the same time. The Sous-Chef also works with the waitstaff, ensuring they get the food in the time they need to serve it together.

Sous-Chefs may also have some role in ordering food and kitchen supplies. They might need to estimate quantities and determine needs for food production or supplies. Also, they make sure that all jobs are being done properly and safety standards are being upheld. They may review and correct the presentation of food before it goes out to the customers.

When chefs first begin professional work, they often start off with cold items such as salads or appetizers and work their way up. Eventually, they will be ready for entrée preparation, the main part of the meal. The Sous-Chef has worked up to that level where he or she can cook or oversee the highlighted items for each restaurant.

Additional responsibilities include:

- utilizing food surplus and leftovers
- overseeing banquet operations
- maintaining health and hygiene regulations and quality control standards
- taking inventory and estimating quantities
- monitoring payroll costs and overtime
- developing work schedules for kitchen staff
- tasting food
- speaking with customers
- working with food and beverage managers and other staff
- instilling safety and sanitation habits in kitchen employees
- negotiating prices for purchasing
- standardizing recipes and portion sizes

Sous-Chefs may work at restaurants, hotels, resorts, and on cruise ships. Depending on their work environment and restaurant type, they may travel for additional training. Weekends, evenings, and holidays are typical work hours, as dinner is the signature meal at most establishments.

The work is often physically demanding, as Sous-Chefs are on their feet most of the time. They lift heavy pots, deal with extreme temperatures, and use technical skills such as slicing and dicing where there is room for injury. Yet, most Sous-Chefs have a great passion for their work. Most aspire to run their own kitchen one day, while some enjoy carrying out direction.

Salaries

Salaries for Sous-Chefs can vary greatly depending on their work setting, geographical location, and experience. According to annual average base salary information on Culinaryed.com, typical earnings are as follows in this range of cities: Los Angeles, $44,700; Chicago, $42,700; New York, $46,800; Miami, $39,600; Washington, D.C., $42,000; Houston, $41,100; and Seattle, $43,600.

According to the Bureau of Labor Statistics (BLS), median annual wage-and-salary earnings of chefs and head cooks were $37,160 as of May 2007. The middle 50 percent earned between $28,020 and $49,790. The lowest 10 percent earned less than $21,560, and the highest 10 percent earned more than $64,550. Sous-Chefs at very prestigious or high-end restaurants and resorts can earn considerably more.

Employment Prospects

Employment prospects are good for Sous-Chefs, although there is tough competition for top jobs. With more restaurants and hotels opening and competing for customers, the need to hire quality Sous-Chefs will grow. The BLS states that the largest market for growth will be in family-oriented establishments, rather than in fine dining. Many Sous-Chefs find opportunities through professional associations, their culinary institutes or training programs, networking/word of mouth, and job listing Web sites.

Advancement Prospects

Sous-Chefs enjoy good advancement prospects. Many aspire to become executive chefs where they will have ultimate decision-making power and might oversee a number of different restaurants, chefs, and kitchen staff. Others ultimately aspire to own their own restaurants. That is a way to make their mark based on their specialty cooking and also to have a larger stake in the profits.

Other Sous-Chefs branch out into other areas including catering or food writing. They also might move to Sous-Chef positions at larger or more prestigious establishments for more money and responsibility.

Education and Training

Most Sous-Chefs have degrees or certificates from culinary schools, institutes, or academies. While experience provides great training, many employers require degrees, increasingly from accredited programs. For a list of programs accredited by the American Culinary Federation, see Appendix I of this book on page X. Sous-Chefs may also complete apprenticeship programs. The American Culinary Federation also offers certification in specialty areas such as executive chef or master chef.

One of the best known schools is the Culinary Institute of America, located in Hyde Park, New York. It offers bachelor's degrees, associate's degrees, and certificates, with courses held in New York and California. See its Web site at www.ciachef.edu for more information.

Experience, Skills, and Personality Traits

Sous-Chefs come to their positions with several years of experience in the industry working as line cooks and/or assisting other chefs. Since they frequently supervise kitchen staff, Sous-Chefs should have strong managerial and supervisory skills. They need to motivate and train workers, thus making customers happy and impacting profits. Additionally, they must be able to take direction well and carry out the vision of the executive chef without resistance or complaint.

Additionally, Sous-Chefs need good attention to detail and strong organizational skills. They must be able to multitask and stay calm under pressure as they oversee many different things at once. Good communication skills help them work with a variety of people ranging from supervisors and staff to customers.

Most importantly, Sous-Chefs should be expert in the technical skills of their job. They should love food and being around food, with good creative and aesthetic sense. Knowledge of wines is also important. Foreign language skills may be useful for international work or recipes as well as work with international clientele.

Unions and Associations

Sous-Chefs may belong to the American Culinary Federation, credited with changing the designation of chef from a service occupation to a professional one. Additionally, they may belong to the International Association of Culinary Professionals and the National Restaurant Association.

Tips for Entry

1. Experiment with different types of cooking to find your niche. For example, do you love preparing Italian dishes or do you have skill with seafood?

2. Before attending culinary school, gain experience working at a restaurant. Try a position as part of the waitstaff and observe the inner workings of the kitchen.

3. Read books about becoming a chef such as *The Professional Chef* by the Culinary Institute of America and *My Daughter Wants to Be a Chef! Everything You Should Know about Becoming a Chef!* by Martin Laprise.

4. Take a culinary course before committing to an entire program. You can focus on a type of cuisine or basic skills. Or consider a wine course.

PASTRY CHEF

CAREER PROFILE

Duties: Preparing, creating, and decorating desserts; overseeing the dessert menu

Alternate Title(s): Chef de Pâtisserie; Baker; Patissier

Salary Range: $30,000 to $70,000 and up

Employment Prospects: Fair to good

Advancement Prospects: Good

Best Geographical Location(s): All, with the greatest opportunities in large cities and heavy tourist regions with many restaurants, resorts, and hotels

Prerequisites:

Education and Training—Degree or certificate from culinary school or institute in baking or pastry arts required for most positions

Experience—Apprenticeship or prior work as a Pastry Chef or baker

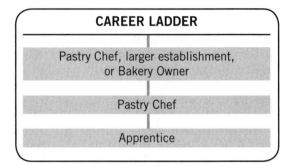

CAREER LADDER

Pastry Chef, larger establishment, or Bakery Owner

Pastry Chef

Apprentice

Special Skills and Personality Traits—Excellent culinary and baking skill with special focus on desserts and pastries; good supervisory skills; ability to work well under pressure and multitask; ability to pay close attention to detail and creativity

Position Description

What could be sweeter than spending your day surrounded by sugar? Pastry Chefs are responsible for what many people consider to be the most enjoyable part of the meal: dessert. They bake, prepare, create, and develop desserts including cakes, candies, pastries, ice cream, pies, cookies, custards, soufflés, and tarts, as well as their frostings, fillings, and decorative touches.

Some Pastry Chefs are also bakers, responsible for bread, muffins, biscuits, scones, strudels, and more. For these Pastry Chefs, their day may begin between 2:00 and 4:00 A.M., as they arrive at their restaurants or bakeries before regular business begins. At this peaceful hour, they begin their work, baking enough goods to last each day. Typically, items must be baked fresh each day to ensure that they will not be stale.

Pastry Chefs are responsible for the desserts at their restaurants. The pastry kitchen is usually slightly separate from the regular kitchen and the Pastry Chef presides, supervising other chefs or apprentices. The Pastry Chef determines the recipes to use, experimenting and developing creations and adapting existing recipes to match his or her style. Creativity comes into play as he or she devises desserts that are unique, delicious, and will become favorites among customers.

Presentation is a huge part of dessert preparation. More so than in any other type of cooking, Pastry Chefs need an artistic sense to decorate their dessert plates in a way that is pleasing and special. This might include drizzling chocolate or raspberry sauce in a pattern on the dish, creating flowers made of sugar and real berries, and other intricate and elaborate designs.

Many Pastry Chefs have specialties in certain types of desserts based on their background and training. Some may be experts in wedding cake decoration, cupcakes, homemade ice cream, flan custards, or bananas flambé. They may become known for their specialties; however, most Pastry Chefs are skilled at preparing a wide range of desserts as well, both domestic and international in origin.

Furthermore, Pastry Chefs often must oversee and supervise apprentices and other dessert cooks. They may prepare items in advance and leave some cooking to others. They must ensure that items are prepared uniformly, consistently, and always meet the same high standards. Pastry Chefs may hire and train others to do this work. They also work with chefs and sommeliers to develop desserts that will complement the food and wine on the menu.

Also, Pastry Chefs are responsible for ordering food and kitchen supplies related to dessert. They may develop budgets for their department and estimate quantities as well as the popularity of different menu items. Pastry Chefs may work with suppliers including growers to get the best prices on seasonal items such as fruit.

Additional duties may include:

- developing menu specials
- creating dessert themes for holidays and other special events
- organizing the kitchen
- meeting health regulations and quality control standards
- taking inventory and estimating quantities
- developing work schedules for kitchen staff
- tasting food
- speaking with customers
- negotiating prices for purchasing
- standardizing recipes and portion sizes
- participating in baking competitions

Pastry Chefs may work at restaurants, bakeries, hotels, resorts, and on cruise ships. Depending on their work environment and restaurant type, they may travel for additional training. Workweeks can be 55 hours or more and can include very nontraditional schedules. For bakers, the day starts in the wee hours of the morning, and Pastry Chefs preparing desserts for the end of the dinner rush can work late into the night. Weekend and holiday work is usually required as well.

Additionally, the work can be physically demanding, as Pastry Chefs are on their feet most of the time. They lift heavy pots, knead dough, deal with extreme temperatures, and use knives and other delicate instruments where there is room for injury. Yet most Pastry Chefs love their work and feel it is the fulfillment of a lifelong dream.

Salaries

Pastry Chefs can have vastly different earnings depending on their work setting, geographical location, and experience. According to annual average base salary information on Culinaryed.com, typical earnings for Pastry Chefs are as follows in this range of cities: Los Angeles, $47,200; Chicago, $45,100; New York, $49,300; Miami, $41,800; Washington, D.C., $44,300; Houston, $43,300; and Seattle, $46,000. However, Pastry Chefs at very prestigious or high-end restaurants and resorts who have developed a strong reputation can earn considerably more.

General chef salary information also comes from the Bureau of Labor Statistics (BLS). The BLS states median annual wage-and-salary earnings of chefs and head cooks were $37,160 as of May 2007. The middle 50 percent earned between $28,020 and $49,790. The lowest 10 percent earned less than $21,560, and the highest 10 percent earned more than $64,550.

Employment Prospects

Employment prospects are fair to good for Pastry Chefs. As more restaurants open and compete for customers, as do coffee houses that serve pastries, the need for quality Pastry Chefs will grow. Competition remains tough for top jobs, however, and the best opportunities will be for Pastry Chefs with strong education and training.

Advancement Prospects

Pastry Chefs have good opportunity for advancement. They can move to become Pastry Chefs at larger or more prestigious establishments where they might enjoy greater creativity, greater impact on menu, and larger salaries. Others might aspire to ultimately own their own bakeries, restaurants, or specialty shops.

Additional opportunities for advancement can include branching into catering where they provide desserts for parties and special events to individual or corporate clients. Pastry Chefs may also write articles or cookbooks about pastries and baking.

Education and Training

To succeed in the current competitive market, most Pastry Chefs have degrees or certificates from culinary schools, institutes, or academies. The three most typical paths are the baking and pastry certificate, the associate's degree in culinary arts, or the bachelor's degree in culinary arts. A one-year baking and pastry certificate prepares candidates for basic entry-level positions and the two-year associate's degree and four-year bachelor's degree provide additional education and training. All courses of study combine academic classes with hands-on experience. Topics covered include handling ingredients such as eggs, cream, and butter, keeping a germ-free kitchen, proper cooking and handling temperatures, and the physiology of taste, as well as the fundamentals of baking and correct methods and tool usage.

The French Culinary Institute in New York City is very well-known for its pastry programs. See its Web site for more information at www.frenchculinary.com.

Experience, Skills, and Personality Traits

Pastry Chefs gain experience through prior work in restaurants and bakeries and apprenticeships during their education. Here, they become experts in the necessary skills of the job and gain exposure to the wide variety of ingredients and tools used in pastry and dessert preparation. Creativity and a good artistic eye are essential. Desserts are visual and aesthetics can go hand in hand with taste.

Furthermore, Pastry Chefs should have excellent attention to detail. Preparing desserts can be a painstaking process involving intricate decorations and details. Pastry Chefs should be well organized to oversee the dessert process and need good managerial skills to supervise workers. They must be able to multitask and stay calm under pressure as they oversee many different things at once.

Good communication skills help Pastry Chefs work with a variety of people ranging from supervisors and staff to customers. Knowledge of food and wines is also important. Foreign language skills may be useful for international work or recipes as well as work with international clientele.

Unions and Associations

Pastry Chefs may belong to professional associations including the American Culinary Federation, the International Association of Culinary Professionals, and the National Restaurant Association.

Tips for Entry

1. Because of the artistic nature of dessert preparation, develop a portfolio of your best work by taking photographs of your signature desserts. Pay careful attention to the presentation and be sure to highlight a range of your abilities.

2. Consider a class in cake decorating to expose you to the dessert field.

3. Try a job in a bakery where you can learn techniques from master bakers.

4. Explore programs in pastry arts and baking. Allculinaryschools.com highlights programs nationwide at www.allculinaryschools.com/featured/bparts.

5. Read books such as *Dessert University: More than 300 Spectacular Recipes and Essential Lessons from White House Pastry Chef Roland Mesnier* by Roland Mesnier, Lauren Chattman, John Burgoyne, and Maren Caruso.

6. There are many niche areas for Pastry Chefs. What type of baked goods or desserts interest you the most? Once you focus on a specialty, gain more experience and exposure to that area.

7. Find a mentor. The best way to learn about the work of a Pastry Chef is by following and observing one at work.

RESTAURANT OWNER

Duties: Owns and operates a restaurant; may own a restaurant as a franchise

Alternate Title(s): Restaurateur

Salary Range: $0 to $100,000 and up

Employment Prospects: Fair

Advancement Prospects: Fair

Best Geographical Location(s): All, with the greatest opportunities in large cities and heavy tourist regions with many restaurants, resorts, and hotels

Prerequisites:

Education and Training—No specific requirements, but courses in business and restaurant management helpful

Experience—Prior food service industry experience very helpful

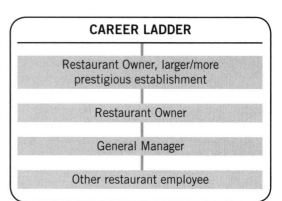

CAREER LADDER

Restaurant Owner, larger/more prestigious establishment

Restaurant Owner

General Manager

Other restaurant employee

Special Skills and Personality Traits—Passion for food and wine; excellent interpersonal skills; good business, accounting, and bookkeeping skills; ability to handle stress and risk

Position Description

Have you ever dreamed of owning your own restaurant? Perhaps you have walked by an empty eatery with a "For Sale" sign in the window, stumbled upon the perfect concept and location, or considered opening a franchise. Becoming a Restaurant Owner can be fulfilling and exciting, but it involves much hard work and careful planning.

Restaurant Owners are responsible for everything in their restaurant, from hiring staff and stocking the bar to negotiating relationships with suppliers and choosing the decor. However, successful Restaurant Owners are also good delegators and they staff their establishment with trusted individuals who can handle these responsibilities. Yet the ultimate bottom line falls to them. Especially at the opening of a restaurant, the Restaurant Owner has to handle all of these duties.

Choosing a location, name, and theme are of utmost importance when one makes the decision to open a restaurant. Restaurant Owners conduct market research to determine what location might be best, the different client bases in each area, and which types of establishments have succeeded and failed.

Furthermore, they need to make the decision as to whether they will take over an existing restaurant, buy a franchise, or open an independent restaurant, and there are advantages and disadvantages to each. Buying a franchise is safe in the sense that you have name

recognition, an instant client base, support from the corporate office, and can usually get better prices on food and supplies. However, Restaurant Owners with franchises have less freedom, having no say in the decor or menu. They must adhere to many rules and regulations set forth by the corporate office. Additionally, the start-up costs are very high.

When Restaurant Owners look to buy a restaurant that is going out of business, it is important for them to determine why this restaurant failed. Was it the location, menu, management, or financial problems? Buying a space that was already a restaurant is easier in the sense that the layout is already set, but can be harder if you are inheriting someone else's problems.

Starting up a new restaurant is the most exciting but most risky avenue for a Restaurant Owner. Once a location, name, and theme/cuisine have been chosen, the Restaurant Owner needs to get funding either from an individual investor or a bank. When a loan has been received, it might seem like the culmination of hard work, but that is really when the hard work begins.

Restaurant Owners report working 80 hours per week or more, especially in the first two years of owning a restaurant. Statistics show that three quarters of all new restaurants fail by the end of the first year, so that beginning time period is crucial to eventual success. Restaurant Owners must hire staff, including a general manager, chef, waitstaff, bartenders, bookkeepers, and many others. They oversee the design and decor, as well as choosing a menu. Additionally, they develop relationships with wholesalers and distributors to negotiate fair prices on food and supplies.

Once they get going, a typical day for a Restaurant Owner is long and tiring. In the morning, Restaurant Owners come in before the restaurant opens to review the previous day's receipts and notes, checking the accounting records and noting any customer complaints. They speak with staff in order to make sure everything is running smoothly. They are on hand during all restaurant hours at the beginning and they spend time speaking to customers.

The customer contact is a part of the job that most Restaurant Owners truly enjoy. Many feel that their restaurant is their baby and they are very proud of their efforts. Working as a host gives them the opportunity to gain feedback and get to know clients. Establishing name and face recognition with customers helps make them want to come back. Furthermore, learning more about customers and their preferences—tables, food orders—will make them have a more personal dining experience and encourage them to become regular patrons as well as tell others about the excellent service.

Additional duties may include:

- seeking additional financing
- consulting with chefs on menus
- resolving customer complaints
- developing a marketing and advertising plan
- soliciting new business
- providing interviews with local media
- getting to know customers and their preferences
- reading food and wine publications, as well as restaurant reviews
- procuring a liquor license

At different times, Restaurant Owners may complete tasks that other staff members also do, such as waiting tables, taking reservations, placing orders, cooking, balancing the books, seating guests, working with suppliers and more. Since ultimately it is their place, they have a vested interest in every aspect. As many Restaurant Owners will tell you, it is not just a job, but a way of life. For those with a passion for the business, all their hard work is worth it.

Salaries
Salaries can very extensively for Restaurant Owners. Typically, it takes almost two years before a restaurant is actually showing a profit and loans are paid off, so earnings can be hard to gauge. Certainly, people make a living as Restaurant Owners, but that can be dependent on luck and timing. Salaries very tremendously based on type of restaurant, price point, expenses, location, and other factors. Money earned in sales needs to be spent toward staff salaries, rent, utilities, food, supplies, and more. However, with a highly successful restaurant, earnings can be quite substantial, $100,000 per year and up.

It is important to remember that with any business, earnings can vary year to year and income is not stable. Restaurant Owners must also take into account the lack of built-in benefits: health insurance, 401(k) plans, and others, and how they will be handled for themselves and their staff.

Employment Prospects
Employment prospects are fair for Restaurant Owners. Although anyone with enough capital can open a restaurant, success is a very risky venture. Many restaurants fail before they start turning a profit. Finding the right location, the decision about franchising, the timing, and getting the financing is difficult. The best prospects are for those with experience in the restaurant industry who have the knowledge to take the right steps. Beginning as waitstaff, bartenders, or other positions are a good way to gain exposure. Some chefs also become Restaurant Owners as well.

Advancement Prospects
Restaurant Owners can advance through the success of their establishment. They may hire larger staffs, expand their menu, or franchise their brand. A few very successful Restaurant Owners, especially those who are also chefs, may establish their brand into a household name through cookbooks, merchandise, and even television appearances. Other Restaurant Owners may serve as consultants to others trying to break into the field.

Education and Training
People become Restaurant Owners from all types of backgrounds and prior careers, so there is no specific education required. Restaurant Owners range from high school graduates to professionals with advanced degrees. Courses in business, accounting, bookkeeping, entrepreneurship, food service, and restaurant management can be very helpful. In fact, those in the field recommend a restaurant management course as a way to learn all the steps needed in planning to open a restaurant from business plan to marketing. Additionally, prior training through restaurant work is valuable.

Experience, Skills, and Personality Traits

Restaurant Owners should have a passion for food and wine that propels them to undertake this labor of love. Experience in the restaurant industry can be extremely helpful. Skills in management and finance will help Restaurant Owners make sound economic and staffing decisions.

Strong interpersonal and communication skills are also required. As a host, the Restaurant Owner must enjoy interfacing with the public and genuinely want to make people happy. Working with people is constant whether they are staff, customers, backers, or the media. High energy is needed for the long hours, as is the ability to deal with stress and handle risk.

Unions and Associations

Restaurant Owners can get valuable tips and advice about opening a restaurant from the National Restaurant Association at www.restaurant.org/business/start.cfm.

Tips for Entry

1. There are many books written with prospective Restaurant Owners in mind. Explore *Running a Restaurant for Dummies* by Michael and Heather Dismore and Andrew Dismore, as well as *The Restaurant Dream* by Lee Simon.

2. Research the legal aspects of running a restaurant at www.legalzoom.com/legal-articles/article14110.html.

3. The following article offers tips for Restaurant Owners about how to expand their customer base; it can be a valuable learning tool: www.bizcovering.com/Business/10-Ways-for-Restaurant-Owners-to-Expand-Their-Customer-Base.192199

4. The Institute of Culinary Education in New York City offers courses on how to open a restaurant. For more information see www.iceculinary.com/professional/restaurants.shtml.

5. This site shares a restaurant business plan, a critical part of the planning process: virtualrestaurant.com/Merchant2/merchant.mvc?Store_Code=VR&Screen=PLAN.

6. Prior restaurant work is essential for success as a Restaurant Owner. Holding different positions, ranging from waitstaff to manager, provides an inside understanding of how restaurants operate.

RESTAURANT MANAGER

CAREER PROFILE

Duties: Oversees the entire operation of a restaurant including kitchen, dining room, and administrative functions

Alternate Title(s): General Manager

Salary Range: $30,000 to $80,000 and up

Employment Prospects: Good

Advancement Prospects: Good

Best Geographical Location(s): All, with the greatest opportunities in large cities and heavy tourist regions with many restaurants, resorts, and hotels

Prerequisites:

Education and Training—Bachelor's degree (food service or restaurant management helpful) may be required at high-end restaurants; others work their way up within the field and/or attend training programs and seminars in restaurant management

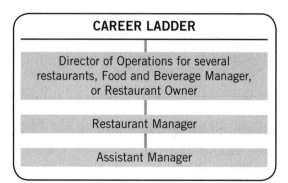

CAREER LADDER

Director of Operations for several restaurants, Food and Beverage Manager, or Restaurant Owner

Restaurant Manager

Assistant Manager

Experience—Prior restaurant experience including as waitstaff, bartender, and assistant manager

Special Skills and Personality Traits—Good leadership and supervisory skills; ability to multitask; strong communication, business, and financial skills; excellent communication; love for food and wine

Position Description

According to the National Restaurant Association, the restaurant industry employs an estimated 13.1 million people, making it the nation's second-largest employer after government. To make sure they are providing quality service to satisfied customers, each restaurant has a Restaurant Manager. Restaurant Managers are responsible for overall restaurant operations from the decor, to the service, to the food. They work with executive chefs to plan menus and oversee the kitchen as well as with assistant managers who supervise the waitstaff and dining room. The ultimate responsibility for the flow and profitability of the restaurant is often in their hands.

At any given time, many things go on at a restaurant and the Restaurant Manager must have his or her hand in all of them. Each day, there are menus to plan, schedules to coordinate, supplies to order, e-mails to answer, and complaints to address. Restaurant Managers handle or delegate these tasks, making sure that everything gets done in a timely fashion. Additionally, there are always the unpredictable daily issues that come up—staff calling in sick, construction in the parking lot, heat not working in the winter—that will cause the Restaurant Manager to spend much time troubleshooting.

The Restaurant Manager is responsible for overseeing food and beverage purchases, ensuring the budget

is being used to the best advantage. They work closely with the executive chef to plan menus, create specials, price menu items, and analyze supply and demand of different items, identifying and estimating food quantities. Restaurant Managers also order supplies in addition to food, including furniture and other items that contribute to the restaurant's overall look and aura.

Furthermore, they handle accounting tasks such as nightly bank deposits, submitting invoices, and budgeting sales projections. A good business sense is necessary to increase profitability and meet costs. Each day, Restaurant Managers may be responsible for totaling receipts and analyzing sales. Weekly, they may look at the labor cost numbers to see if they are profitable and monthly; they develop profit and loss (P&L) statements for the restaurant owner to determine financial success.

Restaurant Managers also supervise staff members, being responsible for personnel issues such as training, hiring, firing, and scheduling. In this customer service–oriented field, an effective, people-centered staff is critical to running a successful restaurant. Restaurant Managers establish and enforce policies and procedures. They ensure all shifts are covered, food is served efficiently, and the kitchen and outer areas are clean, pitching in themselves to complete any tasks necessary. Restaurant Managers should enjoy supervising others in order to motivate their staff and help them develop.

Restaurant Managers must have exceptional people skills as well. Whenever a customer demands, "I want to speak to a manager," regarding a problem with his or her meal or service, it is the Restaurant Manager who must intervene, making a judgment call about how to best handle the problem. Customer satisfaction is ultimately the most important factor in restaurant profitability—if people aren't coming back, it doesn't matter how good the food and service are. Restaurant Managers must be strong decision makers who are able to handle complaints and problems without getting flustered.

Additional duties may include:

- ensuring compliance with health and safety regulations
- scheduling deliveries and checking the quality of incoming deliveries
- directing cleaning of kitchen and dining areas
- maintaining budget and employee records
- preparing payroll and paying bills
- walking the restaurant floor and speaking with customers
- using computer software to monitor inventory and track schedules and payroll
- meeting with sales representatives and other vendors
- arranging for maintenance and repair of equipment and facility
- opening/closing the restaurant

Marketing and promotions may also be the responsibility of some Restaurant Managers, as they seek opportunities to put their restaurant in the spotlight and increase sales. They may work with the media, write press releases or ads, develop promotions, provide interviews, and interact with the public.

Restaurant Managers often work long hours, including evenings and weekends, to reflect the restaurant's hours of operations. A passion for food, wine, and the hospitality industry is instrumental in job satisfaction.

Salaries

Salaries for Restaurant Managers vary greatly depending on the restaurant, location, and cuisine. According to annual average base salary information on Culinaryed.com, typical earnings are as follows in this range of cities: Los Angeles, $53,700; Chicago, $51,300; New York, $56,200; Miami, $47,500; Washington, D.C., $50,400; Houston, $49,300; and Seattle, $52,300.

According to the Bureau of Labor Statistics (BLS), median annual wage-and-salary earnings of food service managers were $44,570 as of May 2007. The middle 50 percent earned between $35,270 and $57,370. The lowest 10 percent earned less than $28,240, and the highest 10 percent earned more than $74,060. Restaurant Managers at very prestigious or high-end restaurants and resorts can earn considerably more.

Employment Prospects

Employment prospects are good overall for Restaurant Managers. The best opportunities are often in full-service restaurants and for those who have degrees in hospitality or food service management. Most Restaurant Managers achieve their positions through working their way up within the food service industry. Opportunities are also good for those who are geographically flexible. The most competition is for positions at high-end restaurants.

Advancement Prospects

Advancement prospects are also good for Restaurant Managers with the right combination of education and experience. They may move to more prestigious restaurants where they enjoy higher salaries and supervise larger staffs. Also, Restaurant Managers at hotels or resorts might advance to become directors of food and beverage, where they oversee several restaurants and other managers. Furthermore, Restaurant Managers may aspire to own their own restaurants where they have final decision making power and control of profits.

Education and Training

Those in the industry agree that the best training and preparation for a career in restaurant management is prior experience in food service. Restaurant Managers have worked as bartenders, waitstaff, assistant managers, cooks, maître d's, and other positions leading them to this point.

In addition to prior experience, a high school diploma is necessary. For positions in high-end, prestigious restaurants, a college degree can be very helpful and even required in some cases. Fields such as food service, restaurant, or hospitality management are valuable, in addition to business courses. Degree programs in restaurant management include courses in hygiene, nutrition, the business aspect of the hospitality industry, food and wine, and more.

Culinary institutes as well as vocational and technical schools often provide training programs in restaurant management; one such is the International Culinary School at the Art Institutes: www.artinstitutes.edu/AreasOfStudy/TheInternationalCulinarySchool.aspx?ID=8.

Experience, Skills, and Personality Traits

To be a successful Restaurant Manager, one needs a combination of strong business skills and a passion for the hospitality industry. An appreciation for food and wine and the desire to work surrounded by it, as well as the acumen and knowledge of accounting, payroll, and strategic planning needed to run a profitable business, are essential. Restaurant Managers should also be excellent decision makers, able to problem-solve and act quickly whether it involves a customer complaint, a staff absence, or an aesthetical judgment about the restaurant atmosphere.

Prior industry experience has taught Restaurant Managers what it takes to run successful restaurant operations. They need patience and the ability to multi-task, and must pay attention to details such as the color coordination of flowers and tablecloths. Strong communications and interpersonal skills enable them to work effectively with owners, staff, and customers alike.

Unions and Associations

The main professional association for Restaurant Managers is the National Restaurant Association, the leading business association for the restaurant industry (www.restaurant.org).

Tips for Entry

1. Voluntary certification as a Certified Restaurant Manager, for those working within hotels or resorts, is available through the American Hotel and Lodging Association. For more information, see www.ei-ahla.org/content.aspx?id=112.

2. Career and educational information in restaurant management, including certification as a food service management professional (FMP) can be found on the Web site of the National Restaurant Association Educational Foundation at www.nraef.org.

3. In order to be an effective restaurant manager, one should be knowledgeable about food and wine. Take culinary and wine courses to advance your skills.

4. Work in the food service industry. To manage others, you garner more expertise and respect from having done those jobs before. The more diverse your restaurant experience the better, so try out different settings ranging from chain family establishments to more high-end options.

5. Conduct an informational interview with a Restaurant Manager to find out more about his or her job and career path.

WAITSTAFF

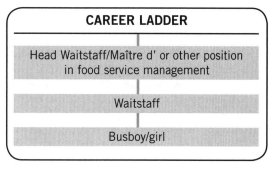

Position Description

"Hello, welcome, may I take your order?" These are the phrases we hear from Waitstaff every time we dine at a restaurant. Whether we are eating breakfast at a casual family establishment or a five-course dinner at a gourmet hot spot, Waitstaff take our orders and bring us our food and beverages, paying utmost attention to making our dining experience a positive one.

The job of Waitstaff can vary depending on the type of restaurant in which they work. In more casual locations, Waitstaff take orders and bring food out in a timely manner. At more elegant restaurants, the job of the Waitstaff can be more involved. Serving must be timed for leisurely dining between courses and customers often ask questions about the menu. The Waitstaff often recommend specials, wines, desserts and more; it is important for them to know about the items on the menu and have tasted a variety of the main dishes.

Customer service is the main focus for Waitstaff. Service affects customers' dining experience as much as the quality of the food sometimes. Bad service is a frequent reason diners will not revisit a restaurant. The Waitstaff has an important job in impacting profits as well. Attentive, knowledgeable, and friendly service is often the deciding factor to encourage customers to become regulars. Since the bulk of Waitstaff salary comes from tips, providing excellent service directly benefits Waitstaff as well. They must adhere to the philosophy "The customer is always right" and try to handle complaints about the food or service with a smile.

Waitstaff is also responsible for preparing the check at the end of the meal, either manually or through computers. They need good memories not only to take orders (although they often write them down), but also to remember which person at each table ordered what meal. Furthermore, they accommodate special requests such as food allergies and bring these requests back to the kitchen.

Additional duties may include:

- preparing special dishes table side, such as guacamole
- serving as host/hostess or bartender as needed
- training new Waitstaff
- working with chefs, sommeliers, cooks, and other kitchen staff
- attending staff meetings
- checking the ID of customers before serving alcohol
- escorting guests to tables
- setting up/cleaning up tables
- dealing with customer complaints
- taking payment for bills and making change
- refilling salt shakers and ketchup bottles

Waitsaff need skills at working with different types of people. On the front line, they interact with children, the elderly and everyone in between. Knowing where to get crayons for a four-year-old or adding an umbrella on a drink for senior citizen are just small touches that make Waitstaff good at their jobs. They may meet a wide variety of people, particularly at high-end restaurants. Many Waitstaff in cities such as New York or Los Angeles have stories about the celebrities they served or the next job opportunity that came from a conversation with a wealthy and successful customer. In heavy tourist restaurants or hotels, customers may ask about local attractions and the more knowledge the Waitstaff have, the better tips might be.

The job can be physically exhausting, as Waitstaff are on their feet almost all of the time, balancing heavy trays and dishes. Many restaurants require some type of dress code for their Waitstaff ranging from specific uniforms to white shirts and dark pants. Shifts are usually centered around mealtimes, with dinner usually the most lucrative shift but often lasting until 11 P.M. or later. However, Waitstaff frequently enjoy the flexibility of their jobs. Many use it as a stepping-stone to other careers in the hospitality or entertainment industry, or as a way to earn money while in school.

Salaries

Salary for Waitstaff comes from a combination of hourly pay and tips. According to the Bureau of Labor Statistics (BLS), as of May 2007, median hourly wage-and-salary earnings (including tips) of waiters and waitresses were $7.62. The middle 50 percent earned between $6.95 and $9.84. The lowest 10 percent earned less than $6.31, and the highest 10 percent earned more than $13.55 an hour. The median annual salary was $15,850 with the range spanning from less than $13,120 to more than $28,180.

However, earnings can be higher depending on the geographic location and prestige of restaurant. Tips usually average between 10 and 20 percent of guests' checks; Waitstaff working in busy, expensive restaurants during the dinner shift earn the most, with 20 percent and higher tips the standard. While many Waitstaff work part-time, combined with school or other jobs, career Waitstaff at fine restaurants can earn considerably more, $75,000 or higher at the nation's top restaurants.

At some restaurants, the policy is for all Waitstaff to pool their tips to be divided evenly among them; at others, they keep what they have been given directly.

Employment Prospects

Employment prospects for Waitstaff are excellent. With high turnover as employees leave to pursue other careers, education, or positions at more prestigious restaurants, opportunities abound. Insiders advise that the best way to find employment is by going directly to the restaurants where one wishes to work. However, it is best to go between mealtimes when things are slow and the manager will have time to talk.

Typically, new Waitstaff will start out working the less lucrative or desirable shifts (such as weekday breakfast) until they have proven themselves to be effective workers.

Advancement Prospects

A wide range of people work as Waitstaff; therefore in the field, advancement prospects vary. There are teens working summer jobs during high school and college, aspiring food and beverage workers, older adults who have had careers as Waitstaff, and actors/actresses and other entertainment/artists looking to earn money as they pursue their other dreams. These groups come to the field with different backgrounds and goals.

Those looking to stay in the food and beverage industry may advance to become head waitstaff or maître d's, eventually seeking positions in management such as restaurant general manager. Others may be interested in wine as bartenders or sommeliers, while others consider different options in the hospitality industry. Additional training or education may be necessary for advancement.

Education and Training

Overall, there are no set educational requirements for Waitstaff. Some establishments require a high school degree; others have Waitstaff with college degrees. For those who are looking to launch a career in the hospitality or food service industry, they may work as part-time Waitstaff while studying for a degree in these fields.

Waitstaff also are trained on the job. They learn the specific policies and procedures of their restaurant, including cleanliness, sanitation, teamwork, customer service, food/drink preparation, and serving. Often, new Waitstaff learn from observing and speaking with experienced Waitstaff.

Experience, Skills, and Personality Traits

Waitstaff are on the front lines of customer service and should genuinely enjoy working with people. They need the ability to be tactful and diplomatic, handling stressed and angry customers without losing their tempers and helping to dispel a negative situation. Good communication and interpersonal skills help them to remember orders and convey information such as specials to customers.

Good physical stamina is needed to keep Waitstaff on their feet, balancing dishes, plates, and trays. Knowledge of numbers and/or computers can also be helpful as they prepare bills and exchange money.

Unions and Associations

Waitstaff may belong to professional associations including the National Restaurant Association. Positions may or may not be unionized, depending on the restaurant, but some Waitstaff are members of local unions.

Tips for Entry

1. Explore the Web site Waiters World at www. watersworld.com/About.htm. The site's mission is to elevate the status of waiters in America to a professional career level.

2. Try a job as Waitstaff at a local restaurant. To get started, you usually do not need much experience, just a positive attitude, especially in a small establishment.

3. Compare and contrast the different Waitstaff who have served you recently. What makes good Waitstaff stand out?

4. Read this article from the *New York Times* food critic Frank Bruni, describing the week he spent a week as a waiter: www.nytimes.com/2006/01/25/dining/25note.html?_r=1&oref=slogin.

5. Consider the specific customer challenges of Waitstaff. How might you approach a cranky child or an adult with food allergies differently?

BARTENDER

Duties: Serves alcoholic and nonalcoholic drinks to customers at a bar or restaurant; prepares specialty drinks

Alternate Title(s): Mixologist

Salary Range: $7.25 per hour to $200–300 per shift

Employment Prospects: Excellent

Advancement Prospects: Good

Best Geographical Location(s): All, with a multitude of opportunities in cities, resort areas, and college towns

Prerequisites:

Education and Training—Varies depending on the position; some bartending classes may be needed or helpful

Experience—Prior experience in the food and beverage industry

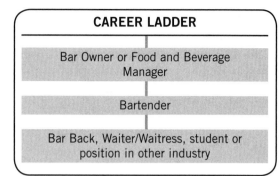

CAREER LADDER

Bar Owner or Food and Beverage Manager

Bartender

Bar Back, Waiter/Waitress, student or position in other industry

Special Skills and Personality Traits—Excellent interpersonal skills; ability to stay calm under pressure; flexibility; knowledge of drink recipes

Position Description

You have seen them depicted in countless movies, most famously, probably, by Tom Cruise in *Cocktail*. They may serve the role of therapist, cheerleader, janitor, and even officer, letting you know when to call it a night. Bartenders say there are many components to their jobs that go way beyond mixing and pouring drinks for customers.

Bartenders serve both alcoholic and nonalcoholic drinks to customers. They pour soda, beer, or wine or other beverages, as well as mix and prepare specialty drinks. Depending on the work setting, these drinks may range from basic martinis to fruity concoctions requiring five or more ingredients. A Bartender may serve 20 to 40 types of drinks in one night, perhaps more depending on where he or she works.

Bartenders become experts in making drinks, familiar with both the specialties of their bar or restaurant as well as other typical cocktails customers may request. They need to know a wide variety of recipes and how to make the drinks quickly and efficiently. Some Bartenders are creative and like to experiment with new drinks.

In addition to mixing drinks, Bartenders often perform other tasks related to the bar and beverage services. They may take inventory or have responsibility for stocking the bar, including ordering the necessary alcohol, juices, and mixes. They may also wash and dry glassware (or load dishwashers), maintain a clean bar area, and refill bar snacks.

Another aspect of the job involves the exchange of money. Usually, customers pay the Bartender directly for their drinks and the Bartender must make change quickly and accurately, often operating a cash register or credit card machine.

Often, customers will have their identification checked when they enter a bar to ensure that they are of legal drinking age. However, in cases when this doesn't happen, Bartenders may check ID to ensure that customers are 21 before they are served an alcoholic beverage.

Additional duties may include:

- opening bottles of wine
- carrying cases
- changing a keg
- opening or closing a bar
- washing countertops
- garnishing drinks and slicing fruit
- arranging displays of bottles and/or glassware
- serving food at the bar
- maintaining appearance of the bar
- handling money and making change

While some Bartenders fill drink orders placed through waitstaff, most interact directly with customers and take their orders. For this reason, Bartenders must be skilled at customer relations. Some customers sit at a bar to escape a bad day at work or personal problems and seek a sympathetic ear. A good Bartender knows how to listen and read people and this can have an effect on the establishment's overall success as well as the Bartender's salary. Customers are more likely to come again to the same place if they feel they had exceptional service.

Bartenders may work at local neighborhood dives, college hangouts, chic urban lounges, restaurants of all kinds, hotels and resorts, and more. There are piano bars, sports bars, pubs and taverns, cruise ship and casino lounges, and beach/pool bars, just to name a few. Bartenders work a variety of hours, including weekends and holidays, with most shifts lasting for several hours. They work mostly evenings, sometimes into the wee hours of the morning.

Typically, Bartenders spend most of their time on their feet, and they work with their hands. Many Bartenders work part-time, combining bartending with a wide variety of other vocations including being a student, actor, and others. Full-time Bartenders working at restaurants or hotels often receive benefits.

Salaries

Most Bartenders make the bulk of their salary on tips from customers. Annual salaries are a combination of hourly pay and tips. At some establishments, tips are pooled among Bartenders and other employees.

Payscale.com lists median salaries for Bartenders in a variety of major cities, ranging from a low of $6.21 per hour in Chicago to a high of $10.24 per hour in New York. Grading salary by work environment, casinos and resorts lead the pack on Payscale.com, with a median of $9.00 per hour.

According to the Bureau of Labor Statistics (BLS), as of May 2007 the mean hourly wage for Bartenders was $9.49 and the mean annual salary was $19,740. The highest paying state for Bartenders was Hawaii, with a mean hourly wage of $14.62 and a mean annual salary of $30,420.

However, these figures might not present a completely accurate portrait of Bartender salaries. Since tips are usually in cash, the accounting might be off depending on what is reported. Some Bartenders can earn up to $200 or $300 per night, especially those with established or wealthy customers working at high-end restaurants or resorts.

Employment Prospects

The BLS says that with the rise of people eating outside their homes as well as the high turnover in the field, employment prospects are excellent for Bartenders. Competition is typically the sharpest at upscale establishments where pay tends to be higher.

To find jobs, insiders say that the best approach is often to apply in person, particularly at places you frequent as a customer. Finding a Bartender who is a good fit for the atmosphere can be a key component in hiring, and looks and personality can play a role in many instances.

Advancement Prospects

Bartenders can advance by moving to more upscale and lucrative locations or working their way up to becoming a manager at their establishment. They also may become directors of beverage services at hotels and resorts, responsible for supervising all Bartenders. Some Bartenders aspire to open their own bars. Through their extensive work with people, Bartenders have tremendous networking opportunities with customers that can have a direct impact on their careers.

Education and Training

There is not one required path to become a Bartender. Although they must all be of legal age to serve liquor, some may have high school diplomas while others might have college or even advanced degrees. Regardless of formal education, Bartenders and managers agree that knowledge of the industry is key. Understanding different wines and beers, the tastes of various liquors, which ingredients go together, and so on, is crucial.

Some Bartenders attend bartending or vocational/technical schools. These schools include hands-on training in a simulated bar, cocktail recipes preparation, and instruction on laws and regulations, as well as some assistance with job placement. However, training schools have a mixed reputation among those in the industry and some feel it is better to learn on the job.

Experience, Skills, and Personality Traits

Skills and personality traits are important for success as a Bartender. A confident and friendly manner is necessary in order to put customers at ease. A sense of humor helps Bartenders joke with customers and the ability to stay calm under pressure helps them to juggle multiple orders and customers at once without getting flustered. A good memory enables Bartenders remember drink orders as well as beverage recipes.

Prior experience in the food and beverage industry is very helpful for becoming a Bartender. Many start out as waiters or waitresses, hostesses, bar backs, or cooks in order to learn more about the industry.

Unions and Associations

Bartenders may belong to the United States Bartenders' Guild or Unite Here, the union representing workers in the hotel, restaurant, and food service industry.

Tips for Entry

1. Visit this Web site for an idea of one person's opinion about the drinks that all Bartenders should know how to make: www.miss-charming.com/recipes/know.htm.

2. Make a connection with a Bartender and find out how he or she got started. The best time to visit a bar is typically between lunch and dinner, when Bartenders often have the most free time to talk.

3. Check out an Amazon.com list for the best books in bartending at www.amazon.com/Best-Books-In-Bartending/lm/2SMGN4X16L435.

4. Explore bartending courses at local community colleges and online programs. Conduct an Internet search and then check with local Bartenders or managers to make sure they feel the program is respected in the industry.

MAÎTRE D'

Duties: Oversees the dining room, typically in a fine dining establishment

Alternate Title(s): Dining Room Manager; Maître d'Hotel

Salary Range: $28,000 to $60,000 and up

Employment Prospects: Fair

Advancement Prospects: Fair

Best Geographical Location(s): All, with the greatest opportunities in large cities and heavy tourist regions with many fine restaurants, resorts, and hotels

Prerequisites:

Education and Training—Varies, but a degree in hospitality or restaurant management can be helpful

Experience—Prior dining room experience

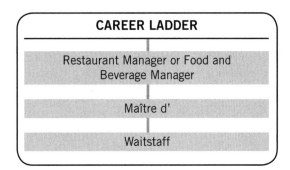

Special Skills and Personality Traits—Knowledge of food and wine; excellent interpersonal, communications, and customer service skills; personable and friendly; strong management skills; well-organized

Position Description

Each member of a restaurant team contributes to the customers' enjoyment of the fine dining experience. Maître d's take pride in managing the front of the house, including all the first contacts that guests have with the establishment. The Maître d' oversees the dining room, including reservations, the host/hostess station, waitstaff, and other food service workers to ensure quality of service.

Maître d's are responsible for the customer experience at their restaurants. They greet customers when they enter, sometimes taking their coats or making small talk. Then, they often escort them to their table, or introduce them to a host or hostess who will take them over to their seats.

At fine restaurants, reservations may book one month in advance or more. Maître d's oversee this process, making sure tables are reserved for guests at the scheduled times and that each night tables are cleared and ready to accommodate guests. They may squeeze in important guests or regular customers who come in without reservations. Managing walk-ins is common at some restaurants, with Maître d's making sure that the front desk clerk is taking names in an orderly fashion and that customers are being seated and satisfied.

At the tables, Maître d's speak to customers, perhaps providing menus and letting them know about specials before the waitstaff arrives to take their order. They circulate through the dining room, stopping at tables and asking if customers have any needs or requests and making sure they are enjoying themselves. Furthermore, they may share information about wines and send over a sommelier when requested.

Maître d's also handle other special requests. If a customer wants to hide an engagement ring in a soufflé or send a bottle of champagne to her parents for their anniversary, the Maître d' is the one who arranges this process. Maître d's enjoy being helpful and finding ways to make events celebrated at their restaurants special. They also oversee and arrange for large parties or other special events.

Much of the job of a Maitre d' involves management. They supervise staff and make sure everything is running smoothly, often coordinating between the front of the house and the dining room. They ensure that enough waitstaff is scheduled for heavy reservation times and sections of the restaurant, assigning tables and stations. Also, Maître d's make sure the restaurant looks clean, warm, and inviting. They may be responsible for ordering and arranging flowers, linens, candles, folded napkins, and other touches, confirming that all tables are set properly and elegantly.

Additional duties include:

• planning the menu with chefs and restaurant managers
• interviewing, hiring, and training dining room staff

- recommending food or wines
- forecasting revenues
- opening and closing the restaurant
- assisting individuals with disabilities
- completing work orders for repairs
- maintaining inventory and ordering supplies
- recommending new procedures to increase efficiency and cut costs
- inspecting the dining room for cleanliness
- personally serving VIP guests

Customer service drives their work and Maître d's are often sought to resolve problems and handle complaints. For example, if a customer grumbles to his waiter that the food is taking too long, the Maître d' might intervene with solutions including asking the cooks to get his meal out early or offering a complimentary appetizer or drink. Just as they escort the customers in, Maître d's walk them out, thank them, and ask about their dining experience.

Hours for Maître d's include evenings, weekends, and holidays, to reflect times when restaurants are open. They may work shifts with other Maître d's so they do not have to cover all these hours. Much of their time is spent on their feet, interacting with people.

Salaries

Salaries for Maître d's are typically in the $30,000 to $60,000 range, but they vary depending on geographical location. Since Maître d's are usually employed only by upscale restaurants, this puts their salary at a higher level than restaurant employees working at less expensive establishments. Maître d's may receive bonuses, as well as tips and gratuities, to add to their incomes. It is not uncommon for Maître d's at top restaurants to earn $85,000 or more.

Employment Prospects

For Maître d's, employment prospects are fair. Unlike other restaurant industry positions such as waitstaff or chefs, only upscale restaurants typically hire Maître d's, thus limiting the number of available positions. However, for Maître d's with good experience, opportunities are available, particularly for those working in big cities or who are geographically flexible.

Advancement Prospects

Maître d's may advance to other positions in the food service or hospitality industry, depending on their backgrounds and interests. Some may advance to become restaurant managers or even food and beverage direc-

tors at hotels. Others might move to be Maître d's at larger and more prestigious restaurants. Advancement can depend on education as well as experience, with more opportunities available for Maître d's with college degrees.

Education and Training

Because it is a management position, some employers require Maître d's to have college degrees, preferably in hospitality or restaurant management. Programs include those at Fairleigh Dickinson University in Madison and Teaneck, New Jersey (view.fdu.edu/default. aspx?id=1562) and Newbury College in Brookline, Massachusetts (www.newbury.edu/academics/schools/ hotel_rest/majors/hotel.shtml).

Most training comes on the job and from previous work experience in the restaurant industry where Maître d's have learned the workings of the dining room and importance of customer service. Culinary and wine courses can also be very helpful.

Experience, Skills, and Personality Traits

Knowledge of food and wine is important for Maitre d's as they interact with customers and make recommendations. Excellent interpersonal, communications, and customer service skills are essential. Maitre d's should be personable and friendly and truly enjoy talking to people and enhancing their dining experience.

Also, Maitre d's need strong management skills to oversee staff and dining room operations. Organization helps them to keep an eye on everything going on and keep track of reservations and staffing. The ability to stay calm under pressure enables Maitre d's to supervise a busy dining room and handle customer and staff requests without getting ruffled.

Most Maitre d's have prior experience as waitstaff and work their way up to progressively more upscale restaurants. Knowledge of a foreign language may be helpful when working with international clientele.

Unions and Associations

While there is no specific professional association for Maitre d's, associations to which they may belong include the National Restaurant Association. More information can also be obtained from the International Council on Hotel, Restaurant, and Institutional Education.

Tips for Entry

1. Explore the Web site of the International Council on Hotel, Restaurant, and Institutional Education

(CHRIE) at www.chrie.org. CHRIE is a nonprofit association for schools, colleges, and universities offering programs in hotel and restaurant management, food service management, and culinary arts.

2. Conduct an informational interview with a Maitre d'. Find out how he or she spends a typical day on the job.

3. Try working as a waiter or waitress in an upscale restaurant where you will interact with the Maitre d'.

4. Take a wine course at a local community college or adult education program. *Wine Spectator* offers a searchable directory of programs at www.winespectator.com/Wine/Educators/Educators_Search_Page/0,3388,,00.html.

VINEYARD MANAGER

Duties: Oversees the process of grape growing for a winery; supervises workers and administrative operations

Alternate Title(s): None

Salary Range: $70,000 to $90,000 and up

Employment Prospects: Fair

Advancement Prospects: Fair

Best Geographical Location: Regions especially fertile for growing wine; the top five wine growing states in the United States are California, New York, Washington, Oregon, and Texas. Top countries producing wine are France, Italy, and Spain, followed by the United States and Argentina.

Prerequisites:

Education and Training—Degree in viticulture or related field

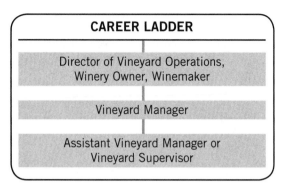

CAREER LADDER

Director of Vineyard Operations, Winery Owner, Winemaker

Vineyard Manager

Assistant Vineyard Manager or Vineyard Supervisor

Experience—Five to 10 years of vineyard experience

Special Skills and Personality Traits—Excellent technical knowledge of agriculture, wine making, viticulture, soil and environmental science; strong leadership, management and communication skills

Position Description

Vineyard Managers are, in essence, chief farmers who oversee all winery operations and grape growing activities for a vineyard. It is their responsibility to manage the fields and crew, guaranteeing that all steps fall into place to make grapes ready for harvest. This requires a fine balance of technical and management skills to ensure grape health.

A typical day in the "office" involves arriving to work at sunrise and creating a plan for the day. Vineyards are hundreds of acres that need monitoring, depending on the season. Vineyard Managers oversee the crews that maintain the vineyards, planting, pruning, spraying, hedging, fertilizing, and picking the crops. They hire and train these workers, motivating them to take ownership of their work by delegating specific areas of responsibility. Furthermore, Vineyard Managers coordinate schedules to ensure that each area is staffed as needed. Scheduling is very important and can change very quickly depending on the season as well as weather conditions.

Wine making is a cyclical business and the careful attention of the Vineyard Manager and communication with the winemaker have a huge impact on each year's output. The winter months are typically the time to recover from winter dormancy and begin the pruning process, which will help the vines grow and produce in future years. March will begin budburst where the first flowers begin to peek through and Vineyard Managers are alert for frost damage. In April and May, the flowers emerge and crops must be fertilized, checked, and tested. The summer months see fruit development, with constant monitoring of grape cluster size and controlling the yield. Fruit must be checked for disease and soil fertilized. In late summer, the cycle focuses on leaf plucking as well as testing sugar content and acidity before harvest. September involves much testing leading into harvest with a close watch of the weather. October is harvest month as the grapes are ready to pick and crush by hand and machine. November sees ground mowing and gearing up for winter as the cycle begins again.

Vineyard Managers must be skilled in soil and environmental analysis in order to determine the growing conditions. Additionally, they need knowledge of pest control and how spraying and pesticides can impact crops. Health of the vines is critical, and Vineyard Managers check for disease. All the while, they are managing the vineyard in a cost-effective manner, looking to maximize profits.

As supervisors, Vineyard Managers are responsible for vineyard budgets. They order supplies as well as maintain equipment. This includes any ordering, repairs, and maintenance on the machines that enable the work to get done. They keep records about vine performance, which help them make projections about the timing of vineyard operations. Each year, the calendar may vary slightly due to weather conditions and other factors. Vineyard Managers keep on top of these changes and can forecast crops, planning accordingly. It is up to them to make those minor adaptations in plan that can produce some of the finest wines.

Additional duties may include:

- managing irrigation systems and schedules
- participating in wine tastings
- attending winery events
- evaluating crop ripeness
- completing seasonal reports related to crush and pesticides
- keeping up to date with viticulture research and technology
- attending meetings with winemakers, owners/general managers, and other vineyard leadership
- developing business plans for vineyard operations
- recommending best practices for viticulture

Safety and health practices are essential vineyard operations. Vineyard Managers must educate and train the crew regarding policy and procedure. They follow field sanitation rules and regulations, as well as Occupational Safety and Health Administration (OSHA) standards.

Since crops vary every season, the job of a Vineyard Manager is constantly changing and always challenging. Vineyard Managers should expect to work outdoors in all types of weather conditions as well as to operate equipment and lift heavy items. Hours are long, especially during and near harvest when Vineyard Managers are monitoring crops closely around the clock. Some Vineyard Managers live on the premises of the winery, while others live close by. Wineries are often family-owned and Vineyard Managers become part of this close-knit culture.

Salaries

According to the 2006 Wine Industry Salary Report, Vineyard Managers' wages have grown 18 percent in the last five years. In 2006 the average salary for a Vineyard Manager was $80,400. While salaries for Vineyard Managers are lower than those of winemakers and other administrative leadership, they vary depending on the winery and location.

Employment Prospects

Even in difficult economic times, wine production is still growing, creating opportunities for Vineyard Managers. With the right combination of education and experience, Vineyard Managers can find positions in major wine growing regions. In the United States, the top five wine producing states are California, New York, Washington, Oregon, and Texas. Positions can be found through networking, as well as Web sites such as www.winejobs.com and www.winebusiness.com.

Advancement Prospects

Depending on their professional goals, Vineyard Managers can advance in several ways. They may want to become involved with the business of making wine as winemakers, which offers a higher salary and direct involvement with creating wine. Others may want to direct all vineyard operations or become general managers, while still others aspire to own their own winery. Vineyard Managers may also advance by moving to different wineries in more desirable locations or for higher salaries.

Education and Training

Positions as a Vineyard Manager require a bachelor's degree or a master's degree in viticulture or enology or a related field, including horticulture, ecology, and botany. Viticulture is the study of grape growing and enology is the study of wine making. A variety of schools offer such programs in viticulture and enology at the undergraduate and graduate level, including Cornell University in Ithaca, New York (www.grapesandwine.cals.cornell.edu/undergraduate), Oregon State University in Corvallis (wine.oregonstate.edu), and the University of California at Davis (wineserver.ucdavis.edu). These programs incorporate all the scientific disciplines that affect grape growing and wine making. Their regional locations will prepare Vineyard Managers for working with the particular grapes of that region.

Experience, Skills, and Personality Traits

Before becoming a Vineyard Manager, one should have five to 10 years of progressively responsible experience working at a winery. This experience, combined with the education needed to provide the technical skills required to do the job, prepares Vineyard Managers. Vineyard Managers must be experts in viticulture and everything related to growing grapes.

Furthermore, Vineyard Managers are supervisors. They need management ability to inspire respect among the crew and to lead them through the grape growing process. Organizational skills help them create schedules and communication/interpersonal skills enable them to work well with others. Depending on the geographical location, familiarity with a foreign language can be helpful. For example, many jobs in California require fluency in Spanish since many crew members speak Spanish. Vineyard Managers should also be familiar with vineyard-specific software and database systems.

Unions and Associations

Vineyard Managers may belong to professional associations including the American Society for Enology and Viticulture, the Wine Institute, and the American Wine Society.

Tips for Entry

1. Read publications such as *Vineyard & Winery Management Magazine* at www.vwm-online.com to learn more about the industry.

2. Type "degrees in viticulture" into a search engine to learn about the variety of programs available.

3. Take tours of wineries and learn about the wine growing process. Spend time in the vineyards, especially during different seasons to note the cycles.

4. Speak to people involved in the wine industry, including Vineyard Managers, winemakers, owners, and crew members. See how they got into the field and what recommendations they have.

5. Try a wine industry internship. Read this article to learn more: www.classicwines.com/articles/getting-a-wine-internship.

CASINOS AND GAMING

CASINO MANAGER

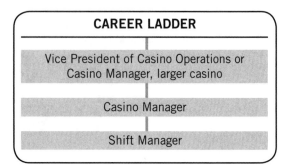

CAREER LADDER

Vice President of Casino Operations or Casino Manager, larger casino

Casino Manager

Shift Manager

Experience—Typically, at least seven years of progressively responsible casino experience

Special Skills and Personality Traits—Strong management skills; excellent financial and customer service ability; knowledge of gaming industry and casino games

Position Description

Casino Managers oversee all daily operations that occur in a casino. Since there are many things happening on the casino floor at any given time, this job carries a lot of responsibility.

Casino Managers must ensure that all table games are being played according to the government rules and regulations for each game. This requires extensive knowledge of both games and federal policy. However, the Casino Manager's objective is also to ensure financial gain for his or her casino. Casino Managers have some leeway in modifying rules to help the casino earn a profit, as long as they are still working within the government regulations.

Supervising staff is also a large part of working as a Casino Manager. Casino Managers are responsible for all floor workers ranging from dealers and floor supervisors to pit bosses and shift managers. They handle staffing issues such as hiring, firing, and scheduling. Training is also important, as casino staff must fully understand casino policy and procedure as well as be able to demonstrate strong customer service ability. Casino Managers also delegate responsibility to their subordinate supervisors.

Casino Managers demonstrate presence in the casino by walking the floor and ensuring that staff is doing their jobs and that guests are enjoying themselves. They observe games, slot machines, and the cash desk in order to minimize security and fraud issues. When problems arise, Casino Managers must step in to resolve them, knowing when to involve security if necessary. They are skilled at handling customer complaints in a way that leaves the customer satisfied while still maintaining profit for the casino.

Developing relationships is also important for Casino Managers. They need strong relationships with their staff to earn trust and respect. They also cultivate relationships with customers, particularly ongoing guests and VIPs. They may work to get or approve special accommodations for these high rollers to keep them coming back for more.

Additional duties may include:

- administering policies set by the CEO and executives
- monitoring customer credit limits
- overseeing a customer rewards program
- enforcing security
- keeping up on new developments with regard to government regulations on gaming
- reviewing financial transactions
- working on casino marketing and promotions
- interpreting and explaining house rules for customers
- reviewing operational expense and collection reports for accuracy

Depending on the casino, Casino Managers may also have some involvement with the hotel or restaurant portion of their property. Casino Mangers may work in casino hotels, riverboat casinos, cruise ship casinos, and other types of gaming facilities. Their hours are typically long and involve evenings, weekends, and holidays.

Salaries

Salaries for Casino Managers tend to be high, based on their large scope of responsibility and the years of experience required. While they do not receive tips like casino floor staff, Casino Managers often earn $100,000 or more. They may receive part of their salary in bonuses. Geography, size, and scope of the casino play a strong role in determining salary range.

Employment Prospects

According to the Bureau of Labor Statistics (BLS), employment in gaming services occupations is projected to grow by 23 percent between 2006 and 2016, which is much faster than the average for all occupations. Increasing popularity and prevalence of Indian casinos and racinos will provide substantial new job openings, and the BLS also suggests that additional job growth will occur in established gaming areas in Nevada and Atlantic City, New Jersey, as they solidify their positions as tourist destinations.

As casino employment continues to grow, so will opportunities for experienced Casino Managers. However, since the economy will drive position availability, employment prospects are only fair for Casino Managers. Although every casino employs a Casino Manager, there is just one manager, not multiple positions. The best options will be for those Casino Managers who are flexible.

Advancement Prospects

Advancement prospects are fair for Casino Managers. They can advance by moving to larger and more prestigious casinos that generate greater revenue. Also, they might seek to further pursue executive management as vice presidents of operations, general managers of casino hotels, and other high-level gaming positions.

Education and Training

Education and training requirements vary for Casino Managers. Some positions, particularly at larger casinos, require a bachelor's degree. Fields of study such as business, finance, and hospitality/gaming management are helpful. Other Casino Managers do not have formal degrees but have extensive experience in the industry. Training as dealers in the different casino games such as blackjack or roulette can also be important. While some Casino Managers come through professional degree programs, others work their way up on the floor, beginning as dealers.

Experience, Skills, and Personality Traits

Prior casino experience is required for all Casino Managers. Usually, one doesn't become a Casino Manager without at least seven years of experience. Many move through the ranks, working as dealers, floor supervisors, pit bosses, or shift managers. Skills and understanding of casino games is required.

Furthermore, Casino Managers need excellent management skills. They supervise large staffs and must be able to manage that responsibility. Strong financial ability coupled with a customer service orientation is essential. Casino Managers should also be observant and aware of activity in the casino, as well as possess good communication skills to maintain relationships.

Unions and Associations

Since there are no specific professional associations for Casino Managers, they can obtain information in several ways. One association for the industry is the American Gaming Association at www.americangaming.org. Also, the Harrah Hotel College at the University of Nevada, Las Vegas, has a list of hospitality industry professional associations at hotel.unlv.edu/IndustResProAsso.html.

Tips for Entry

1. See this article on interesting six-figure jobs at CNNMoney.com that include working as the general manager of a casino hotel: money.cnn.com/2004/09/08/pf/sixfigs_seven/index.htm.
2. Explore degree programs in casino management such as Iowa Lakes Community College (iowalakes.edu/programs_study/business/casino_management.htm) and Morrisville State College in Morrisville, New York (www.morrisville.edu/Academics/Business/Gaming_Casino/index.htm).
3. The College of Southern Nevada offers an online degree in casino management. Research its program at www.csn.edu/pages/202.asp.
4. Conduct an informational interview with a Casino Manager to find out more about the job.
5. Casino management has historically been a male-dominated field, but more women are becoming managers and may mentor others. See this article about female casino executives at www.azcentral.com/business/articles/2008/03/28/20080328biz-casinowomen0329-ON.html.

CASINO DEALER

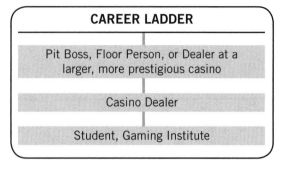

Position Description

If you are interested in casino work that puts you right in the heart of the action, on the floor with players involved in the games, then a job as a Casino Dealer might be right for you. Casino Dealers operate table games such as blackjack, craps, roulette, and baccarat, each according to the game's own set of rules and regulations. They specialize in one game and are experts in how they work.

Casino Dealers stand or sit behind the table and dispense to players either cards, dice, blocks, etc., depending on the game. It is up to them to operate gaming equipment unique to each game, such as spinning the roulette wheel. They represent the house (the casino) against the players, comparing each hand or round to determine the winner. Casino Dealers are responsible for taking bets, collecting losing bets and paying out winning bets, typically in the form of chips.

Blackjack is a card game where the object is to get a 21, or "blackjack." One wins by getting as close to 21 as possible without going over and by beating the dealer. Blackjack dealers work standing behind a table and dealing cards to all players; there is one dealer per table. They add up cards and tell players what they have, allowing players to make the decision whether to stay or hit. Skill at dealing cards and counting quickly is a necessity. Blackjack dealers typically work in a pit

area of blackjack tables and they break after an hour of working their table. Uniforms are required, usually a jacket with the casino logo.

Craps is supervised by several dealers, two standing, one called the stickperson, a replacement dealer, and one or two box persons. Craps is a game played with dice and the stickperson uses a stick to push the dice around the table. The standing dealers are each responsible for the players on their side of the table, changing cash into chips, while the stickperson offers the dice to players (so they can shoot) and calls the game. The box person supervises the process. Craps dealers are also required to wear uniforms and they typically work for 40 minutes before a break.

Roulette is played with a wheel and a ball, and players bet by numbers 0 through 36 or by colors, red and black. There is typically one roulette dealer per table who spins the wheel and releases the ball, although sometimes there may be an assistant. The dealer takes bets, places the marker on the winning number, and calculates payouts. Roulette dealers work standing up and wear uniforms. On average, they work for 40 minute periods before taking a break.

Baccarat is a card game usually run by four dealers—two who sit at the middle of a table, a caller standing across from them, and a ladder man supervising the action from above the table. The caller declares winning and losing hands, while the center dealers oversee bets. No more than 15 people sit at a table and are dealt hands of two to three cards, the total of which needs to exceed nine. Baccarat has long been considered a sophisticated casino game catering to a wealthy crowd, as the Dealers typically wear tuxedos and minimum bets at the tables are high.

Regardless of the game, all Casino Dealers have responsibility for explaining and enforcing the rules of the game to players. They must ensure that all players place their bets before each round begins and they report any problems to supervisors. Casino Dealers answer questions about both game rules and casino policies.

Additional duties may include:

- exchanging currency for chips or the equivalent
- inspecting game cards and equipment to ensure that they are in good condition
- starting and controlling games and gaming equipment
- announce winning numbers or colors
- opening and closing cash floats and game tables
- calculating amounts of players' wins or losses
- scanning winning tickets presented by players to compute the amount of money won
- preparing collection reports for submission to supervisors
- directing players to cashiers to collect winnings
- working as part of a team of dealers in games such as craps or baccarat
- training new dealers

Casino Dealers often work several different tables during a shift. Some Casino Dealers are trained in more than one game and will work different games during a shift as well. The average Casino Dealer works five eight-hour shifts during a workweek. To reflect the 24-hour nature of casinos, these hours often include overnight shifts, especially for beginners. Weekend evening shifts can be the most desirable because tips may be larger.

Salaries
According to the Bureau of Labor Statistics (BLS), median annual wage-and-salary earnings of gaming dealers were $15,610 as of May 2007. The middle 50 percent earned between $14,060 and $18,510. The lowest 10 percent earned less than $12,440, and the highest 10 percent earned more than $28,070. Many Casino Dealers are paid hourly, and the median hourly wage was $7.51, with the range spanning from $5.96 to $13.49.

A large portion of earnings comes from tips from players. If a player is doing well, he or she will often tip the Casino Dealer with tokens. Depending on the policies of the casino for pooling tips, this can have a great impact on a Casino Dealer's salary.

Employment Prospects
The BLS projects that employment in gaming services occupations will grow by 23 percent between 2006 and 2016, which is much faster than the average for all occupations. Casino Dealers enjoy good employment prospects but because so many people train as dealers, those with experience and certification from a gaming institute will have the best opportunities. Furthermore, it can be helpful to have training in more than one casino game, such as craps and blackjack. Since blackjack is one of the most common casino games, prospects are best in this area.

An audition is typical in addition to an interview to get a job so managers can see how Casino Dealers oversee the game and interact with players. Work can be found in casinos worldwide, as well as cruise ships and riverboat facilities.

Advancement Prospects
Working as a Casino Dealer can launch a career in the gaming industry. Many Casino Dealers move on to become floor people, supervisors, pit bosses, and even managers with additional education and training. Some Casino Dealers seek similar positions but at larger, more prestigious casinos, or may move throughout the country.

Education and Training
While there are no formal educational requirements, Casino Dealers are expected to have a high school diploma. Furthermore, those interested in becoming Casino Dealers must attend dealer training schools. These technical schools provide the skills necessary to become expert in one game or more, and they often offer certificates that demonstrate qualification. Programs run from four to 12 weeks in duration and offer daytime and evening class flexibility. Individual casinos also provide training to their new employees.

Additionally, Casino Dealers need a license issued by a regulatory agency such as a state gaming control board or commission. Fees and requirements vary by state.

Experience, Skills, and Personality Traits
Casinos are a fast-paced, high-stress environment. Casino Dealers must thrive on that excitement and be able to work calmly under pressure. Additionally, good

communications and interpersonal skills are required to work with players at tables, dealing with difficult personalities at times. Casino Dealers often bear the brunt of players' frustrations and need to delegate the situation if players become belligerent. People skills help Casino Dealers create a fun atmosphere for customers, which leads to higher gambling and greater tips.

Casino Dealers should also be good with numbers and have strong math skills, as they are required to calculate winnings and add numbers quickly and efficiently. Manual dexterity enables them to deal cards and handle chips. High energy is also needed to work late shifts.

Unions and Associations

There are no specific professional associations for Casino Dealers. Some dealers belong to a union depending on their specialty. For more information, see the American Gaming Association at www.american gaming.org.

Tips for Entry

1. Which casino game interests you the most? Become knowledgeable about that area, playing, reading, and observing Casino Dealers in action.
2. Learn more about dealer training schools at www.ildado.com/casino_dealer_schools.html. This site lists schools by state and provides links to their Web sites for more information.
3. Visit the sites of some major casinos such as the Wynn, Las Vegas (www.wynnlasvegas.com/index.cfm#Casino/) and Mohegan Sun in Connecticut (www.mohegansun.com). Explore their job listings.
4. Speak to Casino Dealers to find out more about their jobs. How do they handle being on their feet, dealing with angry players, and working late nights?

PIT BOSS

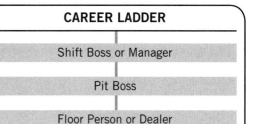

Position Description

At any given time, thousands of dollars are changed hands at a casino. People are winning and losing money at each table, as well as putting more down for additional chips. Pit Bosses monitor operations in their defined area of the casino floor, or pit. They may oversee four to eight tables or more, sometimes with different games in their jurisdiction, including blackjack, craps, or roulette.

Efficiency is key to casino operations and profits. The quicker hands are dealt, the more hands can be played. Pit Bosses circulate in their sections, watching the dealers and coaching them to be as efficient as possible. They also interact with players, ensuring they are having a good time and that the atmosphere at the tables is positive. Pit Bosses also supervise dealers, rotating them at tables and scheduling pit breaks. They serve to motivate them and help them apply their customer service skills to ensure player satisfaction.

When trouble arises at a table, the Pit Bosses are on hand. Whether it is a dealer mistake or a customer complaint, they resolve problems and answer questions. They are always watching the tables and monitoring belligerent or rowdy customers, ready to call for assistance at any time and involve security when necessary. It is essential for Pit Bosses to be experts in the games

they supervise, in order to answer questions, resolve disputes, and make final calls and decisions in the face of controversy.

Theft is a big issue at casinos and the Pit Boss is an important part of the process to protect the casino's assets. Pit Bosses must be constantly alert and aware of any illegal happenings. They monitor customers who are winning excessively and check for foul play such as card counting. This is another reason it is vital for Pit Bosses to know the games they oversee.

Furthermore, Pit Bosses deal and account for great sums of money. They watch all bets, chips, and movement of dollars. At the end of the day, they are responsible to account for every penny. Pit Bosses complete and authorize cash-outs, receipts, and credit slips. They make sure that everything is exactly as it should be.

Additional duties may include:

- ensuring policies and procedures are followed
- awarding complimentaries (comps)
- opening and closing gaming tables
- talking to customers
- intervening in difficult situations

Pit Bosses should be tactful and diplomatic in their work with both dealers and players. A table where the mood is happy is better for business all around, and Pit Bosses work to make conversation, lighten the mood, and resolve disputes before they become ugly.

While dealers typically wear uniforms, Pit Bosses dress in professional clothing such as suits to reflect their supervisory position. They also work shifts that vary. Beginning Pit Bosses may be stuck with the graveyard shift from 2 A.M. to 10 A.M., but with experience, they can work more desirable hours. Other shifts include the day shift, from 10 A.M. to 6 P.M., and the swing shift, from 6 P.M. to 2 A.M. However, casinos operate on a 24/7 basis, so Pit Bosses work evenings, weekends, and holidays. They are on their feet much of the time, but are not restricted to standing behind a table.

Salaries

Salaries for Pit Bosses vary depending on their geographical location, size of casino, and education and experience level. According to the Bureau of Labor Statistics (BLS), gaming supervisors (which would include Pit Bosses) had median annual earnings for $42,980 as of May 2007. The middle 50 percent earned between $34,250 and $52,560. The lowest 10 percent earned less than $26,310 and the highest 10 percent earned more than $64,910. However, insiders say that Pit Bosses at large casinos and resorts can earn $75,000 per year or more.

Employment Prospects

According to the BLS, employment in gaming services occupations is projected to grow by 23 percent between 2006 and 2016, which is much faster than the average for all occupations. The BLS states that the increasing popularity and prevalence of Indian casinos and racinos will provide substantial new job openings, as well as that more states are reconsidering their opposition to legalized gambling and may approve the construction of more casinos and other gaming establishments during the next decade. The BLS also suggests that additional job growth will occur in established gaming areas in Nevada and Atlantic City, New Jersey, as they solidify their positions as tourist destinations. As casino employment continues to grow, so will opportunities for Pit Bosses, particularly those with experience and some gaming management education.

Advancement Prospects

Advancement prospects are also good for Pit Bosses. They may find positions at larger or more prestigious casino resorts with the opportunity for increased earnings. Additionally, they may move further up into casino management, with the next position being a shift manager. Eventually, they may move on to becoming casino managers, with the right combination of education and experience.

Education and Training

Education and training requirements for Pit Bosses may vary. A high school diploma or equivalent is required and those who are seeking to move up in casino management may need associate's or bachelor's degrees. Since many Pit Bosses begin as dealers and extensive knowledge of casino games is required, many have training from schools that train dealers.

Dealer training schools employ instructors who are licensed to teach gaming procedures. Students choose one or two games in which to specialize and classes may run from between four to 12 weeks, depending on the game. Many programs also help with job placement. In most programs, enrollees must be 21 or older. These courses cover the various components of dealing including handling cards/equipment, rules, and taking bets, all in an atmosphere like a simulated casino so students can gain hands-on training.

Schools are in locations nationwide, but many are centered around main casino areas such as Las Vegas, Nevada and Atlantic City, New Jersey. For example, see the Casino Gaming Institute in Pleasantville, New Jersey at www.casinogaminginst.com.

Pit Bosses often benefit from gaming management courses beyond the dealer level. For example, Delta State University in Cleveland, Mississippi offers a degree in gaming management (www.deltastate.edu/pages/1404.asp) as does Northeast Wisconsin Technical College in Green Bay (www.nwtc.edu/Programs/PDFs08-09/Casino_Management.pdf). Other courses and certificates are offered through local community colleges and vocational schools.

Experience, Skills, and Personality Traits

To be successful as a Pit Boss, one must have an excellent grasp of casino games combined with good leadership and management skills. Pit Bosses who have worked their way up from being dealers may now be supervising their former colleagues. They need to be fair and diplomatic, able to manage difficult situations ranging from an agitated customer to a cheating employee. Furthermore, they need to be alert and aware, overseeing many situations at once with close attention to detail.

Like other hospitality employees, Pit Bosses should also have strong customer service skills as they talk with players and help foster a welcoming atmosphere. Knowledge of rules, regulations, policies, and procedures is also essential, as is the ability to keep track of finances.

Unions and Associations

While there is not a professional association specifically for Pit Bosses, those interested in the gaming industry can explore a number of resources. The Harrah Hotel College at the University of Nevada, Las Vegas, has a list of hospitality industry professional associations at hotel.unlv.edu/IndustResProAsso.html. One association for the industry is the American Gaming Association, at www.americangaming.org.

Tips for Entry

1. The University of Nevada, Las Vegas offers a tip sheet on its Web site about casino employment at hotel.unlv.edu/pdf/tips/TipSheet_33.pdf.

2. The Web site JobMonkey lists dealer training schools at www.jobmonkey.com/casino/html/dealer_schools.html.

3. Notice the role of a Pit Boss at a casino. Be aware of how they often stand next to the dealer and observe interactions. Also, keep your eye on the different tables they supervise to get a better idea of the scope of the job.

4. Check out casino jobs online at sites such as www.ildado.com/casino_jobs.html, www.casinojobs.net, and www.gamingfloor.com/employ.

CASINO HOST

Duties: Greets and entertains casino guests; evaluates and provides special services for guests

Alternate Title(s): Executive Casino Host; Host

Salary Range: $30,000 to $65,000 and up

Employment Prospects: Good

Advancement Prospects: Good

Best Geographical Location(s): Locations with legalized gambling and casinos including Las Vegas, Nevada, Atlantic City, New Jersey, locations with Indian gaming facilities such as Connecticut, and riverboat casinos such as in New Orleans

Prerequisites:

Education and Training—High school diploma/GED required; on the job training

Experience—Some prior experience in the gaming industry, typically one to three years as a dealer or floor person

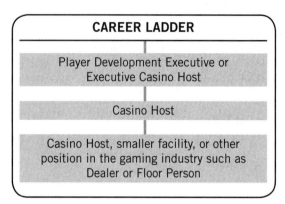

Special Skills and Personality Traits—Excellent communication and interpersonal skills; strong customer service orientation; networking and relationship building skills; organizational skills as well as tact and discretion

Position Description

The excitement of being at a casino is the feeling that anything can happen with a roll of the dice. At any given time, people are winning and losing thousands of dollars. When people go to casinos, part of the experience is the treatment they receive. Whether they are wagering a lot of money or a little, they want to feel valued and like a VIP.

With many different casinos in a given location vying for customers, the position of Casino Host is an essential one. Casino Hosts greet and entertain customers, developing relationships with new clients and building relationships with their current roster of guests. They are vital to their hotels because the services they provide can help attract and retain customers. Casino Hosts can make the difference for a player to chose one casino over another although they may have the same amenities.

Casino Hosts aim to make sure guests of the casino/hotel enjoy their stay. They often spend much of their working hours out on the casino floor, introducing themselves to people and asking if there is anything with which they can help. They answer questions and talk to guests, making conversation about both their gambling experience and personal lives. Furthermore, they help them with aspects that will enhance their

visits such as making dinner reservations and securing show tickets.

When players gamble at a casino, they frequently use a club rating card that they insert into slot machines or give to the floor person in the gaming pit when they sit down at a table. This card is entered into a computer system and tracks their gambling. Casino Hosts may review aspects of gaming play of different guests, including how long they spent gambling on the floor, how much money they lost, and more. This information is used to make decisions about "comps," short for "complimentaries," which are services that are given for free.

Casino Hosts make determinations about comps for guests. These services can include free dinners, hotel rooms, spa services, show tickets, and more. The use of comps is yet another strategy used by Casino Hosts and casinos to recruit and retain guests. Comps used to be granted only to high rollers, but Casino Hosts now might work with all players to enhance their stay and encourage them to come back and keep gambling.

Additionally, Casino Hosts may work in player development. They may have lists of players to contact by phone and e-mail, checking in to invite them back for a stay or special event, perhaps with a free room. Building these relationships is important, as is follow-up. Casino Hosts often send guests thank you notes or e-mails after their stay, always enhancing the positive relationship.

Casino Hosts also prospect for new business, identifying people who might visit and visitors who might become player's club members. Player's clubs entitle members to special benefits and may have different levels; for example, Diamond Level used to identify high rollers. Casino Hosts are often involved with these player's clubs at their casinos, registering target numbers of new members, attending events, and networking with members. They also encourage progression of players into the higher levels.

Some Casino Hosts, usually executive casino hosts, are responsible for greeting special guests including celebrities and high rollers. They might accommodate specific requests such as penthouse suites, limousine transportation, and gourmet room service. Executive casino hosts have many of the same responsibilities of a Casino Host, just at a higher level.

Additional responsibilities may include:

- developing and implementing new promotions
- maintaining player accounts
- entering player information into databases
- attending staff meetings
- participating in property events and promotional activities
- making credit decisions
- resolving problems
- working with assigned lists of clients
- playing golf or attending other events with clients
- recognizing and greeting frequent guests by name
- assisting with telemarketing
- collaborating with other hospitality departments, such as rooms or food and beverage to ensure comps

Casino Hosts work long shifts, usually between 10 and 12 hours, and may work five to six days per week. These hours include evenings, holidays, and weekends, and may extend even longer when they are accommodating requests and questions from high-profile guests. Casino Hosts spend much time on their feet, interacting with people. It is position for those with high levels of energy, enthusiasm, and people skills.

Salaries

According to a salary survey on Salary.com, a typical executive casino host earns a median base salary of $47,244. Half of the people in this job earn between $37,656 and $69,887. However, salaries can vary greatly depending on the size and location of the casino. Most Casino Hosts work on salary and do not receive tips. At the level of player development executive, commission is often part of salary.

Employment Prospects

According to the Bureau of Labor Statistics (BLS), employment in gaming services occupations is projected to grow by 23 percent between 2006 and 2016, which is much faster than the average for all occupations. They state that the increasing popularity and prevalence of Indian casinos and racinos will provide substantial new job openings, as will states that are reconsidering their opposition to legalized gambling and will likely approve the construction of more casinos and other gaming establishments during the next decade. The BLS also suggests that additional job growth will occur in established gaming areas in Nevada and Atlantic City, New Jersey, as they solidify their positions as tourist destinations.

Because Casino Hosts are so important to attracting and retaining guests, employment prospects are good. They will continue to grow as hotels face more competition from one another and as more casinos and casino hotels are built worldwide. Additionally, there is high turnover in the position, with three years as a typical tenure at one hotel. Some Casino Hosts may be required to sign an agreement saying they will not solicit any of their former customers after the end of their employment.

Most Casino Hosts come to their positions through prior experience in the gaming industry. Many have worked for one to three years as dealers or floor people. Insiders say that the best way to start may be as slot casino hosts, and entry level positions may also require more phone work than personal contact.

Advancement Prospects

Advancement prospects are also good for Casino Hosts. The communication and relationship building skills they use are transferable to many other areas. They may move to larger properties and/or into positions as Executive Casino Hosts, with more responsibility and high salaries. Also, they may move into management in positions such as player development executive. In this role, they are responsible for cultivating players, increasing revenue, and marketing. Insiders say that player development executives can earn up to twice as much as Casino Hosts.

Education and Training

While there is no specific educational path required to become a Casino Host, a high school degree or equivalent is required. Some properties prefer candidates with bachelor's degrees and others are willing to substitute education for experience.

Knowledge and training in the gaming industry is needed, and can be obtained through the on-the-job training programs many casinos offer, as well as courses at community colleges or vocational schools. Virginia College in Biloxi, Mississippi (www.vc.edu/site/department.cfm?deptID=16) and San Diego State University in San Diego, California (www.ces.sdsu.edu/casino_online.html) are two of the many schools that offer certificate programs.

Experience, Skills, and Personality Traits

Casino Hosts must, above all, enjoy working with people. They need energy, enthusiasm, and a strong customer service orientation to build and maintain relationships and make conversation. They must like meeting new people and have a good memory for names, faces, and personal details, essential in networking and relationship-building. Schmoozing is crucial as they may be required to play golf and go on other social or sports outings with clients.

Furthermore, Casino Hosts must be organized and able to multitask, as they work with many clients at once. They must employ tact and discretion as they are dealing with people's sensitive financial information and may be entrusted with other personal details. They should always remain professional and calm, especially when dealing with problems.

Unions and Associations

While there is no specific professional association for Casino Hosts, many in the field say they keep in touch with other Casino Hosts informally, and within different geographical locations many get together and know one another. The Harrah Hotel College at the University of Nevada, Las Vegas, has a list of hospitality industry professional associations at hotel.unlv.edu/IndustResProAsso.html.

Tips for Entry

1. To learn more about positions in the gaming industry, conduct an informational interview with a Casino Host. Find out how he or she got involved in the field, as well as what a typical day is like.
2. Read job descriptions for casino jobs at sites such as casinocareers.com/jobsearch.cfm and www.jobmonkey.com/casino.
3. Enhance your customer service skills through courses in public speaking and jobs where you are working with people and answering questions.
4. View the Web sites of major casino chains such as www.harrahs.com.
5. Explore the site www.statescasinos.com, which provides information about casinos and casino hotels in all of the United States.

SURVEILLANCE OFFICER

CAREER PROFILE

Duties: Monitors casinos for illegal activity through watching and analyzing footage from closed-circuit surveillance cameras, as well as in-person observation

Alternate Title(s): Surveillance Agent; Gaming Surveillance Officer; Surveillance Observer; Gaming Investigator

Salary Range: $22,000 to $46,000 per year and up

Employment Prospects: Good

Advancement Prospects: Good

Best Geographical Location(s): Locations with legalized gambling and casinos including Las Vegas, Nevada, Atlantic City, New Jersey, locations with Indian gaming facilities such as Connecticut, and riverboat casinos such as in New Orleans

Prerequisites:

Education and Training—High school diploma or equivalent and surveillance training

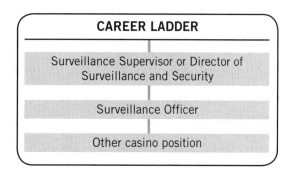

CAREER LADDER

Surveillance Supervisor or Director of Surveillance and Security

Surveillance Officer

Other casino position

Experience—Prior work in casinos and/or security field

Special Skills and Personality Traits—Good judgment; excellent knowledge of casino games, policies, and procedures; attention to detail and strong observation skills and vision

Position Description

An exorbitant amount of money changes hands at a casino at any given time. Bets are taken, winnings paid out, chips cashed in, and more. There is the potential for much illegal activity to occur in the hands of both customers and employees; therefore, casinos take their security very seriously. Surveillance Officers monitor all casino activities to make sure no illegal activities are occurring.

While uniformed security guards are visible on the casino floor to eject belligerent guests and handle other problems, Surveillance Officers work behind the scenes in a surveillance room or office. They are not recognizable as they spend their time in isolated locations, often watching the closed-circuit cameras that are spread out through the casino floor. Video and audio equipment is used to capture this action.

Surveillance Officers study this footage for anything out of the ordinary. They watch customers at the game tables and slot machines, as well as the cashier booths, in addition to watching staff members as they distribute chips and cash. Carefully, they analyze and watch for activities such as cheating, stealing, or any other illegal actions. It is important for Surveillance Officers to organize this footage as it may sometimes be used in police investigations.

Additional duties may include:

- observing employees as they drop money in the count room
- monitoring cashiers and cages
- looking for cheating during table games
- reporting illegal activities
- documenting violations and suspicious behavior
- communicating with uniformed security officers and floor managers to alert them about trouble
- monitoring and recording money transfers
- watching the opening and closing of slot machines

In addition to working in high-tech surveillance offices, Surveillance Officers also may work on the more old-fashioned catwalks with one-way mirrors built over the casino floor for more direct observation. The key is for them not to be seen or recognized, viewing activity when guests and staff believe no one is watching. Surveillance Officers may also sometimes walk the casino floor, but they do not wear uniforms or anything that will make them obvious to patrons.

Knowledge of casino games is important for Surveillance Officers to recognize cheating or discrepancies. Surveillance Officers also ensure that rules and regulations are in compliance with federal and state laws.

Frequently, they work with high-tech equipment such as facial recognition software to identify known cheaters and thieves.

Shifts run around the clock to reflect the 24-hour nature of casinos, and illegal activity can take place at any time. In fact, crimes might be more likely to take place in the middle of the night when fewer people are around. Surveillance Officers spend much time on their feet, as well as watching numerous cameras at once.

Salaries

According to the Bureau of Labor Statistics (BLS), gaming Surveillance Officers had median annual wage-and-salary earnings of $27,440 as of May 2007. The middle 50 percent earned between $22,220 and $36,090. The lowest 10 percent earned less than $19,170, and the highest 10 percent earned more than $46,370. Salaries can vary depending on experience as well as the size and location of the casino.

Employment Prospects

According to the BLS, employment of gaming Surveillance Officers is expected to grow by 34 percent between 2006 and 2016, much faster than the average for all occupations. As more states legalize gambling and the number of casinos grows in states with legalized gambling already, more Surveillance Officers will be needed. This is one area where casinos literally cannot afford to scrimp even during tight times.

Opportunities will be greatest for those with casino experience and knowledge of casino operations and for those with some law enforcement and investigation experience. Additionally, as technology is major factor in stopping casino theft, individuals with technical training will be highly marketable. Surveillance Officers may also work for the government to ensure that casinos are operating according to state regulations.

Advancement Prospects

There are several ways for Surveillance Officers to advance. They may become a surveillance supervisor or director of surveillance and security. Additionally, they may supervise surveillance for a chain of casino hotels at the brand level. Some Surveillance Officers advance to become surveillance consultants to various casinos. Others move to larger and more prestigious casinos for more responsibility and higher salaries.

Education and Training

According to the Bureau of Labor Statistics, Surveillance Officers typically need training beyond high school but not usually a bachelor's degree. Several educational institutes offer certification programs. Classroom training usually is conducted in a casino-like atmosphere and includes the use of surveillance camera equipment, as well as rules of the games and policies and procedures. Previous security experience is a plus, as is training in one or more casino games and/or work as a dealer. Surveillance Officers usually must go through extensive background checks before being hired.

Experience, Skills, and Personality Traits

Surveillance Officers must have good judgment in order to make quick decisions and notice what constitutes wrongdoings. Furthermore, they need good physical skills in case they have to detain individuals before additional help can arrive, as well as strong detail orientation and powers of observation. Surveillance Officers should be responsible, alert, and action oriented. Knowledge of casino games, rules, policies, and procedures help them to spot inconsistencies. Furthermore, they should be able to stay calm under pressure and work with a wide variety of people.

Unions and Associations

While there are no specific professional associations for gaming Surveillance Officers, they can obtain information through the American Gaming Association at www.americangaming.org.

Tips for Entry

1. Take a look at books such as *Casino Surveillance and Security: 150 Things You Should Know* by Gary L. Powell, Louis A. Tyska, and Lawrence J. Fennelly.
2. Gain experience in security by working at a local mall or store in their security or surveillance area.
3. Focus on one casino game and learn all about it through dealer training school.
4. Consider studying fields such as criminal justice or law enforcement. A degree in these subjects can increase marketability and future career advancement.

PLAYER DEVELOPMENT EXECUTIVE

Duties: Develops and cultivates casino players to bring in new business and retain current customers

Alternate Title(s): Director of Casino Player Development; Player Development Manager

Salary Range: $50,000 to $100,000 and up

Employment Prospects: Good

Advancement Prospects: Good

Best Geographical Location(s): Locations with legalized gambling and casinos including Las Vegas, Nevada, Atlantic City, New Jersey, locations with Indian gaming facilities such as Connecticut, and riverboat casinos such as in New Orleans

Prerequisites:

Education and Training—College degree required for many positions; experience can substitute for education in some cases

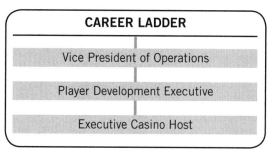

Experience—Prior experience in the gaming industry, typically as a casino host, floor manager, or other position

Special Skills and Personality Traits—Strong business and financial knowledge; excellent communication and interpersonal skills; strong customer service orientation; networking and relationship-building skills; organizational skills

Position Description

Casinos depend on players for their success. One of their primary objectives is to make existing customers into regulars and cultivate new players. Player Development Executives are responsible for developing and cultivating these relationships. They establish new and retain existing gaming customers.

While casino hosts entertain players on the floor and ensure that they are enjoying their experience, Player Development Executives are involved at a higher level. They oversee the process of player development, working with lists of specific contacts that need to be approached by phone and e-mail. Player Development Executives strategize about the best approach to reach these players, such as inviting them to visit for special events such as concerts. Building these relationships is essential to their success.

Player development is a marketing function, and Player Development Executives are constantly devising ways to promote their casino and its programs, as well as tap into the demographics of players they wish to attract. They have access to information about prior casino guests and their gambling records. They use their networking and relationship-building skills to contact these guests, as well as other good prospects, to increase trip frequency. Player Development Executives also drive to develop customers into more profitable customers. They plan and manage the develop strategy, which may include a combination of personal notes/e-mails, invitations, telemarketing, and direct player contact.

Player Development Executives oversee the casino hosts, analyzing and evaluating their productivity and profitability. As managers, they develop goals and budgets for their departments and oversee operations. They may assign casino hosts specific prospects to cultivate, and work on VIP customers themselves. Player Development Executives may also be responsible for hiring, training, and directly supervising casino hosts.

At many casinos, Player Development Executives do not work the casino floor, except when talking specifically to their personal customers. Instead, they are often behind the scenes, on the phone and networking with players. It is typical for Player Development Executives to cultivate social relationships with especially strong customers and they may play golf or attend sporting or other special events together. Developing these relationships not only encourages these players to come back, but also for them to bring their friends and provide new customer leads. Player development is an ongoing process as different players visit the casino where they might win or lose money in varying degrees. The top Player Development Executives are known for attracting especially high-profile, celebrity, and VIP players.

Additional responsibilities may include:

- developing and forecasting budgets
- making decisions related to comps
- representing the casino at special events or VIP functions
- making recommendations to maximize profitability
- working with player tracking software
- resolving problems
- supervising telemarketing
- working with other departments, such as rooms or food and beverage, to ensure comps
- developing policies and procedures
- working on marketing plans
- interacting with slot and table managers to identify areas of concern
- attending to customer needs and issues
- adhering to strict confidentiality
- supervising player ratings or rewards programs

Player Development Executives need high energy and may work five to six days per week. These hours include evenings, holidays, and weekends, working to develop players outside of a typical business context. Work hours may be spent in the casino as well as in corporate offices. Additionally, work hours may be spent fishing, golfing, and participating in other off-site activities to entertain players.

Salaries

Player Development Executives receive salaries that are a combination of base pay and commissions, related to how profitable they are each year or quarter. Typically, they can earn twice as much as the casino hosts they supervise with salaries ranging from $60,000 to $150,000 and above.

Employment Prospects

According to the Bureau of Labor Statistics (BLS), employment in gaming services occupations is projected to grow by 23 percent between 2006 and 2016, which is much faster than the average for all occupations. They state that the increasing popularity and prevalence of Indian casinos and racinos will provide substantial new job openings, as will additional states reconsidering their opposition to legalized gambling that will likely approve the construction of more casinos and other gaming establishments during the next decade. The BLS also suggests that additional job growth will occur in established gaming areas in Nevada and Atlantic City, New Jersey, as they solidify their positions as tourist destinations.

For Player Development Executives who are excellent networkers, employment prospects are good. Casinos are willing to invest in these important positions and hire qualified individuals who can impact profitability and bring in revenue. Player Development Executives with existing lists of contacts and a good following may be recruited from other casinos. There is typically high turnover in player development. Player Development Executives may be required to sign an agreement saying they will not solicit any of their former customers following the end of their employment. However, for those Player Development Executives with strong followings, the customers will contact them anyway without solicitation.

Player Development Executives come to their positions through prior experience in the gaming industry. Many have worked as dealers or floor people/managers, in addition to casino hosts.

Advancement Prospects

Advancement prospects are also good for Player Development Executives. Those who are proved to bring in revenue can move into upper-level management positions such as vice president, overseeing casino operations. Player Development Executives can also advance by moving from smaller casinos to larger ones.

Education and Training

While there is no specific educational path required to become a Player Development Executive, many hold bachelor's degrees. Some properties are willing to substitute education for experience, but courses in casino operations and management can be very helpful. Knowledge and training in the gaming industry is needed, and can be obtained through the on-the-job training programs offered by many casinos, as well as courses at community colleges or vocational schools. Some schools offer degree programs in gaming management such as the bachelor of science in gaming management at the Harrah Hotel College at the University of Nevada, Las Vegas (hotel.unlv.edu/departGameMgt.html) and the associate of science in casino management at the College of Southern Nevada campus with locations throughout the state (www.csn.edu/pages/1319.asp).

Experience, Skills, and Personality Traits

Player Development Executives should enjoy schmoozing and networking with people. They must be skilled at developing and building relationships, comfortable making small talk on a variety of topics. A good memory for names, faces, and personal details help cultivate and nurture these relationships. Player Development Executives also need high energy and enthusiasm.

Additionally, Player Development Executives need experience in the gaming industry. They must understand the psychology of players and what motivates them. Knowledge of business and marketing helps them manage budgets and devise strategic plans. They should also be organized and able to juggle multiple projects at once.

Unions and Associations

There is not a professional association specifically for Player Development Executives, although many in the field say they keep in touch and meet informally within different geographical locations. The Harrah Hotel College at the University of Nevada, Las Vegas, has a list of hospitality industry professional associations at hotel.unlv.edu/IndustResProAsso.html. One association for the industry is the American Gaming Association at www.americangaming.org.

Tips for Entry

1. Check out the Institute for the Study of Gambling and Commercial Gaming at the University of Nevada in Reno at www.unr.edu/gaming/index.asp.
2. Explore the site www.statescasinos.com, which provides information about casinos and casino hotels in all of the United States.
3. Read interesting facts and statistics about the gaming industry from the American Gaming Association at www.americangaming.org.
4. Visit Web sites specifically for casino employment such as www.gamingfloor.com/employ. Also, most casinos have job and internship listings directly on their own sites. For example, see Foxwoods Resort and Casino in Mashantucket, Connecticut (www.foxwoods.com/AboutFoxwoods/Careers.aspx) and the Borgata in Atlantic City, New Jersey (www.borgatajobs.com).

COMMUNICATIONS
AND OTHER

TRAVEL WRITER

CAREER PROFILE

Duties: Writes and reports on travel in a variety of formats, including newspaper, magazine, and online articles, as well as guidebooks

Alternate Title(s): Travel Reporter

Salary Range: $25,000 to $60,000 and up

Employment Prospects: Fair

Advancement Prospects: Fair

Best Geographical Location(s): All

Prerequisites:

Education and Training—Bachelor's degree in English, journalism, or related field

Experience—Previous writing and publishing experience; familiarity with a particular region and/or extensive travel experience needed

Special Skills and Personality Traits—Excellent writing, reporting, and editing skills; passion for

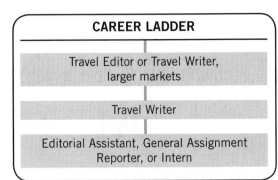

CAREER LADDER

Travel Editor or Travel Writer, larger markets

Travel Writer

Editorial Assistant, General Assignment Reporter, or Intern

travel and visiting new locations; adventurous spirit; respect for other cultures; openness to new experiences and flexibility; good organizational skills; critical eye

Position Description

The last time you took a vacation, how did you make your plans? While many people consult travel agents for some of the particulars, chances are that you read material that helped you to decide what to do, where to stay, and where to eat. Travel Writers transport their audience to a far-off locale. They write pieces that acquaint readers with a specific place, giving them information and advice they need to plan and enjoy their trip.

The work of Travel Writers appears in a variety of formats. They can write for newspapers and/or magazines, including articles profiling cities, beaches, and lesser-known villages around the world. Also, Travel Writers can work for one of the many online sites dedicated to travel planning. Furthermore, some Travel Writers author guidebooks for major travel publishers. Guidebooks include complete information about a region, including tips for getting there, hotels, restaurants, activities, and day trips.

Travel topics can include (among others):

- hotels
- restaurants
- nightlife
- arts and culture
- entertainment
- sports and outdoor activity
- budget/luxury travel
- travel arrangements: air, bus, train, and car; also may include directions
- local history
- adventure travel
- travel for specific groups or populations
- travel to specific areas such as Disney World or Caribbean cruises

Travel Writers may have a variety of specialties. Some find their niche writing for a particular population. There is much special-interest travel including family vacations, traveling with pets, gay- and lesbian-friendly locales, and best spots for singles, to name just a few. Other Travel Writers focus on a specific region. To write extensively about a place for a major publication such as a guidebook, it is necessary for the Travel Writer to have lived there for several years. For a shorter article, however, Travel Writers working for newspapers or magazines might be sent to visit a place where they have never been, offering readers a fresh and critical perspective.

In order to be a Travel Writer, one must obviously love to travel. While that sounds exciting, it also requires a willingness to deal with the not-so-glamorous aspects of travel including dealing with airport security, waiting on long lines for museums, eating at dingy restaurants, and trekking around to find an obscure hotel in the rain. As they enjoy their trips, Travel Writers are always thinking critically and analytically. They try to view their experiences from the point of view of their readers, thinking, "How would I rate this sight, who would most enjoy this activity, and is this hotel worth the price?" When Travel Writers are on location, they are working, rather than on vacation, and many find it hard to relax, especially on shorter trips.

Good travel writing involves careful research and planning. For each story, Travel Writers must determine their focus and what they need to cover. Outlines help them to stay organized and keep track of the sights, hotels, and restaurants they may need to visit in a short period of time. Often, they develop a rating system to help readers make decisions about how to spend their time. Travel Writers strive to offer their opinions in a factual and objective way that can enhance people's travel experience. In a sense, they do the research so the average traveler does not have to.

Articles may be written daily, weekly, and/or monthly depending on the publication. Travel Writers usually complete a combination of stories they have generated on their own, as well as those that have been assigned by their editors. Travel Writers that write guidebooks usually have a set period of time (such as six months to one year) to complete their manuscript.

Additionally, Travel Writers have the responsibility of finding fresh and exciting new things in places that have been visited before. They must keep up to date on the travel industry, aware of new trends and events. Furthermore, they must be up on the news of the regions they visit. Not only should they be aware of tourism-related business news, but also any political, cultural, and economic news that can affect tourism.

Their duties may include:

- traveling domestically and internationally
- working with photographers, including shoots for different articles
- taking photographs to accompany writing
- conducting interviews and speaking with local residents and proprietors
- attending meetings with editors to brainstorm story ideas
- editing articles
- conducting background research using the Internet and other databases
- answering questions from readers

It is important for Travel Writers to know their market and its demographics. Understanding not only what the editors want, but also what the readers need, is essential. For example, certain publications target the wealthy, the adventurous, or the budget-conscious. With each of their trips, Travel Writers need to find the stories that appeal to their population.

The amount of time that a Travel Writer actually travels can vary tremendously. A Travel Writer living in and working on a guidebook about Phoenix, Arizona can spend a year only focusing on local information, while a Travel Writer on staff at a newspaper or magazine may be on a plane more than three times in a month. In most cases, the publication for which the Travel Writer is working provides a budget that covers travel and writing-related expenses.

Salaries

To earn a living as a Travel Writer, one is usually employed by a newspaper or magazine. Salaries vary depending on the level and responsibility of the position. In the newspaper industry, experienced reporters can earn in the $40,000 to $50,000 range. The Newspaper Industry Compensation Survey, conducted annually by the Inland Press Association, shows that experienced reporters earned an average of $43,292 per year in 2004 in total direct compensation.

At magazines and Web sites, Travel Writers can earn comparable salaries, and sometimes even higher ones. Typical ranges are from $25,000 for entry-level positions to $60,000 and above with experience.

Freelance Travel Writers can earn anywhere from several hundred dollars per year up to $50,000 and more, depending on their previous writing experience, connections, and contracts. They may be paid per word, per piece, or per book, possibly including an advance for travel expenses and royalties. However, it is difficult to earn enough money to make a living as a freelancer without extensive prior journalism experience.

However, Travel Writers often receive other perks aside from base salary. The free travel expenses make the job worthwhile for many, especially those who earn at the lower end of the spectrum. In addition to those covered by editors, hotels and restaurants may also offer rooms or meals on the house in exchange for being included in an article or guide. Although accommodations and meals may not be luxurious and only the lucky few are successful enough to jet-set, travel writing offers a way for writers to experience new things. For those with a passion for seeing the world, this is well worth it.

Employment Prospects

Employment prospects are fair for Travel Writers. While anyone with a passion for travel can find a forum to post their opinions, only the fortunate and qualified will be able to earn a living this way. Competition is great for staff jobs at newspapers and magazines. The best opportunities will be in large cities such as New York with big papers and magazine headquarters.

Travel Writers should be willing to start at the bottom to develop their specialty. Positions such as editorial assistant at a travel magazine or general assignment reporter at a newspaper can be good entry points. Travel Writers should expect to get started by writing and reporting on whatever topics are needed, not just travel.

A portfolio of clips is essential for employment. Aspiring Travel Writers should also consider freelancing as a way to get started and develop some published pieces. Insiders say that writing the brief pieces at the front of travel magazines (product reviews, blurbs), rather than trying for lengthy articles can be a good way to get published initially. Trade and regional magazines with small sections on travel may also be good places to begin.

Advancement Prospects

In order to advance, many Travel Writers look to find more lucrative and stable work. Freelancers might look for staff positions at newspapers and magazines, while Travel Writers already employed by publications may try to move to larger markets. Those who are looking for managerial responsibility may also become editors where they run a department or manage a team of staff.

However, most Travel Writers look to continue writing in as financially and personal rewarding a setting as they can. They seek opportunities to travel to more interesting places and reach larger numbers of readers. Travel Writers who develop niche areas may write columns, books, or even travel series.

Education and Training

While most people love to travel, that is not enough to make one a Travel Writer. A bachelor's degree in English, journalism, communications, or a related field is very valuable. Some Travel Writers may also have degrees in other subjects including liberal arts. Internships are also a key way for those interested in travel writing to break in.

Travel Writers who attend journalism school can also make valuable contacts that will help them get a first job at a newspaper or magazine. Other Travel Writers may break in through the hospitality industry, working in public relations or corporate communications within the travel industry.

Experience, Skills, and Personality Traits

Like other writers and critics that offer opinions and advice, Travel Writers must be able to deal with criticism and difficult people. A hotel manager or restaurant chef may be very disappointed if his establishment does not get high marks. Travel Writers need to stick to their guns and remain ethical, doing their duty as journalists rather than advertisers.

Travel Writers must have very strong writing and reporting skills. While a love for travel is required, it does not amount to much without writing talent and ability. They must know how to structure articles or guides with the appropriate balance of information, fact, opinion, and interesting tidbits. The best travel pieces are not dry, but are peppered with amusing anecdotes about people and places.

Furthermore, Travel Writers need initiative and curiosity to help them to generate interesting and informative stories. It is important to be open-minded, respectful, and tolerant, especially when visiting different cultures. Travel Writers need excellent communication skills to speak to a variety of people.

Travel Writers should be passionate not only about travel, but also about people. They must be avid travelers who want to truly experience each place they see rather than stay within their comfort zone. Like all journalists, Travel Writers must be able to work under tight deadline pressure. They need to be flexible in order to adapt to sudden changes of plans and schedules.

Unions and Associations

The North American Travel Journalists Association (www.natja.org) is a professional association dedicated to writers, editors, and photographers in the travel industry. Travel Writers may also belong to professional associations including the regional Outdoor Writers Association of California and the Midwest Travel Writers Association, as well as the International Food, Wine and Travel Writers Association and the Society of American Travel Writers.

Tips for Entry

1. To be a Travel Writer, you must be a consumer of travel information. Plan a trip, either real or fantasy. Once you select your location, read everything you can about this destination. Search the Internet for newspaper and magazine articles, use online sites, and browse through guidebooks. Take note of how the different articles help you make decisions.

2. Check out major guidebook sites such as www.fodors.com, www.frommers.com, and www.lonelyplanet.com. See how they are written and the types of information they include.

3. You do not need a lot of money to be a traveler. As your budget allows, backpack through Europe, study abroad, volunteer for the Peace Corps, visit a museum in your home city, take a road trip, or go camping, to name a few ideas both large and small. These experiences will help you be a better Travel Writer.

4. Read travel magazines such as *Condé Nast Traveler*, *Travel and Leisure*, *National Geographic Traveler*, and others. What types of articles do they include? Look on the masthead to see if most seem to be written by staff members or freelancers.

5. Get started as a freelancer by writing about what you know. How would you advise a visitor to your hometown? Develop an idea for an article and send a query letter outlining the piece to a local publication. See www.poewar.com/archives/2004/10/24/how-to-write-a-query-letter/ and www.fictionwriters.com/tips-query-letters.html for some ideas about writing query letters.

6. Many good links to becoming a Travel Writer can be found at the following site: www.yudkin.com/travel.htm.

TRANSLATOR/INTERPRETER

CAREER PROFILE

Duties: Converts written, oral, or sign language text from one language into another

Alternate Title(s): None, although Translators deal with written language and Interpreters with spoken language only

Salary Range: $30,000 to $65,000 and up

Employment Prospects: Good

Advancement Prospects: Good

Best Geographical Location(s): Urban areas, cities with large international or multilingual populations, major tourist destinations

Prerequisites:

Education and Training—Fluency in two or more languages is required; bachelor's or graduate degree in foreign language or culture helpful

Experience—Familiarity with foreign countries and culture; prior experience using language skills in tourism or hospitality industry

CAREER LADDER

Chief Translator/Interpreter, Consultant, or Head of Translation/ Interpretation Services

Translator or Interpreter

Student or other position involving foreign language skills

Special Skills and Personality Traits—Excellent verbal and written communication skills; cultural sensitivity and awareness; patience; strong listening skills

Position Description

Communication is the link between cultures and enables people to understand each other. Translators and Interpreters have a challenging job of converting languages in order to provide mutual understanding. Whether helping a group of tourists enjoy sightseeing in a foreign language or assisting executives during their meetings with international clients, Translators and Interpreters bridge the gap between people and place them on a level playing field.

Translators deal exclusively with written documents. As they evaluate pieces of writing, they make sure not only to convert the words into another language, but also to ensure they retain their original meaning. Translators may translate different types of writing, including books, articles, and Web sites. An excellent grasp of punctuation, grammar, word usage, spelling, and idioms in their native language, and at least two languages, is necessary. In the travel and hospitality field, translators may translate visitor information at museums, hotels, and attractions, as well as travel documents.

Interpreters are responsible for listening to live speech and converting what the speakers say into a language others can understand (which can be a foreign language or sign language). They may interpret consecutively, where they wait for the speaker to pause, or simultaneously, where they begin interpreting while the speaker is talking. When interpreting for the hearing impaired, Interpreters convert spoken language into the hand signals of sign language. At meetings, they may sit in soundproof booths listening to the original material through headphones and interpreting into a microphone.

In the travel and hospitality industries, Interpreters may work in hotels and resorts, with conference/meeting groups, and in tours and tour operations. They may accompany groups of tourists to explain what they will see in their own language, or they might work for tourist attractions where they provide language-specific tours. Extensive travel may be required, which for many Interpreters is a perk of the job.

It is crucial for Interpreters to be familiar with the material they will translate, whether it is the history of local sites or a question-and-answer session at a conference. Interpreters review background information before beginning a session and they must listen carefully and think quickly. Their familiarity with both languages should be so intuitive that they can anticipate what will come next, especially when interpreting a lecture to a large group.

Additional duties of Translators and Interpreters may include:

- speaking with people to ensure language comprehension
- consulting dictionaries and other material for word usage
- using electronic audio systems to transcribe language
- listening to speaker statements to ascertain meanings
- attending meetings, conferences, and events where more than one language is spoken
- reading material in different languages
- working on a computer to receive assignments electronically

Translators and Interpreters may work irregular hours including evenings and weekends to reflect the schedules of hotels, tours, and conference groups. Some work full-time, but many work on a freelance or part-time basis, providing services by contract for several different groups. This may lead to an erratic schedule and periods without work, but some Translators and Interpreters use that time to pursue other interests and enjoy the flexibility.

The challenge for Translators and Interpreters is not just to literally convert language, but to also make sure the meaning and message is conveyed, and is not "lost in translation," so to speak. For many, this is the aspect they enjoy most about their work.

Salaries

According to the Bureau of Labor Statistics (BLS), salaried Interpreters and Translators had median hourly earnings of $18.10 as of May 2007. The middle 50 percent earned between $13.49 and $24.36. The lowest 10 percent earned less than $10.34, and the highest 10 percent earned more than $32.25. The median annual wage was $37,490.

Salary can depend on several factors, including language, subject matter, skills, experience, and education. Higher earnings also can come from knowledge of a language in great demand. The BLS also says that some highly skilled Translators and Interpreters (such as high-level conference Interpreters) can earn more than $100,000 working full-time. For freelancers, salaries tend to fluctuate.

Employment Prospects

The BLS forecasts that demand for Translators and Interpreters will grow much faster than average over the next decade. Data shows that demand will remain strong for translators of the languages referred to as "PFIGS"—Portuguese, French, Italian, German, and Spanish; Arabic and other Middle Eastern languages; and the principal Asian languages—Chinese, Japanese, and Korean. Demand for American Sign Language Interpreters is also expected to grow rapidly.

Strong opportunities for Translators and Interpreters outside of the traditional hospitality fields include medicine and law, as well as working for the government or with immigrant populations. The BLS also states that 22 percent of Translators and Interpreters are self employed.

Advancement Prospects

Advancement prospects are also good for Translators and Interpreters. As freelancers, they can market themselves and expand their services, developing a strong client base. Those who work for large organizations like the United Nations, the federal government, or international corporations might be promoted to chief translation/interpretation responsibilities.

Education and Training

While no formal training or education is required to become a Translator or Interpreter, most Translators and Interpreters have at least a four-year college degree, especially those that are responsible for more complex language and material. Many also hold advanced degrees, which can help employment prospects.

Although formal education is not required, language fluency is. The ability to speak two languages is paramount, with many Translators and Interpreters knowing additional languages as well. Many Translators and Interpreters were raised bilingual; others lived and studied in foreign countries. A select few may never have lived abroad but have a knack for language through extensive study. Training may come from formal course work, intensive language institutes, or personal experience such as travel.

A limited number of schools offer certificate or degree programs in translating or interpreting. See the Web site for the American Translators Association for more information at www.atanet.org.

Experience, Skills, and Personality Traits

Above all, Translators and Interpreters must have excellent communication skills. They combine their skill in foreign language with the desire to help people and make information clear and accessible. Appreciation for different cultures enables them to work with people from all over the world with sensitivity and tact. They also must be flexible, quick thinkers who can process information easily.

Understanding of spelling, grammar, and word usage also enables them to perform their jobs efficiently. Patience and strong reading and listening skills help Translators and Interpreters pay attention to detail and focus on the information at hand.

Unions and Associations

The main professional association for Translators and Interpreters is the American Translators Association. Additionally, they may belong to other associations such as the Translators and Interpreters Guild and the American Association of Language Specialists. Furthermore, the Registry of Interpreters for the Deaf is a national association for those professionals who interpret sign language.

Tips for Entry

1. Find a mentor to help navigate the Translator/ Interpreter career path. Professional associations can be a great way to link up with people in the field. Try contacting the American Translators Association (www.atanet.org) and the Registry of Interpreters for the Deaf (www.rid.org) for more information.

2. Become an expert in a foreign language. Try studying abroad or at a language institute such as the one offered by the University of Virginia Summer Language Institute; see www.virginia.edu/summer/SLI.

3. Explore the possibility of teaching English in a foreign country. Sites such as www.daveseslcafe.com offer a multitude of job listings.

4. Attend an event where you can observe Interpreters at work. Pay close attention to their body language, mannerisms, and fluency.

5. Whether you are traveling abroad or locally, become aware of Interpreters at major attractions such as museums. Observe how they do their jobs. Are they leading groups, or accompanying other groups and interpreting information?

FOOD WRITER

CAREER PROFILE

Duties: Writes about food and/or wine for a newspaper, magazine, or other publication; offers critiques and ratings

Alternate Title(s): Food Critic; Restaurant Reviewer; Food and Wine Writer

Salary Range: $20,000 to $70,000 and up

Employment Prospects: Poor to fair

Advancement Prospects: Fair

Best Geographical Location(s): All, with the best opportunities in larger cities

Prerequisites:

    Education and Training—Degree in journalism or culinary training

    Experience—Several years of writing and reporting experience and/or culinary work

    Special Skills and Personality Traits—Excellent writing and reporting skills; knowledge of food and wine; an adventurous palate; strong communication skills

CAREER LADDER

Food Writer, larger publication, or Food Editor

Food Writer

General Assignment Reporter, Staff Writer, or Chef

Position Description

Imagine getting paid to eat for a living. In essence, that is what Food Writers do. However, the job entails much more than simple wining and dining. Food Writers offer critiques on new restaurants, wines, eating trends, and more.

Food Writers can work in a variety of settings. At newspapers, they often write for a dining, food and wine, arts, entertainment, or features section. They might review restaurants in a number of different price or food categories, cover openings of new food stores and events, rate wines, interview chefs or restaurant owners, write feature stories related to food, and write pieces that include recipes. They may cover similar topics for general magazines and Web sites; in addition, they can work for specialty publications dedicated to food and wine. Furthermore, some Food Writers work as freelancers and authors.

While not all Food Writers are also critics, many do write restaurant reviews. Like other critics, they devise a rating system to account for all factors that contribute to a restaurant's success—food, service, atmosphere, price/value, cleanliness, noise level, presentation, and overall dining experience. They must be willing to try many things on the menu and to analyze them with an expert's palate, not just based on taste alone. Food Writers consider how the chef prepared the meal, looking for creativity in terms of ingredients and presentation.

They examine the menu, looking for new and innovative ideas and approaches. Some offer a star system as a rating, with five stars being outstanding.

Food Writers may be faced with the challenge of chefs and restaurant owners who expect good publicity in exchange for free meals. Since a review by a prominent critic can have an impact on a restaurant's success, chefs can become very angry about a bad review, questioning the writer's expertise or wanting to strike a deal. Food Writers who develop personal relationships with chefs or proprietors may find it difficult to remain objective. However, it is important for Food Writers to remain professional and detached, offering their ratings as a guide to readers. Some Food Writers may visit a restaurant several times before writing about it, in order to not base their review on only one experience.

Chefs and restaurant staff are often nervous when a critic arrives. If a prominent critic is dining, the staff may feel the need to give special treatment in exchange for a positive review. Some Food Writers report going to restaurants incognito and providing false names on their reservation. While some see this as dishonest, others say it is the only way to judge the restaurant experience for the average person. Their reviews serve to help people decide where to spend their money for dining.

Food Writers offer a combination of facts and opinions to serve as credible sources. In their reviews and articles, they provide tangible facts about prices, menu items, and decor. Furthermore, they share their educated opinion about less tangible factors such as taste and service. Food Writers must have excellent background knowledge of food and culinary history to make their judgments. They use evidence to justify their conclusions and analyze their experience.

In addition to reviewing restaurants, Food Writers cover other issues of importance in dining. They may have specialties in areas such as wine, Italian cooking, budget dining, vegetarian lifestyle, family establishments, or desserts and pastries. Some may focus on food preparation and cooking rather than dining. Furthermore, different communities have various food trends and may focus on issues such as organic produce or free-range farms.

Often, Food Writers conduct interviews and write human-interest pieces that relate in some way to food. They may offer tips about barbecuing in the summer and suggestions about pairing food and drink. Their writing contributes to their readers' lifestyles. Some Food Writers have columns as well.

Their duties may include:

- covering food events
- visiting wineries, farms, or factories where food or wine is produced
- researching and reporting on food trends
- contributing to cookbooks
- trying exotic dishes
- speaking to restaurant patrons and waitstaff
- collaborating with travel or entertainment writers
- working with editors to generate story ideas and complete assignments
- creating a diverse list of restaurant genres and locations to review
- writing books in conjunction with chefs
- answering reader mail
- working with copy editors and page designers on formatting articles
- working with photographers and food stylists

Food Writers may eat in restaurants several times a week. While for many this is one of the best parts about their job, some Food Writers do say that it gets tiring to go out all the time. Others note that they need to exercise in order to balance out the sometime excess of rich and fattening foods.

Although they enjoy their meals, Food Writers cannot merely sit back and relax while they dine. They must take notes and pay attention to every detail of their experience. Staff Food Writers have expenses covered by their publication and may be permitted to bring a guest. Freelance Food Writers and those at small publications typically have much smaller budgets.

An interesting aspect of food writing is that it can combine several types of journalism. Food Writers often include components of travel, entertainment, and health for different stories. With our culture of celebrity chefs and trendy restaurants, a lucky few Food Writers become something of celebrities themselves. The rest, however, are satisfied informing their local communities and doing something they enjoy.

Salaries

Salaries for full-time staff Food Writers vary depending on the level and responsibility of their position. In the newspaper industry, experienced reporters can earn in the $40,000 to $50,000 range. The Newspaper Industry Compensation Survey, conducted annually by the Inland Press Association, shows that experienced reporters earned an average of $43,292 per year in 2004 in total direct compensation.

At magazines, Web sites, and publishing companies, Food Writers can earn comparable salaries, and sometimes even higher ones. Typical ranges are from $25,000 for entry-level positions to $60,000 and above with experience. Freelance Food Writers can earn anywhere from several hundred dollars per year up to $50,000 and more, depending on their previous writing experience, connections, and contracts. However, it is difficult to earn enough money to make a living as a freelancer without extensive prior journalism experience.

In addition to base salary, Food Writers enjoy perks such as expense accounts for dining and related travel. Their work may give them the opportunity to eat in fine restaurants they could never afford on a journalist's salary alone.

Employment Prospects

As a whole, Food Writers love their work. For this reason, staff positions are extremely competitive. Anyone who is persistent may find a way to review new local eateries for their small-town paper, but staff positions that enable Food Writers to make a living this way are not plentiful.

If you love to eat as well as write, be prepared to start small and gather the right combination of skills. Food Writers may start as journalists at local papers, while gathering expertise in the food industry through training and courses. Food Writers may also find positions at magazines, Web sites, and publishing companies that produce cookbooks and restaurant/travel guides, as well as through freelancing.

Advancement Prospects

Although staff positions for Food Writers are very competitive, new restaurants are always opening, creating a buzz and need for reviews. Specialty niches can be important as a way for Food Writers to market themselves. Food Writers can advance by finding bigger markets—larger city newspapers, specialty magazines, and others. They may also supplement staff work with freelance articles, columns, and books.

Education and Training

Food Writers can come to the professional in several different ways. Many have degrees in journalism. These Food Writers usually start out as general assignment reporters and slowly build up experience with entertainment and features in order to switch over to food. Others begin as editorial assistants or staff writers at food-themed magazines.

While some come from journalism and build up food expertise, others come from the food industry and build their writing skills. Food Writers may be former chefs or restaurant owners, as well as amateur cooks. Some may have degrees in culinary arts or certificates from cooking schools. Wine courses and training are also very valuable. A combination of writing and culinary training is ideal.

Experience, Skills, and Personality Traits

Successful Food Writers have a passion for food. They are adventurous eaters who enjoy varied and exotic food and drink. While of course they have particular likes and dislikes, they are generally willing to try most things.

This passion for food must be combined with excellent writing skills. Food Writers need to know how to write a critical analysis, as well as report on news and events. A good command of language and an engaging style makes their pieces enjoyable to read. As journalists, they are able to adhere to tight deadlines and generate creative ideas.

Furthermore, Food Writers need excellent observation skills and a good eye for detail, as they use their senses at all times. Strong communication skills enable them to conduct interviews and interact with "foodies" of all kinds.

Unions and Associations

Food Writers may belong to professional associations including the Association of Food Journalists, the International Food, Wine, and Travel Writers Association, and the International Association of Culinary Professionals.

Tips for Entry

1. Explore and read food and wine magazines such as *Saveur* and *Bon Appetit* (www.epicurious.com) *Food and Wine* (www.foodandwine.com), and *Wine Spectator* (www.winespectator.com). Consider internship opportunities in these settings.

2. Visit the Web site of the Association of Food Journalists at www.afjonline.com. They offer such features as critics'guidelines, recipes and news, and spelling tips for exotic food terms.

3. Browse through the dining section of your local bookstore. Read the bios of cookbook authors and other types of food-related publications to learn more about their professional backgrounds.

4. Try writing restaurant reviews for a campus or local publication. By pitching your ideas, you may find that many would be happy to have you work for free and enable you to build a portfolio.

5. Read the dining section of different newspapers. Take note not only of the restaurant reviews, but also the food news and other components of the section.

6. Take a wine-tasting course. Local courses are often available through college and universities, as well as culinary institutes. See the offering at the University of California at Davis at extension. ucdavis.edu/unit/winemaking/course/listing/ ?unit=WINE&prgList=WAP&coursearea=Wine +Appreciation.

TRAVEL PHOTOGRAPHER

Duties: Takes pictures related to domestic or international travel destinations; may shoot video footage and/or write some captions or copy

Alternate Title(s): Photojournalist; Videographer; Freelance Photographer

Salary Range: $10,000 to $100,000 and up

Employment Prospects: Fair

Advancement Prospects: Fair

Best Geographical Location(s): Major cities such as New York or Los Angeles that are home to magazines and advertising agencies; may travel to many destinations

Prerequisites:

Education and Training—Bachelor's degree not required, but can offer credibility; fields such as photography, media production, and arts are helpful; photography and/or video training necessary

Experience—Prior photography experience including a viable portfolio

CAREER LADDER

Photo Editor, Head Photographer, or Travel Photography Entrepreneur

↑

Photographer

↑

Photo Assistant or Photographer, smaller market

Special Skills and Personality Traits—Creativity and artistic vision; excellent technical photography skills; good visual eye; ability to work with people and work well under pressure; flexibility and willingness to travel

Position Description

Travel Photographers bring readers and viewers along with them to destinations all over the world. Whether on location in Africa filming herds of zebra, or shooting new features of a cruise ship for a brochure to promote sales, Travel Photographers capture images meant to pique the interest of their audience. They tell a visual story using different media and can market their work in a variety of ways.

Some Travel Photographers work for magazines, newspapers, guidebooks, or Web sites. These publications may be travel-focused, such as *Travel & Leisure* or *National Geographic,* or they may be general interest publications, which often feature travel pieces. Travel Photographers at magazines may be staff members or freelancers, paid on a per-assignment basis. They work on the magazine deadlines, weekly or monthly. Travel to locations is often required, but sometimes photos will be shot in studios near the magazine's offices.

Travel Photographers may run entire photo shoots, including scouting locations, deciding what equipment to use, and hiring models when necessary. They may take still pictures or shoot video or other multimedia content. Once the photos are taken or video is filmed,

Travel Photographers may send their images or content digitally back to the studio for editing. Some Travel Photographers edit their own work, while others work with editors responsible for that component.

Additionally, Travel Photographers might work for television programs airing on stations such as the Travel Channel. They set up scenes and film segments. The content may serve as the primary focus of the program, or as scenes meant to serve in the background, what is known as B Roll.

Other Travel Photographers may work in commercial photography, the advertising realm of the travel industry. They may work for hotels, cruise lines, resorts, or tourism bureaus taking pictures to be used in promotional brochures, ads, and other collateral materials.

Their duties may include:

- performing digital photo or video editing
- developing film in a darkroom
- writing articles, captions, or content
- working with writers and editors
- shooting photo essays (series of linked images that tell a story)
- attending meetings with management
- taking direction from photo editors

It is important for Travel Photographers to use their visual skills to tell a story. Their work may be accompanied by articles, captions, or video narration; regardless, their role is to interpret and complement the story. Patience can be highly important for Travel Photographers filming animals or waiting for the right natural lighting to perfect a shot. Since most travel photography is shot outdoors, Travel Photographers must make use of shadows, exposure, and other features to convey the right mood for a shoot.

Travel Photographers may complete specific assignments as directed by editors or producers or they may pitch their own ideas. Many work on a freelance basis. They may work a variety of shifts including evenings and weekends. Travel is frequently a huge component of the job, which many Travel Photographers see as the greatest perk of their work.

Salaries

Salaries for Travel Photographers vary greatly depending on their type of work and years of experience. In-house Travel Photographers typically earn between $20,000 to $70,000 and up. Freelance Travel Photographers are paid per assignment, and pay is determined by experience as well as size and scope of the assignment. Salaries reflect the amount of hours Travel Photographers work, their reputation, and their entrepreneurial skills at marketing themselves.

When considering compensation for Travel Photographers, one must also consider the other aspects that comprise the overall financial rewards. For experienced Travel Photographers on assignment, these can include free travel, free accommodations, free meals, and free access to the world's most exotic destinations and attractions. However, Travel Photographers need to cover many of these expenses themselves when they are first starting out.

Employment Prospects

Employment prospects for Travel Photographers are fair. The field is affected by the economy, as people travel less in hard financial times. The best opportunities are in larger cities and for those who demonstrate an entrepreneurial spirit, marketing themselves and their work on their Internet and through other venues.

Travel Photographers may get started as photo assistants shooting restaurants and hotels for brochures or wall displays. They may also freelance for little or no pay to build up portfolios. Experience through internships or photography classes can be valuable, and help aspiring Travel Photographers make helpful contacts.

Advancement Prospects

Travel Photographers can advance in several ways. They may work their way up to becoming photo editors at magazines, where they have more control over artistic vision and direction, managing a staff of photographers. They also may move to larger, more prestigious publications where they have greater responsibility and salaries. On the video side, they may advance to become television producers, directors of travel segments or programs, or documentary filmmakers.

Furthermore, freelance Travel Photographers may advance by either finding staff positions or by growing and expanding their freelance business. They may focus on images of one city or certain types of landscapes, or a variety of scenic shots. By making direct contact with potential clients, they can build up a network of referrals.

Research and persistence is a key way to build a business and opportunities for potential clients can be found through Internet searches, targeting publishers of travel books and magazines, and checking visitor guides in hotels. Travel Photographers must then query them and offer to send submissions of their work.

Education and Training

While it is not necessary for Travel Photographers to have bachelor's degrees, it can help them break into today's competitive job market. Undergraduate programs in photography or media production can provide the technical skills needed to succeed. Courses in art, digital design, or journalism can also be useful, depending on overall goals.

If formal education based on degrees is not crucial, training in photography is essential for Travel Photographers. Although digital editing is now the norm, most Travel Photographers are also skilled in the traditional darkroom process.

Experience, Skills, and Personality Traits

Above all, Travel Photographers are creative and flexible, with a good eye and strong artistic vision. They must be able to shoot a variety of coverage while managing tight deadlines. Strong communication skills enable Travel Photographers to work with writers, producers, editors, and subjects effectively. Patience and persistence is also needed to work with animals or natural settings, such as sunsets or snowstorms.

Furthermore, Travel Photographers must have the technical skills to follow through on their artistic vision. They need to understand the use of digital and regular cameras, know how to expose film, edit pictures, and use a darkroom. The use of light and its challenges, balancing color, processing digital imaging, and digital editing are also required. Computer programs for editing such as Adobe Photoshop and Final Cut Pro are valuable.

Unions and Associations

Travel Photographers may belong to professional associations including the Professional Photographers of America, the American Society of Media Photographers, the American Society of Picture Professionals, the Stock Artists Alliance, and others.

Tips for Entry

1. Check out Lonely Planet Images, a digital image library with a collection of over 300,000 professional-quality destination photographs: www.lonelyplanetimages.com/homepage.html. Their submission guidelines can be found at this page by clicking on "Prospective Photographers."

2. Photo essays are a great way to get recognition for your work. Choose a topic of interest such as the "Best Bed-and-Breakfasts in the Northeast," or "Top Roadside Restaurants in the Southwest," and write and shoot a travel series you can market.

3. Develop your own style and niche, whether it is a nautical series or work focused on different images of your hometown.

4. Utilize different forms of media such as podcasts to post on the Internet. Create your own travel blog, which can feature multimedia components showcasing your work.

5. Look into the Stock Artists Alliance at www.stockartistsalliance.org. This is the only professional trade association focused on the business of stock photography.

HOSPITALITY PROFESSOR

CAREER PROFILE

Duties: Serves on the faculty of a college or university, teaching courses to undergraduates and/or graduate students; may also conduct research and/or publish scholarly or trade material as well as maintain industry ties

Alternate Title(s): Instructor; Lecturer; Faculty Member

Salary Range: $30,000 to $125,000 and above

Employment Prospects: Fair

Advancement Prospects: Fair to good

Best Geographical Location(s): All (especially college towns and schools that offer hospitality programs)

Prerequisites:

Education and Training—Depending on the program, a combination of academic credentials and professional experience is required; a master's degree in a hospitality field (hotel or restaurant management, tourism) is often the minimum credential, but professionals with extensive accomplishments may have only a bachelor's degree (especially in fields

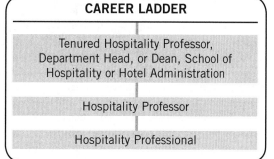

such as culinary arts); a Ph.D. is required at some colleges and universities

Experience—At least five years of professional work or a combination of graduate education, completed dissertation, and experience

Special Skills and Personality Traits—Good communication and leadership skills; teaching ability; writing, research, and/or business background

Position Description

Hospitality Professors are responsible for teaching, training, and mentoring the hotel, restaurant, and tourism specialists of the future. Spanning the hospitality disciplines such as hotel and restaurant administration, culinary arts, special events, tourism management, and others, they leverage their professional expertise to prepare students for careers in the hospitality and travel industry.

A professor in a specific field such as hospitality might have a somewhat different background from the traditional path of an academic. By and large, Hospitality Professors are current or former hospitality professionals. Whether their experience is in hotels, restaurants/culinary arts, gaming, resorts, communications, or business, they frequently have significant experience and accomplishments out in the field. For many positions, management experience, particularly in hotel front office operations, is required. Since hospitality is a professional discipline, its educators need to understand the profession from the inside out.

Hospitality programs may offer concentrations or specializations in the following areas:

- business/management
- tourism
- culinary arts
- gaming/casino management
- pastry/baking
- hotel management
- restaurant/food service management
- special events and convention administration
- ecotourism
- recreation and parks management
- club and resort management
- marketing
- front office operations
- hospitality accounting or law
- ethics, philosophy, and/or history

Depending on what they studied when they were students and the trajectory of their career following their education, Hospitality Professors often specialize in one of these areas. They may teach core courses in addition to their specialty.

Hospitality Professors may work at colleges or universities that do not have separate hotel schools or even departments. They may be part of a business school, geography department, health and physical education department, recreation department, nutrition department, or culinary institute, to name just a few. There are also many hospitality programs at community colleges.

Hospitality Professors may teach exclusively undergraduate students or graduate students, or a combination of both. They have an assigned course load per semester, usually about 12 to 16 teaching hours per week. In addition to the actual teaching of these courses, Hospitality Professors prepare extensively for them. Developing curriculum and syllabi, selecting texts and reading material, designing tests and assignments, and determining grades are all part of the process. In the classroom, Hospitality Professors are able to draw from their experience and use their creativity to devise the most effective methods of teaching their subject according to their own personal style.

Additional duties may include:

- advising and mentoring undergraduate or graduate students
- supervising teaching assistants
- writing grant proposals to fund research
- participating in faculty meetings
- holding office hours for students
- writing textbooks or other publications
- teaching online courses
- serving as faculty advisers to campus restaurants, hotels, or other hospitality ventures
- collaborating with campus administrators
- fulfilling university service requirements
- supervising internships or practical training
- participating in student recruiting
- providing career advice and guidance
- developing online courses

Some Hospitality Professors still work in some capacity as professionals in the industry, serving as consultants, managers, or trainers. With teaching schedules usually not taking up more than 16 hours per week, they are able to use their time flexibly. Teaching may take place during the day, or on evenings and weekends, especially at programs geared toward working professionals or other adult learners. Many Hospitality Professors work a nine- or ten-month year, enjoying reduced course loads or no course assignments over the summer months and during school breaks.

Salaries

Salaries for Hospitality Professors can vary greatly depending not only on the school at which they teach but also according to their own professional background. Well-known hospitality schools may use money as a way to recruit high-profile professionals to come and teach in their program, while those professors at other institutions will follow the traditional academic salary scales.

According to a 2006–07 survey by the American Association of University Professors, the average salary for faculty members with doctorates averaged $83,865. At the master's level, the average salary for all types of professors combined was $64,488 and at the baccalaureate level, $61,951. At two-year colleges with ranks (including full professor, associate professor, assistant professor, lecturer, and instructor), the average was $54,746 and at two-year colleges without ranks, $50,462.

Generally speaking, faculty at private four-year institutions earn higher average salaries than those teaching at community colleges or state colleges and universities.

In addition to their base salaries, Hospitality Professors may earn additional income from writing, consulting, or speaking engagements. They may also receive special university benefits such as tuition for dependents, housing allowances, and other perks.

Employment Prospects

Experienced hospitality professionals who are looking for a change as well as a more regular schedule often covet positions as Hospitality Professors. After the demands of this service-oriented industry, the hours of freedom between course loads and lack of evening work can be very attractive. Because of this, competition for positions can be very tight, especially tenure-track positions, which offer higher salaries, more freedom, and greater security.

One way for professionals to break into the teaching market is through work as an adjunct instructor. Adjunct instructors are not full-time employees of their institutions. While common at two-year colleges, community colleges, and smaller colleges and universities, adjunct positions are also frequent at larger institutions when a working professional only wants to teach one course. This is cost-effective for the school, as they do not have to pay overall salary and benefits and the Hospitality Professor is only paid per class taught.

Working as an adjunct instructor can be a good way for a hospitality professional to gain teaching experience as an entry to a full-time professorship or a way for otherwise-employed professionals to share their skills and teach on the side. Unfortunately, adjunct work alone is not usually financially feasible for most people looking to support themselves.

The job search process for full-time Hospitality Professors is very grueling. Interviews are extensive and a candidate's past writing, research, and professional accomplishments are scrutinized. A selection committee makes final decisions after candidates fully explain their expertise and accomplishments, as well as their teaching methodologies.

For those who are determined to find a position as a Hospitality Professor, it is necessary to be geographically flexible. Positions may open up in small towns and opportunities that get passed up may not come again.

Advancement Prospects

Advancement for Hospitality Professors, as with other university professors, is usually through the tenure process. The time frame for tenure review varies by school, but often occurs after approximately seven years under contract. At this point, the instructor's accomplishments are reviewed and tenure may be awarded.

What this means is that those granted tenure essentially enjoy job stability for the rest of their lives, if they so desire. Hospitality Professors with tenure can feel free to explore new ideas and controversial topics without fear of losing their jobs for being unpopular.

The typical advancement process is from assistant professor to associate professor, and then to full professor status. Once granted tenure, Hospitality Professors can advance to become department heads or even deans of hospitality schools.

Education and Training

Unlike professors in other fields, education for Hospitality Professors will vary. At many schools, career accomplishments are valued more highly than educational credentials. Hospitality Professors may hold bachelor's degrees, master's degrees, or doctoral degrees. Usually, they have a combination of hospitality education and professional experience. The professional experience required in some programs can be extensive, ranging from five to 10 years or more.

The Ph.D. typically takes six to eight years beyond the bachelor's degree, culminating in a significant original research paper called a dissertation. Course work may take up half the time, and the research and writing of the dissertation the other.

Experience, Skills, and Personality Traits

In order to teach their subject well, Hospitality Professors need experience and expertise in their industry. Depending on their specialty, they have worked as chefs, hotel managers, operations directors, marketing specialists, event planners, or other professionals.

To train future professionals, Hospitality Professors must be expert communicators that like to work with people. Speaking and customer service skills are vital, as well as knowledge of a business environment. In addition to having these skills, Hospitality Professors must also be good teachers and have the ability to impart their knowledge to others. They need to motivate students to succeed and must be able to assess students' work fairly and objectively.

Furthermore, Hospitality Professors need organization and management abilities. Not only will these skills help them in their classrooms, but they will also help them lead groups of students.

Unions and Associations

Some Hospitality Professors may belong to academic professional associations such as the American Association of University Professors, the Association of American Colleges and Universities, and the American Association of Community Colleges. Others may belong to hospitality associations such as the International Council on Hotel, Restaurant and Institutional Education or the Hospitality, Marketing and Sales Association International. They may also belong to the International Society of Travel and Tourism Educators.

Tips for Entry

1. Cornell University, in Ithaca, New York, has one of the top hotel schools in the country. Their school of hotel administration offers bachelor's, master's and doctoral degrees. Check out the program at www.hotelschool.cornell.edu.
2. Consider working as a teaching assistant for a course. This will provide valuable experience in standing up in front of a class, devising assignments, and grading.
3. Speak to hospitality professors about their career path. Ask them questions about how they came to academia and where did they work before and for how long. Take the opportunity to benefit from their valuable advice.
4. Take a look at the Web site for the Chronicle of Higher Education (www.chronicle.com), the leading publication in the academic world. Look at its job listings for Hospitality Professors to learn more about requirements. Also, see www.higheredjobs.com for additional listings.

WEDDING PLANNER

CAREER LADDER

```
Wedding Planner, larger market, or
Director of Special Events

Wedding Planner

Special Events Assistant
```

quet halls planning special events, or in bridal shops, before striking out on their own

Special Skills and Personality Traits—Excellent organization skills and attention to detail; ability to work well with people; strong communication skills; leadership and management skills; ability to stay calm under pressure

Position Description

In today's busy world, people try to find ways to outsource many of their daily tasks. A wedding is one of the most exciting and important moments in a couple's life. With time at a premium, many couples seek assistance with planning this special day.

Wedding Planners assist couples with as many or as few aspects of planning their wedding as needed. Some couples simply do not have the time to focus on the details; others want advice from an expert about how to make their event as memorable as possible. Wedding Planners serve as guides—sometimes also as marriage counselors, parents, mediators, and salespeople—to walk them through every step of the process.

Wedding Planners first meet with couples to determine their plan for their wedding. Budgets need to be established early on so Wedding Planners know the limits in which they need to work. Once the budget is determined, Wedding Planners work with various vendors, including florists, invitation suppliers, caterers, musicians, and many others. They may solicit proposals and contract with vendors, presenting all the information to their clients for final approval. Their goal is to get their clients the highest quality of service for the best price, as well as find the particular style that is right for the individual couple.

Some brides and grooms will contact a Wedding Planner as soon as they get engaged, asking for assistance with selecting a wedding date and choosing a venue. Wedding Planners may be hired a year or more before the event, or with the wedding just several months away. A Wedding Planner may help with details including:

- how to obtain a marriage license
- securing the services of a wedding officiate
- selecting music as well as musicians
- planning rehearsals and/or bridal showers
- coordinating venue staff
- determining seating arrangements
- selecting gifts for attendants
- developing a floral theme
- choosing bridesmaid dresses
- helping the bride choose a wedding dress
- selecting rings
- arranging for a photographer/videographer
- choosing invitations
- planning the menu, including the wedding cake
- negotiating contracts

While many meetings and decisions take place in the months leading up to the wedding, on the actual day of the event, a Wedding Planner is very busy. He or she will attend the wedding, coordinating the details of the day, including the processional, setup, hair/makeup/gown, music, flowers, etc. Wedding Planners pay close attention to detail and troubleshoot, finding solutions for last-minute issues that may occur.

Some Wedding Planners may be responsible for planning themed receptions or destination weddings. They may plan specific types of religious or civil ceremonies, both traditional and unique. They must be attuned to people and strike the balance of asserting their expertise yet complying with the wishes of the couple and providing them with the type of event they desire.

For Wedding Planners working as private consultants, some of their time is spent running their own business, including marketing, advertising, merchandising, and bookkeeping. Most Wedding Planners are self-employed, generating business through marketing and advertising, as well as through word of mouth. Most charge a flat fee to the bride and groom that includes an array of services. Typically, a Wedding Planner's fee is 10 to 15 percent the total cost of the wedding. Less common is for Wedding Planners not to charge the bride and groom but instead receive a percentage from their vendors, usually between 8 and 10 percent.

However, Wedding Planners are not only for the wealthy. Typically, through developing a network of vendors, they are able to get better prices for the couple on music, flowers, and other services. Through this concept, the bride and groom actually save money on their overall wedding costs by using a Wedding Planner. It does not always work out this way, but many couples feel it is worth the splurge to have someone knowledgeable handle the process and help them navigate the sometimes overwhelming web of services.

Also, some Wedding Planners are employed by catering facilities or hotels. As soon as a couple selects the venue, they are automatically provided with a Wedding Planner who will help them with the details. In this case, the couple does not pay out of pocket; the Wedding Planner's salary comes from the facility at which he or she works.

Wedding Planners may operate out of a home office, their own office space, or visit clients in their homes. Due to the nature of the work, Wedding Planners must expect to work on evenings and weekends, when most weddings take place. The hours are not traditional and can be long and stressful. However, many Wedding Planners take great satisfaction in attending clients' weddings—seeing everything come together for a happy occasion.

Salaries

Depending on their market, salaries for Wedding Planners can vary greatly. Those who are self-employed may earn salaries ranging from a few thousand dollars to $50,000 and up for those catering to the rich and famous. Yearly salary will depend on how many clients they take on, and success depends on word of mouth and the size of the market in which they work.

For Wedding Planners employed by catering facilities, salaries may range between $40,000 to $70,000 per year depending on the size of the venue and budget of the typical event at that location. They may also be responsible for planning other types of events for their facility.

Employment Prospects

Overall, employment prospects are fair for Wedding Planners. Job opportunities can be somewhat dependent on the economy; while people keep getting married in tough economic times, they often do cut back on their budgets. However, since Wedding Planners provide a service that is always needed, opportunity depends on geographic location as well as marketing success. Larger cities with more affluent and high-powered clients provide the best opportunity for Wedding Planners who are self-employed.

Some Wedding Planners also find more employment opportunities by planning additional events along with weddings, including bar/bat mitzvahs, Sweet Sixteens, corporate events, and other parties.

Advancement Prospects

Wedding Planners might advance by building their business. Additional advertising and marketing techniques can increase client base and allow them to become more selective and charge higher fees. Developing a Web site can be a necessity for Wedding Planners looking to expand their business.

Additionally, Wedding Planners working at catering facilities may advance to become directors of all events, or move to larger facilities for higher-revenue events.

Education and Training

There is no typical educational path to become a Wedding Planner and a college degree is not required. However, many Wedding Planners come from within the hospitality industry, having worked in event planning at hotels, restaurants, or catering halls before developing enough contacts to start their own business. Other Wedding Planners may have experience working in bridal stores or salons, helping brides select gowns, veils, and other accessories.

Courses in business, hospitality, entrepreneurship, management, marketing, event planning, or public relations may be helpful for Wedding Planners looking to build their businesses.

Additionally, there are a number of wedding planner certification courses available. While not required, these courses can help provide credibility and contacts in a competitive market. See the Association of Certified Wedding Consultants at www.acpwc.com for more information.

Experience, Skills, and Personality Traits

While from the outside, wedding planning may appear to be glamorous and fun, the work can be difficult and stressful. Successful Wedding Planners are masters at developing relationships, which they need to do with both clients and vendors. Excellent communication skills enable them to connect with people, so couples will trust them to handle their big day and value their advice and input.

Managing stress is a big part of the job. As Wedding Planners help people prepare for a major emotional event in their lives, they must be able to bear the brunt of disappointments and high expectations. With all events, things can go wrong. A beautiful outdoor ceremony can be marred by unexpected thunderstorms or a florist could bring the wrong color roses. Wedding Planners must remain calm and take control of the situation, alleviating stress for the couple and managing problems as they arise. They must also be prepared to soothe highly emotional brides and grooms who might panic if things do not go exactly as planned.

A wedding is all about details, so Wedding Planners must be highly organized. They must be able to balance multiple tasks and be thorough. Good business sense helps Wedding Planners market themselves and their work. It must be coupled by strong integrity as word of mouth in this business is extremely valuable.

Unions and Associations

There are many professional associations to which Wedding Planners may belong including the Association of Bridal Consultants, the Association of Certified Wedding Consultants, the National Association of Wedding Professionals, June Wedding, Inc., and the Association for Wedding Professionals International.

Tips for Entry

1. Take a look at the Web site for the Association for Wedding Professionals International, afwpi.com, which includes a job board and opportunities for networking and referrals.

2. For fun, rent the 2001 movie *The Wedding Planner* starring Jennifer Lopez. While the Hollywood depiction is very glamorous, it provides a humorous look into the work of a Wedding Planner.

3. Look into the FabJob Guide: How to Become a Wedding Planner at www.fabjob.com/weddingplanner.asp.

4. Entrepreneur.com has an interesting article on starting up a business as a Wedding Planner. Read it at www.entrepreneur.com/startingabusiness/businessideas/startupkits/article41348.html.

5. Go to a bookstore and browse through wedding magazines such as *Martha Stewart Weddings* or *Bridal Guide*. Look at the topics covered, as well as advertisements for vendors and consultants.

WEBMASTER

Duties: Develops, manages, and maintains a Web site for a hotel, resort, or travel-related organization; oversees programming and content for the site

Alternate Titles: Web Site Administrator; Web Developer; Web Producer; Web Site Manager

Salary Range: $40,000 to $70,000 and up

Employment Prospects: Fair

Advancement Prospects: Fair

Best Geographical Location(s): All, with the greatest opportunities in large cities and heavy tourist regions with many resorts and hotels

Prerequisites:

Education and Training—Bachelor's degree in computer science preferred, but not required; knowledge of computer programming

Experience—Related experience creating and managing Web sites through full-time work or internships

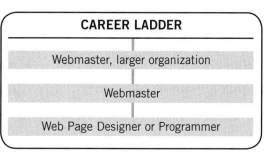

CAREER LADDER

Webmaster, larger organization

Webmaster

Web Page Designer or Programmer

Special Skills and Personality Traits—Excellent computer programming skills; understanding of Internet and online communication technologies; strong organizational skills; ability to meet deadlines and work well under pressure; knowledge of graphic design

Position Description

Web sites are an essential part of the hospitality and travel industries. The Web site of a hotel or resort can be crucial to its success, as people book reservations online and learn about amenities and specials. Furthermore, visitors conduct much of their travel research online as well, reading reviews of different destinations and attractions, as well as arranging for transportation, meals, lodging and more. Webmasters create and implement these Internet visions.

Starting from scratch, Webmasters strategize as to what will make a successful Web site for their organization, whether it is a beach resort, hotel or restaurant chain, small bed-and-breakfast, a travel review site, or large tour operation. They gather information from all the departments and key players to determine the overall structure of the site. Their aim is to command the attention of visitors and to make them want to linger on the site. A user-friendly site can mean a considerable difference in success.

The job of a Webmaster is often defined differently at varying sites. It may include programming, graphic design and determining the appearance of the site, content development, and production. Most Webmasters continuously maintain and update their sites after development, troubleshooting problems. They create

the links that visitors use to navigate the site. Also, they record the "hits" so they know the parts of the site people most often visit and whether they complete online registrations.

Additionally, Webmasters may work on both the back end and the front end of a Web site. The back end involves the database and hardware infrastructure that supports the site, requiring the Webmaster to be skilled at programming. The front end relates to the aspects that users can see, such as design and navigation tools, which requires the Webmaster to be up to speed on graphics and content development. Webmasters must decide on the hardware needed to build the site and the software needed to make it work properly.

Webmasters must continuously communicate with the different departments at their organization (including public relations, sales/marketing, and many others) to make sure that the information on the Web site is up-to-date and reflects the most current information. Information gets outdated in the blink of an eye, so they must be on top of all new developments such as reduced rates, special events, promotions, and news. Usually, they serve as internal liaisons and do little work with external vendors.

Furthermore, Webmasters create the documents—Web pages—that constitute the site. They may supervise the content writers and computer programmers that develop the text and graphics. Always, they are guided both by what will work as well as what will look aesthetically pleasing. Web design and Web development may also be components of the Webmaster's job. Web design involves the visual art and graphic design that defines the look of the site. Web development focuses more on the site's structure and interactivity.

Their duties may include:

- setting up and managing internal and external Listservs
- fixing software bugs
- brainstorming ideas
- adding new features such as discussion boards and registration capabilities
- researching Web sites of similar organizations
- writing code
- responding to visitor feedback
- supporting users nationwide and worldwide
- posting content pages
- editing and reviewing content
- testing the links on the site to make sure they work properly
- dealing with security issues

Webmasters use their technical skills to make information accessible to the public. Most Webmasters are passionate about the Internet and are very involved in their work, getting paid to indulge in one of their favorite hobbies. Since the Internet does not function on a nine-to-five schedule, neither do most Webmasters. Their jobs may involve long, nontraditional hours to enable sites to go live and fix any problems.

Salaries

Salaries of Webmasters vary based on where they work, as well as their job responsibilities. As the position continues to change and get redefined in new media, salaries will differ. Typical ranges can be anywhere from $40,000 to $70,000 and up for those with considerable experience. These figures demonstrate the large range for these types of positions.

Employment Prospects

Employment prospects for Webmasters are fair. However, growth is promising as even small hotels and restaurants are developing and building on their Web sites to make themselves competitive and known in this tight market. Sometimes, the Webmaster role is combined with that of a Web designer or other specialist. Opportunities are best for those with a wide range of skills including programming, writing, management, and graphic design. Some Webmasters work on a freelance basis, which may be a good way to gain experience in the field.

Advancement Prospects

Webmasters may advance by moving to larger organizations with more complex Web sites. They may seek out positions that enable them to build more online features such as reservation features and discussion boards, and even cutting-edge technologies such as streaming videos. Webmasters at larger organizations can earn higher salaries. Webmasters may also decide to become self-employed, working as new-media consultants. Those who have built experience working in the hospitality industry can develop a niche area for themselves as consultants.

Education and Training

While formal education is less important for Webmasters than having the required skill sets, most position listings require bachelor's degrees. Fields such as computer science, programming, or information technology are especially helpful. Some positions require additional skills, such as writing and graphic design.

The best training for the field comes from actually doing the work. Most Webmasters gain experience through internships and part-time jobs while they are students. As they design Web sites for campus organizations or companies, they receive the valuable training needed to perform this job on a regular basis. Furthermore, constant training is needed to keep skills up-to-date with new technologies.

Experience, Skills, and Personality Traits

Excellent computer skills are required to become a Webmaster. Depending upon the position, different programming languages may be needed. Some common requirements may include HTML, XML, CGL, SQL, Java, JavaScript, ASP, ColdFusion, and C++. Web development and design tools such as Acrobat, Dreamweaver, Flash animation, and Photoshop can also be required. Webmasters should be experienced and familiar with Internet technologies, having already had the experience of personally building and maintaining several Web sites in order to get hired.

In addition to technical skills, Webmasters need to be excellent organizers. They need to have creative vision combined with the ability to manage projects, meet deadlines, and work well under pressure. Those Webmasters who write and develop content should have strong writing skills as well.

Unions and Associations

Webmasters may belong to a variety of professional associations including the World Organization of Webmasters and the Internet Society, as well as to regional groups. Others who are involved with online news may belong to the Online News Association. New associations form frequently since the field is still so new.

Tips for Entry

1. View a wide range of travel Web sites ranging from online guides to travel reviews to hotel chains. A few to try include www.fodors.com, www.tripadvisor.com, and www.ritzcarlton.com. Notice the features they have in common.

2. Volunteer to create and maintain the Web site for a student organization on campus. This will provide firsthand experience in the work of a Webmaster.

3. Courses that enhance your computer skills can be very valuable. In addition to those offered by local universities, there are hundreds of online tutorials. Conduct a search engine query for the programs you want to learn to explore the options.

4. Apply for a formal internship in Web development. This will provide you with skills as well as mentors who may be able to help you find a job.

CORPORATE COMMUNICATIONS SPECIALIST

CAREER PROFILE

Duties: Creates, writes, edits, and/or oversees communications for a hotel or resort; may be responsible for one specific area such as brochures, Internet copy, or public relations, or might manage overall communication strategy

Alternate Title(s): Writer; Consultant; Communications Specialist; Media Relations Officer; Director of Corporate Communications

Salary Range: $40,000 to $85,000 and up

Employment Prospects: Fair to good

Advancement Prospects: Good

Best Geographical Location(s): All, with the greatest opportunities in large cities and heavy tourist regions with many resorts and hotels

Prerequisites:

Education and Training—Bachelor's degree; useful fields include communications, English, journalism, public relations, media studies, or business

Experience—Positions range from entry-level assistants to senior-level managers

Special Skills and Personality Traits—Excellent writing and editing skills; strong verbal communications; media savvy; persuasive skills; good attention to detail and the ability to be organized

CAREER LADDER

Director of Corporate Communications or Vice-President of Corporate Communications

Corporate Communications Specialist

Corporate Communications Assistant

Position Description

Writing is used by companies in the hospitality industry to get their message across in a variety of ways. Externally, a Web site promotes hotels and their services. It offers information to visitors, inviting them to learn about special packages and make reservations. Hotel and resort chains also may have external written material including newsletters and brochures, as well as communications that will be shared verbally such as speeches, presentations, and proposals. On the internal side, many organizations have written and verbal presentations as well. Particularly at large chains, there are internal newsletters, memos, and other communications that are produced regularly. Corporate Communications Specialists are involved with writing and promoting this material.

The job of a Corporate Communications Specialist can involve public relations—activities and communications designed to enhance their company's image. They may be responsible for helping define their hotel or resort's image through written material. This means that Corporate Communications Specialists must understand their properties and brands very well. They must fully know

the goals and objectives they are trying to convey through communications. Every type of writing, from memos to Web copy, must promote the same image and goals.

Corporate Communications Specialists frequently spend much time writing. Some have specific responsibilities, such as writing and editing an internal newsletter. This can include brainstorming content, assigning material to other staff members, working on layout, and editing the finished product. Other Corporate Communications Specialists handle writing Internet copy or marketing material such as brochures or advertising information. Writing skills are key here, for regardless of the material, catchy and persuasive content is necessary.

In addition to written materials, many Corporate Communications Specialists handle the verbal aspect of communications. They may write speeches and presentations for top management to use internally or externally. Furthermore, they may represent their hotel to the media, acting as spokespeople and putting a positive spin on recent events. In this way, their communication strategies can directly affect their company's success.

Some Corporate Communications Specialists work directly for the CEO or general manager of their hotel.

Especially at a large company, the communication approach of this leader is crucial to its image. The Corporate Communications Specialist might write letters, memos, and other correspondence on the managers's behalf. In addition to writing speeches, he or she may also advise on overall communication strategy. It can be almost like being a White House speechwriter, who targets and projects a cultivated image.

Additional duties may include:

- running publicity campaigns
- building community relationships
- offering training and seminars
- writing press releases
- organizing media tours
- creating media and analyst pitches
- developing collateral marketing materials
- coaching other staff members with regard to communcations strategy
- overseeing Internet copy and making updates
- coordinating interviews
- conducting research
- organizing and planning special events
- enforcing brand compliance
- serving as a liaison with the news media
- developing diversity initiatives

Corporate Communications Specialists in leadership positions have much supervisory and management responsibility. They often manage a department and oversee both professional and support staff in several communications areas that can include public relations, media, employee relations, marketing, advertising, and others. Moreover, they participate in the overall communications vision and strategy for their organization at an upper level.

A position in corporate communications enables those with a skill and interest in writing to work in the hospitality industry. Whether they are overseeing a brochure promoting a new 10,000-square-foot spa or helping the general manager write a proposal to investors to finance expansion to a new property location, Corporate Communications Specialists use their writing skills to make a strong contribution.

Salaries

Salaries vary for Corporate Communications Specialists depending on the level of their position. Entry-level positions or those requiring one to three years of experience may pay in the $40,000 range, while management positions can be considerably more. A corporate communications manager with more than five years of experience and supervisory responsibility can earn an average of $70,000. Surveys say that a typical salary for an experienced Corporate Communications Specialist is between $60,000 and $85,000 per year.

Employment Prospects

Employment prospects are fair to good for Corporate Communications Specialists. As competition and public expectation increases, hotels seek ways to make themselves stand out, as well as to improve and safeguard their image. Corporate Communications Specialists help these chains and properties enhance the way they are seen by the public. Furthermore, the Internet continues to grow as another media outlet for organizations, and more Corporate Communications Specialists will be needed to write, edit, and promote this content. However, this position is usually a corporate one, in the corporate offices of large chains rather than in smaller individual hotels.

Advancement Prospects

Corporate Communications Specialists bring with them and further develop a skill set that can be used in a variety of areas. Writing, editing, research, public relations, and marketing skills can be applied in a number of ways. Some Corporate Communications Specialists advance by moving into management positions for their hotel chain such as communications director or vice president of communications. Others become specialized in one area such as public relations or new-media content writing.

Education and Training

Corporate Communications Specialists hold bachelor's degrees in variety of fields. As one might expect, communications fields are particular helpful, including communications, journalism, public relations, and English, as well as business and marketing. Some hotel management courses can also be helpful for understanding the hospitality industry.

Some schools offer specific programs in corporate communications. Courses hone strategic writing, persuasive writing, and presentation skills. These degree programs include the bachelor of arts in corporate communication in St. Louis, Missouri (www.fontbonne.edu) and degrees in strategic communication from Ithaca College in Ithaca, New York (www.ithaca.edu/rhp/depts/stratcomm).

Experience, Skills, and Personality Traits

Successful Corporate Communications Specialists must be skilled at writing. They must know how to use words to persuade and catch people's attention. In addition to good use of language, they also need editing skills to review their own work, as well as the work of others, and research skills to validate their material.

Prior relationships with the media can be helpful for Corporate Communications Specialists. For this reason, it may be a common career transition for journalists who are looking to use their writing skills in a different venue. Others come to the field from public relations firms. Those who enter corporate communications directly from school usually begin in assistant level positions where they can learn the ropes.

Corporate Communications Specialists must be team players. The business world emphasizes teamwork and they must be able to lead as well as to work independently. Additionally, their verbal communication skills must be top-notch as well, as they build relationships and manage projects.

Unions and Associations

There are a variety of professional associations to which Corporate Communications Specialists may belong, depending on their specialty. These include the Association for Business Communication, the International Association of Business Communicators, the National Council for Marketing and Public Relations, the Public Relations Society of America, and the Association for Women in Communications.

Tips for Entry

1. Try an internship for a large hotel chain. Here, you can learn more about their communications strategy and the role of different department members.

2. Conduct an informational interview with a Corporate Communications Specialist. Often you can find contact names in the Media Inquiries section of a hotel chain's Web site.

3. Your cover letter provides a great opportunity for you to showcase your writing skills and is even more important when the position involves writing. Get some cover letter tips at sites such as www.careerlab.com/letters/default.htm and jobstar.org/tools/resume/cletters.php.

4. Hone your communication skills through courses that require considerable writing, as well as courses in public speaking.

INTERNATIONAL JOURNALIST

Duties: Covers world issues for a newspaper, television station, or new-media outlet, reporting from foreign locations

Alternate Title(s): Foreign Correspondent; International Reporter; Foreign Affairs Reporter

Salary Range: $40,000 to $100,000 and up

Employment Prospects: Poor

Advancement Prospects: Fair

Best Geographical Location(s): Major world cities and newsworthy regions

Prerequisites:

    Education and Training—Bachelor's degree in journalism or related field; background in international affairs, politics, or language helpful

    Experience—Several years of news reporting experience

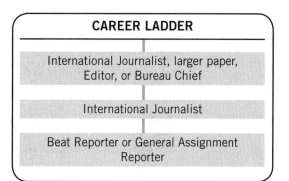

CAREER LADDER

International Journalist, larger paper, Editor, or Bureau Chief

International Journalist

Beat Reporter or General Assignment Reporter

Special Skills and Personality Traits—Excellent writing and reporting skills; international exposure; knowledge of at least one foreign language; willingness to travel; flexibility, independence, and initiative; understanding of international culture, news, and politics

Position Description

The world is a much smaller place in the 21st century thanks to the media. Newspapers, television, radio, and the Internet keep us informed around the clock about breaking news across the globe. International Journalists cover these international stories, bringing world news into our homes. They are there, on location, telling the stories of what is really happening abroad.

International Journalists may report from one overseas post for a set period of time, or they may travel frequently to various international locations. As reporters, they often cover a combination of stories. They handle breaking news, but most also write and broadcast longer investigative/enterprise pieces. They conduct interviews, visit scenes of events, check in with sources, and scan local media just as domestic reporters do. However, this all must be done with international savvy and sensibility. Not only are languages different in foreign lands, but so are the methods to access information.

Some foreign language skills, as well as knowledge of the politics, history, and culture of their region, are necessary for International Journalists. Equally important is the ability to work in a country very different from home. International Journalists often work with local translators that do more than merely help them with words. These locals, who are often journalists themselves, serve as guides to help International Journalists

get information, connect with sources, conduct interviews, and cut through red tape. They also may help them with practical needs such as securing transportation and finding places to stay on assignment. These relationships are crucial to good reporting.

Unlike domestic reporters, International Journalists may not have an editor to check with daily who hands out assignments. They may not have an office with a computer where they can collaborate with colleagues. International Journalists must be independent and resourceful. They have the initiative to generate stories and the curiosity to follow through with leads. Furthermore, they have the ambition to handle difficult topics with professionalism.

International Journalists are often sent to areas of conflict. Many U.S. newspapers and television stations can only report on major world events involving war, political unrest, disaster, or business. International Journalists who cover these conflicts, particularly those relating to war or political unrest, may put themselves at risk for their work. However, the desire to uncover the truth as danger beckons is typically part of the excitement.

Not all International Journalists handle dangerous assignments. Another major area for specialty is business. While business reporting does not have the glamour and intrigue of other types of international journalism, it provides a way to work overseas in a more controlled environment. As long as issues of international business affect the world economy, International Journalists will be needed to cover this news. Other issues might include trade, immigration, and global finance.

Additional duties may include:

- writing/broadcasting features about people's lives
- conducting interviews
- working with state departments and U.S. embassies
- meeting with other foreign journalists in their region
- keeping abreast of new developments in their region
- learning one or more foreign languages
- taking photographs or video footage
- staying informed about local culture
- reading, watching, and listening to all news media from their region
- checking in with local sources

For most International Journalists, the travel required is the most exciting aspect of the job. It can be an opportunity to see the world and live in different environments. However, International Journalists do not necessarily get to choose their assignments. They may need to uproot themselves (and their families, if applicable) to move to undesirable regions for extended periods of time. Many positions require a specific time period overseas, as well as time working domestically on international issues. Some International Journalists report that for their first few years, they were never home for more than six weeks at a time. However, in spite of the negatives, most thrive on the sheer excitement of their work and the ability to gain insight into different cultures and make an impact.

Salaries

Salaries for International Journalists vary depending on experience. Earnings also vary depending on whether they work for newspapers, television stations, or new-media outlets. Typically, International Journalist positions go to reporters with experience. Salaries may range from $40,000 to $100,000 and up depending on these factors.

Employment Prospects

Jobs for International Journalists are highly competitive. With the newspaper industry experiencing increased mergers and layoffs, employment prospects in print are limited to papers large enough to have reporters overseas. On-air reporting jobs are even more competitive.

Job seekers need to gain as much experience as possible as reporters and consider their areas of expertise. Which countries would you want to target and why? Have you spent time living in these regions? Can you speak the language? These are important questions to ask in order to get started. Business reporting may also be a good way to transition to international news. Some International Journalists find opportunities through freelance work as well.

Advancement Prospects

International Journalists may advance through moving to larger markets with more high-profile posts. However, extensive travel causes some International Journalists to burn out after several years in the field. As transitions, they may try to take on semipermanent positions at international bureaus of their news organization. Others might work for journalism schools as professors training future International Journalists. Still other International Journalists might advance to become news editors or bureau chiefs.

Education and Training

The majority of International Journalists starting in the field have bachelor's degrees in journalism or related fields. Many hold master's degrees in journalism as well. These degrees and courses provide a foundation in writing and reporting, as well as an entry into reporting jobs. A liberal arts curriculum that emphasizes history, political science, and culture is also important. International affairs, international relations, and foreign language and culture courses are very helpful.

The best training for International Journalists comes from a combination of reporting and international experience. Time spent living, working, or studying abroad develops a cultural understanding, as well as a network of contacts that is invaluable.

Experience, Skills, and Personality Traits

In addition to having excellent writing and reporting skills, it is essential for International Journalists to be interested in travel and living abroad. Knowledge of at least one foreign language may be required, as is the ability to be adaptable and function in different environments. International Journalists must be comfortable with risk and potentially dangerous situations. They should be confident, with excellent news and personal judgment.

Furthermore, International Journalists must be able to work independently. They need to be flexible and resourceful with an insatiable curiosity that drives them to uncover breaking stories and issues that can hold the world's attention. At the same time, they are sensitive to people and their differences. International Journalists should be nonjudgmental and committed to telling the accurate story. Working under tight deadline pressure is a daily reality for International Journalists. They can juggle many tasks at once, taking photos or video as necessary. Persistence and thick skin enable them to persevere, even in tough conditions.

Unions and Associations

There are a variety of professional associations for International Journalists, including the Overseas Press Club of America, serving the interests of International Journalists since 1939. They may also belong to associations based on their specialty region including the Foreign Correspondents' Association for journalists working in Australia and the South Pacific and the Foreign Press Association in London.

Tips for Entry

1. Explore journalism internships on sites such as www.journalismjobs.com and www.mediabistro.com for an introduction to the field.

2. Consider study abroad as a way to live and learn in another country. There are a variety of programs available that include internships and language institutes. Get started by looking on sites such as www.studyabroad.com.

3. Take courses in journalism to hone your writing and communication skills, as well as courses in a foreign language. Choose a language of a region with a history, culture, and politics where you might want to live or specialize.

4. Constantly read and stay up on world news. It is essential for a career in international journalism to stay abreast of current events and take note of different types of coverage.

EVENT PLANNER

CAREER PROFILE

Duties: Plans meetings, social, and business events for corporations, nonprofit organizations, and individuals

Alternate Title(s): Special Events Coordinator; Meeting Planner; Party Planner

Salary Range: $26,000 to $76,000 and up

Employment Prospects: Good

Advancement Prospects: Good

Best Geographical Location(s): All

Prerequisites:

Education and Training—Varies; education in hospitality, business, or public relations can be helpful

Experience—Prior experience planning events in a particular section or working in catering sales

Special Skills and Personality Traits—Excellent organizational skills and attention to detail; cre-

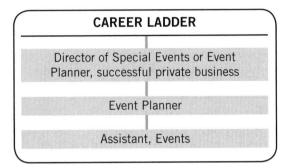

ativity and vision; good interpersonal, communications, and relationship-building skills; management ability

Special Requirements—Voluntary certification is available as a certified meeting planner (CMP) or certified special events professional (CSEP)

Position Description

Every event we attend, whether a benefit for the American Heart Association, a corporate golf retreat, or an anniversary dinner for 50 at a catering hall, requires much hard work and planning behind the scenes to make it happen. Event Planners organize a wide variety of events, attending to all the details and delegating tasks in order to make the occasion a success.

Event Planners may work in many different settings, enjoying a range of job tasks depending on their work environment. Corporations have Event Planners that work in special events departments. These Event Planners may plan executive retreats, holiday parties, employee recognition receptions, large training meetings, and more. Furthermore, some Event Planners in the corporate sector work directly for hotels and catering facilities planning the special events held in these locations. They may also plan promotional events to market particular products.

Event Planners who specialize in planning meetings work on selecting a destination and venue and making travel arrangements. They work with hotels, airlines, car rental agencies, and local chambers of commerce. They ensure that the destination will offer attractions for attendees and may develop a schedule of activities for their leisure time. Event Planners also evaluate the

venue to make sure that there are a variety of rooms for lectures, exhibitions, dining, and more. Furthermore, they oversee preparation of all materials including brochures, name tags, collateral material, and giveaways, as well as secure audiovisual and technical equipment for presentations as needed.

Additionally, Event Planners may work for nonprofit organizations, including professional associations, universities, hospitals, charitable organizations, political parties, and religious organizations. These Event Planners organize benefits such as black tie galas or silent auctions designed to raise money for their cause. Additionally, Event Planners at professional associations often work to arrange the annual convention for members, as well as other smaller meetings and conferences throughout the year.

Furthermore, many Event Planners are self-employed, running their own event planning businesses. They are frequently hired by individuals, but also can contract their services to corporations and nonprofits. These Event Planners work with multiple clients to plan a variety of events depending on their clients' needs. In one month, they may work on a wedding, a fund-raiser, a promotional launch party, and a meeting. Event Planners in private business also spend time promoting their services, including marketing, advertising, merchandising, and bookkeeping. Generating business comes through marketing and advertising, as well as through word of mouth.

Regardless of their setting, there are many components that go into planning an event. First and foremost, Event Planners work with their clients to assess their needs. What is their vision for the event? What do they hope to achieve? And very important: What is their budget? Event Planners use their expertise to work within these constraints to develop an event that will satisfy their clients.

After assessing the client needs and creating both a vision and a plan, Event Planners continue to work closely with their clients. A venue and a date must be chosen, as well as invitations or publicity material for guests or attendees. Event Planners may have a hand in the menu, the decor, the linens, and the theme of the event. If guests or attendees are coming in from out of town, Event Planners will help secure hotel rooms.

Part of their work involves developing relationships with suppliers. By working with caterers and catering halls, convention centers, invitation suppliers, designers, florists, musicians, local hotels, and more, Event Planners can secure the best rates for their clients. Through their network of vendors, they can actually save clients money, even with their own fee taken into account.

Additional duties may include:

- selecting and tasting menus
- negotiating contracts
- soliciting requests for proposals
- listening to bands, orchestras, and previewing other entertainment
- overseeing support staff
- maintaining financial records
- visiting and researching various event locations and destinations
- developing event time lines
- conducting follow-up surveys and evaluations
- securing speakers for events

Planning is only the first part of the Event Planner's job. Supervising on-site is essential and most Event Planners attend all their own events, although some may delegate this to subordinates. There are many things that can go wrong the day of an event, and Event Planners must be excellent troubleshooters to tap into their network of contacts if the flowers do not arrive, the name tags are missing, or the tablecloths are the wrong color.

Event Planners with their own businesses may work out of a home office, their own office space, or visit clients in their homes. Due to the timing of special events on weekends and evenings, the hours are not traditional and can be long and stressful. However, most Event Planners find it very satisfying to see their hard work come together in a successful event.

Salaries

According to the Bureau of Labor Statistics, median annual earnings of Event Planners that are wage-and-salary meeting and convention planners as of May 2007 were $43,530. The middle 50 percent earned between $33,900 and $57,310. The lowest 10 percent earned less than $26,880, and the highest 10 percent earned more than $74,740. Additional information comes from Salary.com, which states that in January 2008, the national average base salary for an Event Planner fell between $45,000 and $63,000 per year.

However, Event Planners in the corporate sector or who are self-employed can earn considerably more, especially if they plan very costly and high-end events for multiple clients. Some Event Planners charge a flat fee that includes an array of services; this fee may be 10 to 15 percent the cost of the total event. Other Event Planners may receive a commission from their vendors.

Employment Prospects

Employment prospects are good for Event Planners. In difficult economic times, individuals may scale back private events, but corporations and nonprofits will still need professionals to plan meetings and programs. Corporations may count on Event Planners to work within a limited budget and associations will still hold conventions and conferences. Event Planners with experience have marketable skills that can be applied in many different work environments.

Advancement Prospects

Because of their transferable skills, advancement options are good for Event Planners. They may move from corporate to nonprofit and vice versa, directing departments of special events. They may work for hotels as directors of convention services. Furthermore, Event Planners can always advance by starting and growing their own private businesses.

Education and Training

Event Planners come to the field from a variety of educational backgrounds. Those coming into the field at entry level typically have degrees in public relations, sales, marketing, business, communications, or hospitality management. There are a limited number of degree and certificate programs specifically in event management. One such program, the event management certificate program, is offered through George Washington University's School of Business in Washington, D.C. (www.gwutourism.org/eventmanagement/index.html). Also, San Jose State University in San Jose, California, offers a bachelor of science degree in hospitality, tourism, and event management; see info.sjsu.edu/web-dbgen/catalog/departments/HRTM-section-1.html.

Experience, Skills, and Personality Traits

Event Planners must be highly organized. Excellent communication and interpersonal skills help them develop relationships with clients and vendors and to inspire their trust. Attention to detail is a necessity, as is creativity to distinguish events and give them each a personal touch. They must be good delegators and managers who can budget their time wisely. Furthermore, patience and flexibility helps them stay calm under pressure and troubleshoot when problems arise. For Event Planners in their own businesses, financial and entrepreneurial skills are also needed.

Special Requirements

Event Planners can seek voluntary certification as a certified meeting planner (CMP) from the Convention Industry Council or certified special events professional (CSEP) from the International Special Events Society.

Unions and Associations

There are a variety of professional associations for Event Planners. These include the International Special Events Society, the Convention Industry Council, Meeting Professionals International, the International Association of Exhibitions and Events, the Professional Convention Management Association, the Society of Government Meeting Professionals, the Association of Collegiate Conference and Events Directors–International, Financial and Insurance Conference Planners, and the Association for Convention Management, among others.

Tips for Entry

1. Learn more about CMP certification at www.conventionindustry.org/cmp/index.htm and CSEP certification at www.ises.com/Default.aspx?tabid=87.
2. Gain experience planning events on campus or for associations and groups with which you are involved. Offer to plan fund-raisers, pledge drives, and other programs.
3. To explore the social side of event planning, organize a party for family or friends. Go through every aspect of the process from making the guest list to securing the location and menu.
4. Read about event planning and starting an event planning business on sites such as About.com (eventplanning.about.com) and Entrepreneur.com (www.entrepreneur.com/startingabusiness/businessideas/startupkits/article37892.html).
5. Take courses and seminars in Event Management through schools including Stratford University in Falls Church, Virginia (www.stratford.edu/?page=eventmgmt).
6. Look for jobs on sites such as www.meetingjobs.com/ and eventplanningjob.com/Event_planning_jobs.htm.

ACCOUNT EXECUTIVE

Duties: Oversees a client's entire advertising account as well as serves as a liaison between the client and the advertising agency

Alternate Title(s): Account Manager

Salary Range: $50,000 to $100,000 and up

Employment Prospects: Fair

Advancement Prospects: Fair

Best Geographical Location(s): All, with the most opportunities in large cities with many advertising agencies such as New York, Chicago, Boston, and Los Angeles

Prerequisites:

  Education and Training—Bachelor's degree; fields such as advertising, public relations, marketing, sales, business, journalism, or communications helpful

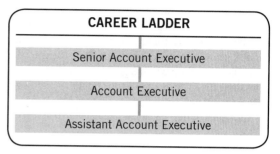

Experience—Several years of advertising industry experience

Special Skills and Personality Traits—Excellent communication and interpersonal skills; good business, sales, and negotiation skills; creativity and writing skills; ability to juggle multiple tasks at once

Position Description

Advertising is what determines the success of hotels, resorts, restaurants, casinos, and other hospitality businesses. It is the medium through which the company showcases its offerings to the public in order for sales to take place. Hotels and other organizations spend much money in order to promote their brand and show what makes them unique. Account Executives manage the advertising campaigns for their clients in the hospitality industry. They work to oversee their clients' accounts, ensuring that communication between the client and the agency takes place and goals are being met.

Account Executives work to get the word out for their hospitality clients. They develop strategies such as where to place ads, how often, and what their message should accomplish. Account Executives work with other parts of the advertising agency team including the creative and media departments in order to get the client's message across. Furthermore, they determine where to place the ads, including newspapers, magazines, billboards, television, radio, direct mail, and the Internet.

Whether a restaurant chain wants to promote its new healthy choices or a luxury hotel needs customers to know about its new full-service spa, the advertising campaign is crucial. Account Executives for agencies who specialize in the hospitality industry know

how to target the best avenues to reach their desired demographic. They begin by meeting with clients and learning more about their strategy and ideas. They also discuss the budget within which they have to work. Together, Account Executives and clients work on a plan as well as the desired types of placements, publicity, and media.

It is up to the Account Executive to manage the relationship between the client and the agency (particularly the creative department), and often they manage multiple accounts at the same time. They are the point person and the one responsible for making sure their desired campaign is executed. The entire campaign plan includes publicity, promotions, market research, and public relations. Also, the best timing for the ads as well as placement must be determined. For certain clients, television ads may be worth the expense, while for others, Internet or print ads will be more appropriate. The type of audience they want to attract—families, upscale older travelers, single partygoers—will influence all aspects of the campaign.

After developing the campaign, Account Executives work with the other people at the agency responsible for these different components. The media planners recommend how to spend the budget, including which geographic locations to target the heaviest as well as the best mediums. Media buyers make sure the ads run as they are planned. The creative team creates the sample ad for client approval, including written copy, slogans, taglines, artwork, music, video, and special effects. Creative directors supervise the filming of a commercial or photography for print ads. The public relations team handles getting the word out about their client to the media as well as the brand image, while market research helps determine which populations might respond best to advertisements.

Additional duties may include:

- conducting research on the type of ads that will attract consumers
- attracting new clients
- recommending strategies for sales
- managing pitches for the client
- presenting concepts to the client for approval
- checking the status of clients' jobs and communicating with them

Some of the special features of advertising in the hospitality industry may be letting the public know about these properties, their amenities, new locations or features, and special attractions or discounts.

Client satisfaction and relationship building are essential for Account Executives. They meet with their client constantly in order to ensure that the campaign is meeting objectives. Typically, an Account Executive at a midsize advertising agency may juggle four distinct clients at a time. Account Executives keep details about their work hours so that clients are billed accordingly. The job can involve long hours and may require travel to meet with clients, visit properties, and scope markets and placements.

Salaries

According to the Bureau of Labor Statistics (BLS), median annual earnings as of May 2007 were $78,250 for advertising and promotions managers. Additional sources say that average salaries are between $52,000 and $70,500 for Account Executives and between $66,000 and $90,000 for senior account executives. Earnings can vary greatly depending on geographic location, size of agency, budget of clients, and other factors. Account Executives often receive bonuses as part of overall earnings. Starting salaries in the advertising field can be very low, but often rise quickly.

Employment Prospects

Average growth is predicted for positions in the advertising industry. As hotels, restaurants, resorts, and casinos continue to open, the need for specialized Account Executives will grow in order to promote these properties. Competition will be tight and the best opportunities are for those Account Executives with experience. A background in both advertising and hospitality can provide an extra edge.

Advancement Prospects

There are many opportunities for advancement for Account Executives. They can rise within their agencies to become senior account executives, account supervisors, and eventually vice presidents. Furthermore, they can decide to go in-house to direct advertising for a hotel, resort, casino, or restaurant. They may work for individual properties or chains in executive positions. Additionally, some Account Executives may aspire to open their own advertising agencies catering to hospitality clients.

Education and Training

To get into the field of advertising, a bachelor's degree is needed. Common and helpful majors include advertising, public relations, marketing, sales, business, journalism, or communications. Some Account Executives have graduate degrees as well, which can be helpful for advancement. Others may have studied hospitality management at either the undergraduate or graduate level and have some work experience in that area. While not necessary, this can be helpful for gaining credibility with the clients.

Experience, Skills, and Personality Traits

Account Executives usually have at least three years of experience in an advertising agency before reaching this level. They need strong communication and interpersonal skills to work with clients and as part of their agency team. Furthermore, excellent business, sales, and negotiation skills help them manage budgets and projects, while creativity and writing skills help them offer recommendations about goals and directions. Account Executives need the ability to juggle multiple tasks at once as they handle accounts for multiple clients. Computer literacy is important for billing spreadsheets as well as design or editing work.

Unions and Associations

Advertising Account Executives may belong to professional associations including the American Advertising Federation and the Advertising Club of New York. Agencies may belong to the American Association of Advertising Agencies.

Tips for Entry

1. Since positions in advertising are highly competitive, internships are essential to gain necessary experience. The American Advertising Federation lists internships on its Web site at www.aaf.org/default.asp?id=148, as does New York Women in Communications at www.nywici.org/foundation/internships.advertising.html.

2. Read through a travel-oriented magazine, such as *Travel & Leisure*. Notice all the print ads in the publication and how their approaches vary.

3. Pay attention to hospitality-related commercials and other advertisements as well. Do you notice billboards and other materials? What are they trying to achieve?

4. Take courses in advertising to learn more about the field.

5. Speak to Account Executives specializing in the travel and hospitality fields to find out about their jobs. What are the unique challenges about this industry that differ from other specialties?

APPENDIXES

APPENDIX I
EDUCATIONAL PROGRAMS

I. TRAVEL AND HOSPITALITY MANAGEMENT

Here you will find degree programs in travel and hospitality, including administration, tourism, hotel/restaurant, food service, and management. Degrees available include associate's degrees, bachelor's degrees, and graduate degrees.

ALABAMA

Alabama State University
Department of Health and
    Physical Education: Recreation
    Management
915 South Jackson Street
Montgomery, AL 36195-0301
Phone: (334) 229-4502
http://www.alasu.edu

Auburn University
Hotel and Restaurant Management
    Program
328 Spindle Hall
Auburn, AL 36849
Phone: (334) 844-1333
Fax: (334) 844-3268
http://www.auburn.edu

**Faulkner State Community
    College**
Hotel and Restaurant Management
    Program
1900 U.S. Highway 31 South
Bay Minette, AL 36507
Phone: (203) 257-2100 or
    (800) 231-3752
http://www.faulknerstate.edu

University of South Alabama
Department of Health, Physical
    Education, and Leisure Studies
307 University Boulevard
Mobile, AL 36688
Phone: (334) 460-7131
http://www.southalabama.edu

ALASKA

Alaska Pacific University
Outdoor Studies Department
4101 University Drive
Anchorage, AK 99508
Phone: (907) 564-8243
Fax: (907) 562-4276
http://www.alaskapacific.edu

**University of Alaska–
    Fairbanks**
Hospitality and Tourism,
    School of Management
P.O. Box 757520
Fairbanks, AK 99775
Phone: (907) 474-6525
http://www.uaf.edu

ARIZONA

Arizona State University
Recreation and Tourism
    Management Department
P.O. Box 37100
Phoenix, AZ 85069-7100
Phone: (602) 543-6603
Fax: (602) 543-6612
http://www.asu.edu

Central Arizona College
Business Division, Hotel and
    Restaurant Management
8470 North Overfield Road
Coolidge, AZ 85228
Phone: (520) 426-4403
http://www.centralaz.edu

Northern Arizona University
School of Hotel and Restaurant
    Management
P.O. Box 5638
Flagstaff, AZ 86011
Phone: (928) 523-1705
Fax: (928) 523-5233
http://www.nau.edu/hrm

Pima Community College
Hospitality and Tourism
1255 North Stone Avenue
Tucson, AZ 85709-3030
Phone: (520) 206-6278
Fax: (520) 206-6162
http://www.pima.edu

ARKANSAS

Arkansas Tech University
Hospitality Administration
100 Williamson Hall
Russellville, AR 72801
Phone: (501) 968-0687
Fax: (501) 968-0600
http://www.atu.edu

Henderson State University
Health, Physical Education and
    Recreation Department
HSU Box 7552
Arkadelphia, AR 71999-0001
Phone: (870) 230-5192
Fax: (870) 230-5073
http://www.hsu.edu

**National Park Community
    College**
Hospitality Administration

101 College Drive
Hot Springs, AR 71913
Phone: (501) 760-4222
http://www.npcc.edu

CALIFORNIA

Butte College
Tourism and Travel Department
3536 Butte Campus Drive
Oroville, CA 95965
Phone: (530) 895-2396
Fax: (530) 895-2411
http://www.butte.edu

California State Polytechnic University
Collins School of Hospitality
  Management
3801 West Temple Avenue
Pomona, CA 91768
Phone: (909) 869-2275
http://www.csupomona.edu/~cshm

California State University, Chico
Department of Recreation
  Administration and Parks
  Management
400 West First Street
Chico, CA 95929-0560
Phone: (530) 898-INFO
http://www.csuchico.edu

California State University, Long Beach
Department of Recreation and
  Leisure Studies
1250 Bellflower Boulevard
Long Beach, CA 90840-4903
Phone: (562) 985-4071
http://www.csulb.edu

California State University, Northridge
Department of Leisure Studies and
  Recreation
18111 Nordhoff Street
Northridge, CA 91330-8269
Phone: (818) 677-3202
Fax: (818) 677-2695
http://www.csun.edu

City College of San Francisco
Culinary Arts and Hospitality
  Management Program
50 Phelan Avenue, SW 156
San Francisco, California 94112
Phone: (415) 239-3152
Fax: (415) 239-3913
http://www.ccsf.edu

Empire College
Tourism, Hospitality & Wine
  Industries Program
3035 Cleveland Avenue
Santa Rosa, CA 95403
Phone: (707) 546-4000
Fax: (707) 546-4058
http://www.empcol.edu

Foothill College
Travel Careers Program
12345 El Monte Road
Los Altos Hills, CA 94022
Phone: (650) 949-7263
Fax: (650) 949-7287
http://www.foothill.fhda.edu/index.
  php

Golden Gate University
Hotel, Restaurant and Tourism
  Management
536 Mission Street, Room 493
San Francisco, CA 94105
Phone: (415) 442-6508
Fax: (415) 442-7049
http://www.ggu.edu

Long Beach City College
Programs in Hospitality, Tourism,
  and Restaurant & Catering
  Management
4901 East Carson Street
Long Beach, CA 90808
Phone: (562) 938-4325
Fax: (562) 938-4118
http://www.lbcc.edu

Loyola Marymount University
Travel and Tourism Management
College of Business Administration
1 LMU Drive, Suite 100
Los Angeles, CA 90045-8350
Phone: (310) 338-2750

Fax: (310) 338-2797
http://www.lmu.edu

Miracosta College
Tourism Program
One Barnard Drive
Oceanside, CA 92056-3899
Phone: (760) 795-6841
Fax: (760) 795-6804
http://www.miracosta.edu

Mission College
Hospitality Management,
  Commercial Services
3000 Mission College Boulevard
Santa Clara, CA 95054
Phone: (408) 855-5252 or
  (888) 509-7040
Fax: (408) 855-5452
http://www.missioncollege.org

San Bernadino Valley College
Restaurant Management
701 South Mount Vernon Avenue
San Bernadino, CA 92410
Phone: (909) 888-6511
http://www.valleycollege.edu

San Diego Mesa College
Hospitality/Hotel Management
  Program
7250 Mesa College Drive
San Diego, CA 92111
Phone: (858) 627-2600
http://www.sdmesa.sdccd.cc.ca.us

San Francisco State University
Hospitality and Tourism
  Management Department
P.O. Box 27188
San Francisco, CA 94127
Phone: (415) 586-6888
http://www.sfsu.edu

Santa Barbara City College
School of Culinary Arts & Hotel
  Management
721 Cliff Drive
Santa Barbara, CA 93109-2394
Phone: (805) 965-0581
http://www.sbcc.edu/
  hotelrestaurantculinary

Travel University International

Hospitality/Hotel Management and
Travel/Meeting Planner
3870 Murphy Canyon Road,
Suite 310
San Diego, CA 92123
Phone: (858) 292-9755
Fax: (858) 292-8008
http://www.traveluniversity.edu

University of San Francisco

Hospitality Industry Management
Program
2130 Fulton Street MCL 115
San Francisco, CA 94117-1080
Phone: (415) 422-6236
http://www.usfca.edu

West Los Angeles College

Travel Department
4800 Freshman Drive
Culver City, CA 90230
Phone: (310) 287-4369
Fax: (310) 841-0396
http://www.wlac.edu

COLORADO

Colorado State University

Warner College of Natural Resources,
Park Management and Tourism
300 West Drake
Fort Collins, CO 80523-1480
Phone: (970) 491-6591
Fax: (970) 491-2255
http://welcome.warnercnr.colostate.
edu

Fort Lewis College

Tourism and Resort Management,
Business Administration
1000 Rim Drive
Durango, CO 81301
Phone: (970) 247-7550
http://www.fortlewis.edu

Johnson & Wales University

College of Culinary Arts
The Hospitality College
7150 Montview Boulevard
Denver, CO 80220
Phone: (303) 256-9300
http://www.jwu.edu

Mesa State College

Business Department
Culinary Arts, Travel and Tourism
2508 Blichmann Avenue
Grand Junction, CO 81505
Phone: (970) 255-2632
Fax: (970) 255-2650
http://www.mesastate.edu

Metropolitan State College of Denver

Department of Hospitality, Tourism
and Events
P.O. Box 173362, Campus Box 60
Denver, CO 80217-3362
Phone: (303) 556-3152
Fax: (303) 556-8046
http://www.mscd.edu/~hmt

University of Denver

School of Hotel, Restaurant and
Tourism Management
2030 East Evans Avenue
Denver, CO 80208
Phone: (303) 871-4275
Fax: (303) 871-4260
http://www.dcb.du.edu/HRTM.aspx

CONNECTICUT

Briarwood College

Hotel and Restaurant Management
Program
2279 Mount Vernon Road
Southington, CT 06790
Phone: (860) 628-4751
Fax: (860) 628-6444
http://www.briarwood.edu

Clemens College

Programs in Hospitality
Management / Culinary Arts
Management
1760 Mapleton Avenue
Suffield, CT 06078
Phone: (800) 955-0809 /
(860) 668-3515
Fax: (860) 668-7369
http://www.clemenscollege.edu

Gateway Community College

Hotel-Motel Management, Business
Department

60 Sargent Drive
New Haven, CT 06511
Phone: (203) 285-2175
Fax: (203) 285-2180
http://www.gwcc.commnet.edu

Mitchell College

Hospitality and Tourism
Department
437 Pequot Avenue
New London, CT 06320
Phone: (860) 701-5000
Fax: (860) 701-5090
http://www.mitchell.edu

Naugatuck Valley Community College

Hospitality Management, Business
Division
750 Chase Parkway
Waterbury, CT 06708
Phone: (203) 578-8175
http://www.nvcc.commnet.edu

Norwalk Community College

Hospitality & Culinary Arts
Department
188 Richards Avenue
Norwalk, CT 06854
Phone: (203) 857-7355
Fax: (203) 857-3327
http://www.nctc.commnet.edu

University of New Haven

Tourism & Hospitality
Administration
Hotel & Restaurant Management
300 Boston Post Road
West Haven, CT 06516
Phone: (800) 342-5864
http://www.newhaven.edu

DELAWARE

Delaware State University

School of Management
Hospitality & Tourism
Management
1200 North Dupont Highway
Dover, DE 19901
Phone: (302) 857-6980
Fax: (302) 857-6983
http://www.desu.edu

Delaware Technical & Community College
Hotel, Restaurant & Institutional
    Management
100 Campus Drive
Dover, DE 19904-1383
Phone: (302) 857-1000
http://www.dtcc.edu

University of Delaware
Hotel, Restaurant & Institutional
    Management
Raub Hall
14 West Main Street
Newark, DE 19716
Phone: (302) 831-6077
Fax: (302) 831-6395
http://www.hrim.udel.edu

DISTRICT OF COLUMBIA

George Washington University
Department of Tourism and
    Hospitality Management
2201 G Street, NW
Suite 301
Washington DC 20052
Phone: (202) 994-6281
http://www.gwutourism.org

FLORIDA

Bethune-Cookman University
Department of Hospitality
    Management
640 Dr. Mary McLeod Bethune
    Boulevard
Daytona Beach, FL 32114
Phone: (386) 481-2800
Fax: (386) 481-2802
http://www.cookman.edu

Broward Community College
Hospitality, Restaurant and Tourism
111 East Las Olas Boulevard
Fort Lauderdale, FL 33301
Phone: (954) 201-7350
http://www.broward.edu

Daytona State College
Hospitality Management
1200 West International Speedway
    Boulevard

Daytona Beach, FL 32114
Phone: (386) 506-3000
http://www.daytonastate.edu

Everest University
Hospitality Management Program
225 North Federal Highway
Pompano Beach, FL 33062
Phone: (954) 783-7339
Fax: (954) 943-2571
http://www.everest.edu

Florida Atlantic University
Hospitality and Tourism
    Management Program
777 Glades Road
Boca Raton, FL 33431
Phone: (561) 297-3666
Fax: (561) 297-3935
http://www.fau.edu

Florida Community College at Jacksonville
Institute of the South for Hospitality
    and Culinary Arts
North Campus, 4501 Capper Road
Jacksonville, FL 32218
Phone: (904) 766-6703
http://www.fccj.org

Florida International University
School of Hospitality & Tourism
    Management
Biscayne Bay Campus
3000 Northeast 151st Street
North Miami, FL 33181
Phone: (305) 919-4500
http://hospitality.fiu.edu

Florida National College
Hospitality Management
4425 West 12th Avenue
Hialeah, FL 33012
Phone: (305) 821-3333
http://www.fnc.edu

Florida State University
College of Business, Dedman
    School of Hospitality
P.O. Box 3062541
Tallahassee, FL 32306-2541
Phone: (850) 644-4787

Fax: (850) 644-5565
http://www.cob.fsu.edu/dsh

Johnson & Wales University
College of Culinary Arts
The Hospitality College
1701 NE 127th Street
North Miami, FL 33181
Phone: (305) 892-7000
http://www.jwu.edu

Miami Dade College
Hospitality Management/Travel &
    Tourism Management
300 NE Second Avenue
Miami, FL 33132-2297
Phone: (305) 237-3267
Fax: (305) 237-7074
http://www.mdc.edu

Palm Beach Community College
Hospitality and Tourism
    Management
4200 Congress Avenue
Lake Worth, FL 33461
Phone: (561) 868-3353
http://www.pbcc.edu

Saint Thomas University
Tourism & Hospitality Program
16401 NW 37th Avenue
Miami Gardens, Florida 33054
Phone: (305) 628-6535
http://www.stu.edu

Schiller International University
International School of Tourism
    and Hospitality Management
300 East Bay Drive
Largo, Florida 33770
Phone: (727) 736-5082
Fax: (727) 734-0359
http://www.schiller.edu

University of Central Florida
Rosen College of Hospitality
    Management
9907 Universal Boulevard
Orlando, FL 32819
Phone: (407) 903-8000
Fax: (407) 903-8105
http://www.hospitality.ucf.edu

Webber International University
Hospitality & Tourism Management
  Program
1201 North Scenic Highway
Babson Park, FL 33827
Phone: (800) 741-1844
http://www.webber.edu

GEORGIA

Georgia Southern University
Department of Hospitality, Tourism,
  and Family & Consumer Sciences
P.O. Box 8034
Statesboro, GA 30460
Phone: (912) 681-5345
http://www.georgiasouthern.edu

Georgia State University
J. Mack Robinson College of
  Business
Cecil B. Day School of Hospitality
35 Broad Street, Suite 220
Atlanta, GA 30303
Phone: (404) 413-7615
Fax: (404) 413-7625
http://robinson.gsu.edu/hospitality/
  index.htm

HAWAII

**Brigham Young University–
  Hawaii**
The School of Business—Hospitality
  and Tourism Program
55-220 Kulanui Street
P.O. Box 1956
Laie, HI 96762
Phone: (808) 293-3211
http://www.byuh.edu

Hawaii Pacific University
Travel Industry Management
  Program
1164 Bishop Street
Honolulu, HI 96813
Phone: (808) 544-0200
http://www.hpu.edu

Kapiolani Community College
Hotel/Restaurant Operations, Travel
  and Tourism Program
Olapa Building, Room 121

4303 Diamond Head Road
Honolulu, HI 96816-4421
Phone: (808) 743-9716
http://www.kcc.hawaii.edu

University of Hawaii at Manoa
School of Travel Industry
  Management
2560 Campus Road, George Hall 346
Honolulu, HI 96822
Phone: (808) 956-8946
Fax: (808) 956-5378
http://www.tim.hawaii.edu

IDAHO

College of Southern Idaho
Business and Economics Degree
  Department
Hospitality Management
315 Falls Avenue
P.O. Box 1238
Twin Falls, ID 83303
Phone: (208) 732-6221
Fax: (208) 736-4705
http://www.csi.edu

University of Idaho
College of Natural Resources
Resource Recreation and Tourism
P.O. Box 441139
Moscow, ID 83844-1139
Phone: (208) 885-7911
Fax: (208) 885-6226
http://www.uihome.uidaho.edu/
  uihome/default.aspx

ILLINOIS

College of DuPage
Hospitality Administration, Hotel
  and Lodging Management,
  Travel and Tourism
425 Fawell Boulevard
Glen Ellyn, IL 60137-6599
Phone: (630) 942-2380
http://www.cod.edu

Elgin Community College
Culinary Arts and Hospitality
  Institute
1700 Spartan Drive
Elgin, IL 60123-7193

Phone: (847) 697-1000
http://www.elgin.edu

Kendall College
Les Roches School of Hospitality
  Management
900 N. North Branch Street
Chicago, IL 60622
Phone: (866) 667-3344
http://www.kendall.edu

Lexington College
Hospitality Management Program
310 South Peoria Street
Chicago, IL 60607
Phone: (312) 226-6294
Fax: (312) 226-6405
http://www.lexingtoncollege.edu

**Moraine Valley Community
  College**
Restaurant/Hotel Management and
  Culinary Arts Program
9000 West College Parkway
Palos Hills, IL 60465-0937
Phone: (708) 974-5597
Fax: (708) 274-3745
http://www.morainevalley.edu/
  Hospitality

Northern Illinois University
School of Family, Consumer, and
  Nutrition Science
Nutrition, Dietetics & Hospitality
  Administration
Wirtz Hall
DeKalb, IL 60115
Phone: (815) 753-6351
http://www.niu.edu

Parkland College
Hotel/Motel Management
Department of Business and Agri-
  Industries
2400 West Bradley Avenue
Champaign, IL 61821
Phone: (217) 351-2200
http://www.parkland.edu/bai/
  hospitality

Robert Morris College
Institute of Culinary Arts
401 South State Street

Chicago, IL 60605
Phone: (312) 935-6835
http://www.robertmorris.edu/
culinary

Southern Illinois University at Carbondale

Hospitality and Tourism
  Specialization
Department of Animal Science,
  Food & Nutrition
Mailcode 4417
Carbondale, IL 62901
Phone: (618) 453-2329
Fax: (618) 453-5231
http://www.siu.edu/departments/
  coagr/animal/program.htm

Triton College

Division of Career Education
Hospitality Industry
  Administration
2000 Fifth Avenue
River Grove, IL 60171
Phone: (708) 456-0300
http://www.triton.edu

University of Illinois at Urbana-Champaign

Department of Food Science and
Human Nutrition
Hospitality Management Program
260 Bevier Hall
905 South Goodwin Avenue
Urbana, IL 61801
Phone: (217) 244-4498
Fax: (217) 265-0925
http://www.fshn.uiuc.edu

Western Illinois University

Hotel and Restaurant Management
Recreation, Park and Tourism
  Administration
1 University Circle
Macomb, IL 61455
Phone: (309) 298-1414
http://www.wiu.edu

INDIANA

Ball State University

Geography Department–Travel and
  Tourism

2000 West University Avenue
Muncie, IN 47306
Phone: (765) 285-1776
Fax: (765) 285-2351
http://www.bsu.edu/geog

Indiana University

Department of Recreation, Park,
  and Tourism Studies
1025 East 7th Street, HPER 133
Bloomington, IN 47405
Phone: (812) 855-4711
http://www.indiana.edu/~recpark/
  index.shtml

Indiana University–Purdue University Fort Wayne

Consumer & Family Sciences–
  Hospitality and Tourism
  Management
2101 Coliseum Boulevard, Neff 330
Fort Wayne IN 46805-1499
Phone: (260) 481-6562
http://www.ipfw.edu/cfs

Indiana University-Purdue University Indianapolis

School of Physical Education and
  Tourism Management
IUPUI, PE 251
901 West New York Street
Indianapolis, IN 46202-5192
Phone: (317) 274-2599
Fax: (317) 278-2041
http://www.iupui.edu/~indyhper

Ivy Tech Community College

School of Public and Social Services
Hospitality Administration
P.O. Box 1763
Indianapolis, IN 46206
Phone: (317) 921-4797
http://www.ivytech.edu

Purdue University

College of Consumer and Family
  Sciences
Hospitality and Tourism
  Management
Stone Hall, Room 106
700 West State Street
West Lafayette, IN 47907-2059
Phone: (765) 494-4643

Fax: (765) 494-0327
http://www.cfs.purdue.edu/HTM

IOWA

AIB College of Business

Travel and Hospitality Department
2500 Fleur Drive
Des Moines, IA 50321
Phone: (515) 244-4221
http://www.aib.edu

Iowa Lakes Community College

Hotel & Restaurant Management/
  Casino Management Programs
3200 College Drive
Emmetsburg, IA 50536
Phone: (712) 852-3554
http://www.iowalakes.edu

Iowa State University

Department of Apparel, Education
  Studies and Hospitality
  Management
31 MacKay Hall
Ames, IA 50011-1121
Phone: (515) 294-7474
http://www.aeshm.hs.iastate.edu

Kirkwood Community College

Hospitality Programs
6301 Kirkwood Boulevard, SW
Cedar Rapids, IA 52406
Phone: (319) 398-5517
http://www.kirkwood.edu

KANSAS

Johnson County Community College

Hospitality Management Program
12345 College Boulevard
Overland Park, KS 66210-1299
Phone: (913) 469-8500
http://www.jccc.edu

Kansas State University

Department of Hotel, Restaurant,
  Institution Management &
  Dietetics
104 Justin Hall
Manhattan, KS 66506-1404
Phone: (785) 532-5521

Fax: (785) 532-5522
http://www.humec.k-state.edu/hrimd

KENTUCKY

Sullivan University

National Center for Hospitality
    Studies
3101 Bardstown Road
Louisville, KY 40205
Phone: (502) 456-6505
http://www.sullivan.edu

University of Kentucky

Department of Nutrition and Food
    Science
Hospitality Management and
    Tourism
204 Funkhouser Building
Lexington, KY 40506-0054
Phone: (859) 257-3800
Fax: (859) 257-3707
http://www.ca.uky.edu/hes/?p=34

Western Kentucky University

Consumer & Family Sciences
    Department–Hospitality
    Management
1906 College Heights Boulevard
Building #11037
Bowling Green, KY 42101
Phone: (270) 745-4352
Fax: (270) 745-3999
http://www.wku.edu/hospitality

LOUISIANA

Grambling State University

Family & Consumer Sciences
    Department–Hotel/Restaurant
    Management
P.O. Box 4248
Grambling, LA 71245
Phone: (318) 274-2249
Fax: (318) 274-6049
http://www.gram.edu/arts%20and%
    20sciences/consumersci/hotel
    mgmnt.asp

University of Louisiana at Lafayette

B. I. Moody III College of Business
    Administration

Department of Marketing &
    Hospitality
P.O. Box 43490
Lafayette, LA 70504-3490
Phone: (337) 482-6347
Fax: (337) 482-1051
http://cobweb.louisiana.edu/New/
    academics/mkt_hosp.htm

University of New Orleans

Lester E. Kabacoff School of
    Hotel, Restaurant and Tourism
    Administration
5919 Pratt Drive
New Orleans, LA 70122
Phone: (504) 286-6385
http://business.uno.edu/hrt

MAINE

Andover College

Travel and Hospitality Management
    Program
901 Washington Avenue
Portland, ME 04103
Phone: (888) 242-5314
http://www.andovercollege.edu

Southern Maine Community College

Career and Technical Programs
Lodging and Restaurant
    Management
2 Ford Road
South Portland, ME 04106
Phone: (207) 741-5500
http://www.smccme.edu

University of Maine

Forestry Program
Parks, Recreation and Tourism
215 Nutting Hall
Orono, ME 04469
Phone: (207) 581-2850
http://www.umaine.edu

MARYLAND

Anne Arundel Community College

Hospitality Culinary Arts and
    Tourism Institute
101 College Parkway
Arnold, MD 21012-1895

Phone: (410) 777-2398
http://www.aacc.edu/hcat

Baltimore International College

School of Hotel Restaurant &
    Catering Management
School of Culinary Arts
17 Commerce Street
Baltimore, MD 21202
Phone: (410) 752-4710, ext. 120
http://www.bic.edu

Chesapeake College

Hotel/Restaurant Management
    Program
P.O. Box 8
Wye Mills, MD 21679
Phone: (410) 822-5400
http://www.chesapeake.edu

Montgomery College

Hospitality Management Program
51 Mannakee Street
Rockville, MD 20850
Phone: (240) 567-5000
http://www.montgomerycollege.
    edu/Departments/hospitality/
    home.html

Morgan State University

Earl G. Graves School of Business
    and Management
Hospitality Management
1700 East Cold Spring Lane
Baltimore MD 21251
Phone: (443) 885-3160
http://www.morgan.edu/academics/
    sbm/academic/BUAD/
    homgmajor.html

University of Maryland Eastern Shore

School of Business and Technology
Department of Hotel and
    Restaurant Management
Princess Anne, MD 21853
Phone: (410) 651-2200
http://www.umes.edu/hrm

MASSACHUSETTS

Bay State College

Travel and Hospitality Management
    Program

122 Commonwealth Avenue
Boston, MA 02116
Phone: (617) 236-8000
Fax: (617) 536-1735
http://www.baystate.edu

Becker College

Hospitality and Tourism
    Management
61 Sever Street
Worcester, MA 01609
Phone: (508) 791-9241
http://www.becker.edu

Boston University

School of Hospitality
    Administration
928 Commonwealth Avenue
Boston, MA 02215
Phone: (617) 353-3261
http://www.bu.edu/hospitality

Cape Cod Community College

Hotel Restaurant Management
2240 Iyannough Road
West Barnstable, MA 02668-1599
Phone: (508) 362-2131
http://www.capecod.mass.edu

Lasell College

Hospitality and Event Management
    Program
1844 Commonwealth Avenue
Newton, MA 02466
Phone: (617) 243-2000
Fax: (617) 243-2380
http://www.lasell.edu/majors/
    hospitality.asp

Marian Court College

Business Administration Program
Hospitality Management
35 Little's Point Road
Swampscott, MA 01907
Phone: (781) 595-6768
Fax: (781) 595-3560
http://www.mariancourt.edu

Massachusetts Bay Community College

Hospitality Management
Social Sciences and Professional
    Studies

50 Oakland Street
Wellesley Hills, MA 02481-5307
Phone: (781) 239-3000
http://www.massbay.edu

Massasoit Community College

Travel and Tourism Department
One Massasoit Boulevard
Brockton, MA 02302
Phone: (508) 588-9100
Fax: (508) 497-1250
http://www.massasoit.mass.edu

Newbury College

Roger A. Saunders School of Hotel
    & Restaurant Management
129 Fisher Avenue
Brookline, MA 02146
Phone: (617) 730-7000
http://www.newbury.edu

Quinsigamond Community College

Hotel and Restaurant Management
670 West Boylston Street
Worcester, MA 01606
Phone: (508) 853-2300
http://www.qcc.edu

Salem State College

Bertolon School of Business–
    Hospitality Management
    Concentration
352 Lafayette Street
Salem, MA 01970
Phone: (978) 542-6000
http://www.salemstate.edu/
    business/mgt.php

University of Massachusetts

Department of Hospitality &
    Tourism Management
107 Flint Lab
90 Campus Center Way
Amherst, MA 01003-9247
Phone: (413) 545-2535
Fax: (413) 545-1235
http://www.isenberg.umass.edu/htm

MICHIGAN

Central Michigan University

Hospitality Services Administration

Mount Pleasant, MI 48859
Phone: (989) 774-4000
http://www.cmich.edu

Eastern Michigan University

Hotel and Restaurant Management
    Program
206 Roosevelt Hall
Ypsilanti, MI 48197
Phone: (734) 487-7087
http://www.emich.edu/sts/hrm

Ferris State University

Hospitality Programs
West Commons 106
1319 Cramer Circle
Big Rapids, MI 49307
Phone: (231) 591-2382
http://www.ferris.edu

Grand Valley State University

Department of Hospitality &
    Tourism Management
2249 Mackinac Hall
1 Campus Drive
Allendale, MI 49401
Phone: (616) 331-3118
Fax: (616) 331-3115
http://www.gvsu.edu/htm/index.
    cfm

Henry Ford Community College

Hospitality Professional
    Management
5101 Evergreen Road
Dearborn, MI 48128-1495
Phone: (313) 845-9600
http://www.hfcc.edu

Lansing Community College

Hospitality, Travel and Tourism
    Program
Business Department
Gannon Building, Room 190
Lansing, MI 48901
Phone: (517) 483-1983
http://www.lcc.edu/business/hosp_
    tourism

Michigan State University

The School of Hospitality Business
232 Eppley Center

East Lansing, MI 48824
Phone: (517) 353-9211
Fax: (517) 432-1170
http://www.bus.msu.edu/shb/about/
index.cfm

Northern Michigan University
School of Technology & Applied
Sciences–Hospitality
1401 Presque Isle Avenue
Marquette, MI 49855
Phone: (906) 227-2190
Fax: (906) 227-1549
http://webb.nmu.edu/TechnologyAnd
AppliedSciences

Western Michigan University
Department of Geography–Tourism
and Travel
3219 Wood Hall
Kalamazoo, MI 49008
Phone: (269) 387-3410
Fax: (269) 387-3442
http://www.wmich.edu/geography/
tour.htm

MINNESOTA

Alexandria Technical College
Hotel-Restaurant Management
Program
1601 Jefferson Street
Alexandria, MN 56308
Phone: (320) 762-0221
Fax: (320) 762-4501
http://www.alextech.edu

Central Lakes College
Ecotourism Program
510 West College Drive
Brainerd, MN 56401-4096
Phone: (800) 933-0346
http://www.clcmn.edu

Dakota County Technical College
Tourism and Travel Program
1300 145th Street East
Rosemount, MN 55068-2999
Phone: (651) 423-8301
http://www.dctc.edu

Minneapolis Business College
Travel and Hospitality Program

1711 West County Road B
Roseville, MN 55113
Phone: (800) 279-5200 or
(651) 636-7406
http://www.minneapolisbusiness
college.edu

Normandale Community College
Hospitality Management Programs
9700 France Avenue South
Bloomington, MN 55431
Phone: (952) 787-8200
http://www.normandale.edu

Southwest Minnesota State University
Hospitality Management
1501 State Street
Marshall, MN 56258
Phone: (800) 642-0684
http://www.southwestmsu.edu/
Academics/Programs/Hotel
RestaurantAdministration/
Index.cfm

St. Cloud State University
Geography Department–Travel and
Tourism
359 Stewart Hall
720 Fourth Avenue South
St. Cloud, MN 56301-4498
Phone: (320) 308-3160
Fax: (320) 308-1660
http://www.stcloudstate.edu/geog

University of Minnesota–Crookston
Business Department Hotel,
Restaurant, and Institutional
Management Program
2900 University Avenue
Crookston, MN 56716
Phone: (218) 281-8176
http://www.2.crk.umn.edu/
academics/Bus/HRI/

MISSOURI

Missouri State University
Hospitality and Restaurant
Administration Department
901 South National Avenue

Springfield, MO 65897
Phone: (417) 836-5744
Fax: (417) 836-7673
http://www.missouristate.edu/hra

St. Louis Community College
Hospitality Studies Program
5600 Oakland Avenue
St. Louis, MO 63110-1393
Phone: (314) 644-9100
http:///www.stlcc.edu

University of Central Missouri
Department of Health & Human
Performance
Hotel and Restaurant
Administration/Tourism
Humphreys Building, Room 216
Warrensburg, MO 64093
Phone: (660) 543-4256
http://www.ucmo.edu/x67245.xml

University of Missouri
Hotel & Restaurant Management
122 Eckles Hall
Columbia, MO 65211
Phone: (573) 882-4114
Fax: (573) 882-0596
http://hrm.missouri.edu

MONTANA

University of Montana
College of Forestry and
Conservation, Department of
Society and Conservation
Recreation Management–Nature
Based Tourism
32 Campus Drive
Missoula, MT 59812
Phone: (406) 243-5521
Fax: (406) 243-4845
http://www.cfc.umt.edu/RECM

University of Montana Western
Business and Technology
Department
Tourism and Recreation
710 South Atlantic Street
Dillon, MT 59725
Phone: (406) 683-7331
http://www.umwestern.edu

NEBRASKA

Central Community College
Hospitality Management and
　　Culinary Arts Program
East Highway 6
P.O. Box 1024
Hastings, NE 68902-1024
Phone: (402) 463-9811
Fax: (402) 461-2454
http://www.cccneb.edu

Metropolitan Community College
Institute for the Culinary Arts
Hospitality and Restaurant
　　Leadership Program
P.O. Box 3777
Omaha, NE 68103
Phone: (402) 457-2510
http://www.mccneb.edu/culinary

University of Nebraska at Kearney
Recreation, Park and Tourism
　　Management Program
905 West 25th Street
Kearney, NE 68849
Phone: (308) 865-8626
http://www.unk.edu/acad/hperls/
　　index.php?id=7807

NEVADA

College of Southern Nevada
Department of Hospitality
　　Management
Casino Management
6375 West Charleston Boulevard
Las Vegas, NV 89146
Phone: (702) 651-5000
http://www.csn.edu/pages/
　　1307.asp

Sierra Nevada College
Department of Business
Ski Resort Business and
　　Management/Hospitality and
　　Tourism Management
999 Tahoe Boulevard
Incline Village, NV 89451-9500
Phone: (775) 831-1314
http://www.sierranevada.edu

University of Nevada, Las Vegas
William F. Harrah College of Hotel
　　Administration
Box 456013
4505 Maryland Parkway
Las Vegas, NV 89154-6013
Phone: (702) 895-3161
Fax: (702) 895-4109
http://hotel.unlv.edu

NEW HAMPSHIRE

Nashua Community College
Restaurant Management Program
505 Amherst Street
Nashua, NH 03063
Phone: (603)882-6923
Fax: (603) 882-8690
http://www.nashua.nhctc.edu

NHTI—Concord's Community College
Hospitality and Tourism
　　Management Program
31 College Drive
Concord, NH 03301-7412
Phone: (603) 271-6484
http://www.nhti.edu

Plymouth State University
Nature and Heritage Tourism
17 High Street
Plymouth, NH 03264-1595
Phone: (603) 535-2335
http://www.plymouth.edu

University of New Hampshire
Tourism Planning and
　　Development, College of Life
　　Sciences and Agriculture
Department of Hospitality
　　Management, Whittemore
　　School of Business and
　　Economics
College Road
Durham, NH 03824
Phone: (603) 862-2711 (tourism);
　　(603) 862-3303 (hospitality)
http://www.dred.unh.edu and
　　http://wsbe.unh.edu/bs-
　　hospitality-management

NEW JERSEY

Atlantic Cape Community College
Hospitality Management
Food Service Management
Academy of Culinary Arts
5100 Black Horse Pike
Mays Landing, NJ 08330
Phone: (609) 343-4900
http://www.atlantic.edu

Bergen Community College
Hotel/Restaurant/Hospitality
　　Management
400 Paramus Road
Paramus, NJ 07652
Phone: (201) 447-7100
http://www.bergen.edu

County College of Morris
Hospitality Management Program
214 Center Grove Road
Randolph, NJ 07869-2086
Phone: (973) 328-5000
http://www.ccm.edu

Fairleigh Dickinson University
International School of Hospitality
　　and Tourism Management
College at Florham
285 Madison Avenue
Madison, NJ 07940
Phone: (973) 443-8500
Metropolitan Campus
1000 River Road
Teaneck, NJ 07666
Phone: (201) 692-2000
http://view.fdu.edu/default.
　　aspx?id=80

Georgian Court University
Tourism, Hospitality and Recreation
　　Management Program
900 Lakewood Avenue
Lakewood, NJ 08701-2697
Phone: (732) 987-2760
Fax: (732) 987-2000
http://www.georgian.edu

Middlesex County College
Hotel, Restaurant and Institution
　　Management Program

2600 Woodbridge Avenue
Edison, NJ 08818-3050
Phone: (732) 906-2538
http://www.middlesexcc.edu

Montclair State University
School of Business
Leisure Industries & Tourism
Hospitality Management
1 Normal Avenue
Montclair, NJ 07043
Phone: (973) 655-4000
http://sbus.montclair.edu

NEW MEXICO

Doña Ana Community College
Business and Information Systems
 Division
Hospitality Services
2800 North Sonoma Ranch
 Boulevard
Las Cruces, NM 88011
Phone: (575) 528-7250
Fax: (575) 527-7515
http://dabcc.nmsu.edu

New Mexico State University
School of Hotel, Restaurant and
 Tourism Management
Gerald Thomas Hall, Room 119,
 College Street
Box 30003, MSC 3HRTM
Las Cruces, NM 88003
Phone: (575) 646-5995
Fax: (575) 646-8100
http://hrtm.nmsu.edu

NEW YORK

Adirondack Community
 College
Hospitality and Tourism
640 Bay Road
Queensbury, NY 12804
Phone: (518) 743-2200
Fax: (518) 745-1433
http://www.sunyacc.edu

Buffalo State College
Hospitality and Tourism
 Department
Caudell Hall 207

1300 Elmwood Avenue
Buffalo, NY 14222
Phone: (716) 878-5913
Fax: (716) 878-5834
http://www.buffalostate.edu/
 hospitality

Cornell University
School of Hotel Administration
Ithaca, NY 14853-6902
Phone: (607) 255-9393
Fax: (607) 255-0021
http://www.hotelschool.cornell.edu

The Culinary Institute of
 America
1946 Campus Drive
Hyde Park, NY 12538-1499
Phone: (845) 452-9430
http://www.ciachef.edu

Erie Community College
Business and Public Service
 Division
Hotel Restaurant Management/
 Culinary Arts
6205 Main Street
Williamsville, NY 14221
Phone: (716) 634-0800
http://www.ecc.edu

Finger Lakes Community
 College
Hotel and Resort Management
4355 Lake Shore Drive
Canandaigua, NY 14424
Phone: (716) 394-3500
http://www.fingerlakes.edu

Genesee Community College
Tourism and Hospitality
 Management Program
One College Road
Batavia, NY 14020
Phone: (585) 343-0055
Fax: (585) 343-4541
http://www.genesse.edu

Herkimer County Community
 College
Travel & Tourism Program:
 Hospitality & Events Management
Reservoir Road

Herkimer, NY 13350
Phone: (315) 866-0300
http://www.herkimer.edu

Jefferson Community College
Hospitality and Tourism Program
1220 Coffeen Street
Watertown, NY 13601
Phone: (315) 786-2277
http://www.sunyjefferson.edu

Kingsborough Community
 College
Tourism & Hospitality Department
2001 Oriental Boulevard
Manhattan Beach
Brooklyn, NY 11235
Phone: (718) 368-5143
Fax: (718) 368-4880
http://www.kingsborough.edu

LaGuardia Community College
Travel and Tourism
33-10 Thomson Avenue
Long Island City, NY 11101
Phone: (718) 482-5606
Fax: (718) 609-2060
http://www.lagcc.cuny.edu/
 accountingms

Monroe Community College
Department of Food, Hotel, and
 Tourism Management
1000 East Henrietta Road
Rochester, NY 14623
Phone: (585) 292-2000
http://www.monroecc.edu/depts/
 fhtm

Morrisville State College
Travel and Tourism: Hospitality
 Management Program
Gaming and Casino Management
 Program
P.O. Box 901
Morrisville, NY 13408
Phone: (800) 258-0111
http://www.morrisville.edu

Nassau Community College
Hospitality/Business
One Education Drive
Garden City, NY 11530-6793

Phone: (516) 572-7344
Fax: (516) 572-9739
http://www.ncc.edu

New York Institute of Technology

School of Management
    Hospitality Management
26 West 61st Street
New York, NY 10023
Phone: (212) 261-1529
http://www.nyit.edu

New York University

Preston Robert Tisch Center for
    Hospitality, Tourism, and Sports
    Management
School of Continuing and
    Professional Studies
145 Fourth Avenue, Room 201
New York, NY 10003
Phone: (212) 998-7100
http://www.scps.nyu.edu/areas-of-
    study/tisch

Niagara University

College of Hospitality and Tourism
    Management
Niagara University, NY 14109
Phone: (716) 285-1212
http://www.niagara.edu/hospitality

Paul Smith's College

Division of Hospitality, Resort and
    Culinary Management
P.O. Box 265
Paul Smiths, NY 12970-0265
Phone: (518) 327-6227
Fax: (518) 327-6016
http://www.paulsmiths.edu/hrcm/

Rochester Institute of Technology

School of Hospitality and Service
    Management
14 Lomb Memorial Drive
Rochester, NY 14623
Phone: (585) 475-2867
Fax: (585) 475-5099
http://www.rit.edu/cast/hsm

Rockland Community College

Hospitality and Tourism Program

145 College Road
Suffern, NY 10901
Phone: (845) 574-4486
http://www.sunyrockland.edu

Schenectady County Community College

Department of Hotel, Culinary Arts
    & Tourism
78 Washington Avenue
Schenectady, NY 12305
Phone: (518) 381-1200
http://www.sunysccc.edu/academic/
    cularts

State University of New York at Cobleskill

Culinary Arts, Hospitality and
    Tourism Division
State Route 7
Cobleskill, NY 12043
Phone: (518) 255-5425
Fax: (518) 255-6325
http://www.cobleskill.edu/
    BUS3overview.html

State University of New York at Delhi

Hospitality Department
111 Alumni Hall
Delhi, NY 13753
Phone: (607) 746-4400
Fax: (607) 746-4769
http://www.delhi.edu/academics/
    hospitality/default.asp

State University of New York at Oneonta

Food Service and Restaurant
    Administration
Department of Human Ecology
Ravine Parkway
Oneonta, NY 13820
Phone: (607) 436-2705
http://www.oneonta.edu/academics/
    huec/FSRA3.asp

State University of New York at Plattsburgh

Hotel, Restaurant, and Tourism
    Management Program
101 Broad Street
Sibley Hall

Plattsburgh, NY 12901
Phone: (518) 564-3260
Fax: (518) 564-3263
http://www.plattsburgh.edu/
    academics/hrtm

St. Johns University

Division of Hospitality, Tourism,
    and Sport Management
Bent Hall, 201
8000 Utopia Parkway
Queens, NY 11439
Phone: (718) 990-7391
http://www.stjohns.edu/
    academics/undergraduate/
    professionalstudies/
    departments/hotel

Suffolk County Community College

Culinary Arts Program
533 College Road
Selden, NY 11784-2899
Phone: (631) 451-4000
http://www.sunysuffolk.edu

Sullivan County Community College

Hospitality Management Program
112 College Road
Loch Sheldrake, NY 12759
Phone: (800) 577-5243; (845) 434-
    5750
Fax: (845) 434-4806
http://www.sullivan.suny.edu

Syracuse University

College of Human Ecology—
    Nutrition and Hospitality
    Management
119 Euclid Avenue
Syracuse, NY 13244
Phone: (315) 443-2027
http://humanecology.syr.edu/
    schools/nhm

NORTH CAROLINA

Appalachian State University

Walker College of Business—
    Hospitality and Tourism
    Management
Room 4135 Raley Hall

ASU Box 32037
Boone, NC 28608-2037
Phone: (828) 262-2057
http://www.business.appstate.edu/
about

Asheville-Buncombe Technical Community College

Hotel and Restaurant Management
Program
340 Victoria Road
Asheville, NC 28801
Phone: (828) 254-1921
http://www.abtech.edu

Blue Ridge Community College

Travel and Tourism Technology
180 West Campus Drive
Flat Rock, NC 28731
Phone: (828) 694-1700
Fax: (828) 694-1690
http://www.blueridge.cc.nc.us

Cape Fear Community College

Hotel and Restaurant Management
Programs
411 North Front Street
Wilmington, NC 28401
Phone: (910) 362-7000
http://cfcc.edu

Central Piedmont Community College

Hospitality Education
P.O. Box 35009
Charlotte, NC 28235
Phone: (704) 330-2722
http://www1.cpcc.edu/hospitality-
education

East Carolina University

Department of Hospitality
Management
College of Human Ecology
152 Rivers Building
Greenville, NC 27858-4353
Phone: (252) 737-1603
http://www.ecu.edu/che/hmgt

Johnson & Wales University

College of Culinary Arts
The Hospitality College
801 West Trade Street

Charlotte, NC 28202
Phone: (980) 598-1000
http://www.jwu.edu

North Carolina Central University

Hospitality & Tourism
Administration Program
1801 Fayetteville Street
Durham, NC 27707
Phone: (919) 530-7389
http://www.nccu.edu

Southwestern Community College

Culinary Technology Program
447 College Drive
Sylva, NC 28779
Phone: (828) 586-4091 or
(800) 447-4091
Fax: (828) 586-3129
http://www.southwesterncc.edu

University of North Carolina at Greensboro

Hospitality and Tourism
Management Program
420 J HHP Building,
P.O. Box 26170
Greensboro, NC 27402-6170
Phone: (336) 334-5327
Fax: (336) 334-3238
http://www.uncg.edu/rth

University of North Carolina at Wilmington

Department of Health and Applied
Human Sciences
Parks and Recreation Management
601 South College Road
Wilmington, NC 28403
Phone: (910) 962-3250
Fax: (910) 962-7073
http://www.uncw.edu/hahs

Wake Technical Community College

Business Technologies Division
Hotel & Restaurant Management
9101 Fayetteville Road
Raleigh, NC 27603
Phone: (919) 866-5951
http://hrm.waketech.edu

Western Carolina University

Hospitality and Tourism Program
391 Belk Building
Cullowhee, NC 28723
Phone: (828) 227-3316
http://www.wcu.edu/cob/HT/index.
htm

Wilkes Community College

Business and Public Services
Technologies Division
Culinary Technology
P.O. Box 120
1328 South Collegiate Drive
Wilkesboro, NC 28697
Phone: (336) 838-6100
Fax: (336) 838-6277
http://www.wilkescc.edu/wcccms

OHIO

Bowling Green State University

Sport Management, Recreation, and
Tourism Division
Bowling Green, OH 43403-0248
Phone: (419) 372-6902
Fax: (419) 372-0383
http://www.bgsu.edu/colleges/edhd/
hmsls

Central State University

College of Business and Industry
Hospitality Management
P.O. Box 1004
1400 Brush Row Road
Wilberforce, OH 45384
Phone: (937) 376-6011
http://www.centralstate.edu

Columbus State Community College

Hospitality Management
Department
Columbus, OH 43215
Phone: (614) 287-5353
http://www.cscc.edu

Cuyahoga Community College

Hospitality Management
700 Carnegie Avenue
Cleveland, OH 44115
Phone: (216) 987-4000
http://www.tri-c.edu

Kent State University

School of Exercise, Leisure and
    Sport
Recreation, Park and Tourism
    Management
Kent, OH 44242
Phone: (330) 672-2012
Fax: (330) 672-4106
http://www.ehhs.kent.edu/els

Lakeland Community College

Social Science and Public Service
    Department
Hotel and Lodging Management
7700 Clocktower Drive
Kirtland, OH 44094-5198
Phone: (440) 525-7832
http://www.lakelandcc.edu

Ohio State University

College of Education and Human
    Ecology
Hospitality Management
231 Campbell Hall
1787 Neil Avenue
Columbus, OH 43210
Phone: (614) 247-7243
Fax: (614) 688-8133
http://ehe.osu.edu/cs/programs/
    undergraduate

Ohio University

School of Human and Consumer
    Sciences
Restaurant, Hotel and Tourism
Grover Center W324
Athens, OH 45701-2979
Phone: (740) 593-0700
http://www.ohiou.edu/humanand
    consumer/foodservicemgt.htm

Sinclair Community College

Hospitality Management and
    Tourism Department
444 West Third Street
Dayton, OH 45402-1460
Phone: (800) 315-3000
http://www.sinclair.edu

Tiffin University

Management Major—Hospitality
    and Tourism Program
155 Miami Street

Tiffin, OH 44883
Phone: (800) 968-6446
http://www.tiffin.edu/management

OKLAHOMA

Northeastern State University

Hospitality and Tourism
    Management
600 North Grand Avenue
Tahlequah, OK 74464
Phone: (918) 456-5511
http://arapaho.nsuok.edu/%7Emdm

Oklahoma State University

College of Human Environmental
    Sciences
School of Hotel and Restaurant
    Administration
210 Human Environmental
    Sciences–West
Stillwater, OK 74078-6173
Phone: (405) 744-7651
Fax: (405) 744-6299
http://ches.okstate.edu/hrad

Tulsa Community College

Hospitality and Gaming Operations
    Program
West Campus
7505 West 41st Street
Tulsa, OK 74107
Phone: (918) 595-7000
http://www.tulsacc.edu

OREGON

Central Oregon Community College

Hotel, Tourism Recreation
    Management and Cascade
    Culinary Institute
2600 Northwest College Way
Bend, OR 97701
Phone: (541) 383-7700
http://www.cocc.edu

Chemeketa Community College

Hospitality & Tourism Management
    Programs
4000 Lancaster Drive NE
P.O. Box 14007

Salem, OR 97309
Phone: (503) 399-5186
http://www.hsm.org

Mount Hood Community College

Hospitality & Tourism Management
    Program
26000 SE Stark Street
Gresham, OR 97030
Phone: (503) 491-7486
http://www.mhcc.edu

Oregon State University–Cascades

Tourism and Outdoor Leadership
    Program
2600 Northwest College Way
Bend, OR 97701
Phone: (541) 322-3100
http://www.osucascades.edu/
    academics/orlt

Southern Oregon University

School of Business—Hospitality
    and Tourism Management
Central 144
1250 Siskiyou Boulevard
Ashland, OR 97520
Phone: (541) 552-6484
http://www.sou.edu

PENNSYLVANIA

Bucks County Community College

Department of Business Studies
Hospitality & Tourism
275 Swamp Road
Newtown, PA 18940
Phone: (215) 968-8249
http://www.bucks.edu

California University of Pennsylvania

Department of Earth Science
Parks and Recreation Management
    Program
250 University Avenue
California, PA 15419
Phone: (724) 938-4000
http://www.cup.edu

Central Pennsylvania College

Travel and Tourism Operations
    Program
College Hill and Valley Roads
Summerdale, PA 17093
Phone: (800) 759-2727
http://www.centralpenn.edu

Delaware County Community College

Hotel and Restaurant Management
    Program
901 South Media Line Road
Media, PA 19063-1094
Phone: (610) 359-5000
http://www.dccc.edu

Drexel University

Goodwin College of Professional
    Studies
Hospitality Management
101 North 33rd Street
Academic Building Suite 110
Philadelphia, PA 19104
Phone: (215) 895-2411
Fax: (215) 895-2426
http://www.drexel.edu/goodwin

East Stroudsburg University

Hospitality Management Center
Hotel Restaurant & Tourism
    Management
East Stroudsburg, PA 18301
Phone: (570) 422-3511
Fax: (570) 422-3198
http://www4.esu.edu/academics/
    majors2/programs/hrtm/hrtm.
    cfm

Harrisburg Area Community College

Hospitality and Tourism
    Department
125 Hall Technology Building
One HACC Drive
Harrisburg, PA 17110-2999
Phone: (717) 780-3248
http://wwww.hacc.edu

Indiana University of Pennsylvania

Academy of Culinary Arts
1012 Winslow Street

Punxsutawney, PA 15767
Phone: (800) 438-6424
Fax: (814) 938-1158
http://www.iup.edu/admissions/
    culinary/default.aspx

Indiana University of Pennsylvania

Hospitality Management
    Department
Ackerman Hall, Room 11
911 South Drive
Indiana, PA 15705
Phone: (724) 357-2626
Fax: (724) 357-7582
http://www.iup.edu/hospitality-
    mgt/default.aspx

Keystone College

Hotel and Restaurant Management
Culinary Arts
One College Green
La Plume, PA 18440
Phone: (570) 945-8000
http://www.keystone.edu

Lehigh Carbon Community College

Hotel/Resort Management
Food Service Management
4525 Education Park Drive
Schnecksville, PA 18078
Phone: (610) 799-1508
http://www.lccc.edu

Luzerne County Community College

Hospitality Business Management
    Department
1333 South Prospect Street
Nanticoke, PA 18634-3899
Phone: (800) 377-LCCC
http://www.luzerne.edu

Mansfield University

Business & Economics
    Department—Travel & Tourism
106 Elliott Hall
Mansfield, PA 16933
Phone: (570) 662-4481
Fax: (570) 662-4111
http://www.mansfield.edu/
    %7Ebusecon

Marywood University

Business and Managerial Science
    Programs
Hospitality Management
2300 Adams Avenue
Scranton, PA 18509
Phone: (570) 348-6274
Fax: (570) 961-4762
http://www.marywood.edu

Mercyhurst College

Hotel, Restaurant and Institutional
    Management
501 East 38th Street
Erie, PA 16546
Phone: (814) 824-2356
http://www.mercyhurst.edu

Northampton Community College

Hotel/Restaurant Management
    Program
3835 Green Pond Road
Bethlehem, PA 18020
Phone: (610) 861-5300
http://www.northampton.edu

Pennsylvania State University

College of Health and Human
    Development
School of Hospitality Management
201 Mateer Building
University Park, PA 16802
Phone: (814) 865-1853
http://www.hhdev.psu.edu/shm

The Restaurant School at Walnut Hill College

Culinary/Pastry Arts; Restaurant/
    Hotel Management
4207 Walnut Street
Philadelphia, PA 19104
Phone: (215) 222-4200
http://www.therestaurantschool.com

Robert Morris University

Hospitality and Tourism
    Management
6001 University Boulevard
Moon Township, PA 15108
Phone: (412) 397-3278
Fax: (412) 397-2172
http://www.robert-morris.edu

Temple University
School of Tourism and Hospitality
  Management
1700 North Broad Street,
  Room 412
Philadelphia, PA 19122-0843
Phone: (215) 204-8701
Fax: (215) 204-8705
http://sthm.temple.edu

**Westmoreland County
  Community College**
Hotel/Motel Management; Culinary
  Arts
145 Pavilion Lane
Youngwood, PA 15697
Phone: (724) 925-4000
http://www.wccc.edu

Widener University
School of Hospitality Management
Academic Center North
One Place University
Chester, PA 19013
Phone: (610) 499-1101
Fax: (610) 499-1106
http://www.widener.edu/shm/
  default.asp

York Technical Institute
Hospitality Program
1405 Williams Road
York, PA 17402
Phone: (717) 757-1100
Fax: (717) 757-4964
Culinary Arts/Restaurant
  Management Program
3040 Hempland Road
Lancaster, PA 17601
Phone: (717) 295-1135
Fax: (717) 295-1135
http://www.yti.edu

RHODE ISLAND

Johnson & Wales University
College of Culinary Arts
The Hospitality College
8 Abbott Park Place
Providence, RI 02903
Phone: (401) 598-2352
http://www.jwu.edu

SOUTH CAROLINA

Clemson University
Department of Parks, Recreation
  and Tourism Management
263 Lehotsky Hall
Clemson, SC 29634
Phone: (864) 656-3400
http://www.hehd.clemson.edu/
  PRTM

**Horry-Georgetown Technical
  College**
Hospitality/Tourism Management
  Program
2050 Highway 501 East
Conway, SC 29528-6066
Phone: (843) 477-2000
http://www.hgtc.edu

**Technical College of the
  Lowcountry**
Business Technologies Department
921 Ribaut Road
Beaufort, SC 29901
Phone: (843) 525-8211
Fax: (843) 525-8285
http://www.tcl.edu

Trident Technical College
Culinary Institute of Charleston:
  Hospitality, Tourism & Culinary
  Arts
P.O. Box 118067
Charleston, SC 29423
Phone: (843) 574-6111
http://www.tridenttech.edu/culinary_
  institute_of_charleston.htm

University of South Carolina
School of Hotel, Restaurant and
  Tourism Management
108-B Carolina Coliseum
Columbia, SC 29208
Phone: (803) 777-4658
http://www.hrsm.sc.edu

SOUTH DAKOTA

Black Hills State University
Tourism and Hospitality
  Management Program
1200 University Street

Spearfish, SD 57799
Phone: (800) ALL-BHSU
http://www.bhsu.edu

TENNESSEE

**Southwest Tennessee
  Community College**
Hospitality Management Program
5983 Macon Cove
Memphis, TN 38134
Phone: (901) 333-5000
http://www.southwest.tn.edu

University of Tennessee
Department of Retail, Hospitality,
  and Tourism Management
1215 West Cumberland Avenue
110 Jessie Harris Building
Knoxville, TN 37996-1911
Phone: (865) 974-2141
Fax: (865) 974-5236
http://rhtm.utk.edu

**Volunteer State Community
  College**
Hotel/Restaurant Management
  Program
1480 Nashville Pike
Gallatin, TN 37066
Phone: (615) 230-3466
http://www.volstate.edu/Hotel
  Restaurant

TEXAS

Del Mar College
Department of Hospitality
  Management
101 Baldwin Boulevard
Corpus Christi, TX 78404
Phone: (361) 698-1200
http://www.delmar.edu/hospmgmt

El Paso Community College
Travel and Tourism Program
Culinary Arts Program
P.O. Box 20500
El Paso, TX 79998
Phone: (915) 831-3722
http://www.epcc.edu

Richland College

Travel, Exposition and Meeting
    Management Program
12800 Abrams Road
Dallas, TX 75243-2199
Phone: (972) 238-6097
Fax: (972) 238-6333
http://www.rlc.dcccd.edu/travel

St. Philip's College

Department of Tourism, Hospitality
    and Culinary Arts
1801 Martin Luther King Drive
San Antonio, TX 78203
Phone: (210) 531-3200
http://www.accd.edu/spc

Tarrant County College

Hospitality Management–Southeast
    Campus
2100 Southeast Parkway
Arlington, TX 76018
Phone: (817) 515-8223
http://www.tccd.edu

Texas A&M University

Department of Recreation, Park &
    Tourism Sciences
2261 TAMU
College Station, TX 77843-2261
Phone: (979) 845-5411
Fax: (979) 845-0446
http://www.rpts.tamu.edu/index.
    shtml

Texas State Technical College

Food Service/Culinary Arts
Golf Course/Landscape Management
3801 Campus Drive
Waco, TX 76705
Phone: (254) 867-4868
Fax: (254) 867-3663
http://www.tstc.edu

Texas Tech University

College of Human Sciences
Restaurant, Hotel and Institutional
    Management
NHR Department Box 41240
Lubbock, TX 79409-1240
Phone: (806) 742-3068, ext. 252
http://www.depts.ttu.edu/hs/nhr/
    rhim

University of Houston

Conrad N. Hilton College of Hotel
    and Restaurant Management
229 C. N. Hilton Hotel & College
Houston, TX 77204-3028
Phone: (713) 743-2655
http://www.hrm.uh.edu

University of North Texas

School of Merchandising and
    Hospitality Management
P.O. Box 311100
Denton, TX 76203-1100
Phone: (940) 565-2436
Fax: (940) 565-4348
http://www.smhm.unt.edu

The University of Texas at San Antonio

College of Business—Tourism
    Management Program
One UTSA Circle
San Antonio, TX 78249-0631
Phone: (210) 458-4313
Fax: (210) 458-4308
http://tourism.utsa.edu

Wiley College

Hospitality and Tourism
    Administration
711 Wiley Avenue
Marshall, TX 75670
Phone: (903) 927-3300
http://www.wileyc.edu

UTAH

Brigham Young University

Department of Geography—Travel
    and Tourism Studies
690 Spencer W. Kimball Tower
Provo, UT 84602
Phone: (801) 422-3851
Fax: (801) 422-0266
http://www.byu.edu

University of Utah

College of Health
Department of Parks, Recreation
    and Tourism
1901 East South Campus Drive
    Annex C, Room 1085

Salt Lake City, UT 84112
Phone: (801) 581-8542
Fax: (801) 581-4930
http://www.health.utah.edu/prt

Utah Valley State College

School of Business—Hospitality
    Management
800 West University Parkway
Orem, UT 85058
Phone: (801) 863-8098
http://www.uvsc.edu/business/hosp

VERMONT

Champlain College

Hospitality Industry Management
    Program
163 South Willard Street
Burlington, VT 05402
Phone: (802) 860-2700
http://www.champlain.edu/majors/
    hospitality/index.php

New England Culinary Institute

Hospitality and Restaurant
    Management
56 College Street
Montpelier, VT 05602
Phone: (877) 223-NECI
Fax: (802) 225-3280
http://www.neci.edu

University of Vermont

The Rubenstein School of
    Environment and Natural
    Resources—Recreation
    Management
330 George D. Aiken Center
Burlington, VT 05405
Phone: (802) 656-4380
http://www.uvm.edu/~envnr

VIRGINIA

Blue Ridge Community College

Culinary Arts and Management
Box 80, One College Lane
Weyers Cave, VA 24486
Phone: (540) 234-9261
http://www.brcc.edu

George Mason University
School of Recreation, Health, and
 Tourism
Tourism and Events Management
MS 4E5, 10900 University
 Boulevard
Manassas, VA 20110
Phone: (703) 993-4698
http://rht.gmu.edu/tem

James Madison University
College of Business
Hospitality and Tourism
 Management
MSC 0202
Harrisonburg, VA 22807
Phone: (540) 568-5168
Fax: (540) 568-3273
http://www.jmu.edu/hospitality

**Northern Virginia Community
 College**
Business and Public Services
Hospitality Management
8333 Little River Turnpike
Annandale, VA 22003
Phone: (703) 323-3000
http://www.nvcc.edu

Old Dominion University
Darden College of Education
Recreation and Tourism Studies
Education Building, Room 120
Norfolk, VA 23529
Phone: (757) 683-3938
Fax: (757) 683-5083
http://education.odu.edu/esper/
 academics/degrees/rts/rts.
 shtml

**Virginia Polytechnic Institute
 and State University**
Department of Hospitality and
 Tourism Management
362 Wallace Hall (0429)
Blacksburg, VA 24061
Phone: (540) 231-5515
Fax: (540) 231-8313
http://www.htm.pamplin.vt.edu

Virginia State University
School of Agriculture
Hospitality Management

1 Hayden Drive
Petersburg, VA 23806
Phone: (804) 524-6753
http://www.vsu.edu/pages/751.asp

WASHINGTON

**Central Washington
 University**
Recreation and Tourism Program
400 East University Way
Ellensburg, WA 98926-7565
Phone: (509) 963-1968
http://www.cwu.edu

Washington State University
School of Hospitality Business
 Management
Todd Hall, Room 470
P.O. Box 644742
Pullman, WA 99164-4742
Phone: (800) 239-4095 or
 (509) 335-5766
Fax: (509) 335-3857
http://www.business.wsu.edu/
 academics/Hospitality/Pages/
 index.aspx

WEST VIRGINIA

Concord University
Recreation and Tourism
 Management
Division of Social Sciences
Vermillion Street
P.O. Box 1000
Athens, WV 24712-1000
Phone: (800) 344-6679
http://www.concord.edu

Davis and Elkins College
Business Administration &
 Economics—Hospitality
 Management
Recreation Management and
 Tourism Program
Elkins, WV 26241
Phone: (304) 637-1975 (hospitality
 management)
Phone: (304) 637-1803 (recreation
 management and tourism)
http://www.davisandelkins.edu

Fairmont State University
Hospitality Management Program
1201 Locust Avenue
Fairmont, WV 26554
Phone: (304) 367-4892
http://www.fairmontstate.edu

West Liberty University
School of Business
Hospitality and Tourism
 Management Program
P.O. Box 295
West Liberty, WV 26074
Phone: (304) 336-8159
http://www.westliberty.edu

WISCONSIN

Gateway Technical College
Hotel/Hospitality Management
3520 30th Avenue
Kenosha, WI 54144
Phone: (262) 564-2200
http://www.gtc.edu

**Milwaukee Area Technical
 College**
Hotel/Hospitality Management
700 West State Street
Milwaukee, WI 53233
Phone: (414) 297-MATC
http://www.matc.edu

**University of Wisconsin–
 Stout**
Hospitality and Tourism
 Department
429 Home Economics Building
Menomonie, WI 54751
Phone: (715) 232-1203
Fax: (715) 232-2588
http://www.uwstout.edu/chd/
 hosptour

**Waukesha County Technical
 College**
Hotel and Restaurant Management
 Program
800 Main Street
Pewaukee, WI 53072
Phone: (262) 691-5566
http://www.wctc.edu

WYOMING

Northwest College
Travel and Tourism Program
231 West 6th Street
Powell, WY 82435

Phone: (307) 754-6459
http://www.northwestcollege.edu

Sheridan College
Hospitality Management

P.O. Box 1500
Sheridan, WY 82801
Phone: (307) 674-6446;
    (800) 913-9139
http://www.sheridan.edu

II. CULINARY ARTS AND FOOD SERVICE

The following is a list of American Culinary Federation Education Foundation Accrediting Commission–accredited institutions that offer culinary and food service programs by state. For updated listings, please visit www.acfchefs.org/Content/Education/Accreditation/PostSecondary/postsecondary.htm.

ALABAMA

Bishop State Community College
414 Stanton Street
Mobile, AL 36617
AAS Degree in Commercial Food
    Service
Certificate in Commercial Food
    Service
Contact: Chef Herman Packer,
    CEC, CCE, AAC
Phone: (334) 473-8692, ext. 49
Fax: (334) 471-5961
http://www.bscc.cc.al.us

Culinard
65 Bagby Drive
Birmingham, AL 35209
AOS Degree in Culinary Arts
AOS Degree in Baking and Pastry
Contact: Anthony Osbourne
Phone: (205) 802-1200
http://www.culinard.com

**Faulkner State Community
    College**
Highway 31 South
Bay Minette, AL 36507
AAS Degree in Culinary Arts /
    Food Service Management
Certificate in Culinary Arts / Food
    Service Management
AAS and Certificate in Baking and
    Pastry
Contact: Ron Koetter, CEC, CCE,
    AAC
Phone: (334) 968-3108
Fax: (334) 968-3120
http://www.faulkner.cc.al.us

**Jefferson State Community
    College**
Pinson Valley Parkway at 2601
    Carson Road
Birmingham, AL 35215
AAS Degree in Hospitality
    Management / Culinary
    Apprentice Option
AOS Degree in Baking and Pastry
Contact: Joseph Mitchell, CEPC,
    CCE
Phone: (205) 856-7898
Fax: (205) 853-0340
http://www.jeffstateonline.com

**Trenholm State Technical
    College**
1225 Air Base Boulevard
Montgomery, AL 36108
AAT Degree in Culinary Arts
Culinary Apprentice
Contact: Mary Ann Campbell,
    CEC, CCE, AAC
Phone: (334) 420-4495
Fax: (334) 420-4495
http://www.trenholmtech.cc.al.us

ALASKA

**Alaska Vocational Technical
    Center (AVTEC)**
P.O. Box 889
Seward, AK 99664-0889
Certificate in Culinary Arts
Certificate in Baking and Pastry
Contact: Robert Wilson, CEC, CCE
Phone: (800) 478-5389
http://www.avtec.alaska.edu

ARIZONA

Art Institute of Phoenix
2233 West Dunlap Avenue
Phoenix, AZ 85251
AAS Degree in Culinary Arts
Contact: Joseph LaVilla
Phone: (602) 678-4300

Scottsdale Community College
9000 East Chaparral Road
Scottsdale, AZ 85256
AAS in Culinary Arts
Certificate in Culinary Arts
Contact: Karen Chalmers
E-mail: karen.chalmers@sccmail.
    maricopa.edu
Phone: (480) 423-6241
Fax: (480) 423-6091

Scottsdale Culinary Institute
8100 East Camelback Road
Scottsdale, AZ 85251
AOS Degree in Le Cordon Bleu
    Culinary Arts
AOS Degree in Le Cordon Bleu
    Patisserie & Baking
AOS Degree in Restaurant
    Management
Certificate in Baking and Pastry
Contact: Mary Malasky Mules
Phone: (480) 990-3773
Fax: (480) 990-0351
http://www.scichefs.com

CALIFORNIA

Art Institute of San Diego
7650 Mission Valley Road

San Diego, CA 92108
AS Degree in Culinary Arts
Contact: Mark Sullivan, CCA -
masullivan@aii.edu
Phone: (858) 598-1281

California Culinary Academy
625 Polk Street
San Francisco, CA 94102
AOS Degree in Culinary Arts
Certificate in Baking and Pastry
Contact: Dalace Bubemyre
Phone: (415) 216-4376
Fax: (415) 292-8290
http://www.baychef.com

City College of San Francisco
50 Phelan Avenue
San Francisco, CA 94112
AS Degree in Hotel and Restaurant
Operation
Contact: Edward Hamilton
Phone: (415) 239-3154
Secretary: Kathleen Manning
Phone: (415) 239-3152
Fax: (415) 705-1776
http://www.ccsf.edu

Columbia College
11600 Columbia College Drive
Senora, CA 95370
AS Degree in Hospitality
Management, Emphasis
in Culinary Arts, Hotel
Management, or Restaurant
Management
Contact: Gene Womble
Phone: (209) 588-5135
http://columbia.yosemite.cc.ca.us

Diablo Valley College
321 Golf Club Road
Pleasant Hill, CA 94523
Certificate in Culinary Arts
Certificate in Baking and Pastry
Contact: Robert Eustes
Phone: (925) 685-1230, ext. 252
Fax: (925) 825-8412
http://www.dvc.edu

Institute of Technology–Clovis
564 West Herndon Avenue
Clovis, CA 93612-0105

Professional Diploma in Culinary
Arts
Contact: Don Waddell, CC
E-mail: waddell@it.email.com
Phone: (559) 323-4216

Institute of Technology–
Modesto
5737 Stoddard Road
Modesto, CA 95356-9000
Professional Diploma in Culinary
Arts
Phone: Contact: Paul Topping
E-mail: ptopping@it.email.com
Phone: (209) 545-3100

Institute of Technology–
Roseville
333 Sunrise Avenue
Suite 510
Roseville, CA 95661-3482
Professional Diploma in Culinary
Arts
Contact: Don Dickinson, CEC,
CCA, AAC
Phone: (916) 797-6337
Fax: (916) 797-6338
E-mail: ddickinson@it-email.com

Los Angeles Trade–Tech
College
400 West Washington Boulevard
Los Angeles, CA 90015
AA Degree in Culinary Arts
AA Degree in Professional Baking
Certificate in Culinary Arts
Certificate in Professional Baking
Contact: Steve Kasmar
Phone: (213) 763-7331
Fax: (213) 748-7334
http://www.lattc.cc.ca.us

Orange Coast College
2701 Fairview Road
Costa Mesa, CA 92625
Certificate in Advanced Culinary
Arts and Cook Apprentice
AA Degree in Culinary Arts
Cook's Apprentice Certificate of
Achievement
Contact: Bill Barber
Phone: (714) 432-5835, ext. 2
Fax: (714) 432-5609

http://www.occ.cccd.edu/
departments/culinary/culinary.
htm

Quality College of Culinary
Careers, Inc.
1776 North Fine Street
Fresno, CA 93727
Certificate in Culinary Arts—Food
and Beverage Management
Contact: John Moore, Ph.D., CEC,
CCE
Phone: (866) 373-2466 or
(559) 497-5050
E-mail: qcchefjohn@aol.com

San Joaquin Delta College
5151 Pacific Avenue
Stockton, CA 95207
AS Degree in Baking and Pastry
AS Degree in Culinary Arts
Basic and Advanced Certificate in
Culinary Arts
Advanced Certificate in Baking and
Pastry
Contact: Robert Halabicky
Phone: (209) 954-5151
Fax: (209) 954-5516
http://www.deltacollege.org

Santa Barbara City College
721 Cliff Drive
Santa Barbara, CA 93109
AS Degree in Hotel, Restaurant and
Culinary
Certificate in Hotel Restaurant and
Culinary
Contact: Randy Bublitz, CCE,
Culinary Arts Department
Phone: (805) 965-0581
http://www.sbcc.cc.ca.us

COLORADO

Art Institute of Colorado
675 South Broadway
Denver, CO 80209
AAS Degree in Culinary Arts
Contact: Chef Matthew Bennett,
CEC, CCE, CHE
Phone: (303) 824-3850
Fax: (303) 778-8312
http://www.aic.aii.edu

Pikes Peak Community College

5675 South Academy Boulevard
CC17
Colorado Springs, CO 80906
AAS Degree in Culinary Arts
Culinary Arts Certificate, Baking
Certificate
Contact: Rob Hudson, CEC, CCE
Phone: (719) 473-0937
Fax: (719) 540-7453
E-mail: rob.hudson@ppcc.edu
http://www.ppcc.cccoes.edu

Pueblo Community College

900 West Orman Avenue
Pueblo, CO 81004
AAS Degree in Culinary Arts
Certificate in Culinary Arts
Contact: Carol Himes
Phone: (719) 549-3071
Fax: (719) 543-7566
http://www.pcc.cccoes.edu/welcome.
htm

CONNECTICUT

Connecticut Culinary Institute–Hartford

85 Sigourney Street
Hartford, CT 06105
Contact: Tad Graham-Handley
Phone: (860) 668-3515
http://www.ctculinary.com

Connecticut Culinary Institute–Suffield

1760 Mapleton Avenue
Suffield, CT 06078
Advanced Culinary Arts Program
Diploma
Contact: Tad Graham-Handley
Phone: (860) 668-3515
http://www.ctculinary.com

Manchester Community College

60 Bidwell Street
Manchester, CT 06045
Certificate in Culinary Arts
AS Degree in Food Service
Management
Contact: Jayne Pearson
Phone: (860) 512-2785
Fax: (860) 533-5249
http://www.mcc.commnet.edu

Lincoln Technical Institute Center for Culinary Arts– Cromwell

Center for Culinary Arts
106 Sebethe Drive
Cromwell, CT 06416
Diploma in Culinary Arts
Phone: (860) 613-3350
http://www.centerforculinaryarts.com

Lincoln Technical Institute Center for Culinary Arts– Shelton

Diploma in Culinary Arts
8 Progress Drive
Shelton, CT 06484
Phone: (860) 613-3350
E-mail: centerchefs@aol.com

DELAWARE

Delaware Technical and Community College

400 Stanton-Christiana Road
Newark, DE 19713
AAS Degree in Culinary Arts
Technology
AAS Degree in Food Service
Management Technical
Contact: David Nolker, CCE
Phone: (302) 453-3757
Fax: (302) 368-6620
E-mail: dnolker@dtcc.edu
http://www.dtcc.edu

DISTRICT OF COLUMBIA

Art Institute of Washington in Arlington, VA

1820 North Fort Myer Drive (Ames
Building)
Arlington, VA 22209
Diploma in Culinary Arts or Baking
and Pastry
AAS Degree in Culinary Arts
Contact: Paul Magnant
Phone: (703) 247-6860
http://www.artinstitute.edu

FLORIDA

Art Institute of Fort Lauderdale

1799 Southeast 17th Street

Fort Lauderdale, FL 33316
AS Degree in Culinary Arts
Contact: John (Jack) Kane, MS,
CEC, CCE, CCA, CHE
Phone: (954) 308-2639 or
(800) 275-7603, ext. 2639
Fax: (954) 760-6219
http://www.aifl.artinstitutes.edu

Atlantic Technical Center

4700 Coconut Creek Parkway
Coconut Creek, FL 33066
Certificate in Commercial Foods
and Culinary Arts
Contact: Martin Wilcox, CEC, CCE
Phone: (754) 321-9516
Fax: (754) 321-5252
E-mail: martin.wilcox@
browardschools.com
http://www.atlantictechcenter.com

First Coast Technical Institute (Southeast Institute of Culinary Arts)

Division of St. Augustine Technical
Center
2980 Collins Avenue
St. Augustine, FL 32095
Commercial Foods / Culinary Arts
Diploma
Certificate and Apprenticeship
Programs
Contact: Noel Ridsdale, CEC, CCA
Phone: (904) 824-4401
Fax: (904) 824-1089
E-mail: risdan@fcti.org
http://www.fcti.org

Florida Community College at Jacksonville

4501 Capper Road
Jacksonville, FL 32218
AS Degree in Commercial Foods
and Culinary Management
AAS Degree in Hospitality and
Culinary Arts
Certificate in Hospitality and
Culinary Arts
Contact: Bob Mark
Phone: (904) 766-6703
Fax: (904) 713-4858
E-mail: wmark@fccj.edu
http://www.fccj.edu

Florida Culinary Institute
A Division of Lincoln College
2400 Metro Centre Boulevard
West Palm Beach, FL 33407
BS Degree in Culinary Management
Contact: David Pantone, CEPC,
CEC, CCE, AAC
Phone: (800) 826-9986 or
(561) 842-8324
Fax: (561) 688-9882
E-mail: dpantone@floridaculinary.
com

Gulf Coast Community College
5230 West US Highway 98
Panama City, FL 32401
AS Degree in Culinary Management
Contact: Paul Ashman
Phone: (850) 769-1551
Fax: (850) 747-3259
E-mail: pashman@gulfcoast.edu
http://www.gc.cc.fl.us

Hillsborough Community College
4001 Tampa Bay Boulevard
Tampa, FL 33614
AS Degree in Culinary
Management–Restaurant
Management Option
AS Degree in Culinary
Management–Culinary Arts
Option
Contact: Anne White
Phone: (813) 253-7316
Fax: (813) 253-7226
http://www.hcc.cc.fl.us

Keiser College–Capital Culinary Institute
1700 Halstead Boulevard
Tallahassee, FL 32309
AS Degree in Culinary Arts
Contact: Kevin Keating, CEC, CCE
Phone: (850) 906-9494 or
(877) CHEF-123 (U.S. only)
Fax: (850) 906-9497
E-mail: admissions-tal@
keisercollege.edu
http://www.capitalculinaryinstitute.
com
http://www.keisercollege.edu/
culinary.html

Lake Culinary Institute
2001 Kurt Street
Eustis, FL 32726
Certificate in Culinary Arts
Certificate in Chef Apprentice
Contact: Kenneth Koenig, CCC,
CCE
Phone: (352) 589-2250, ext. 212
E-mail: koenighk@lake.k12.fl.us

Manatee Technical Institute
5603 34th Street West
Bradenton, FL 34210-3509
Certificate in Culinary Arts
Contact: Gary Colpitts, CEC
Phone: (941) 751-7900

Orlando Culinary Academy
8511 Commodity Circle
Orlando, FL 32819
AAS Degree in Le Cordon Bleu
Culinary Arts
Contact: David Weir, CEC, CCE
Phone: (866) 622-2433

Pensacola Junior College
1000 College Boulevard
Pensacola, FL 32404-8998
AAS Degree in Culinary
Management
Contact: Travis Herr, CCE, CEC
Phone: (850) 484-1422
E-mail: therr@pjc.edu
http://www.pjc.cc.fl.us
http://www.itech.pjc.edu/therr

Pinellas Technical Education Center–Clearwater Campus
6100 154th Avenue
North Clearwater, FL 33760
Certificate / Diploma in Commercial
Foods / Culinary Arts
Contact: Rose Audibert
Phone: (727) 538-7167, ext. 1141
Fax: (727) 538-7203
http://www.ptecclw.pinellas.k12.
fl.us/default.htm

Sheridan Technical Center
5400 Sheridan Street
Hollywood, FL 33021
Commercial Foods / Culinary Arts
Certificate

Contact: Odis Herring, CEC, CCE
Phone: (754) 321-5400
Fax: (754) 321-5680
E-mail: odisherring@
browardschools.com
http://www.sheridantechnical.com

GEORGIA

Art Institute of Atlanta
6600 Peachtree Dunwoody Road
100 Embassy Row
Atlanta, GA 30328
BS Degree in Culinary Arts
Management
AA Degree in Culinary Arts with
concentration in Baking and
Pastry
Degree in Culinary Arts
Contact: Sarah Gorham, CEC
Phone: (770) 394-8300, ext. 4809 or
(800) 275-4242
Fax: (678) 579-9124
E-mail: gorhams@aii.edu
http://www.sheridantechnical.com

Chattahoochee Technical College - Mountain View Campus
2680 Gordy Parkway
Marietta, GA 30066
AAS Degree in Culinary Arts
Diploma Culinary Arts
Certificate Culinary Arts
Contact: Michael Bologna, CEC
Phone: (770) 509-6329
www.chattcollege.com

Coastal Georgia Community College
3700 Altama Avenue
Brunswick, GA 31520-3644
Culinary Arts Certificate
Contact: Walter Wright, CHA, CHE
Phone: (912) 280-6899
E-mail: wwright@cgcc.edu

Le Cordon Bleu–Atlanta– College of Culinary Arts
1927 Lakeside Drive
Tucker, GA 30084
AOS Degree in Culinary Arts
Contact: Todd Kazenske

Phone: (770) 938-4711
E-mail: tkazenske@atlantaculinary.
com

North Georgia Tech College
434 Meeks Avenue
Blairsville, GA 30512-2983
Culinary Arts Diploma
AAS Degree in Culinary Arts
Contact: Alan J. Tholen, CEC
Phone: (706) 439-6337
Fax: (706) 439-6301

Savannah Technical Institute
5717 White Bluff Road
Savannah, GA 31499
Culinary Arts Diploma
AAS Degree in Culinary Arts
Contact: Marvis Hinson, CCE
Phone: (912) 303-1833
Fax: (912) 352-4362
http://www.savtec.org

HAWAII
Hawaii Community College
200 West Kawili Street
Hilo, HI 96720-4091
AAS Degree in Food Services
Contact: Jim Lightner
Phone: (808) 974-7311
E-mail: lightner@hawaii.edu
http://hawaii.hawaii.edu

Kapiolani Community College
University of Hawaii Suite 114
4303 Diamond Head Road
Honolulu, HI 96816
AS Degree in Food Service Culinary
Arts
AS Degree in Food Service
Program, Patisserie
Contact: Ron Takahashi
Phone: (808) 734-9485
Fax: (808) 734-9212
http://www.kcc.hawaii.edu

Kauai Community College
3-1901 Kaumualii Highway
Lihue, HI 96766-9591
AAS Degree in Culinary Arts
Contact: Susan Uchida
Email: suchida@hawaii.edu

Leeward Community College
96-045 Ala Ike
Pearl City, HI 96782
AAS Degree in Food Service Program
Contact: Tommylynn Benavente
Phone: (808) 455-0687
Fax: (808) 455-0626
E-mail: tlbenave@hawaii.edu
http://www.lcc.hawaii.edu

Maui Community College
Food Services Department
310 Kaahamanu Avenue
Kahului, HI 96732
AAS Degree in Food Service
AAA Degree in Culinary Arts—
Baking
Contact: Karen Tanaka, CCE
Phone: (808) 984-3225
Fax: (808) 984-3314
http://mauiculinary.com

IDAHO
Boise State University
1910 University Drive
Boise, ID 83725
AAS Degree in Culinary Arts
Contact: Kelli Dever
Phone: (208) 426-1957
Fax: (208) 426-1948
http://selland.boisestate.edu

Idaho State University
777 Memorial Drive
Campus Box 8380
Pocatello, ID 83209
AAS in Culinary Arts Technology
Certificate in Culinary Arts
Technology
Contact: David Miller
Phone: (208) 282-3327
http://www.isu.edu/ctech

ILLINOIS
College of Dupage
22nd Street and Lambert Road
Glen Ellyn, IL 60137
AAS Degree in Foodservice
Administration
AAS Degree in Culinary Arts
Contact: Chris Thielman

Phone: (630) 942-2800
Fax: (630) 942-2315
http://www.cod.edu

Cooking and Hospitality
Institute of Chicago, Inc.
361 West Chestnut
Chicago, IL 60610
AAS Degree in Le Cordon Bleu
Culinary Arts
Certificate in Baking and Pastry
Certificate in Professional Cooking
Contact: Marshall Shafkowitz
Phone: (312) 944-0882
Fax: (312) 944-8557
http://www.chicnet.org

Illinois Institute of Art–
Chicago
180 North Wabash Avenue
Chicago, IL 60601
AAS Degree in Culinary Arts
Certificate in Professional Cooking
Certificate in Professional Baking
and Pastry
Contact: Bart Lindstrom
Phone: (312) 280-3500
Fax: (312) 364-9451
http://www.ilic.artinstitutes.edu

Joliet Junior College
1216 Houbolt Avenue
Joliet, IL 60436
AAS Degree in Culinary Arts
Contact: Michael J. McGreal, CEC,
CCE
Phone: (815) 280-2639
Fax: (815) 280-2696
http://www.jjc.edu

Kendall College
900 N. North Branch Street
Chicago, IL 60622
AAS Degree in Culinary Arts
Contact: Christopher Koetke, CEC,
CCE, Dean
Phone: (312) 752-2302
Fax: (312) 752-2303
http://www.kendall.edu

Southwestern Illinois College
2500 Carlyle Avenue
Belleville, IL 62221

AAS Degree Hospitality Food
Service Management
Certificate Culinary Arts
Contact: Lisa Brockman
Phone: (618) 235-2700, ext. 5321
Fax: (618) 222-8964
http://www.southwestern.cc.il.us

INDIANA

Ivy Tech Community College Northwest–Gary

1440 East 35th Avenue
Gary, IN 46409
AAS Degree in Culinary Arts
AAS Degree in Baking and Pastry
Certificates in Culinary Arts
Certificates in Baking and Pastry
Contact: Terry Zych, Hospitality
Program Chair
Phone: (219) 981-1111, ext. 2377
http://nwi.ivytech.edu

Ivy Tech Community College of Indiana–Indianapolis

1 West 26th Street
Indianapolis, IN 46208
AAS Degree in Hospitality
Administration with Specialties
in Culinary Arts
Specialties in Baking and Pastry
Contact: Jeff Bricker, CEC
Phone: (317) 921-4619
Fax: (317) 921-4753
http://www.ivytech.edu/
indianapolis

Ivy Tech State College–Fort Wayne

3800 North Anthony Boulevard
Fort Wayne, IN 46805
AAS Degree in Culinary Arts
Specialty
Contact: Alan Eyler
Phone: (219) 482-9171
Fax: (219) 480-4177
http://www.ivytech.edu/fortwayne

Ivy Tech State College–South Bend

220 Dean Johnson Boulevard
South Bend, IN 46601-3415

AAS in Hospitality Administration—
Culinary Arts Specialty
Contact: Tim Carrigan
Phone: (219) 289-7001
http://www.ivytech.edu/SouthBend/
south_bend

IOWA

Des Moines Area Community College

2006 South Ankeny Boulevard
Building #7
Ankeny, IA 50021
AAS Degree in Culinary Arts
Contact: Robert Anderson
Phone: (515) 964-6532
Fax: (515) 965-7129
http://www.dmacc.cc.ia.us

Indian Hills Community College

525 Grand View
Ottumwa, IA 52521
AAS in Culinary Arts
Diploma of Culinary Arts
Contact: Mary Kivlahan
Phone: (641) 683-5197
http://www.ihcc.cc.ia.us

Iowa Western Community College

2700 College Road
Box 4-C
Council Bluffs, IA 51503
AAS Restaurant and Hospitality
Management
Contact: Robert Graunke
Phone: (712) 325-3238
Fax: (712) 325-3736
http://iwcc.cc.ia.us

Kirkwood Community College

6301 Kirkwood Boulevard S.W.
P.O. Box 2068
Cedar Rapids, IA 52406
AAS Degree in Culinary Arts
AAS Degree in Restaurant
Management
Certificate in Baking
Contact: Mary Jane German
Phone: (319) 398-4981
Fax: (313) 398-5667
http://www.kirkwood.cc.ia.us

KANSAS

Johnson County Community College

12345 College Boulevard
Overland Park, KS 66210
AAS Degrees in Hospitality
Management
AAS Degree in Chef Apprenticeship
Contact: Lindy Robinson
Phone: (913) 469-8500, ext. 3250
Fax: (913) 469-2560
http://www.jccc.net/home

KENTUCKY

Bowling Green Technical College

1845 Loop Drive
Bowling Green, KY 42101
AAS Degree in Culinary Arts
Diploma in Culinary Arts
Contact: Michael Riggs, MAE,
CEC, FMP
Phone: (270) 901-1009
E-mail: mike.riggs@kctcs.edu

Jefferson Community College

109 East Broadway
Louisville, KY 40202
AAS Degree in Culinary Arts
Certificate in Advanced Culinary
Arts
Contact: Gail Crawford
Phone: (502) 584-0181, ext. 2317
Fax: (502) 585-4425
http://www.jcc.kctcs.net

Sullivan University–National Center for Hospitality Studies

3101 Bardstown Road
Louisville, KY 40205
AS Degree in Culinary Arts
AS Degree in Baking and Pastry
Contact: Tom Hickey, CEC, CCE
Derek Spendlove, CEPC, CCE
Phone: (502) 456-6504, ext. 123
Fax: (502) 454-4880
http://www.sullivan.edu/nchs

Sullivan University–Lexington Campus

2355 Harrodsburg Road

Lexington, KY 40505
AS Degree in Culinary Arts
Contact: Tom Hickey
Phone: (502) 456-6504, ext. 123
E-mail: thickey@sullivan.edu

LOUISIANA

Bossier Parish Community College

6220 East Texas Street
Bossier City, LA 71111
Certificate in Culinary Arts
Contact: Elizabeth Dickson, CEPC
Phone: (318) 678-6115
Fax: (318) 678-6408
E-mail: edickson@bpcc.edu
http://www.bpcc.cc.la.us

Delgado Community College

615 City Park Avenue
New Orleans, LA 70119-4399
AA Degree in Culinary Arts
Certificate in Culinary Arts
Apprenticeship
Contact: Dr. Mary Bartholomew
Phone: (504) 483-4208
Fax: (504) 483-4893
http://www.dcc.edu

Louisiana Technical College– Baton Rouge Campus

3250 North Acadian Thruway
East Baton Rouge, LA 70805
Diploma in Culinary Arts and
Occupations
Contact: Michael Travasos, CCE
Phone: (225) 359-9226
E-mail: mtravasos@theltc.net
http://www.theltc.net/batonrouge

Louisiana Technical College– Lafayette Campus

1101 Bertrand Drive
P.O. Box 4909
Lafayette, LA 70502
Diploma in Culinary Arts and
Occupations
Contact: Jerry Sonnier, CCE
Phone: (337) 262-5962, ext. 232
Fax: (337) 262-1782
http://www.lafayette.tec.la.us

Louisana Technical College– Shreveport Campus

2010 N. Market
Shreveport, LA 71107
Culinary Arts and Occupations
Diploma
Contact: Danny Beavers
Phone: (318) 676-7811
Fax: (318) 676-7805
www.ltc.edu/shreveport

MARYLAND

Anne Arundel Community College

101 College Parkway
Arnold, MD 21012-1895
AAS in Hotel / Restaurant
Management—Culinary Arts
Option
http://www.aacc.edu

Baltimore International College

17 Commerce Street
Baltimore, MD 21201
AAS Degree in Professional
Cooking
AAS Degree in Cooking and
Baking,
AAS Degree in Baking and Pastry
Culinary Arts Certificate
Contact: Chef Charles Talucci, CEC
Susan Sykes Hendee, Ph.D., CCE
Phone: (410) 752-4710

MASSACHUSSETTS

Holyoke Community College

303 Homestead Avenue
Holyoke, MA 01040
Certificate in Culinary Arts
Contact: Mark Antsel, CEC, CCE
Phone: (413) 552-2548
http://www.hcc.mass.edu/
CATALOG/HOSPITALITY
CULINARYARTS.htm

MICHIGAN

Baker College

1903 Marquette Avenue
Muskegon, MI 49442

ABA Degree in Culinary Arts
Contact: Rob White
Phone: (231) 777-5321
http://www.baker.edu

Grand Rapids Community College

151 Fountain Street N.E.
Grand Rapids, MI 49503
AAAS Degree in Culinary Arts
AAAS Degree in Culinary
Management
Certificate in Baking and Pastry
Contact: Randy Sahajdack
Phone: (616) 234-3690
Fax: (616) 234-3698
http://www.grcc.edu/hospitality

Henry Ford Community College

5101 Evergreen Road
Dearborn, MI 48128
AS Degree in Hospitality Studies /
Culinary Arts
Contact: Dennis Konarski, CCE
Phone: (313) 845-6390
Fax: (313) 845-9784
http://www.henryford.cc.mi.us

The Macomb Culinary Institute at Macomb Community College

44575 Garfield Road
Clinton Township, MI 48038-1139
AAS Degree in Culinary Arts
AAS Degree in Pastry Arts
Certificate in Culinary
Management
Certificate in Pastry Arts
Skill Specific Certificates in
Assistant Baker and Prep Cook
Contact: David Schneider, CEC,
CCE
Phone: (586) 286-2088
Fax: (586) 226-4725
http://www.macomb.edu

Monroe County Community College

1555 South Raisinville Road
Monroe, MI 48161
Certificate in Culinary Skills and
Management

Associate of Commerce (AC)
Degree in Culinary Skills and
Management
Contact: Kevin Thomas, CEC, CCE
Phone: (734) 242-9711
Fax: (734) 242-9711
http://www.monroe.cc.mi.us

Northwestern Michigan College–Great Lakes Culinary Institute
1701 East Front Street
Traverse City, MI 49686
AAS Degree in Culinary Arts
Contact: Fred Laughlin, CCE
Phone: (231) 922-1000;
(800) 748-1566
Fax: (231) 922-1134
http://www.nmc.edu

Oakland Community College
The Culinary Studies Institute
27055 Orchard Lake Road
Farmington Hills, MI 48018
AAS Degree in Culinary Arts
Certificate in Apprenticeship
Contact: Kevin Enright
Phone: (248) 522-3700
Fax: (248) 522-3706
http://www.occ.cc.mi.us

Washtenaw Community College
4800 E. Huron River Drive
P.O. Box D1
Ann Arbor, MI 48106-0978
AAS Degree in Culinary Arts and
Hospitality Management
Certificate in Baking and Pastry
Certificate in Culinary Arts
Contact: Terry Herrera
Phone: (734) 973-3549
http://www.washtenaw.cc.mi.us

MINNESOTA

Art Institutes International– Minnesota
15 South 9th Street
Minneapolis, MN 55402
AAS Degree in Culinary Arts
Certificate in Culinary Arts
Contact: John Cappellucci, CFM,
CFBE

Phone: (612) 656-6905
Fax: (612) 338-2351
E-mail: jcappellucci@aii.edu
http://www.aim.artinstitutes.edu

Hennepin Technical College– Brooklyn Park Campus
9000 Brooklyn Boulevard
Brooklyn Park, MN 55445
Diploma or AAS Degree in
Culinary Arts
Contact: David Eisenreich
Phone: (763) 488-2458
E-mail: david.eisenreich@
hennepintech.edu
http://www.hennepintech.edu/
career/service/culinary.htm

Hennepin Technical College– Eden Prairie Campus
13100 College View Drive
Eden Prairie, MN 55347
Diploma or AAS Degree in
Culinary Arts
Contact: Richard Forpahl, CEC,
CCE
Phone: (952) 995-1557
E-mail: rick.forpahl@hennepintech.
edu
http://www.hennepintech.edu/
career/service/culinary.htm

Le Cordon Bleu College of Culinary Arts Minneapolis/ St. Paul
1315 Mendota Heights Road
Mendota Heights, MN 55120
AAS Degree in Culinary Arts
AAS Degree in Baking and Pastry
Contact: William Niemer, CEC, CCE
Phone: (651) 675-4756
Fax: (651) 675-4775
E-mail: wniemer@browncollege.edu
http://www.twincitesculinary.com

St. Paul College
235 Marshall Avenue
St. Paul, MN 55102
Diploma or AAS Degree in
Culinary Arts
Contact: Manfred Krug
Phone: (651) 846-1398
Marilyn Krasowski

Phone: (651) 846-1314
http://www.saintpaul.edu

MISSOURI

East Central College
1964 Prairie Dell Road
Union, MO 63084
AAS Degree in Culinary Arts
Contact: Ted Hirschi, CEC, CCE,
FMP
Phone: (636) 583-5195, ext. 2401
E-mail: hirschi@eastcentral.edu or
chefted55@yahoo.com
http://www.eastcentral.edu

Ozark Technical College
P.O. Box 5958
Springfield, MO 6501-5958
AAS Degree in Culinary Arts
Contact: Lou Rice, CCC
Phone: (417) 895-7282

St. Louis Community College
5600 Oakland Avenue
St. Louis, MO 63110
AAS Degree in Management /
Culinary / Baking & Pastry
Certificate in Baking and Pastry
Contact: Robert Hertel, CCE, AAC,
FMP
Phone: (314) 644-9617
http://www.stlcc.edu

MONTANA

University of Montana
College of Technology in Missoula
909 South Avenue West
Missoula, MT 59801
ASA Degree in Food Service
Management
Certificate in Culinary Arts
Contact: Tom Campbell, CEC
Phone: (406) 243-7816
Fax: (406) 243-7899
http://www.umt.edu

NEBRASKA

The Institute for the Culinary Arts at Metropolitan Community College
P.O. Box 3777

Omaha, NE 68103
AAS Degree in Food Arts and
Management in Food Arts
AAS Degree in Food Arts &
Management in Supervisory
Management, Chef
Apprenticeship and Bakery Arts
Option
Contact: Jim Trebbien, CCE
Phone: (402) 457-2510
Fax: (402) 457-2515
http://www.mccneb.edu

Southeast Community College
8800 O Street
Lincoln, NE 68520
AAS Degree in Food Service /
Culinary Arts
Contact: Bernardine Jo Taylor
Phone: (402) 437-2465
Fax: (402) 437-2465
http://www.southeast.edu

NEVADA

**Community College of
Southern Nevada**
3200 East Cheyenne Avenue S2D
North Las Vegas, NV 89030-4296
AAS Degree in Hotel, Restaurant,
Casino Management Culinary
Arts
AAS Degree in Food and Beverage
Management
Contact: John Metcalf
Phone: (702) 651-4656
Tom Rosenberger
Phone: (702) 657-4193
Fax: 702-651-4116
http://www.ccsn.nevada.edu

**The Culinary Institute of
Las Vegas–Art Institute of
Las Vegas**
2350 Corporate Circle
Henderson, NV 89074
AAS Degree in Culinary Arts
Contact: David Hendrickson
Phone: (702) 992-8500
Fax: (702) 992-8564
E-mail: fav@aii.edu

**Truckee Meadows Community
College**
Culinary Arts Department
7000 Dandini Boulevard RDMT–207
Reno, NV 89512-3999
AAS Degree in Culinary Arts
Certificate in Culinary Arts
Certificate in Baking and Pastry
Contact: Karen Cannan
Phone: (775) 673-7160
http://www.tmcc.edu

NEW HAMPSHIRE

**Atlantic Culinary Academy–
McIntosh College**
181 Silver Street
Dover, NH 03820
AS Degree in Culinary Arts
Contact: Jim Gallivan, CCA

**Southern New Hampshire
University**
School of Hospitality, Tourism, and
Culinary Management
2500 North River Road
Manchester, NH 03106-1045
AAS Degree in Culinary Arts
AAS Degree in Baking and Pastry
Contact: Dean John Knorr
Phone: (603) 688-2211, ext 3296
Fax: (603) 645-9693
http://www.snhu.edu

NEW JERSEY

**Hudson County Community
College**
161 Newkirk Street
Jersey City, NJ 07306
AAS Degree in Hospitality
Management.
Certificate in Culinary Arts
Contact: Paul Dillon
Phone: (201) 360-4631
Fax: (201) 656-1522
E-mail: pdillon@hccc.edu
http://www.hccc.edu

NEW MEXICO

**Central New Mexico
Community College**
525 Buena Vista S.E.

Albuquerque, NM 87106
AAS Degree in Culinary Arts
Contact: Donna Diller, Culinary
Arts, Hospitality and Tourism
Director
Phone: (505) 224-3896
E-mail: ddiller@cnm.edu
http://www.cnm.edu

NEW YORK

Art Institute of New York City
75 Varick Street
16th Floor
New York, NY 10013-1917
AOS Degree in Culinary Arts and
Restaurant Management
AOS Degree in Baking and Pastry
Certificate in Culinary Arts and
Restaurant Management
Certificate in Pastry Arts
Contact: Dave Moughilian, Dean of
Education
Phone: (212) 226-5500
http://ainyc.artinstitutes.edu

**New York Institute of
Technology**
300 Carlton Avenue
P.O. Box 9029
Central Islip, NY 11722-9029
AOS Degree in Culinary Arts
Contact: James Turley
Phone: (631) 348-3290
Fax: (631) 348-3247
http://iris.nyit.edu/culinary

Paul Smith's College
P.O. Box 265
Routes 86 & 30
Paul Smiths, NY 12970
AAS Degree in Culinary Arts
Contact: Lucille Baker
Phone: (518) 327-6215
Fax: (518) 327-6369
http://www.paulsmiths.edu

**Schenectady County
Community College**
Department of Hotel, Culinary Arts
& Tourism
78 Washington Avenue
Schenectady, NY 12035

AOS Degree in Culinary Arts
Contact: Toby Strianese, CCE
Phone: (518) 381-1391
Fax: (518) 327-6369
http://www.sunysccc.edu

Sullivan County Community College

Hospitality Department
112 College Road
Loch Sheldrake, NY 12759
AAS Degree in Professional Chef
AAS Degree in Hotel Technology
AOS Degree in Culinary Arts
Contact: Art Rega
Phone: (914) 434-5750, ext. 309
Fax: (914) 434-4806
E-mail: ariegal@sullivan.suny.edu
http://www.sullivan.suny.edu

SUNY Cobleskill Agriculture and Technical College

P.O. Box 4002
Cobleskill, NY 12043
AOS Degree in Professional Chef
Contact: David G. Campbell, CCC, CCE
Phone: (518) 255-5822
Fax: (518) 255-6325
E-mail: camped@cobleskill.edu
http://www.cobleskill.edu

SUNY Delhi–College of Technology

2 Main Street
Delhi, NY 13753
AAS Degree in Culinary Arts
Contact: Michael J. Petrillose, Ph.D., Dean, Business and Hospitality Management
Phone: (607) 746-4402
E-mail: petrilmj@delhi.edu

NORTH CAROLINA

Alamance Community College

P.O. Box 8000
Graham, NC 27253
AAS Degree in Culinary Technology
Contact: Doris Schomberg, CCE
Phone: (336) 506-4241

Fax: (336) 578-1987
E-mail: schombed@alamance.cc.nc.us
http://www.alamance.cc.nc.us

Asheville Buncombe Technical College

340 Victoria Road
Asheville, NC 28801
AAS Degree in Culinary Technology
Contact: Sheila Tillman, ME
Phone: (828) 254-1921, ext. 232
E-mail: stillman@abtech.edu
http://www.abtech.edu

Central Piedmont Community College

P.O. Box 35009
Charlotte, NC 28235
AAS Culinary Technology
Contact: James Bowen, CEC, CFBE
Jeff LaBarge CEC, CCE
Phone: (704) 330-6721
http://www.cpcc.edu/hospitality-education

Guilford Technical Community College

601 High Point Road
P.O. Box 309
Jamestown, NC 27282
AAS Degree in Culinary Technology
Contact: Keith Gardiner, CEC
Phone: (336) 454-1126, ext. 2302
Fax: (336) 819-2013
http://technet.gtcc.cc.nc.us

Wake Technical Community College

9101 Fayetteville Road
Raleigh, NC 27603
AAS Degree in Culinary Technology
Certificate in Culinary Technology
Contact: Penny Prichard, MBA, MEd
Phone: (919) 662-3400
E-mail: plprichard@waketech.edu
http://www.waketech.edu

OHIO

Columbus State Community College

550 East Spring Street
Columbus, OH 43215
AAS Degree in Food Service
AAS Degree in Restaurant Management
AAS Degree in Chef Apprenticeship
Contact: Jim Taylor, CEC, AAC for Apprenticeship
Margaret Steiskal, CCE for Culinary Arts
Phone: (614) 287-5188;
(800) 621-6407
http://www.cscc.edu

Cuyahoga Community College

2900 Community College Avenue
Cleveland, OH 44115-3196
AAB in Hospital Management—Culinary Arts
AAB in Hospital Management—Restaurant Management.
Certificate in Professional Culinarian
Certificate in Professional Baking
ACF Apprenticeship
Contact: Chris Moir
Phone: (216) 987-4082
http://www.tri-c.edu

Hocking Technical College

3301 Hocking Parkway
Nelsonville, OH 45764
AAS Degree in Baking and Pastry
AAS Degree in Culinary Arts
Certificate in Cooking
Certificate in Baking and Pastry
Contact: Clarence Steadman
Phone: (740) 753-3531, ext. 300
Fax: (740) 753-9018
http://www.hocking.edu

Midwest Culinary Institute at Cincinnati State

3520 Central Parkway
Cincinnati, OH 45223
AAB Degree in Chef Technology
Contact: Jeffrey Sheldon, CCE, CCE
Phone: (513) 569-1637
Fax: (513) 569-1467
http://culinary.cincinnatistate.edu

Sinclair Community College

444 West Third Street
Dayton, OH 45402-1460
AAS Degree in Hospitality
  Management
AAS Degree in Hospitality
  Management with Culinary Arts
Contact: Steven Cornelius, M.Ed.,
  CEC, CCE, FMP
Phone: (937) 512-5197
Fax: (937) 512-5396
E-mail: steve.cornelius@sinclair.edu
http://www.sinclair.edu/academics/
  bus/departments/hmt

Zane State College

1555 Newark Road
Zainesville, OH 43701
AB Degree in Culinary Arts
Contact: Marco Adornetto, CEC
Phone: (800) 686-TECH, ext. 225
http://www.matc.tec.oh.us

OKLAHOMA

Culinary Institute of Platt College

2727 West Memorial Road
Oklahoma City, OK 73134
AOS Degree in Culinary Arts
Contact: Rob Ferris
Phone: (405) 749-2433
E-mail: rferris@plattcollege.org
http://www.plattcollege.org

Tri-County Technical School

6101 S.E. Nowata Road
Bartlesville, OK 74006
Culinary Arts Diploma (Dual
  Program)
Contact: Culinary Arts Department
Phone: (981) 331-3325
E-mail: pgarmy@tctc.org or tpoe@
  tctc.org
Fax: (918) 331-3200

OREGON

Cascade Culinary Institute - Central Oregon Community College

2600 N.W. College Way
Bend, OR 97702
Culinary Arts Certificate Program

Contact: Jim Kress
Phone: (541) 383-7712
http://culinary.cocc.edu

Lane Community College

4000 East 30th Avenue
Building 19, Room 202
Eugene, OR 97405
AA Degree in Culinary Arts
Contact: Lynn Nakamura
Phone: (541) 463-3500
E-mail: nakamural@lanecc.edu

Southwestern Oregon Community College

1988 Newmark Avenue
Coos Bay, OR 97420-2911
AAS Degree in Culinary
  Management
Contact: Linda Kridelbaugh
Shawn Hanlin, CEC
Phone: (541) 888-7265
http://www.lanecc.edu

Western Culinary Institute

600 S.W. 10th Avenue
Suite 400
Portland, OR 97205
Diploma in Culinary Arts
AOS Degree in Le Cordon Bleu
  Culinary Arts
AOS Degree in Patisserie and Baking
Certificate in Patisserie and Baking
Contact: Ray Colvin, Vice President
  of Academic Affairs
Phone: (503) 223-2245; toll-free:
  (800) 666-0312
Fax: (503) 223-5554
http://www.westernculinary.com

PENNSYLVANIA

Art Institute of Philadelphia

2300 Chestnut Street
Philadelphia, PA 19103
AS Degree in Culinary Arts
Contact: William Tillinghast, CEC,
  AAC
Phone: (215) 405-6757
http://www.aiph.artinstitutes.edu

Arts Institute of Pittsburgh

420 Boulevard of the Allies

Pittsburgh, PA 15219
AS Degree in Culinary Arts
Contact: Michael T. Zappone, CCM
Phone: (412) 291-6248

Indiana University of Pennsylvania (IUP)– Academy of Culinary Arts

125 South Gilpin Street
Punxsutawney, PA 15767
Certificate in Culinary Arts
Baking and Pastry Certificate
Contact: Al Wutsch, CEC, CCE
Phone: (877) 645-7910
Fax: (814) 938-1155
http://www.iup.edu

Pennsylvania College of Technology

One College Avenue
Williamsport, PA 17701
AAS Degree in Culinary Arts
  Technology
AAS Degree in Baking and Pastry
  Arts
Contact: Fred Becker, Dean
Phone: (570) 327-4503
Fax: (570) 320-5260
http://www.pct.edu

Pennsylvania Culinary Institute

700 Clark Building
717 Liberty Avenue
Pittsburgh, PA 15222
AST Degree in Le Cordon Bleu
  Culinary Arts
AST Degree in Le Cordon Bleu
  Pâtisserie and Baking
Contact: Bill Hunt
Phone: (412) 566-2444
Fax: (412) 391-4224
http://www.pci.edu

Westmoreland County Community College

Founders Hall Room #700
Armbrust Road
Youngwood, PA 15697
AAS Degree in Culinary Arts
Apprenticeship option & Non-
  apprenticeship option
AAS Degree in Food Service
  Management

Baking and Apprenticeship / Non-apprenticeship
Foodservice Management
Contact: Dr. Robert Myers
Phone: (724) 925-4177
http://www.wccc-pa.edu

Winner Institute of Arts and Sciences Culinary Education

1 Winner Place
Transfer, PA 16154
Diploma in Culinary Arts
Contact: Sandra McBride
Phone: (724) 646-2433
Fax: (724) 646-0218
E-mail: wininst@nauticom.net
http://www.winner-institute.com

SOUTH CAROLINA

Culinary Institute of Charleston at Trident Technical College

7000 Rivers Avenue
North Charleston, SC 29423
AS Degree in Culinary Arts
Diploma in Culinary Arts
Contact: Michael Carmel, CEC, CCE
Phone: (843) 820-5090
E-mail: michael.carmel@ tridenttech.edu
http://www.tridenttech.edu

Greenville Technical College

P.O. Box 5616
Greenville, SC 19606
AA Degree in Food Service Management
AA Degree in Food Service Management / Culinary Arts Path
Contact: Alan Scheidhauer, CEC
Phone: (864) 250-8303, ext. 8404
Fax: (864) 250-8455
http://www.greenvilletech.com

Horry-Georgetown Technical College

2050 Highway 501 East
P.O. Box 261966
Conway, SC 29526
AB Degree in Culinary Arts Technology
Contact: Mr. Carmen Catino
Phone: (843) 349-5333

Fax: (843) 347-4207
http://www.hor.tec.sc.us

Spartanburg Technical College

P.O. Box 4386
Spartanburg, SC 29305
Certificate in Culinary Arts
Contact: Holly Boyce
Phone: (864) 591-3836
E-mail: boyceh@stcsc.edu
http://www.stcsc.edu

TENNESSEE

Nashville State Technical Community College

120 White Bridge Road
Nashville, TN 37209
AAS Degree in Culinary Arts
Contact: Tom Loftis
Phone: (615) 353-3783
http://www.nscc.edu

Walters State Community College

Rel Maples Institute For Culinary Arts
1720 Old Newport Highway
Sevierville, TN 37876
AAS Degree, Management Concentration—Culinary Arts
Technical Certificate in Culinary Arts
Contact: Catherine Hallman, Culinary Arts Department
Phone: (865) 774-5817
http://www.ws.edu

TEXAS

Art Institute of Dallas

8080 Park Lane, Suite 100
Dallas, TX 75231-5993
AS Degree in Culinary Arts
Certificate in Culinary Arts
Contact: Larry Matson, CEC, CCE
Phone: (214) 692-8080
http://www.aid.artinstitutes.edu

Austin Community College–Eastview Campus

3401 Webberville Road
Austin, TX 78702

AAS Degree in Culinary Arts
Certificate in Basic Culinary Arts
Contact: Virginia Stipp Lawrence
Phone: (512) 223-5173
Fax: (512) 223-5125
http://www.austin.cc.tx.us

Del Mar College

101 Baldwin Boulevard
Corpus Christi, TX 78404-3897
AAS Degree in Culinary Arts
Certificate in Cook / Baker
Contact: Mark Carpenter, CEC
Phone: (361) 698-1734
Fax: (361) 698-1829
http://www.delmar.edu

El Centro College

Main and Lamar
Dallas, TX 75202
AAS Degree in Food / Hospitality Service
AAS Degree in Culinary Arts
AAS Degree in Baking and Pastry
Contact: Chris Lalonde
Phone: (214) 860-2209
E-mail: clalonde@dcccd.edu
http://www.ecc.dcccd.edu

Lamar University

2111 Redbird Lane
Beaumont, TX 77710
Culinary Arts Certificate Program
Contact: Molly Dahm, M.S.
Phone: (409) 880-1744
http://www.lamar.edu

School of Culinary Arts at the Art Institute of Houston

1900 Yorktown
Houston, TX 77056
AAS Degree in Culinary Arts
Contact: Gary Eaton
Phone: (713) 623-2040
E-mail: geaton@edmc.edu
http://www.aih.aii.edu

St. Philip's College

1801 Martin Luther King Drive
San Antonio, TX 78203
AAS Degree in Hospitality Operations—Culinary Arts Option

AAS Degree in Hospitality
Operations—Restaurant Option
Certificate in Chef's Apprentice
Contact: Mary Kunz
Phone: (210) 531-3315
Fax: (210) 531-3351
http://www.accd.edu/spc/spcmain/
spc.htm

Texas Culinary Academy
11400 Burnet Road
Austin, TX 78758
AAS Degree in Le Cordon Bleu
Culinary Arts
Contact: Marc Dunham
Phone: (512) 837-2665
Fax: (512) 977-9753

UTAH

Salt Lake Community College
4600 South Redwood Road
Salt Lake City, UT 84130
AAS Degree in Apprentice—Chef-
Full-time Program Degree /
Certificate
Apprentice Chef—Part-time
Program Degree / Certificate
Contact: Ricco Renzetti, CEC,
CCE
Phone: (801) 957-4066
Fax: (801) 957-4895
http://www.slcc.edu

VIRGINIA

J. Sargeant Reynolds
Community College
700 East Jackson Street
Richmond, VA 23219
AAS Degree in Culinary Arts
Contact: David Barrish
Phone: (804) 523-5069
E-mail: dbarrish@jsr.vccs.edu

Stratford University
7777 Leesburg Pike
Falls Church, VA 22043
AAS Degree in Advanced Culinary
Arts
Diploma in Advanced Culinary
Arts Professional
Contact: Dean Glenn Walden,
Culinary Department

Phone: (800) 444-0804
Fax: (703) 734-5336
E-mail: gwalden@stratford.edu
http://www.stratford.edu

Tidewater Community
College–Thomas W. Moss,
Jr. Campus
300 Grandby Street
Norfolk, VA 23510-1910
AAS Degree in Hospitality
Management—Specialization
Culinary Arts
Contact: Don Adverso
Phone: (757) 822-1350
E-mail: averso@tcc.edu
http://www.tcc.edu

WASHINGTON

Art Institute of Seattle
2323 Elliot Avenue
Seattle, WA 98121
AAA Degree in Culinary Arts
Contact: Culinary Arts
Department
Phone: (206) 448-6600;
(800) 275-2471
http://www.ais.edu

Bellingham Technical College
3028 Lindbergh Avenue
Bellingham, WA 98225
AAS Degree in Culinary Arts
Certificate in Culinary Arts
Contact: Michael Baldwin, CCE
Phone: (360) 738-3105 ext. 400
Fax: (360) 676-2798
http://www.btc.ctc.edu

Inland North West Culinary
Academy at Spokane
Community College
North 1810 Greene Street
Spokane, WA 99207
AAS Degree in Culinary Arts
Contact: Doug Fisher, CEC, CCE
Phone: (509) 533-7284
Fax: (509) 533-8108
E-mail: scchospitality@scc.spokane.
edu
http://www.scc.spokane.edu/bh/
culinary

Lake Washington Technical
College
11605 132nd Avenue N.E.
Kirkland, WA 98034-8506
AAS Degree in Culinary Arts
AAS Degree in Baking Arts
Certificate in Culinary Arts
Certificate in Baking and Pastry
Contact: Alan Joynson, CCE, CEC
Phone: (425) 739-8310
http://www.lwtc.ctc.edu

Olympic College
1600 Chester Avenue
Bremerton, WA 98337-1699
Certificate in Specialization /
Culinary Arts
ATA Degree in Culinary Arts and
Hospitality Management
Contact: Nicholas Giovanni
Phone: (360) 475-7570
E-mail: ngiovanni@oc.ctc.edu
http://www.oc.ctc.edu/AboutOC

Renton Technical College
3000 N.E. Fourth Street
Renton, WA 98056
AAS Degree in Culinary Arts
Certificate in Culinary Arts
Contact: John Fisher, CEC, CCE,
AAC
Phone: (425) 235-2352, ext. 5708
Fax: (425) 235-7832
http://www.renton-tc.ctc.edu

Seattle Central Community
College
1701 Broadway
Seattle, WA 98122
AAS Degree in Culinary Arts
AAS Degree in Specialty Desserts
and Breads
Certificate in Specialty Desserts and
Breads
Certificate in Culinary Arts
Contact: Linda Chauncey
Phone: (206) 344-4386
Fax: (206) 344-4323
E-mail: lchauncey@sccd.ctc.edu
http://www.seattleculinary.com

Skagit Valley College
2405 East College Way

Mount Vernon, WA 98273
ATA Degree in Culinary Arts and
    Hospitality Management
Contact: Lyle Hildahl
Phone: (360) 416-7890
Fax: (360) 416-7890
http://www.skagit.edu

South Puget Sound
Community College
2011 Mottman Road S.W.
Olympia, WA 98512-6292
ATA Degree in Culinary Arts
Certificate in Culinary Arts
Contact: Bill Wiklendt, CEC, CCE,
    AAC
Phone: (360) 596-5392
E-mail: bwiklendt@spscc.ctc.edu
http://www.spscc.ctc.edu

South Seattle Community
College
6000 16th Avenue S.W.
Seattle, WA 98106
AAS Degree and Certificate in
    Restaurant and Food Service
    Production
AAS Degree and Certificate
    in Catering and Banquet
    Operations
AAS Degree and Certificate in
    Pastry and Specialty Baking
Contact: Robert Hester
Phone: (206) 764-5344
Fax: (206) 768-6728
E-mail: rhester@sccd.ctc.edu
http://south.seattlecolleges.com

WEST VIRGINIA

Pierpont Community and
Technical College
1201 Locust Avenue
Fairmont, WV 26554
AAS Degree in Food Service
    Management—Culinary Arts
    Option
Contact: Brian Floyd
Phone: (304) 367-4409 or
    (304) 367-4297
Fax: 304-367-4587
E-mail: bfloyd@fairmontstate.edu
http://www.fscwv.edu

Mountain State University–
Culinary Arts
410 Neville Street
P.O. Box 9003
Beckley, WV 25802-9003
AS Degree in Culinary Arts
Contact: Leonard Bailey II
Phone: (304) 929-1386
E-mail: lbailey@mountainstate.edu
http://www.mountainstate.edu

West Virginia Northern
Community College
1704 Market Street
Wheeling, WV 26003
AAS Degree in Culinary Arts
Certificate in Culinary Arts
Contact: Marian Gruber
Phone: (304) 233-5900
http://www.wvnorthern.edu

WISCONSIN

Blackhawk Technical College
6004 Prairie Road, P.O. Box 5009
Janesville, WI 53547
AAS Degree in Culinary Arts
Contact: Joe Wollinger, CEC, CCE
Phone: (608) 757-7696
Fax: (608) 743-4407
http://www.blackhawk.edu

Fox Valley Technical College
1825 North Bluemound Drive
P.O. Box 2277
Appleton, WI 54913-2277
AAS Degree in Culinary Arts
Technical Diploma in Foodservice
Contact: Jeffrey Igel, CCC, CCE
Phone: (920) 735-5643
Fax: (920) 735-5643
http://www.foxvalleytech.com/prog/
    CulinaryArts_Hospitality

Madison Area Technical
College
3550 Anderson Street
Madison, WI 53704
AAS Degree in Culinary Arts
Technical Diploma Baking and
    Pastry Arts
Contact: Dr. Loren Toepper, Dean
Phone: (608) 246-6368

Fax: (608) 246-6316
http://matcmadison.edu/matc/ASP/
    showprogram.asp?ID=1559

Milwaukee Area Technical
College
1015 North Sixth Street
Milwaukee, WI 53203
AAS Degree in Culinary Arts
AAS Degree in Cook Apprentice
Contact: Pat Whalen
Phone: (414) 297-6836
Fax: (414) 297-7733

Moraine Park Technical
College
235 North National Avenue
Fond du Lac, WI 54935
AS Degree in Culinary Arts
Contact: Dean Pat Olson
Phone: (920) 924-3333
Fax: (920) 929-3124
http://www.moraine.tec.wi.us/
    academics/programs/culinaryarts

Waukesha County Technical
College
800 Main Street
Pewaukee, WI 53072
AAS Degree in Culinary
    Management
Certificate in Culinary Apprentice
Contact: Timothy Graham,
    Associate Dean
Phone: (262) 691-5254
Fax: (262) 691-5123
http://www.witechcolleges.com

PHILIPPINES

Center for Culinary Arts, Manila
287 Katipunan Avenue, Loyola
    Heights
Quezon City, Philippines 1102
Diploma and Certificate in Culinary
    Arts and Technology
Certificate in Baking and Pastry Arts
Contact: Chef James Antolin
Phone: (632) 426-4840 to 41 or
    (632) 426-4825
Fax: (632) 426-4836
E-mail: marketing@cca-manila.com
http://www.cca-manila.com

SWITZERLAND

DCT–International Hotel and Business Management School

Seestrasse, CH 6354
Vitznau, Switzerland
Diploma in European Culinary Arts
Advanced Diploma in European
    Culinary Management

Contact: Dr. Birgit Black
E-mail: admissions@dct.ch
http://www.culinaryschool.ch

III. TRAVEL AGENT PROGRAMS

Below is the most recent list of the American Society of Travel Agents (ASTA) member schools. If you are interested in becoming a travel agent and there is not a program in your area, many of these schools offer online or correspondence courses.

CALIFORNIA

Academy of Travel and Tourism
2534 Lincoln Boulevard
Marina Del Rey, CA 90292
Phone: (310) 574-6820
Fax: (310) 574-6801
http://www.weteachtheworld.com

Foothill College Travel Careers
4000 Middlefield Road
Palo Alto, CA 94303
Phone: (650) 949-6971
Fax: (650) 949-6968
http://www.foothill.edu/bss/tc

Galileo Travel School
1700 South Winchester Boulevard,
    Suite# 102
Campbell, CA 95008
Phone: (408) 558-7000
Fax: (408) 228-0530
www.galileotravelschool.com

Los Medanos Community College Travel Program
2700 East Leland Road
Pittsburg, CA 94565-5107
Phone: (925) 439-2181
http://www.losmedanos.edu

West Los Angeles College
9000 Overland Avenue
Culver City, CA 90230-5002
Phone: (310) 287-4529
Fax: (310) 841-0396
http://www.wlac.edu

FLORIDA

Mid Florida Tech
2900 West Oak Ridge Road
Orlando, FL 32809-3799
Phone: (407) 251-6000, ext. 2500
Fax: (407) 251-6009
http://www.mft.ocps.net/corporate_
    learning/online_travel.html

ILLINOIS

Career Quest Training Center, Inc.
P.O. Box 849
New Lenox, IL 60451-0849
Phone: (815) 723-9475
Fax: (815) 723-9486
http://www.careerquesttraining.
    com/asta.html

College of DuPage
IC 2026
425 Fawell Boulevard
Glen Ellyn, IL 60137-6599
Phone: (630) 942-2556
Fax: (630) 858-7263
http://www.cod.edu/academic/
    acadprog/occ_voc/Travel/

Moraine Valley Community College
10900 South 88th Avenue
Palos Hills, IL 60465-0937
Phone: (708) 974-5569
Fax: (708) 974-0185
http://www.morainevalley.edu

Wilder Training and Design
117 South Cook Street, #151

Barrington, IL 60010-4311
Phone: (847) 381-5159
Fax: 847-381-5583

MAINE

Andover College
265 Western Avenue
South Portland, ME 04106
Phone: (207) 774-6126
Fax: (207) 774-1715
http://www.andovercollege.edu

MASSACHUSETTS

Northern Essex Community College
100 Elliott Way
Haverhill, MA 01830-2399
Phone: (978) 556-3312
http://www.necc.mass.edu

MISSOURI

St. Louis Community College
5600 Oakland Avenue
St. Louis, MO 63110-1316
Phone: (314) 644-9590
Fax: (314) 951-9405
http://www.stlcc.edu

NEW YORK

State University of New York at Delhi
Alumni Hall 111
Delhi, NY 13753-1144
Phone: (607) 746-4400
Fax: (607) 746-4769
http://www.delhi.edu

NORTH CAROLINA

Travel Agent Training Center, Inc.
607 Trail Ridge Road
Matthews, NC 28105-2061
Phone: (704) 844-8237
Fax: (704)-846-2849
http://www.TravelAgentTraining
    Center.com

OHIO

Columbus State Community College
Hospitality Management
550 East Spring Street
Columbus, OH 43215-1722
Phone: (614) 287-2572
Fax: (614) 287-5973
http://www.cscc.edu

Sinclair Community College
444 West 3rd Street Room 13-420
Dayton, OH 45402-1421
Phone: (937) 512-5197
Fax: (937) 512-5396
http://www.sinclair.edu/
    departments/hos/Findex.htm

PENNSYLVANIA

Penn Foster Career School
925 Oak Street
Scranton, PA 18515-0999
Phone: (570) 342-7701
Fax: (570) 961-4038
http://www.educationdirect.com

Pittsburgh Technical Institute / Boyd School
1111 McKee Road
Oakdale, PA 15071-3211
Phone: (412) 809-5200
Fax: (412) 299-2222
http://www.boydschool.com

RHODE ISLAND

Community College of Rhode Island
400 East Avenue
Warwick, RI 02886-1805
Phone: (401) 825-2061
Fax: (401) 825-2283
http://www.ccri.edu

TEXAS

El Paso Community College
Rio Grande Campus Box 20500
El Paso, TX 79998-0500
Phone: (915) 831-4082
Fax: (915) 831-4114

International Travel Institute
6363 Richmond Avenue
Houston, TX 77057-5914
Phone: (713) 785-4268
Fax: (713) 268-2626
http://www.internationaltravel
    institute.com

UTAH

Education Systems / Travel Campus
11038 Longdale Circle
Sandy, UT 84092-7013
Phone: (801) 572-3454
Fax: (801) 572-0701
http://www.educationsystems.com

VIRGINIA

Northern Virginia Community College
Travel & Tourism
Annandale, VA 22003-3743
Phone: (703) 323-3175
Fax: (703) 323-3509
http://www.nvcc.edu

INDIA

Career Weavers Consultants Private Limited
SCO 405–406 Sector 35
C Chandigarh 160036
Phone: +91 172-4695000
Fax: +91 172-4695099
http://www.careerweavers.co.in

Achariya International Management College
1-18 Gholakachari Road
West Bengal 700124
Phone: +33 2552-6012
Fax: +33 2584-2093

NETHERLANDS

World Travel School Herengracht
501 Den Haag 2597 LA
Phone: +31 20-6201715
Fax: +31 20-6389193
http://www.wts.nl

United Kingdom

Traveltrain Global Education
156 Homesdale Road
London BR1 2RA
Phone: +44 798 405 9381
http://www.imtt.org.uk

APPENDIX II
PROFESSIONAL ASSOCIATIONS

Actors' Equity Association
165 West 46th Street
New York, NY 10036
Phone: (212) 869-8530
Fax: (212) 719-9815
http://www.actorsequity.org

The Advertising Club of New York
235 Park Avenue South, #6
New York, NY 10003
Phone: (212) 533-8080
Fax: (212) 533-1929
http://www.theadvertisingclub.org

Aerobics and Fitness Association of America
15250 Ventura Boulevard, Suite 200
Sherman Oaks, CA 91403
Phone: (877) 968-7263
http://www.afaa.com

American Academy of Family Physicians
P.O. Box 11210
Shawnee Mission, KS 66207-1210
Phone: (800) 274-2237 or
(913) 906-6000
Fax: (913) 906-6075
http://www.aafp.org

American Advertising Federation
1101 Vermont Avenue NW, Suite 500
Washington, DC 20005
Phone: (800) 999-2231
Fax: (202) 898-0159
E-mail: aaf@aaf.org
http://www.aaf.org

American Alliance for Health, Physical Education, Recreation and Dance
1900 Association Drive
Reston, VA 20191-1598
Phone: (703) 476-3400 or
(800) 213-7193
http://www.aahperd.org/aapar

American Association of Advertising Agencies
405 Lexington Avenue
New York, NY 10174-1801
Phone: (212) 682-2500
http://www.aaaa.org

American Association of Community Colleges
One Dupont Circle NW
Washington, DC 20036
Phone: (202) 728-0200
Fax: (202) 833-2467
http://www.aacc.nche.edu

American Association of Language Specialists
P.O. Box 39339
Washington, DC 20016
http://www.taals.net

American Association of Museums
1575 Eye Street NW, Suite 400
Washington, DC 20005
Phone: (202) 289-1818
Fax: (202) 289-6578
http://www.aam-us.org

American Association of Snowboard Instructors
133 South Van Gordon Street, Suite 200
Lakewood, CO 80228
Phone: (303) 987-2700
Fax: (303) 987-9489
http://www.aasi.org

American Association of University Professors
1012 Fourteenth Street NW, Suite #500
Washington, DC 20005
Phone: (202) 737-5900
Fax: (202) 737-5526
http://www.aaup.org

American Bar Association
Chicago location
321 North Clark Street
Chicago, IL 60654-7598
Phone: (312) 988-5000
Washington, DC location
740 15th Street NW
Washington, DC 20005-1019
Phone: (202) 662-1000
http://www.abanet.org

The American College of Emergency Physicians
P.O. Box 619911
Dallas, TX 75261-9911
Phone: (800) 798-1822 or
(972) 550-0911
Fax: (972) 580-2816
https://www.acep.org

American Council on Exercise
4851 Paramount Drive
San Diego, CA 92123
Phone: (858) 279-8227; toll free:
(888) 825-3636
Fax: (858) 279-8064
http://www.acefitness.org

American Culinary Federation
180 Center Place Way
St. Augustine, FL 32095
Phone: (800) 624-9458
Fax: (904) 825-4758
E-mail: acf@acfchefs.net
http://www.acfchefs.org

American Dietetic Association
120 South Riverside Plaza, Suite 2000
Chicago, IL 60606-6995

Phone: (800) 877-1600
http://www.eatright.org

American Disc Jockey Association

20118 North 67th Avenue, Suite 300-605
Glendale, AZ 85308
Phone: (888) 723-5776
http://www.adja.org

American Fitness Professionals and Associates

P.O. Box 214
Ship Bottom, NJ 08008
Phone: (609) 978-7583
Fax: (609) 978-7582
E-mail: afpa@afpafitness.com
http://www.afpafitness.com

American Gaming Association

1299 Pennsylvania Avenue NW, Suite 1175
Washington, DC 20004
Phone: (202) 552-2675
Fax: (202) 552-2676
http://www.americangaming.org

American Guild of Musical Artists

1430 Broadway, 14th Floor
New York, NY 10018
Phone: (212) 265-3687
Fax: (212) 262-9088
http://www.musicalartists.org

American Hotel and Lodging Association

1201 New York Avenue NW, Ste. 600
Washington, DC 20005-3931
Phone: (202) 289-3100
http://www.ahla.com

The American Institute of Architects

1735 New York Avenue NW
Washington, DC 20006-5292
Phone: (800) AIA-3837 or (202) 626-7300
Fax: (202) 626-7547
http://www.aia.org

American Institute of Architecture Students

1735 New York Avenue NW
Washington, DC 20006
Phone: (202) 626-7472
Fax: (202) 626-7414
E-mail: mailbox@aias.org
http://www.aias.org

American Massage Therapy Association

500 Davis Street, Suite 900
Evanston, IL 60201-4695
Phone: (847) 864-0123; toll-free (877) 905-2700
Fax: (847) 864-1178
E-mail: info@amtamassage.org
http://www.amtamassage.org

American Medical Association

515 North State Street
Chicago, IL 60654
Phone: (800) 621-8335
http://www.ama-assn.org

American Resort Development Association

1220 L Street NW, Suite 500
Washington, DC 20005
Phone: (202) 371-6700
Fax: (202) 289-8544
E-mail: webmaster@arda.org
http://www.arda.org

American Society for Enology and Viticulture

P.O. Box 1855
Davis, CA 95617-1855
Phone: (530) 753-3142
Fax: (530) 753-3318
http://www.asev.org

American Society for Training and Development

1640 King Street
P.O. Box 1443
Alexandria, VA 22313-1443
Phone: (703) 683-8100
Fax: (703) 683-8103
http://www.astd.org

American Society of Interior Designers

608 Massachusetts Avenue, NE
Washington, DC 20002-6006
Phone: (202) 546-3480
Fax: (202) 546-3240
E-mail: asid@asid.org
http://www.asid.org

American Society of Media Photographers

150 North Second Street
Philadelphia, PA 19106
Phone: (215) 451-2767
Fax: (215) 451-0880
http://www.asmp.org

American Society of Picture Professionals

117 South Saint Asaph Street
Alexandria, VA 22314
Phone: (703) 299-0219
http://www.aspp.com

American Society of Travel Agents (ASTA)

1101 King Street
Alexandria, VA 22314
Phone: (703) 739-8710
http://www.asta.org

American Translators Association

225 Reinekers Lane, Suite 590
Alexandria, VA 22314
Phone: (703) 683-6100
Fax: (703) 683-6122
E-mail: ata@atanet.org
http://www.atanet.org

American Wine Society

113 South Perry Street
Lawrenceville, GA 30045
Phone: (678) 377-7070
Fax: (678) 377-7005
http://www.americanwinesociety.org

Associated Bodywork and Massage Professionals.

1271 Sugarbush Drive
Evergreen, CO 80439
Phone: (800) 458-2267; (303) 674-8478
Fax: (800) 667-8260
E-mail: expectmore@abmp.com
http://www.abmp.com

Associated Landscape Contractors of America
150 Elden Street
Herndon, VA 20170
Phone: (703) 736-9666
Fax: (703) 736-9668
www.alca.org

Association for Business Communication
P.O. Box 6143
Nacogdoches, TX 75962-0001
Phone: (936) 468-6280
Fax: (936) 468-6281
http://www.businesscommunication.org

Association for Experiential Education
3775 Iris Avenue, Suite 4
Boulder, CO 80301-2043
Phone: (303) 440-8844
http://www.aee.org

Association for Wedding Professionals International
6700 Freeport Boulevard, Suite 202
Sacramento, CA 95822
Phone: (800) 242-4461
http://afwpi.com

Association for Women in Communications
3337 Duke Street
Alexandria, VA 22314
Phone: (703) 370-7436
Fax: (703) 370-7437
http://www.womcom.org

Association of American Colleges and Universities
1818 R Street NW
Washington, DC 20009
Phone: (202) 387-3760
Fax: (202) 265-9532
http://www.aacu.org

Association of American Medical Colleges
2450 N Street NW
Washington, DC 20037-1126
Phone: (202) 828-0400
Fax: (202) 828-1125
http://www.aamc.org

Association of Bridal Consultants
56 Danbury Road, Suite 11
New Milford, CT 06776
Phone: (860) 355-7000
Fax: (860) 354-1404
http://www.bridalassn.com

Association of Certified Wedding Consultants
7791 Prestwick Circle
San Jose, CA 95135
Phone: (408) 528-9000
Fax: (408) 528-9333
http://www.acpwc.com

Association of Corporate Counsel
1025 Connecticut Avenue NW, Suite 200
Washington, DC 20036
Phone: (202) 293-4103
Fax: (202) 293-4701
http://www.acc.com

Association of Destination Management Executives
11 West Monument Avenue, Suite 510
P.O. Box 2307
Dayton, OH 45401-2307
Phone: (937) 586-3727
Fax: (937) 586-3699
E-mail: info@adme.org
http://www.adme.org

Association of Food Journalists
7 Avenida Vista Grande, Suite B7
Santa Fe, NM 87508
Phone: (505) 466-4742
E-mail: caroldemasters@yahoo.com
http://www.afjonline.com

Association of Retail Travel Agents
c/o Travel Destinations
4320 North Miller Road
Scottsdale, AZ 85251
Phone: (800) 969-6069
Fax: (615) 985-0600
E-mail: info@artaonline.com
http://www.artaonline.com

Association of Science-Technology Centers
1025 Vermont Avenue NW, Suite 500
Washington, DC 20005-6310
Phone: (202) 783-7200
Fax: (202) 783-7207
http://www.astc.org

Building Officials Association of New Jersey
E-mail: info@boanj.com
http://www.boanj.com

Canadian Association of Tour Operators
7-B Pleasant Boulevard, Suite 1011
Toronto, ON M4T 1K2
Canada
Phone: (416) 485-8232
Fax: (416) 485-0112
E-mail: info@cato.ca
http://www.cato.ca/apply.php

The Center for Hospitality Research at the Cornell School of Hotel Administration
535 Statler Hall
Ithaca, NY 14853
Phone: (607) 255-9780
Fax: (607) 254-6787
E-mail: hosp_research@cornell.edu
http://www.hotelschool.cornell.edu/chr

Club Managers Association of America
1733 King Street
Alexandria, VA 22314
Phone: (703) 739-9500
Fax: (703) 739-0124
E-mail: cmaa@cmaa.org
http://www.cmaa.org

Convention Industry Council
700 North Fairfax Street, Suite 510
Alexandria, VA 22314
Phone: (571) 527-3116
Fax: (571) 527-3105
https://www.conventionindustry.org

Court of Master Sommeliers, American Chapter

P.O. Box 6170
Napa, CA 94581
Phone: (707) 255-5056
http://www.mastersommeliers.org

Cruise Lines International Association

910 SE 17th Street, Suite 400
Fort Lauderdale, FL 33316
Phone: (754) 224-2200
Fax: (754) 224-2250
E-mail: info@cruising.org
http://www.cruising.org

Dance/USA

1111 16th Street NW, Suite 300
Washington, DC 20036
Phone: (202) 833-1717
Fax: (202) 833-2686
http://www.danceusa.org

Day Spa Association

310 17th Street
Union City, NJ 07087
Phone: (201) 865-2065
Fax: (201) 865-3961
E-mail: info@dayspaassociation.
com
http://www.dayspaassociation.com

Environmental Careers Organization

30 Winter Street, 6th Floor
Boston, MA 02108
Phone: (617) 426-4783
http://www.eco.org

Financial and Insurance Conference Planners

401 North Michigan Avenue, 22nd
floor
Chicago, IL 60611
Phone: (312) 245-1023
Fax: (312) 673-6920
http://www.ficpnet.com

Foreign Correspondents' Association

P.O. Box 974
Potts Point NSW, 1335
Australia
http://www.foreigncorrespondents.
org

Foreign Press Association

11 Carlton House Terrace
London SW1Y 5AJ
United Kingdom
Phone: +44 (0) 20 7930 0445
Fax: +44 (0) 20 7925 0469
http://www.foreign-press.org.uk

Golf Course Superintendents Association of America

1421 Research Park Drive
Lawrence, KS 66049-3859
Phone: (800) 472-7878 or
(785) 841-2240
http://www.gcsaa.org

Hospitality Financial and Technology Professionals

11709 Boulder Lane, Suite 110
Austin, TX 78726
Phone: (512) 249-5333; toll-free:
(800) 646-4387 (US)
Fax: (512) 249-1533
http://www.hftp.org

Hospitality, Sales and Marketing Association International

1760 Old Meadow Road, Suite 500
McLean, VA 22102
Phone: (703) 506-3280
Fax: (703) 506-3266
E-mail: info@hsmai.org
http://www.hsmai.org

IDEA Health and Fitness Association

10455 Pacific Center Court
San Diego, CA 92121-4339
Phone: (800) 999-4332, ext. 7
Fax: (858) 535-8234
E-mail: contact@ideafit.com
http://www.ideafit.com

Interior Design Educators Council

9100 Purdue Road, Suite 200
Indianapolis, IN 46268-3165
Phone: (317) 328-4437
Fax: (317) 280-8527
E-mail: info@idec.org
http://www.idec.org

International and American Associations of Clinical Nutritionists

15280 Addison Road, Suite 130
Addison, TX 75001
Phone: (972) 407-9089
Fax: (972) 250-0233
E-mail: iaacnddc@clinicalnutrition.
com
http://www.iaacn.org

International Association of Amusement Parks and Attractions

1448 Duke Street
Alexandria, VA 22314
Phone: (703) 836-.4800
Fax: (703) 836-6742
www.iaapa.org

International Association of Business Communicators

One Hallidie Plaza, Suite 600
San Francisco, CA 94102
Phone: (415) 544-4700; toll-free:
(800) 776-4222
Fax: (415) 544-4747
http://www.iabc.com

International Association of Culinary Professionals

455 South Fourth Street, Suite 650
Louisville, KY 40202
Phone: (502) 581-9786; toll-free:
(800) 928-4227
Fax: (502) 589-3602
E-mail: info@iacp.com
http://www.iacp.com

International Association of Exhibitions and Events (IAEE)

12700 Park Central Drive, Suite 308
Dallas, TX 75251
Phone: (972) 458-8002
Fax: (972) 458-8119
E-mail: news@iaee.com
http://www.iaee.com

International Code Council

500 New Jersey Avenue NW,
6th floor
Washington, DC 20001-2070

Phone: (888) 422-7233
Fax: (202) 783-2348
http://www.iccsafe.org

International Council on Hotel, Restaurant and Institutional Education
2810 North Parham Road, Suite 230
Richmond, VA 23294
Phone: (804) 346-4800
Fax: (804) 346-5009
http://www.chrie.org

International Food, Wine, and Travel Writers Association
1142 South Diamond Bar
Boulevard, #177
Diamond Bar, CA 91765-2203
Phone/Fax: (877) 439-8929
International Phone: (909) 860-6914
Fax: (909) 396-0014
E-mail: admin@ifwtwa.org
http://www.ifwtwa.org

International Foundation of Employee Benefit Plans
18700 West Bluemound Road
Brookfield, WI 53045
Phone: (888) 334-3327
http://www.ifebp.org

International Society of Travel and Tourism Educators
23220 Edgewater Street
St. Clair Shores, MI 48082
Phone/Fax: (586) 294-0208
http://www.istte.org

International Sommelier Guild
4109 NW 88th Avenue, Suite 101
Coral Springs, FL 33065
Phone: (302) 622-3811; (866) 412-0464
Fax: (954) 272-7377
https://www.internationalsommelier.com/links/list

International Spa Association
2365 Harrodsburg Road, Suite A325
Lexington, KY 40504
Phone: (888) 651-4772

Fax: (859) 226-4445
E-mail: ispa@ispastaff.com
http://www.experienceispa.com/ISPA

International Special Events Society
401 North Michigan Avenue, Suite 2200
Chicago, IL 60611-4267
Phone: (800) 688-4737 or
(312) 321-6853
Fax: (312) 673-6953
E-mail: info@ises.com
http://www.ises.com

International Sports Sciences Association
1015 Mark Avenue
Carpinteria, CA 93013
Phone: (800) 892-4772
Fax: (805) 745-8119
E-mail: webmaster@issaonline.com
https://www.issaonline.com

June Wedding, Inc.
19375 Pine Glade
Guerneville, CA 95446
Phone: (707) 865-9894
http://www.junewedding.com

Les Clefs d'Or USA, Ltd.
68 Laurie Avenue
Boston, MA 02132
Phone: (617) 469-KEYS
Fax: (617) 469-4397
E-mail: info@lcdusa.org
http://www.lcdusa.org

Los Angeles Concierge Association
269 South Beverly Drive, Suite 701
Beverly Hills, CA 90212
Phone: (310) 712-2688
Fax: (310) 858-2353
E-mail: info@thelaca.com
http://www.thelaca.com

Meeting Professionals International
3030 Lyndon B. Johnson Freeway, Suite 1700
Dallas, TX 75234-2759

Phone: (972) 702-3000
Fax: (972) 702-3070
http://www.mpiweb.org

Midwest Travel Writers Association
P.O. Box 83542
Lincoln, NE 68501-3542
Phone: (402) 438-2253
Fax: (866) 365-4851
http://www.mtwa.org

National Architectural Accrediting Board
1735 New York Avenue NW
Washington DC 20006
Phone: (202) 783-2007
Fax: (202) 783-2822
http://www.naab.org

National Association of Catering Executives
9881 Broken Land Parkway, Suite 101
Columbia, MD 21046
Phone: (410) 290-5410
Fax: (410) 290-5460
http://www.nace.net
http://www.hmea.com/hmea.html.

National Association of Childcare Professionals
P.O. Box 90723
Austin, TX 78709
Phone: (800) 537-1118
E-mail: admin@naccp.org
http://www.naccp.org

National Association of Underwater Instructors
P.O. Box 14650
Montclair, CA 91763
Phone: (909) 621-5801; toll-free:
(800) 553-6284
Fax: (901) 621-6405
http://www.naui.org

National Association of Wedding Professionals
2150 Sebastian Circle
Alva, FL 33920
Phone: (239) 728-2592
Fax: (239) 728-5452
http://www.nawp.com

National Business Travel Association
110 North Royal Street, 4th Floor
Alexandria, VA 22314
Phone: (703) 684-0836
Fax: (703) 684-0263
E-mail: info@nbta.org
http://www.nbta.org

National Concierge Association
Phone: (612) 253-5110
E-mail: info@nationalconcierge
associaton.com
http://www.nationalconcierge
association.com

National Council for Marketing and Public Relations
P.O. Box 336039
Greeley, CO 80633
Phone: (970) 330-0771
Fax: (970) 330-0769
http://www.ncmpr.org

National Council of Interior Design Qualification
1200 18th Street NW, Suite 1001
Washington, DC 20036-2506
Phone: (202) 721-0220
Fax: (202) 721-0221
E-mail: info@ncidq.org
http://www.ncidq.org

The National Hotel Motel Engineering Association
P.O. Box 965
Huffman, TX 77736
Phone: (800) 222-8134
http://www.hmea.com/hmea.html

National Recreation and Park Association
22377 Belmont Ridge Road
Ashburn, VA 20148-4150
Phone: (703) 858-0784
http://www.nrpa.org

National Restaurant Association
1200 17th Street NW
Washington, DC 20036
Phone: (202) 331-5900; toll free:
(800) 424-5156

Fax: (202) 331-2429
http://www.restaurant.org

National Restaurant Association Educational Foundation
175 West Jackson Boulevard,
Suite 1500
Chicago, IL 60604-2702
http://www.nraef.org

National Retail Federation
325 7th Street NW, Suite 1100
Washington, DC 20004
Phone: (202) 783-7971 or
(800) 673-4692
Fax: (202) 737-2849
http://www.nrf.com

National Strength and Conditioning Association
1885 Bob Johnson Drive
Colorado Springs, CO 80906
Phone: (719) 632-6722; toll-free
(800) 815-6826
Fax: (719) 632-6367
E-mail: nsca@nsca-lift.org
http://www.nsca-lift.org

National Tour Association
546 East Main Street
Lexington, KY 40508
Phone: (859) 226-4444; toll-free:
(800) 682-8886
Fax: (859) 226-4414
E-mail: joinnta@ntastaff.com
http://www.ntaonline.com

The Nature Conservancy
4245 North Fairfax Drive,
Suite 100
Arlington, VA 22203-1606
Phone: (703) 841-5300
http://www.nature.org

North American Travel Journalists Association
531 Main Street, #902
El Segundo, CA 90245
Phone: (310) 836-8712
Fax: (310) 836-8769
http://www.natja.org

Outdoor Industry Association
4909 Pearl East Circle, Suite 200

Boulder, CO 80301
Phone: (303) 444-3353
Fax: (303) 444-3284
E-mail: info@outdoorindustry.org
http://www.outdoorindustry.org

Outdoor Writers Association of California
E-mail: owac.director@gmail.com
http://www.owac.org

Overseas Press Club of America
40 West 45th Street
New York, NY 10036
Phone: (212) 626-9220
Fax: (212) 626-9210
E-mail: info@opcofamerica.org
http://www.opcofamerica.org

PADI International (Professional Association of Diving Instructors)
1251 East Dyer Road, Suite 100
Santa Ana, CA 92705-5605
Phone: (714) 540-7234
Fax: (714) 540-2609
http://www.padi.com

Pilates Method Alliance
P.O. Box 370906
Miami, FL 33137-0906
Phone: (305) 573-4946; toll-free
(866) 573-4945
Fax: (305) 573-4461
E-mail: info@pilatesmethod
alliance.org
http://www.pilatesmethodalliance.
org

Professional Association of Innkeepers International
207 White Horse Pike
Haddon Heights, NJ 08035
Phone: (856) 310-1102;
toll-free: (800) 468-7244
Fax: (856) 310-1105
http://www.paii.org

Professional Convention Management Association
2301 South Lake Shore Drive, Suite
1001
Chicago, IL 60616-1419

Phone: (312) 423-7262; toll-free:
(877) 827-7262
Fax: (312) 423-7222
http://www.pcma.org

Professional Photographers of America
229 Peachtree Street NE, Suite 2200
Atlanta, GA 30303
Phone: (404) 522-8600
Fax: (404) 614-6400
http://www.ppa.com

Professional Ski Instructors of America
133 South Van Gordon Street,
Suite 200
Lakewood, CO 80228
Phone: (303) 987-9390
Fax: (303) 988-9489
http://www.psia.org

Public Relations Society of America
33 Maiden Lane, 11th floor
New York, NY 10038-5150
Phone: (212) 460-1400
Fax: (212) 995-0757
http://www.prsa.org

Registry of Interpreters for the Deaf
333 Commerce Street
Alexandria, VA 22314
Phone: (703) 838-0030;
TTY: (703) 838-0459
Fax: (703) 838-0454
http://www.rid.org

Resort and Commercial Recreation Association
P.O. Box 1564
Dubuque, IA 52004-1564
Fax: (563) 690-3296
http://www.rcra.org

The Screen Actors Guild
5757 Wilshire Boulevard, 7th floor
Los Angeles, CA 90036-3600
Phone: (323) 954-1600
http://www.sag.org

Scuba Schools International
2619 Canton Court
Fort Collins, CO 80525
Phone: (970) 482-0883
E-mail: admin@divessi.com
http://www.divessi.com

Seattle Hotel Concierge Association
P.O. Box 1008
Seattle, WA 98111-1008
http://www.seattlehotelconcierge.com

Society for Human Resource Management
1800 Duke Street
Alexandria, VA 22314
Phone: (800) 283-7476 (U.S.);
(703) 548-3440 (International)
TTY/TDD: (703) 548-6999
Fax: (703) 535-6490
http://www.shrm.org

Society of American Travel Writers
7044 South 13th Street
Oak Creek, WI 53154
Phone: (414) 908-4949
Fax: (414) 768-8001
http://www.satw.org

Stock Artists Alliance
175 Main Street
Glen Gardner, NJ 08826
http://www.stockartistsalliance.org

Society of Government Meeting Professionals (SGMP)
908 King Street, Lower level
Alexandria, VA 22314
Phone: (703) 549-0892, ext. 15
Fax: (703) 549-0708
http://www.sgmp.org

Sommelier Society of America
P.O. Box 20080, West Village Station
New York, NY 10014
Phone: (212) 679-4190
Fax: (212) 255-8959
http://www.sommeliersocietyof
america.org

Stage Managers' Association
P.O. Box 275, Times Square Station
New York, NY 10108-0275
E-mail: info@stagemanagers.org
http://www.stagemanagers.org

Student and Youth Travel Association
3048 Clarkston Road
Lake Orion, MI 48362
Phone: (248) 814-7982;
toll-free: (800) 509-SYTA
Fax: (248) 814-7150
E-mail: info@syta.org
http://www.syta.org

Themed Entertainment Association
150 East Olive Avenue, Suite 306
Burbank, CA 91502
Phone: (818) 843-8497
Fax: (818) 843-8477
E-mail: info@teaconnect.org
http://www.themeit.com

Translators and Interpreters Guild of the Communications Workers of America
501 Third Street NW
Washington, DC 20001
Phone: (202) 434-1100
http://www.cwa-union.org

The Travel Institute
148 Linden Street, Suite 305
Wellesley, MA 02482
Phone: (781) 237-0280;
toll-free: (800) 542-4282
Fax: (781) 237-3860
E-mail: info@thetravelinstitute.com
http://www.thetravelinstitute.com

United States Bartenders' Guild
P.O. Box 82241
Las Vegas, NV 89180
Phone: (702) 248-3383
http://www.usbg.org

The United States Golf Association
P.O. Box 708

Far Hills, NJ 07931
Phone: (908) 234-2300
Fax: (908) 234-9687
http://www.usga.org

United States Professional Tennis Association

1 USPTA Centre
3535 Briarpark Drive
Houston, TX 77042
Phone: (713) 97-USPTA
Fax: (713) 978-7780
http://www.uspta.org

United States Professional Tennis Registry

P.O. Box 4739
Hilton Head Island, SC 29938
Phone: (803) 785-7244 or toll-free:
(800) 421-6289
Fax: (803) 686-2033
http://www.ptrtennis.org

United States Tennis Association

70 West Red Oak Lane
White Plains, NY 10604
Phone: (914) 696-7000
http://www.usta.com

United States Tour Operators Association

275 Madison Avenue, Suite 2014
New York, NY 10016
Phone: (212) 599-6599
Fax: (212) 599-6744
E-mail: information@ustoa.com
http://www.ustoa.com/index.cfm

Unite Here

275 Seventh Avenue
New York, NY 10001-6708
Phone: (212) 265-7000
http://www.unitehere.org

Washington Association of Building Officials

P.O. Box 7310
Olympia, WA 98507-7310
Phone: (360) 586-6725
Fax: (360) 586-5538
E-mail: wabo@wabo.org
http://www.wabo.org

The Wine Institute

425 Market Street Suite 1000
San Francisco, CA 94105
Phone: (415) 512-0151

Fax: (415) 442-0742
http://www.wineinstitute.org

World at Work Society of Certified Professionals

14040 North Northsight Boulevard
Scottsdale, AZ 85260
Phone: (480) 922-2020; toll-free:
(877) 951-9191
Fax: (480) 483-8352; toll-free: (866)
816-2962
E-mail: certification@
worldatworksociety.org
http://www.worldatworksociety.
org/society/home/html/home-
entry.jsp

The Yoga Alliance

7801 Old Branch Avenue, Suite 400
Clinton, MD 20735
Phone: (301) 868-4700; toll-free
(877) 964-2255
Fax: (301) 868-7909 or
(240) 846-0898
http://www.yogaalliance.org

APPENDIX III
USEFUL WEB SITES, INDUSTRY PUBLICATIONS, AND INTERNSHIP PROGRAMS

There are a variety of publications, Web sites, and other sources of information valuable to travel and hospitality job seekers. Read through this section to determine resources that will help you learn more about travel and hospitality careers. Additional Web sites and publications are found within each of the career profiles.

A. JOB LISTINGS AND CAREER INFORMATION WEB SITES

CASINOS

Casino Careers Online
http://www.casinocareers.com

Casino Jobs Network
http://www.casinojobs.net

Harrah's Entertainment
http://www.harrahs.com/harrahs-corporate/careers-home.html

Il Dado Casino Jobs
http://www.ildado.com/casino_jobs.html

Las Vegas Jobs
http://www.lasvegasjobs.com

World Casino Jobs
http://www.worldcasinodirectory.com/jobs

CRUISE SHIPS

Carnival Casino Recruitment
http://www.oceancasinojobs.com

Cruise International Cruise Line Employment Services
http://www.cruiseshipjob.net

Cruise Line Employment
http://www.shipjobs.com

Cruise Ship Job Finder
http://www.cruisejobfinder.com

Cruise Ship Jobs
http://www.cruiseshipjob.com

Free Guide to Cruise Ship Jobs
http://www.cruiselinesjobs.com

GENERAL HOSPITALITY/ OTHER

Club Jobs
http://www.clubjobs.net

Cornell Hotel School Industry Guides
http://www.hotelschool.cornell.edu/research/library/tools/industry

Hcareers Hospitality Jobs
http://www.hcareers.com

Hospitality Jobs Online
http://www.hospitalityonline.com

Hospitality, Recreation, and Tourism Career Guide
http://www.khake.com/page61.html

Hospitality Resource Network
http://hospitalityresourcenetwork.com

Hotel Restaurant Jobs
http://www.hotelrestaurantjobs.com

Jobs in Food, Tourism, Hospitality and Travel
http://www.quintcareers.com/hospitality_jobs.html

JobMonkey
http://www.jobmonkey.com

Meeting Jobs
http://www.meetingjobs.com

Resort Jobs
http://www.resortjobs.com

HOTELS/RESORTS

Hotel Career Solutions
http://www.hotelcareersolutions.com

Hotel Job Resource
http://www.hoteljobresource.com

Hoteljobs.com
http://www.hoteljobs.com

Hotel Jobs Network
http://www.hoteljobsnetwork.com

Hoteltraveljobs.com
http://www.hoteltraveljobs.com

Resortjobs.com
http://www.resortjobs.com

RESTAURANTS/FOOD SERVICE

Chef Jobs Network
http://chefjobsnetwork.com

CulinaryEd.com
http://www.culinaryed.com

Food and Drink Jobs.com
http://www.foodanddrinkjobs.com

Food Industry Jobs.com
http://www.foodindustryjobs.com

Food Service.com
http://www.foodservice.com/
employment

HospitalityHR.com: Restaurant Jobs Recruiters
http://www.hospitalityhr.com

Need Waitstaff.com
http://www.needwaitstaff.com

Restaurant Recruit
http://www.restaurantrecruit.com

Star Chefs Jobfinder.com
http://www.starchefsjobfinder.com

Wine and Hospitality Jobs.com
http://wineandhospitalityjobs.com

TRAVEL/TOURISM/INTERNATIONAL

Adventure Travel Jobs
http://www.great-adventures.com/
know/plan/work.html

Council on International Educational Exchange
http://www.ciee.org

International Job Opportunities
http://www.jobsabroad.com/search.cfm

Jobs Abroad
http://www.jobsabroad.com/search.cfm

Transitions Abroad
http://www.transitionsabroad.com/
listings/work/index.shtml

Travel Agent Jobs
http://www.travels.com/articles/
travel-agents/travel-agent-jobs

Working Abroad
http://www.workingabroad.org

B. PUBLICATIONS

Amusement Today magazine
http://www.amusementtoday.com

Bon Appetit magazine
http://www.bonappetit.com

Brides magazine
http://www.brides.com

Budget Travel magazine
http://www.budgettravel.com

Business Traveller magazine
http://www.businesstraveller.com

Business Travel News magazine
http://www.btnonline.com/
businesstravelnews/index.jsp

Casino Connection magazine
http://www.casinoconnection
nevada.com

Catering magazine
http://www.cateringmagazine.com

Club & Resort Business magazine
http://www.clubandresortbusiness.com

Condé Nast Traveler magazine
http://www.concierge.com/cntraveler

Cooking Light magazine
http://www.cookinglight.com

Cornell Hospitality Quarterly
The Center for Hospitality Research
http://www.hotelschool.cornell.edu/
research/chr/pubs/quarterly/

Cruise Travel magazine
http://www.cruisetravelmag.com

Developments Magazine
American Resort Development
Association
http://www.arda.org/AM/
Template.cfm?Section=About_
Developments

Event Solutions Magazine and Resource
http://www.event-solutions.com

Food & Beverage Magazine
http://www.fb101.com

Food and Wine magazine
http://www.foodandwine.com

Food Arts magazine
http://www.foodarts.com/Foodarts/
Home

Global Hoteliers' Community
http://ehotelier.com

Hispanic Meetings & Travel magazine
http://www.hispanicmeetingstravel.com

Hospitality Net
http://www.hospitalitynet.org/index.html

Hospitality Technology **magazine**
http://www.htmagazine.com/ME2/Splash.asp

Hospitality Upgrade **magazine**
http://www.hospitalityupgrade.com

Hotel Business **magazine**
http://www.hotelbusiness.com/hb/main.asp

Hotel Executive **magazine**
http://www.hotelexecutive.com

Hotel F&B **magazine**
http://www.hotelfandb.com

Hotel Interactive **magazine**
http://www.hotelinteractive.com/home_hi.aspx

Hotel Management International **magazine**
http://www.hmi-online.com

HotelMarketing.com
http://www.hotelmarketing.com

Hotel Online
http://www.hotel-online.com

Hotels—The Magazine of the Global Hotel Industry
http://www.hotelsmag.com

Hotel Resource **magazine**
http://www.hotelresource.com

Hotel World Network **magazine**
http://www.hotelworldnetwork.com/site-redirect

The Journals of Hospitality and Tourism Education
http://www.chrie.org/i4a/pages/Index.cfm?pageID=3392

Lodging Hospitality **magazine**
http://lhonline.com

Lodging **magazine**
http://www.lodgingmagazine.com/ME2/Default.asp

Meeting and Convention **magazine**
http://www.mcmag.com

Meeting Source **magazine**
http://www.meetingsource.com

National Geographic and National Geographic Traveler **magazines**
http://www.nationalgeographic.com
http://traveler.nationalgeographic.com

Native American Casino **magazine**
http://www.nacasino.com

Outside **magazine**
http://outside.away.com/index.html

Restaurant Startup and Growth **magazine**
http://www.restaurantowner.com

Restauranteurs Marketplace **magazine**
http://www.restaurateursmarketplace.com

Ski Area Management **magazine**
http://www.saminfo.com

Special Events **magazine**
http://specialevents.com

Theme Parks Magazine
http://www.themeparksmagazine.com

Travel and Hospitality Industry Digest
http://www.e-tid.com

Travel & Leisure **magazine**
http://www.travelandleisure.com

Travel 50 & Beyond **magazine**
http://travel50andbeyond.com

Travel Weekly **magazine**
http://www.travelweekly.com

Vacations **magazine**
http://vacationsmagazine.com

Vineyard & Winery Management Magazine
http://www.vwm-online.com

Wine Spectator **magazine**
http://www.winespectator.com/Wine/Home

Wine Enthusiast **magazine**
http://www.winemag.com/homepage/index.asp?adid=WEMAGTAB

Wired Hotelier **magazine**
http://www.wiredhotelier.com/index.html

C. INTERNSHIP PROGRAMS

Internships are one of the best ways to determine if a career is right for you, as well as gain valuable experience necessary to break into the field. In addition to the resources below, contact any organization directly if you are interested in interning there. Most companies (including hotels, resorts, restaurant corporations, and casinos) offer internships and often you can find the information directly on their Web site.

The Broadmoor
http://www.broadmoor.com/internships.php

Cool Summer Jobs
http://www.coolsummerjobs.com

Cool Works Summer and Seasonal Jobs
http://www.coolworks.com

Crowne Plaza Hilton Head Island
http://www.cphiltonhead.com/cp/Career-Opportunities-Internships-Hilton-Head-Island-SC.htm

Disney Professional Internships
http://disney.go.com/disneycareers/internships/home.html

Hershey Entertainment and Resorts
http://www.hersheyjobs.com/internships/hospitality.php

Hyatt Hotels & Resorts
http://www.hyatt.com/hyatt/careers/internships/index.jsp

International Guild of Hospitality and Restaurant Managers
http://www.hospitalityguild.com/internship.htm

International Internships: Intern Abroad
http://www.internabroad.com/search.cfm

JobMonkey
http://www.jobmonkeyjobs.com/GetJobs.rs

MGM Mirage
http://www.mgmmiragecareers.com/college-recruiting/internships.aspx

New York Palace
http://www.newyorkpalace.com/career_opportunities/internship.html

Resort Intern Connection
http://www.resortinternconnection.com/

Starwood/Westin Internships
http://www.starwoodhotels.com/westin/careers/recruiting/internships.html

Trump Employment
http://www.trumpemployment.com/internship/default.asp

APPENDIX IV
MAJOR EMPLOYERS

The following appendix lists major U.S. hotel chains, cruise lines, full-service restaurant chains, casinos, and other resorts and amusement parks. This can be used as a reference for jobs, internships, and other useful career information.

MAJOR U.S. HOTEL CHAINS

America's Best Inns & Suites
50 Glenlake Parkway, Suite 350
Atlanta, GA 30328
Phone: (800) 237-8466
http://www.americasbestinn.com

Americas Best Value Inn by Vantage
Guest Relations Department
3300 North University Drive, Suite 500
Coral Springs, FL 33065
Phone: (877) 311-2378
Fax: (954) 575-8275
http://www.bestvalueinn.com

Best Western International
6201 North 24th Parkway
Phoenix, AZ 85016
Phone: (602) 957-4200
http://www.bestwestern.com

Carlson Hotels Worldwide
P.O. Box 59159
Minneapolis, MN 55459
Phone: (763) 212-5000
http://www.carlson.com/brands/hotels.cfm
Includes Regent Hotels and Cruises, Radisson, Park Plaza, Country Inns and Suites, and Park Inn

Choice Hotels International
10750 Columbia Pike
Silver Spring, MD, 20901
Phone: (301) 592-5000
http://www.choicehotels.com
Includes Comfort Inn & Suites, Clarion, Quality, Sleep Inn, Cambria Suites, Main Stay Suites, Econo Lodge, Suburban, and Rodeway Inn

Drury Inns
721 Emerson Road, Suite 400
St. Louis, MO 63141
Phone: (314) 429-2255
Fax: (314) 429-5166
http://www.druryhotels.com

Hilton Hotels Corporation World Headquarters
9336 Civic Center Drive
Beverly Hills, CA 90210
Phone: (310) 278-4321
http://hiltonworldwide1.hilton.com
Includes Conrad Hotels, Doubletree, Embassy Suites, Hampton Inn & Suites, and Homewood Suites

Hyatt Hotels
71 South Wacker Drive
Chicago, IL 60606
Phone: (312) 750-1234
Fax: (312) 750-8550
http://www.hyatt.com
Includes Amerisuites

InterContinental Hotels Group
3 Ravinia Drive, Suite 100
Atlanta, GA 30346-2149
Phone: (770) 604 -2000
http://www.ihgplc.com
Includes Crowne Plaza, Holiday Inn, Hotel Indigo, Staybridge Suites, Candlewood Suites, and Priority Club

Loews Hotels
667 Madison Avenue
New York, NY 10065
Phone: (212) 521-2000
http://www.loewshotels.com

Mandarin Oriental Hotel Group
345 California Street, Suite 1250
San Francisco, CA 94104
Phone: (415) 772-8880
Fax: (415) 782-3778
1775 Broadway, Suite 310
New York, NY 10019
Phone: (212) 399-3938
Fax: (212) 399-7189
E-mail: americas-enquiry@mohg.com
http://www.mandarin-oriental.com

Marriott International
Marriott Drive
Washington, DC 20058
Phone: (301) 380-3000
http://www.marriott.com
Includes JW Marriott, Renaissance Hotels & Resorts, Courtyard, Residence Inn, Fairfield Inn, TownePlace Suites, SpringHill Suites, and Grand Residences

Omni Hotels
420 Decker Drive, Suite 200
Irving, TX 75062
Phone: (972) 730-6664
Fax: (972) 871-5669
http://www.omnihotels.com

The Ritz-Carlton Hotel Company
4445 Willard Avenue, Suite 800

Chevy Chase, MD 20815
Phone: (301) 547-4700
Fax: (301) 547-4723
http://www.ritzcarlton.com

Starwood Hotels and Resorts Worldwide

1111 Westchester Avenue
White Plains, NY 10604
Phone: (914) 640-8100
Fax: (914) 640-8310
http://www.starwoodhotels.com/
Includes Le Meridien, Westin,
Sheraton, St. Regis, W, Luxury
Collection, and Aloft

Wyndham Worldwide Corporation

7 Sylvan Way
Parsippany, NJ 07054
http://www.wyndhamworldwide.
com
Includes Ramada, Days Inn,
Travelodge, Super 8, Wingate,
Baymont Inn & Suites, Howard
Johnson, Knights Inn, and
AmeriHost

MAJOR U.S. CRUISE LINES

American Cruise Lines

741 Boston Post Road, Suite 200
Guilford, CT 06437
Phone: (800) 230-7039
Fax: (203) 453-0417
E-mail: careers@
americancruiselines.com.
http://www.americancruiselines.
com

Carnival Cruise Lines

3655 NW 87th Avenue
Miami, FL 33178
http://www.carnival.com

Celebrity Cruises

1050 Caribbean Way
Miami, FL 33132
Phone: (305) 539-6000
http://www.celebritycruises.com

Costa Cruises

200 South Park Road, Suite 200

Hollywood FL 33021
Phone: (800) 462-6782
http://www.costacruise.com

Crystal Cruises

2049 Century Park East,
Suite 1400
Los Angeles, CA 90067
Phone: (866) 446-6625
http://www.crystalcruises.com

Disney Cruise Line

P.O. Box 10238
Lake Buena Vista, FL 32830
Phone: (407) 566-3500
http://disneycruise.disney.go.com/

Holland America Line

300 Elliott Avenue West
Seattle, WA 98119
Phone: (877) 932-4259
http://www.hollandamerica.com

Imperial Majesty Cruise Line

4161 NW Fifth Street, Suite 200
Plantation, FL 33317
Phone: (954) 453-4625
http://www.imperialmajesty.com

Norwegian Cruise Line

NCL Corporation Ltd.
7665 Corporate Center Drive
Miami, FL 33126
Phone: (305) 436-4000
http://www.ncl.com/nclweb/home.
html

Oceania Cruises, Inc.

8300 NW 33rd Street, Suite 308
Miami, FL 33122
Phone: (305) 514-2300; toll-free:
(866) 765-3630
http://www.oceaniacruises.com

Princess Cruises

24844 Avenue Rockefeller
Santa Clarita, CA 91355
http://www.princess.com

Regent Seven Seas Cruises

1000 Corporate Drive, Suite 500
Fort Lauderdale, FL 33334
Phone: (800) 477-7500

E-mail: information@RSSC.com
http://www.rssc.com/employment/
home.jsp?link=employment

Royal Caribbean International

1050 Caribbean Way
Miami, FL 33132-2096
Phone: (305) 539-6000
http://www.royalcaribbean.com

Voyages of Discovery

1800 SE 10th Avenue, Suite 205
Fort Lauderdale, FL 33316
Phone: (866) 623-2689;
(954) 761-7878
http://us.voyagesofdiscovery.com

Windstar Cruises

2101 4th Avenue, Suite 1150
Seattle, WA 98121
Phone: (206) 292-9606
Fax: (206) 340-0975
www.windstarcruises.com

MAJOR U.S. FULL SERVICE RESTAURANT CHAINS

Applebee's

11201 Renner Boulevard
Lenexa, KS 66219
Phone: (888) 59-APPLE
http://www.applebees.com

Benihana

8685 NW 53rd Terrace
Miami, FL 33166
Phone: (305) 593-0770
Fax: (305) 592-6371
http://www.benihana.com

Bertucci's Corporation

Franchise Department
155 Otis Street
Northborough, MA 01532
http://www.bertuccis.com

Brinker International

6820 LBJ Freeway
Dallas, TX 75240
Phone: (972) 980-9917
http://www.brinker.com
Chili's, Macaroni Grill, On the
Border, Maggiano's

B. R. Guest Restaurants
206 Spring Street
New York, NY 10012
Phone: (212) 529-0900
http://www.brguestrestaurants.com

California Pizza Kitchen
6053 West Century Boulevard, Suite 1100
Los Angeles, CA 90045-6430
Phone: (310) 342-5000
Fax: (310) 342-4640
http://www.cpk.com

Denny's
203 East Main Street P-8-6
Spartanburg, SC 29319
Phone: (864) 597-8000
http://www.dennys.com

Elephant Bar Restaurants
Restaurant Support Center
14241 Firestone Boulevard, Suite 315
La Mirada, CA 90638
Phone: (562) 207-6200
http://www.elephantbar.com

Friendly Ice Cream Corporation
1855 Boston Road
Wilbraham, MA 01095
Phone: (800) 966-9970
http://www.friendlys.com

Hard Rock Cafe
6100 Old Park Lane
Orlando, FL 32835
Phone: (407) 445-ROCK
http://www.hardrock.com

Hillstone Restaurant Group
147 South Beverly Drive
Beverly Hills, CA 90212
Phone: (800) 230-9787
Fax: (310) 385-7119
http://www.hillstone.com
Includes Houston's, Gulfstream, Bandera, and others

IHOP Corporation
450 North Brand Boulevard
Glendale, CA 91203
Phone: (818) 240-6055

Fax: (818) 637-3131
http://www.ihop.com

Landry's Restaurants
1510 West Loop South
Houston, TX 77027
Phone: (800) 5-LANDRY or (713) 850-1010
http://www.landrysrestaurants.com
Rainforest Café, the Chart House, the Crab House, and others

Legal Sea Foods
Quality Control Center
One Seafood Way
Boston, MA 02210
Phone: (617) 530-9000
http://www.legalseafoods.com

The Melting Pot
8810 Twin Lakes Boulevard
Tampa, FL 33614
Phone: (800) 783-0867
http://www.themeltingpot.com

Mimis Café General Office
17852 East 17th Street
South Building, Suite 108
Tustin, CA 92780
Phone: (714) 544-4826; toll-free: (866) 56-MIMIS
http://www.mimiscafe.com

Olive Garden Italian Restaurant
P.O. Box 592037
Orlando, FL 32859-2037
Phone: (800) 331-2729
Fax: (407) 245-5189
http://www.olivegarden.com

OSF International, Inc. (The Old Spaghetti Factory)
0715 S.W. Bancroft Street
Portland, OR 97239
Phone: (503) 225-0433
Fax: (503) 226-6214
http://www.osf.com

P.F. Chang's China Bistro, Inc.
7676 East Pinnacle Peak Road
Scottsdale, AZ 85255
Phone: (480) 888-3000

http://www.pfchangs.com

Pick Up Stix
1330 Calle Avanzado
San Clemente, CA 92673
Phone: (800) 400-7849
http://www.pickupstix.com

Planet Hollywood Corporate Headquarters
7598 West Sand Lake Road
Orlando, FL 32819
http://www.planethollywood.com

Real Mex Restaurants
5660 Katella Avenue
Cypress, CA 90630
Phone: (562) 346-1200
http://www.realmexrestaurants.com
Includes Chevy's Fresh Mex, El Torito Grill, Casa Gallardo, Acapulco

Red Lobster
5900 Lake Ellenor Drive
Orlando, FL 32809
Phone: (407) 245-4000
http://www.redlobster.com

Ruby Tuesday Support Center
150 West Church Avenue
Maryville, TN 37801
Phone: (865) 379-5700
http://www.rubytuesdays.com

T.G.I. Friday's
4201 Marsh Lane
Corrollton, TX 75007
Phone: (972) 662-5400
http://www.tgifridays.com

MAJOR U.S. CASINOS

Ameristar Casinos
3773 Howard Hughes Parkway
490 South
Las Vegas, NV 89169
Phone: (702) 567-7000
http://www.ameristarcasinos.com

Bellagio
3600 Las Vegas Boulevard South
Las Vegas, NV 89109

Phone: (702) 693-8279
Fax: (702) 693-8577
E-mail: employment@bellagioresort.
com
http://www.bellagio.com

Borgata Hotel Casino & Spa
One Borgata Way
Atlantic City, NJ 08401
Phone: (609) 317-1000
http://www.borgatajobs.com

Cypress Bayou Casino
832 Martin Luther King Road
Charenton, LA 70523
Phone: (800) 284-4386
http://www.cypressbayou.com

Foxwoods Resort Casino
Route 2, P.O. Box 3777
Mashantucket, CT 06338
Phone: (866) 4-FOXJOB
http://www.foxwoods.com

Harrah's Entertainment
One Caesars Palace Drive
Las Vegas, NV 89123
Phone: (702) 494-4829
http://www.harrahs.com/harrahs-
corporate/careers-home.html

Island Resort and Casino
West 399, Highway 2 & 41
Harris, MI 49845
Phone: (906) 466-2941; toll-free:
(800) 682-6040
http://www.islandresortandcasino.
com

Mandalay Bay Resort and Casino
3950 Las Vegas Boulevard South
Las Vegas, NV 89119
Phone: (702) 891-1602
http://www.mgmmiragecareers.com/
mandalaybay/mandalaybay-
las-vegas-jobs.aspx

MGM Grand Hotel & Casino
3799 Las Vegas Boulevard South
Las Vegas, NV 89109
Phone: (702) 891-1602
http://www.mgmgrand.com/
bestplacetowork

Mohegan Sun
1 Mohegan Sun Boulevard
Uncasville, CT 06382
Phone: (888) 226-7711
http://mtga.com/mtga/employment

Seneca Allegany Casino & Hotel
777 Seneca Allegany Boulevard
Salamanca, NY 14779
Phone: (888) 913-3377
http://www.senecaalleganycasino.
com

Soaring Eagle Casino & Resort
6800 Soaring Eagle Boulevard
Mount Pleasant, MI 48858
Phone: (888) 732-4537
http://www.soaringeaglecasino.com

Station Casinos
1505 South Pavilion Center Drive
Las Vegas, NV 89135
Phone: (702) 495-3000
http://www.stationcasinos.com/
corp/careers

Sunset Station Hotel and Casino
1301 West Sunset Road
Henderson, NV 89014
Phone: (702) 547-7777 or
(888) 786-7389
http://www.sunsetstation.com

Tropicana Casino & Resort
2831 Boardwalk
Atlantic City, NJ 08401-6338
Phone: (609) 340-4000
http://www.tropicana.net

Wynn Las Vegas
3131 Las Vegas Boulevard South
Las Vegas, NV 89109
Phone: (702) 770-3900
http://www.wynnlasvegas.com

SELECTED U.S. SPECIALTY RESORTS AND THEME PARKS

Anheuser-Busch's Theme Parks
http://www.becjobs.com

- ## Busch Gardens Tampa and Adventure Island
  3605 Bougainvillea
  Tampa, FL 33612
  Phone: (813) 987-5400

- ## Busch Gardens Williamsburg and Water Country USA
  One Busch Gardens Boulevard
  Williamsburg, VA 23187
  Phone: (757) 253-3020

- ## SeaWorld of California
  500 SeaWorld Drive
  San Diego, CA 92109
  Phone: (619) 226-3842

- ## SeaWorld of Florida and Discovery Cove
  7007 SeaWorld Drive
  Orlando, FL 32821
  Phone: (407) 370-1562

- ## SeaWorld of Texas
  10500 SeaWorld Drive
  San Antonio, TX 78251
  Phone: (210) 523-3198

- ## Sesame Place
  100 Sesame Road
  Box L579
  Langhorne, PA 19047
  Phone: (215) 752-7070, ext. 231

California's Great America
P.O. Box 1776
Santa Clara, CA 95052
Phone: (408) 986-5825
http://www.cagreatamerica.com/
jobs/jobs.cfm

Cedar Fair Entertainment Company
One Cedar Point Drive
Sandusky, OH 44870
Phone: (419) 627-2233
Fax: (419) 627-2260
http://www.cedarfair.com/ir/
careers/permanent.cfm

Club Med
http://www.clubmedjobs.com

Great Wolf Lodge
122 West Washington Avenue
Madison, WI 53703
Phone: (608) 661-4700
Fax: (608) 661-4701
http://www.greatwolf.com

Hershey Entertainment and Resorts
Employee Resource Center
75 East Derry Road
Hershey, PA 17033
Phone: (717) 520-5627
http://www.hersheyjobs.com/index.php

The Homestead
1766 Homestead Drive
Hot Springs, VA 24445
Phone: (540) 839-1766
http://www.thehomestead.com

Kiawah Island Golf Resort
One Sanctuary Beach Drive
Kiawah Island, SC 29455
Phone: (800) 654-2924
http://www.kiawahresort.com/about-the-resort/careers.php

Knott's Berry Farm
8039 Beach Boulevard
Buena Park, CA 90620
Phone: (714) 220-5200
http://www.knotts.com/jobs/index.asp

KSL Resorts
50-905 Avenida Bermudas
La Quinta, CA 92253
Phone: (760) 564-8000
http://www.kslresorts.com

Mohonk Mountain House
1000 Mountain Rest Road
New Paltz, NY 12561
Phone: (845) 255-1000
http://www.mohonkjobs.com

Sandals and Beaches Resorts
Unique Vocation, Inc.
4950 SW 72nd Avenue
Miami, FL 33155
Phone: (305) 284-1300, ext. 4344

Fax: (305) 668-2782
http://www.beaches.com/general/employment.cfm

Smugglers' Notch Resort
4323 Vermont Route 108 South
Smugglers' Notch, VT 05464-9537
Phone: (800) 419-4615
Fax: (802) 644-1230
E-mail: smuggs@smuggs.com
http://www.smuggs.com/pages/universal/jobs/index.php

Six Flags
http://www.sixflags.com

- **La Ronde**
  22, Chemin MacDonald
  Ile Sainte-Helene
  Montreal, QC H3C 6A9
  Canada
  Phone: (514) 397-2000

- **The Great Escape & Splashwater Kingdom**
  P.O. Box 511
  Lake George, NY 12845
  Phone: (518) 792-3500

- **Six Flags America**
  P.O. Box 4210
  Largo, MD 20775
  Phone: (301) 249-1500

- **Six Flags Discovery Kingdom**
  2001 Marine World Parkway
  Vallejo, CA 94589
  Phone: (707) 644-4000

- **Six Flags Fiesta Texas**
  17000 IH-10 West
  San Antonio, TX 78257
  Phone: (210) 697-5000
  Guest Relations (210) 697-5050

- **Six Flags Great Adventure**
  Route 537, P.O. Box 120
  Jackson, NJ 08527
  Phone: (732) 928-1821

- **Six Flags Great America**
  P.O. Box 1776

Gurnee, IL 60031
Phone: (847) 249-4636

- **Six Flags Hurricane Harbor–Arlington, Texas**
  1800 Lamar Boulevard
  Arlington, TX 78006
  Phone: (817) 265-3356

- **Six Flags Hurricane Harbor–Los Angeles**
  26101 Magic Mountain Parkway
  Valencia, CA 91355
  Phone: (661) 255-4527

- **Six Flags Hurricane Harbor–New Jersey**
  Route 537, P.O. Box 120
  Jackson, NJ 08527
  Phone: (732) 928-2000

- **Six Flags Kentucky Kingdom**
  937 Phillips Lane
  Louisville, KY 40209
  Phone: (502) 366-2231

- **Six Flags Magic Mountain**
  26101 Magic Mountain Parkway
  Valencia, CA 91355
  Phone: (661) 255-4100

- **Six Flags Mexico**
  Carretera Picacho al Ajusco #1500
  Col. Heroes de Padierna
  Mexico, D.F. C.P. 14200
  Phone: +52(55) 53 39 36 00

- **Six Flags New England**
  1623 Main Street
  Agawam, MA 01001
  Phone: (413) 786-9300

- **Six Flags New Orleans**
  12301 Lake Forest Boulevard
  New Orleans, LA 70129
  Phone: (504) 253-8100

- **Six Flags over Georgia**
  P.O. Box 43187
  Atlanta, GA 30336
  Phone: (770) 739-3400

- **Six Flags over Texas**
  P.O. Box 90191
  Arlington, TX 76004
  Phone: (817) 640-8900

- **Six Flags St. Louis**
  P.O. Box 60
  Eureka, MO 63025
  Phone: (636) 938-4800

- **Six Flags White Water**
  250 North Cobb Parkway #100
  Marietta, GA 30062
  Phone: (770) 948-9290

- **Six Flags Wild Safari**
  Route 537, P.O. Box 120
  Jackson, NJ 08527
  Phone: (732) 928-1821

- **Six Flags Corporate Offices**
  1540 Broadway
  New York, NY 10036
  924 Avenue J East
  Grand Prairie, TX 75050

Storybook Land
6415 Black Horse Pike
  (Routes 40 / 322)
Egg Harbor Township, NJ 08234
Phone: (609) 646-0103, ext. 5
Fax: (609) 646-4533
http://www.storybookland.com

Universal Orlando Resort
1000 Universal Studios Plaza
Orlando, FL 32819-7610
Phone: (407) 363-8000
http://www.universalorlandojobs.com

Universal Studios Hollywood
Universal City, CA 91608
http://www.universalstudios
  hollywood.com/jobs.html

The Walt Disney Company
500 South Buena Vista Street
Burbank, CA 91521
Phone: (818) 560-1000
http://corporate.disney.go.com/
  careers/index.html

Woodloch Resort
RR 1, Box 280
Hawley, PA 18428
Phone: (800) 966-3562
http://www.woodlochpines.com/
  employment

BIBLIOGRAPHY

TRAVEL AND TOURISM/GENERAL HOSPITALITY

Braidwood, Barbara, Susan M. Boyce, and Richard Cropp. *Start and Run a Profitable Tour Guiding Business.* 2nd ed. Bellingham, Wash.: Self-Counsel Press, 2000.

Brymer, Robert A., ed. *Hospitality and Tourism: An Introduction to the Industry.* 8th ed. Dubuque, Iowa: Kendall/Hunt Publishing, 1998.

Colbert, Judy. *Career Opportunities in the Travel Industry.* New York: Ferguson, 2004.

Dittmer, Paul R., and Gerald R. Griffin. *Dimensions of the Hospitality Industry: An Introduction.* 3rd ed. Hoboken, N.J.: John Wiley & Sons, 2002.

Dreith, Rae, and Sharon Scott, eds. *Computer Reservation Systems–SABRE.* New York: Education Systems, 2008.

Eberts, Marjorie, Linda Brothers, and Ann Gisler. *Careers in Travel, Tourism, & Hospitality.* 2nd ed. New York: McGraw-Hill, 2005.

Ferguson Publishing. *Travel and Hospitality.* New York: Ferguson, 2006.

Gagnon, Patricia, and Shelly M. Houser. *Travel Career Development.* 8th ed. Wellesley, Mass.: The Travel Institute, 2005.

Getz, Donald. *Event Management and Event Tourism.* Elmsford, N.Y.: Cognizant Communications, 1997.

———. *Explore Wine Tourism.* Elmsford, N.Y.: Cognizant Communications, 2001.

Krannich, Ron. *Jobs for Travel Lovers: Opportunities at Home and Abroad.* 5th ed. Manassas Park, Va.: Impact Publications, 2005.

Mancini, Marc. *Conducting Tours: A Practical Guide.* Florence, KY: Delmar Cengage Learning, 2000.

Mitchell, Gerald E. *Global Travel and Tourism Career Opportunities.* Charleston, S.C.: The GEM Institute of Tourism Career Development, 2006.

Reigel, Carl, and Melissa Dallas. *Hospitality and Tourism Careers: A Blueprint for Success.* Upper Saddle River, N.J.: Prentice Hall, 1999.

Samuels, Jack B., and Reginald Foucar-Szocki. *Guiding Your Entry into the Hospitality and Tourism Mega-Profession.* Upper Saddle River, N.J.: Prentice Hall, 1999.

Slaton, Hunter. *Vault Guide to the Top Hospitality & Tourism Industry Employers* Vault Career Library. 3rd ed. New York: Vault, 2008.

HOTELS

Craig, Susannah, and Park Davis. *The Complete Idiot's Guide to Running a Bed and Breakfast.* New York: Alpha Books, 2001.

Davies, Mary E., with Pat Hardy, Jo Ann M. Bell, and Susan Brown. *So—You Want to Be an Innkeeper: The Definitive Guide to Operating a Successful Bed and Breakfast or Country Inn.* San Francisco: Chronicle Books, 2004.

Henkin, Shepard. *Opportunities in Hotel & Motel Careers.* New York: McGraw-Hill, 2006.

Hotch, Ripley, and Carl A. Glassman. *How to Start and Run Your Own Bed and Breakfast Inn.* Mechanicsburg, Penn.: Stackpole Books, 1992.

Levine, Karen, and Alan Gelb. *A Survival Guide for Hotel and Motel Professionals.* Clifton Park, N.Y.: Thomson Delmar Learning, 2005.

Raza, Ivo. *Heads in Beds: Hospitality and Tourism Marketing.* Upper Saddle River, N.J.: Prentice Hall, 2004.

Rutherford, Denney G. *Hotel Management and Operations.* 3rd ed. Hoboken, N.J.: John Wiley & Sons, 2002.

Stankus, Jan. *How to Own and Operate a Bed & Breakfast.* 8th ed. Guilford, Conn.: Globe Pequot Press, 2007.

Vallen, Gary K. and Jerome J. Vallen. *Check-In Check-Out: Managing Hotel Operations.* 8th ed. Upper Saddle River, N.J.: Prentice Hall, 2008.

Venison, Peter J. *100 Tips for Hoteliers: What Every Successful Hotel Professional Needs to Know and Do.* Bloomington, Ind.: AuthorHouse, 2004.

SPECIALTY RESORTS AND CRUISE SHIPS

Kennedy, Don H., and Steve Hines, eds. *How to Get a Job on a Cruise Ship.* Atlanta: CareerSource Publications, 2000.

Mancini, Marc. *Cruising: A Guide to the Cruise Line Industry.* 2nd ed. Florence, KY: Delmar Cengage Learning, 2003.

Marin, Richard B. *Cruise Ship Jobs: The Insiders Guide to Finding and Getting Jobs on Cruise Ships around the World.* Verona, Wisc.: Portofino Publications, 1998.

Mihaylov, Bogdan. *Cruise Ship Job in 14 Days: The LASER Strategy for Next Generation Applying.* Bloomington, Ind.: AuthorHouse, 2004.

Mill, Robert Christie. *Resorts: Management and Operation.* Hoboken, N.J.: John Wiley & Sons, 2007.

Pybus, Victoria. *Working in Ski Resorts—Europe & North America.* 5th ed. Surrey, England: Vacation Work Publications, 2003.

RESTAURANT/CULINARY ARTS

Alonzo, Roy. *The Upstart Guide to Owning and Managing a Bar or Tavern.* Chicago: Kaplan Publishing, 2006.

Bilderback, Leslie. *The Complete Idiot's Guide to Success as a Chef.* New York: Alpha Books, 2007.

Chalmers, Irena. *150 Great Jobs for Culinary Students, Career Changers and Food Lovers.* New York: Beaufort Books, 2008.

Chemelynski, Carol Caprione. *Opportunities in Restaurant Careers.* New York: McGraw-Hill, 2004.

The Culinary Institute of America. *At Your Service: A Hands-On Guide to the Professional Dining Room.* Hoboken, N.J.: John Wiley & Sons, 2005.

The Culinary Institute of America. *The Professional Chef.* Hoboken, N.J.: John Wiley & Sons, 2006.

Dornenburg, Andrew, and Karen Page. *Becoming a Chef.* Hoboken, N.J.: John Wiley & Sons, 2003.

Foley, Ray and Heather Dismore. *Running a Bar for Dummies.* Hoboken, N.J.: John Wiley & Sons, 2007.

Garvey, Michael, and Heather Dismore and Andrew Dismore. *Running a Restaurant for Dummies.* Hoboken, N.J.: John Wiley & Sons, 2004.

Halvorsen, Francine. *Catering Like a Pro: From Planning to Profit.* Hoboken, N.J.: John Wiley & Sons, 2004.

Laprise, Martin. *My Daughter Wants to be a Chef! Everything You Should Know About Becoming a Chef!* Victoria, B.C., Canada: Trafford Publishing, 2006.

Matasar, Ann B. *Women of Wine: The Rise of Women in the Global Wine Industry.* Berkeley: University of California Press, 2006.

Mesnier, Roland, Lauren Chattman, and John Burgoyne. *Dessert University: More than 300 Spectacular Recipes and Essential Lessons from White House Pastry Chef Roland Mesnier.* New York: Simon & Schuster, 2004.

McKinney, Anne. *Real-Resumes for Restaurant, Food Service & Hotel Jobs: Including Real Resumes Used to Change Careers and Transfer Skills to Other Industries.* Real-Resumes Series. Fayetteville, N.C.: Prep Publishing, 2002.

Parry, Chris. *The Food Service Professionals Guide to Bar & Beverage Operation: Ensuring Maximum Success.* Ocala, Fla.: Atlantic Publishing Company, 2002.

Simon, Lee. *The Restaurant Dream?* Ocala, Fla.: Atlantic Publishing Group, 2006.

Weinberg, Joyce. *The Everything Guide to Starting and Running a Catering Business: Insider's Advice on Turning Your Talent into a Career.* Cincinnati, Ohio: Adams Media, 2007.

GAMING

Field, Shelly. *Career Opportunities in Casinos and Casino Hotels, Second Edition.* New York: Facts on File, 2009.

Kilby, Jim, Jim Fox, and Anthony F. Lucas. *Casino Operations Management.* 2nd ed. Hoboken, N.J.: John Wiley & Sons, 2004.

McLean, Andrew James. *How to Get a Casino Job.* Evansville, Ind.: Scotwrite Productions, 1998.

University of Nevada, Las Vegas, William F. Harrah College of Hotel Administration International Gaming Institute. *The Gaming Industry: Introduction and Perspectives.* Hoboken, N.J.: John Wiley & Sons, 1996.

EVENT PLANNING/OTHER

Allen, Judy. *The Business of Event Planning: Behind-the-Scenes Secrets of Successful Special Events.* Toronto: John Wiley & Sons Canada, 2002.

Beck, Shari. *The Sandcastles Guide to Starting and Managing Your Own Wedding-Planning Business: How to Enjoy a Career in One of Today's Most Exciting Professions.* Lincoln, Neb.: iUniverse-Indigo, 2007.

Camenson, Blythe. *Opportunities in Event Planning Careers.* New York: McGraw-Hill, 2003.

Craven, Robin, and Lynn Johnson Golabowski. *The Complete Idiot's Guide to Meeting & Event Planning.* New York: Alpha Books, 2006.

Entrepreneur Press. *Start Your Own Event Planning Business.* Irvine, Calif.: Entrepreneur Press, 2007.

Friedmann, Susan. *Meeting and Event Planning for Dummies.* Hoboken, N.J.: Wiley, 2003.

Goldblatt, Joe, and Frank Supovitz. *Dollars & Events: How to Succeed in the Special Events Business.* Hoboken, N.J.: Wiley, 1999.

Moran, Jill. *How to Start a Home-Based Event Planning Business.* Guildford, Conn.: Globe Pequot Press, 2004.

Peragine, John. *How to Open & Operate a Financially Successful Wedding Consultant & Planning Business: With Companion CD-ROM.* Ocala, Fla.: Atlantic Publishing Company, 2008.

Phillips, Cho and Sherrie Wilkolaski. *How to Start a Wedding Planning Business.* Lulu Enterprises, Inc. (Lulu.com), 2003.

INDEX

Page numbers in **boldface** indicate main articles.